Persian Historiography across Empires

Persian served as one of the primary languages of historical writing over the period of the early modern Islamic empires of the Ottomans, Safavids, and Mughals. Historians writing under these empires read and cited each other's works, some moving from one empire to another, writing under different rival dynasties at various points in time. Emphasizing the importance of looking beyond the confines of political boundaries in studying this phenomenon, Sholeh A. Quinn employs a variety of historiographical approaches to draw attention to the importance of placing these histories within not only their historical context but also their historiographical context.

This comparative study of Persian historiography from the sixteenth to the seventeenth centuries presents in-depth case analyses alongside a wide array of primary sources written under the Ottomans, Safavids, and Mughals to illustrate that Persian historiography during this era was part of an extensive universe of literary-historical writing.

SHOLEH A. QUINN is Associate Professor of History at the University of California, Merced. She is the author of *Historical Writing during the Reign of Shah 'Abbas: Ideology, Imitation, and Legitimacy in Safavid Chronicles* (2000) and *Shah Abbas: The King Who Refashioned Iran* (2015). She co-edited *History and Historiography of Post-Mongol Central Asia and the Middle East: Studies in Honor of John E. Woods* (2006).

Persian Historiography across Empires

The Ottomans, Safavids, and Mughals

SHOLEH A. QUINN
University of California, Merced

CAMBRIDGE
UNIVERSITY PRESS

CAMBRIDGE
UNIVERSITY PRESS

University Printing House, Cambridge CB2 8BS, United Kingdom

One Liberty Plaza, 20th Floor, New York, NY 10006, USA

477 Williamstown Road, Port Melbourne, VIC 3207, Australia

314–321, 3rd Floor, Plot 3, Splendor Forum, Jasola District Centre, New Delhi – 110025, India

79 Anson Road, #06–04/06, Singapore 079906

Cambridge University Press is part of the University of Cambridge.

It furthers the University's mission by disseminating knowledge in the pursuit of education, learning, and research at the highest international levels of excellence.

www.cambridge.org
Information on this title: www.cambridge.org/9781108842211
DOI: 10.1017/9781108906975

First published 2021

A catalogue record for this publication is available from the British Library.

Library of Congress Cataloging-in-Publication Data
Names: Quinn, Sholeh Alysia, author.
Title: Persian historiography across empires : the Ottomans, Safavids, and Mughals / Sholeh A. Quinn, University of California, Merced.
Description: First edition. | New York : Cambridge University Press, 2020. | Includes bibliographical references and index.
Identifiers: LCCN 2020021031 (print) | LCCN 2020021032 (ebook) | ISBN 9781108842211 (hardback) | ISBN 9781108820387 (paperback) | ISBN 9781108906975 (epub)
Subjects: LCSH: Iran–Historiography–History–16th century. | Iran–Historiography–History–17th century. | Iran–History–Şafavid dynasty, 1501-1736–Historiography. | Turkey–History–Ottoman Empire, 1288-1918–Historiography. | Mogul Empire–Historiography.
Classification: LCC DS292 .Q565 2020 (print) | LCC DS292 (ebook) | DDC 950/.3072–dc23
LC record available at https://lccn.loc.gov/2020021031
LC ebook record available at https://lccn.loc.gov/2020021032

ISBN 978-1-108-84221-1 Hardback

For my husband
Stephen N. Lambden

Contents

List of Tables — *page* viii
Acknowledgments — ix

1 Introduction — 1

2 Continuity and Transformation: The Timurid Historiographical Legacy — 20

3 Historiography and Historians on the Move: The Significance of the Number Twelve — 73

4 The First King of the World: Kayumars in Universal Histories — 107

5 Mirrors, Memorials, and Blended Genres — 155

6 Conclusion — 202

Appendix — 208
Bibliography — 222
Index — 239

Tables

2.1 Ibn Funduq's list of "famous" histories *page* 43
2.2 Bibliography in Khunji-Isfahani's *Tarikh-i 'alam-ara-yi Amini* 45
2.3 Mirkhvand and Muslih al-Din Lari's bibliographies (cross-listed) 48
2.4 Bibliography in Nizam al-Din's *Tabaqat-i Akbari* 51
3.1 Khvandamir's compositions 76
4.1 The earliest chronicles written under the Safavids 109
4.2 Chapter 4 chronicles 111
4.3 General organizational scheme of Shukr Allah's *Bahjat al-tavarikh* 118
4.4 General organizational scheme of the *Rawzat al-safa* and the *Habib al-siyar* 127
4.5 General organizational scheme of the *Lubb al-tavarikh* 137
5.1 Biographies in the *Habib al-siyar* 176
5.2 Named sources in the biographical sections of the *Habib al-siyar* 178
5.3 Number of biographies by ruler in Khvandamir's *Habib al-siyar* 181

Acknowledgments

This book has been a long time in the making, and it would not have been possible for me to complete it without a great deal of support and assistance from family, friends, and colleagues. I am grateful to Necati Alkan, Susan Amussen, Ali Anooshahr, Sussan Babaie, Shahzad Bashir, Jennifer Berry, Evrim Binbaş, Aditi Chandra, Ferenc Csirkés, Devin DeWeese, Novin Doostdar, Massumeh Farhad, Kioumars Ghereghlou, Mana Kia, Nobuaki Kondo, Paul Losensky, Louise Marlow, Charles Melville, Firuza Melville, Colin Mitchell, Ruth Mostern, Judith Pfeiffer, Kaya Şahin, Hamid Samandari, Ron Sela, Tunç Şen, Marta Simidchieva, Sunil Sharma, Tilmann Trausch, Audrey Truschke, and Ernest Tucker for their assistance with various aspects of this project.

Many thanks to Maria Marsh, Daniel Brown, Atifa Jiwa, Thomas Haynes, and the team at Cambridge University Press, and Vinithan Sethumadhavan and his team at SPi Global for all of their assistance in helping this project reach completion. I am grateful to Pierke Bosschieter for preparing the Index. The three anonymous reviewers of my manuscript made many helpful comments and suggestions for improvement, and I am very thankful to them for their time and expertise. I take full responsibility, of course, for all errors and oversights.

I thank the University of California (UC) Merced Center for the Humanities and the UC Merced Faculty Senate Grant Program for providing research support for this project. UC Merced is a very special place. My distinguished colleagues in the Interdisciplinary Humanities Graduate Group, and the History and Critical Race and Ethnic Studies Department have always been very encouraging and supportive. The remarkable students at UC Merced, past and present, graduate and undergraduate, have been a constant source of inspiration.

My professor and friend, John Woods, has always provided me with wonderful advice and generously shared with me his vast knowledge of the Persianate world. Thank you so much.

The love and support from my family continues to sustain me in a deep and profound way. I am grateful to my precious parents, Robert Quinn and Manijeh Samandari Quinn; my sister, Laleh Quinn; and her partner, Doug Nitz. Finally, my beloved and learned husband, Stephen Lambden, has not only helped me through every step of this journey but also filled it with laughter and happiness.

1 *Introduction*

In 933/1527, after an eventful career as a diplomat, historian, administrator, and writer under multiple rulers – a career that included composing a variety of texts for multiple patrons – Ghiyas al-Din Khvandamir (ca. 880–942/ca. 1475–1535/1536) left Herat, a town which had recently come under Safavid control, and made his way to Qandahar and Mughal territory. There, he authored his final composition: a short historical treatise for the Mughal emperor Humayun (r. 937–963/1530–1556). Khvandamir's career represents movement in a number of ways. In addition to his physical journey from Khurasan to India, he moved effortlessly, it seems, from genre to genre in his writing, and from patron to patron, some of whom were distantly related to each other and others who ruled over rival empires. Khvandamir was not unique in terms of his movements. The early modern Persianate world was one connected by a common Persian language and a body of texts familiar to an elite that existed across empires. However, while we know what, where, and when Khvandamir wrote, we have only started to understand how and why.

This book is a study of Persian historiography during the period of the Ottoman, Safavid, and Mughal empires. Beginning in approximately 1500, three empires formed in Southwest Asia, South Asia, and North Africa out of the political fragmentation that followed the dissolution of the Timurid Empire. The Ottomans, Safavids, and Mughals became three of the most powerful empires of the seventeenth century. After their establishment, a series of dynastic kings built elaborate capital cities or expanded already established ones; surrounded themselves with a dizzying array of artists, architects, and intellectuals; developed bureaucracies that allowed their empires to continue expanding without losing administrative control over their provinces; and formed disciplined and effective armies. They engaged in diplomacy, ruled over multiethnic and multireligious communities, and created conditions through which new literary, artistic, philosophical, and social movements could thrive. At the same time, rulers of these empires also engaged in warfare, massacre, religious persecution, and the forced resettlement of peoples.

The Ottomans managed to accomplish what no Islamic dynasty or ruler had previously been able to do: capture Constantinople and transform it into Istanbul, which became the imperial seat of the Ottoman sultanate. From there, they launched a series of successful military campaigns that brought them into direct contact with the peoples of Europe and Iran. Eventually bringing Arabia and the holy cities of Mecca and Medina under their control, they came to see themselves as the champions and guardians of Sunni Islam while sharing an eastern border with their rival Shiʿi Safavid neighbors.

The Safavids, whose origins trace back to a Sufi dynasty in the northern Iranian city of Ardabil, eventually ruled from Isfahan, a purpose-built capital city that they filled with mosques, bazaars, bathhouses, and more. Having established Twelver/Imami Shiʿism as the official state religion, they proceeded to "convert" Iran, bringing together religious scholars and clerics and establishing religious institutions to help them carry out this project. Like the Ottomans, they engaged in international trade and international diplomacy. Under the Safavids, a philosophical school flourished and so too, eventually, new styles of art and poetry.

At nearly the same time that the Safavid state was founded, the Mughal dynasty established itself in India, and as Muslims, ruled over a Hindu majority population. A series of Mughal emperors situated Agra and then Delhi as their capitals where they used their tremendous wealth to build edifices such as the Taj Mahal. In addition, they attracted large numbers of poets, artists, and other intellectuals to their territory with the promise of financial reward and patronage. The Mughals engaged in unique religious experiments designed to reconcile the different religious communities over which they ruled. They eventually managed, through their effective army, to extend their rule over the entire Indian subcontinent.

Each of these empires cultivated their own unique identities, as rulers tried to ensure the strength of their political borders and boundaries. They squashed rebellions and attempts at defection, waged military and propaganda wars against each other, and competed with each other in terms of their kingship and their legitimacy. However, this was also a period of great movement, exchange, and synthesis. People traveled from one empire to another, living under different dynasties, and as people moved, so too did their religious beliefs, artistic styles, languages, poetry, and practices of historical writing, which in turn interacted with local traditions.

Historical Writing in Persian

Given the magnitude of these empires, it should come as no surprise that their kings made certain that historians would record their accomplishments. The period thus witnessed a significant output of historical writing of many kinds, much of it in the same Persian language, although some of the earliest Ottoman chronicles and most of the later ones were written in Ottoman Turkish.[1] During the Middle Periods of Islamicate history, "new Persian" had spread across the eastern portion of the Islamic heartlands and become the vehicle through which social norms of refined etiquette (*adab*) were communicated. By the early modern period, secretaries (*munshī*s), poets, courtiers, and other writers adhered to models that became familiar to a literate class who composed their own texts in light of these models.[2] Mughal emperors, starting with Humayun, actively encouraged scholars in Iran to go to India, and Persian became the language associated with Mughal kingship and administration.[3]

This study focuses on histories written in Persian because this "lingua franca" served not only as the language of administration and culture across the empires but also the primary language of historical writing for nearly the entirety of the Safavid and Mughal periods and for the earliest phase of Ottoman rule. Persian histories were also composed under the Shaybani Uzbeks in Central Asia and for various

[1] For more background on early Ottoman historiography, see Halil Inalcik, "The Rise of Ottoman Historiography," in *Historians of the Middle East*, ed. Bernard Lewis and P. M. Holt, 152–167 (London: Oxford University Press, 1986). Turkish also played an important role in Central Asia and the Mughal Empire during this time.

[2] Brian Spooner and William L. Hanoway, "Introduction: Persian As *Koine*: Written Persian in World-Historical Perspective," in *Literacy in the Persianate World: Writing and the Social Order*, ed. Brian Spooner and William L. Hanoway, 1–69 (Philadelphia: University of Pennsylvania Press, 2012).

[3] Muzaffar Alam, "The Pursuit of Persian: Language in Mughal Politics," *Modern Asian Studies* 32 (1998): 317–349. See also Sanjay Subrahmanyam, "Iranians Abroad: Intra-Asian Elite Migration and Early Modern State Formation," *The Journal of Asian Studies* 51 (1992): 340–363.

other local rulers and patrons in the region. Since Persian histories form such an essential source of information for this period, scholars often make extensive use of this material, especially for the Safavid and Mughal dynasties.[4] Knowing more about these indispensable texts, including the methods of their composition and how they relate to each other across political boundaries, remains a matter of paramount importance as we use them to understand the past.

The following chapters demonstrate that Persian historiography during this era was part of an extensive universe of literary-historical writing that drew on earlier established models and historiographical traditions, most immediately Timurid. As heirs to the Timurid historiographical legacy, historians of the Ottomans, Safavids, and Mughals modified and further developed these traditions across all three empires. Furthermore, they also read and sometimes cited each other's works, thereby connecting their histories not only to the earlier tradition but also to each other's compositions. Some, like Khvandamir, even physically moved from one empire to another, writing under different and rival dynasties and patrons at various points in time. For these reasons, in studying Persian historical writing, it is important to look beyond the confines of political boundaries and instead focus on the Persianate world.

Connected Histories and the Persianate World

The present volume complements research undertaken in the last few decades on connected histories and notions of the "Persianate world." Such scholarship has suggested that the study of historiographical traditions should not be straightjacketed into the confines of modern nation-states or even the early modern dynastic empires where they were written.[5] Instead, as Sanjay Subrahmanyam has noted, histories, while diverse in terms of genre and other elements, were part of a connected world in which their influence was felt across great

4 Due to the survival of the extensive Ottoman archives, it has been possible to write a social and economic history of the Ottoman Empire in ways that have not been as possible for the Safavids or the Mughals. See Douglas E. Streusand, *Islamic Gunpowder Empires: Ottomans, Safavids, and Mughals* (Boulder, CO: Westview Press, 2011), 6–10.

5 Sanjay Subrahmanyam, "Connected Histories: Notes towards a Reconfiguration of Early Modern Eurasia," *Modern Asian Studies* 31 (1997): 759.

distances.[6] Subrahmanyam further outlines a circulation of legendary material, such as those associated with Alexander the Great, and ideas and concepts, such as the notion of the appearance of a *mujaddid*, or "renewer," who according to Islamic tradition (*ḥadīth*) would appear at the beginning of each century to renew the faith.[7] The chronicles under examination, as will be demonstrated, were used and traveled across empires, as Persian was the primary language of transmission in the early modern era. They thus form part of the circuit or circulation of historiographical traditions. The primary purpose here is to demonstrate in a detailed manner what happened to such texts as they circulated. How exactly were they utilized and rewritten by later generations of chroniclers writing across empires? This is where taking a comparative approach becomes useful. In order to understand the relationship between the chronicles and what happened as they moved from, say, Safavid Iran to the Ottoman Empire or to the Mughal Empire, it is necessary to compare them to each other, not only to establish their dependency, but also to understand the transformations that they underwent. Such an approach does not "compartmentalize" the chronicles but rather allows us to understand them in a more nuanced manner.

In addition to being "connected histories" in ways that subsequent chapters will demonstrate, the chronicles were produced in the "Persianate" world, a notion that, like connected histories, has also received considerable recent scholarly attention. While the renowned University of Chicago historian Marshall G. S. Hodgson was responsible for coining the term "Persianate," a sibling term to his rather more

6 For example, the late Timurid world history, Mirkhvand's *Rawzat al-safa*, while an extremely important text for the Ottomans, Safavids, and Mughals alike, was mentioned in a Portuguese world history completed in 1530. See Sanjay Subrahmanyam, "Intertwined Histories: *Crónica* and *Tārīkh* in the Sixteenth-Century Indian Ocean World," *History and Theory, Theme Issue* 49 (2010): 135, 140.

7 For the Alexander legends, see Subrahmanyam, "Connected Histories," 757. For more on the notion of the *mujaddid* in Ottoman, Safavid, and Mughal chronicles, see Cornell H. Fleischer, *Bureaucrat and Intellectual in the Ottoman Empire: The Historian Mustafa Ali (1541–1600)* (Princeton, NJ: Princeton University Press, 1986), 281 (Ottomans); Sholeh A. Quinn, *Historical Writing during the Reign of Shah 'Abbas: Ideology, Imitation and Legitimacy in Safavid Chronicles* (Salt Lake City: University of Utah Press, 2000), 81–83, 86 (Safavids); A. Azfar Moin, *The Millennial Sovereign: Sacred Kingship and Sainthood in Islam* (New York: Columbia University Press, 2012), 9, 134, 171, 198–204, 209 (Mughals).

popular "Islamicate," this concept has been more recently revisited in an attempt to define it more consciously and explore its implications.[8] These studies suggest that looking beyond and decentering Iran would be useful in helping us to understand the nature of the Persianate world and culture.[9] This study contributes to such scholarship by examining Persian chronicles that were written beyond the borders of the Safavid Empire, across territory spanning from Western Anatolia to the Indian subcontinent, including Iran and Central Asia. Such an approach is particularly effective when applied to the early modern period, as this was a time when each of the Ottoman, Safavid, and Mughal zones "earned a discrete personality of its own," as Persianate culture interacted with Ottoman Turkish in the west and with Hindu and Sanskrit cultures in India.[10] As these empires became "epicenters for a transregional Persianate experience,"[11] the question remains as to how historical writing fits into this paradigm. Do chronicles written across the early modern empires possess something unique that distinguishes them by the dynasty under which they were written, or can we discern more homogenizing characteristics? How does historiography change over time?

The Historiographical Context

The best way to address the questions that theoretical discussions on connected histories and notions of the Persianate world raise is by closely reading and analyzing the chronicles themselves. While

8 An unexhaustive list of such works include the following: *The Persianate World: The Frontiers of a Eurasian Lingua Franca*, ed. Nile Green (Berkeley: University of California Press, 2019); *Medieval Central Asia and the Persianate World: Iranian Tradition and Islamic Civilisation*, ed. A. C. S. Peacock and D. G. Tor (London: I. B. Tauris, 2015); *The Persianate World: Rethinking a Shared Sphere*, ed. Abbas Amanat and Assef Ashraf (Leiden: Brill, 2019); Richard M. Eaton, *India in the Persianate Age 1000–1765* (London: Allen Lane, 2019). In explaining the importance of the period from 111 to 1274, Marshall G. S. Hodgson notes the significance of the Persian language, distinguishing "cultural traditions, carried in Persian or reflecting Persian inspiration" as "Persianate." See Marshall G. S. Hodgson, *The Venture of Islam: Conscience and History in a World Civilization*, 3 vols. (Chicago: University of Chicago Press, 1974), 2: 293–294.

9 See Peacock and Tor, *Medieval Central Asia and the Persianate World*, xix–xxi; Green, *The Persianate World*, xiv–xv.

10 Abbas Amanat, "Remembering the Persianate," in *The Persianate World: Rethinking a Shared Sphere*, 28–29.

11 Amanat, "Remembering the Persianate," 51.

historical chronicles form a body of what we might consider "traditional sources," they certainly should not be dismissed for that reason but rather examined in a sophisticated manner.[12] Throughout this work, I draw attention to the importance of placing these histories not only in historical but also in historiographical contexts. It is the latter of these contexts, the historiographical, that still has not received enough scholarly attention, which is emphasized in this study. Its importance lies in the fact that so many early modern writers employed a method of imitative writing in which they drew heavily on an earlier work or works, modifying the earlier model texts in significant ways. Without identifying these models, it is likely that scholars will read a particular history without realizing whose words they are actually reading. Imitative writing is one of the most important features of Persian historiography when chroniclers narrate their past. In other words, when historians could find earlier texts that covered a particular past period and place, they usually used one or more such sources as the basis upon which they wrote their own accounts. Taking that earlier text, they would modify it by rewriting it in different ways, such as adding new language, changing the wording, removing certain passages, or reproducing the earlier text verbatim. If enough chroniclers chose to carry forward the same portions or sections of an earlier narrative, those sections became conventional elements.

In my earlier study, *Historical Writing during the Reign of Shah ʻAbbas: Ideology, Imitation and Legitimacy in Safavid Chronicles*, I analyzed this process in Safavid chronicle prefaces and accounts of the early Safavid Sufi order, pointing to the highly conventional elements in the prefaces and noting how certain stories originating in the fourteenth-century hagiography of Shaykh Safi al-Din (650–735/1252–1334), founder of the Safaviyyah Sufi order, were reproduced and then significantly rewritten in order to make Shaykh Safi and his followers appear as practicing Twelver Shiʻi Muslims. Chroniclers from the period of Shah Ismaʻil (r. 907–930/1501–1524) later engaged in this rewriting process. When comparing the passages in these various chronicles, it became very clear that the historians chose particular texts as models that they imitated. In some cases, by skillfully adding a

12 Peacock and Tor, "Preface," xxi. See also Assef Ashraf, "Introduction: Pathways to the Persianate," in *The Persianate World: Rethinking a Shared Sphere*, 10.

single word or a short phrase, they completely changed the meaning of the earlier narrative. In other instances, they added significant passages, thereby making their political agendas very clear.[13] Through this creative process of interacting with an earlier text, the chronicler maintained an active engagement and dialog with the past. It is essential to keep this process in mind and read a historical work comparatively alongside its model. Failing to do so may be likened to listening to half of a conversation with the resulting dialog incomplete and difficult to understand.

The phenomenon of imitation has been studied not only in relation to historiography but also to Persian poetry. Paul Losensky analyzed Safavid–Mughal poetry in light of various forms of imitation in which a poet pays tribute to earlier poems through, for example, reproducing the same meter or rhyme. The practice was popular with Safavid–Mughal poets such as Baba Fighani.[14] In the case of both poetry and history, the practice that earlier modern writers engaged in cannot be labeled plagiarism, because to do so ignores the creative and innovative elements inherent in the process of composing a poem or writing and rewriting the past.

The State of the Field

Despite the tremendous historiographical output spanning three empires and the significance that body of writing has for our understanding of early modern history, little research across empires has taken place thus far. This is not surprising for the study of Persian historiography within each of these three dynasties has only recently reached a point where such work can proceed. Nevertheless, a number of books have been recently published that provide the necessary background for the kind of "across empires" approach used in this study. In 2012, a volume entitled *Persian Historiography*, edited by Charles Melville as part of Ehsan Yarshater's *History of Persian Literature* series, brought together numerous essays on Persian historiography from its origins to the Pahlavi period.[15] The chapters in this

[13] Quinn, *Historical Writing*, 63–91.

[14] Paul E. Losensky, *Welcoming Fighānī: Imitation and Poetic Individuality in the Safavid-Mughal* Ghazal (Costa Mesa, CA: Mazda Publishers, 1998), 12, 15, 100–114.

[15] *Persian Historiography*, ed. Charles Melville (London: I. B. Tauris, 2012).

volume provide general overviews of the main sources and main features of historical writing for each time period/dynasty. *Persian Historiography* includes separate chapters on Ottoman, Safavid, and Mughal historiographies. These essays build on several monographs and articles that had been recently published, such as Julie Meisami's *Persian Historiography*, Ernest Tucker's *Nadir Shah's Quest for Legitimacy in Post-Safavid Iran*, numerous articles published by Charles Melville on Mongol and Timurid historiographies, and *Historical Writing during the Reign of Shah 'Abbas.*[16]

Since the publication of *Persian Historiography*, and in one instance before, several monographs have been published that emphasize primarily dynastic and occasionally interdynastic history, making heavy use of historical narratives.[17] Tilmann Trausch's study on Safavid historiography, *Formen höfischer Historiographie im 16. Jahrhundert*, focuses on the rise of Safavid historiography.[18] Kaya Şahin's *Empire and Power in the Reign of Süleyman: Narrating the Sixteenth-Century Ottoman World*, a study that brings a much-needed focus on narrative sources for the reign of the Ottoman sultan Süleyman, emphasizes histories written in Ottoman Turkish rather than Persian texts.[19] Ali Anooshahr's *The Ghazi Sultans and the Frontiers of Islam: A Comparative Study of the Late Medieval and Early Modern Periods* examines three key historical figures: Mahmud of Ghazna (r. 388–421/998–1030), the Mughal founder Babur (r. 932–937/1526–1530), and the Ottoman sultan Murad II

[16] Julie Scott Meisami, *Persian Historiography to the End of the Twelfth Century* (Edinburgh: Edinburgh University Press, 1999); Ernest Tucker, *Nadir Shah's Quest for Legitimacy in Post-Safavid Iran* (Gainsville: University Press of Florida, 2006); Quinn, *Historical Writing*, and numerous articles published by Charles Melville on Mongol and Timurid historiographies, several of which are listed in the Bibliography.

[17] Space does not allow for a comprehensive list of recent scholarship in Arabic historiography, which has made tremendous progress in recent years. See, for example, Konrad Hirschler, *The Written Word in the Medieval Arabic Lands: A Social and Cultural History of Reading Practices* (Edinburgh: Edinburgh University Press, 2012). See also Konrad Hirschler, *Medieval Arabic Historiography: Authors As Actors* (London and New York: Routledge, 2006).

[18] Tilmann Trausch, *Formen höfischer Historiographie im 16. Jahrhundert: Geschichtsschreibung unter den frühen Safaviden: 1501–1578* (Wien: Verlag der Österreichischen Akademie der Wissenschaften (ÖAW), 2015).

[19] Kaya Şahin, *Empire and Power in the Reign of Süleyman: Narrating the Sixteenth-Century Ottoman World* (Cambridge: Cambridge University Press, 2013).

(r. 824–848/1421–1444; 850–855/1446–1451).[20] The book makes use of a wide range of narrative sources from multiple dynasties. For the Mughals, A. Azfar Moin's *The Millennial Sovereign: Sacred Kingship and Sainthood in Islam* similarly makes use of historical narratives, looking particularly at what they have to say about Mughal kingship.[21] Muzaffar Alam and Sanjay Subrahmanyam's *Writing the Mughal World: Studies on Culture and Politics* contains many chapters that deal with Mughal historiography.[22] Audrey Truschke's *Culture of Encounters: Sanskrit at the Mughal Court* examines Persian texts, paying particular attention to understanding the impact of Sanskrit on texts written under the Mughals.[23] Finally, Ali Anooshahr's *Turkestan and the Rise of Eurasian Empires* examines the broad historiographical traditions surrounding the origin narratives of the Ottomans, Safavids, Uzbeks, Mongols, and Mughals.[24]

In addition to this body of scholarship, several recently published books focus on the historiography of the early and middle periods of Islamicate history, providing further context and background for later developments. These include Sarah Bowen Savant's *The New Muslims of Post-Conquest Iran: Tradition, Memory, and Conversion*, which examines Persian historiography immediately following the early Islamic conquests; Blain H. Auer's *Symbols of Authority in Medieval Islam: History, Religion, and Muslim Legitimacy in the Delhi Sultanate*, which analyzes Persian sources written under the Delhi sultanate; and Mimi Hanoaka's *Authority and Identity in Medieval Islamic History*, which focuses on local Persian chronicles.[25]

[20] Ali Anooshahr, *The Ghazi Sultans and the Frontiers of Islam: A Comparative Study of the Late Medieval and Early Modern Periods* (London and New York: Routledge, 2009).

[21] Moin, *Millennial Sovereign.*

[22] Muzaffar Alam and Sanjay Subrahmanyam, *Writing the Mughal World: Studies on Culture and Politics* (New York: Columbia University Press, 2012).

[23] Audrey Truschke, *Culture of Encounters: Sanskrit at the Mughal Court* (New York: Columbia University Press, 2016).

[24] Ali Anooshahr, *Turkestan and the Rise of Eurasian Empires: A Study of Politics and Invented Traditions* (Oxford: Oxford University Press, 2018).

[25] Sarah Bowen Savant, *The New Muslims of Post-Conquest Iran: Tradition, Memory, and Conversion* (Cambridge: Cambridge University Press, 2013); Blain H. Auer, *Symbols of Authority in Medieval Islam: History, Religion and Muslim Legitimacy in the Delhi Sultanate* (London: I. B. Tauris, 2012); Mimi Hanaoka, *Authority and Identity in Medieval Islamic Historiography: Persian Histories from the Peripheries* (New York: Cambridge University Press, 2016).

Organization and Parameters

This book is organized into six chapters, the first and sixth forming the introduction and conclusion. Chapters 2–5 should be viewed as separate "case studies" in the sense that each offers strategies for reading the chronicles to make them provide information that the chronicler may not have intended to reveal. While reading texts in light of their models lies at the heart of the analyses in all four of these chapters, I also explore themes such as historiographical conventions, the movement of the chroniclers themselves across empires, and genres of historical writing and other Islamicate literatures. Each chapter, then, provides the reader with a set of tools to further explore the different forms of historical writing and the ways we might make use of this important body of source material.

Due to the massive historiographical output of this period, it has been necessary to limit the number and types of sources that are analyzed in this study and to provide a rationale for those texts that have been excluded. In terms of genre, the texts that form the basis of this book are predominantly Persian prose historical chronicles that are historiographically related to each other and/or to earlier works. While entire categories of Persianate literature, such as epic poems, contain a great deal of valuable historical information, they require separate study in order to understand their relationships, sources, and the methods used to compose them. One important group of Ottoman histories, the *Şehnames*, has not been included for the same reason.[26] Other important genres, such as biographical compendia (*taẕkirah*) and advice literature/mirrors for princes, while important in their own right, will be discussed in light of their serving as sources that informed the historical chronicles.

In terms of time period, the following chapters focus on a series of related themes or historiographical features that are closely analyzed.

[26] On this important group of historical works, see, for example, Christine Woodhead, "An Experiment in Official Historiography: The Post of Şehnāmeci in the Ottoman Empire," *Wiener Zeitschrift für die Kunde des Morgenlandes* 75 (1983): 157–182; Christine Woodhead, "Reading Ottoman 'Şehnames': Official Historiography in the Late Sixteenth Century," *Studia Islamica* 104–105 (2007): 67–80; and Emina Fetvaci, "The Office of the Ottoman Court Historian," in *Studies on Istanbul and Beyond*, ed. Robert G. Ousterhout (Philadelphia: University of Pennsylvania, Museum of Archaeology and Anthropology, 2007), 7–21.

In some cases, the earliest chronicles to contain particular features do not appear until, for example, the seventeenth century. This is why, for example, Abu al-Fazl 'Allami's (958–1101/1551–1602) *Akbarnamah* (1011/1602) is discussed in Chapter 2, because it contains one of the earliest examples of a Mughal dream narrative associated with dynastic origins. Similarly, Iskandar Beg Munshi's (968 or 969–ca. 1043/1560 or 1561–ca. 1633) famous history of Shah 'Abbas (995–1038/1587–1629), the *Tarikh-i 'alam-ara-yi 'Abbasi* (1028/1628–1629), while not an early Safavid chronicle by any means, is nevertheless one of the earliest chronicles written after the *Habib al-siyar* to include a separate biographical section, one of the themes in Chapter 5.

Turning now to the relative number of chronicles analyzed in light of the dynasties under which they were written, it is important to note first that while there was a truly massive amount of historical writing produced under the Ottomans, Safavids, and Mughals, the number of chronicles per dynasty chosen for analysis here varies overall and from chapter to chapter. This is partially due to the fact that, while Ottoman historiography is extensive and rich, the majority of these chronicles were composed in Ottoman Turkish. Therefore, this study has not incorporated those sources. Despite, however, the comparatively fewer number of Ottoman Persian sources, it is still important to incorporate the Ottoman tradition, as it helps us understand how various elements in pre-Ottoman Persian historiography came to be used by Ottoman chroniclers who chose to write in Persian prose.

While this book focuses on the historiography of Ottoman, Safavid, and Mughal empires, a number of Persian histories that were not written under these dynasties also appear in this study. These include two Central Asian histories, Muhammad Haydar Dughlat's (905–958/1499–1551) *Tarikh-i Rashidi* (952/1546) and Mas'udi b. 'Usman Kuhistani's *Tarikh-i Abu al-Khayr Khani* (sometime between 947–959/1540–1551), both of which include the specific elements and themes covered in Chapters 2 and 4, respectively. For the same reason, I have also incorporated in Chapter 2 a discussion of one section of Sharaf Khan Bidlisi's (949–1012/1543–1603/1604) *Sharafnamah* (1005/1596), even though his chronicle may be characterized as a Kurdish history occupying space between the Safavid and Ottoman traditions, and Ziya al-Din Barani's (684–758/1285–1357) *Tarikh-i Firuzshahi* (ca. 684–758/1285–1357), a history of the Delhi Sultanate. While inclusion of these histories cannot do justice to the entirety of Central Asian chronicles or the historiography of Persian narratives written in the Deccan, Gujarat, Malwa, and other sultanates of the Central Indian plateau, the histories discussed here allow us to understand better just how influential certain histories were across and between dynasties and states.

Finally, because I primarily focus on historiographically connected chronicles, a number of historical works are not included in this study. For example, I do not cover at least one Ottoman Persian chronicle, Muhammad b. Hajji Khalil Qunavi's *Tavarikh-i Al-i Osman*, for this reason.[27] This is also the case for other very well-known works, such as the Safavid chronicle by Fazli Isfahani, the *Afzal al-tavarikh* (1045/1635), and the Mughal *Tarikh-i alfi* (997/1588–1589). I have provided brief general overviews of the early modern histories utilized in this study when they first appear throughout the chapters, but they are all listed and described in chronological order in the Appendix. Some of them are very well known and others exist only in manuscript form and have hardly been used.

Chapter Overviews

Chapter 2, "Continuity and Transformation: The Timurid Historiographical Legacy," explores how the Timurid historiographical tradition survived into the early modern period by examining some of the formal conventional elements in a number of Persian histories. By conventional element is meant certain themes or discussions that appear in similar structural positions, and sometimes articulated in similar language in the chronicles. The specific conventional elements that undergo analysis are (1) benefits of history, (2) bibliographies, (3) genealogies, and (4) dream narratives.[28]

[27] On this important chronicle, see Robert Anhegger, "Mehmed b. Haci Halil ül-kunevi'nin Tarih-i Âl-i Osman'i," *Tarih Dergisi* 2 (1951): 51–66. This chronicle is utilized in, for example, Hüseyin Yılmaz, *Caliphate Redefined: The Mystical Turn in Ottoman Political Thought* (Princeton: Princeton University Press, 2018). For a discussion of how Qunavi fits into the Ottoman historiographical tradition, see Murat Cem Mengüç, "Histories of Bayezid I, Historians of Bayezid II: Rethinking Late Fifteenth-Century Ottoman Historiography," *Bulletin of the School of Oriental and African Studies* 76 (2013): 373–389. For the manuscript itself, see Muhammad b. Hajji Khalil Qunavi, *Tavarikh-i al-i 'Usman*, Kayseri Raşit Efendi Eski Eserler Kütüphanesi, Ms. Raşid Efendi Eki 11243.

[28] In some instances, these analyses build on my previous research. See Quinn, *Historical Writing*.

The chapter demonstrates two important points. First, the survival of conventional elements depends to a very great extent on whether or not a chronicler modeled his history on an earlier work that contains a similar conventional element. In other words, certain information appears in our sources due to established conventions and because of the historiographical choices that the chroniclers made. Second, such conventional elements appear in Persian chronicles across empires. Early modern chroniclers, regardless of the dynasty under which they wrote or the patron who sponsored them, tapped into a common earlier tradition which they then modified and reshaped according to the political and dynastic expediencies of the time. The fact that these conventions were shared across imperial boundaries shows how widely histories were read and rewritten in different contexts. It also suggests a shared historiographical consciousness in the Persianate world at this time, reflecting a tradition that goes back to the tenth century, but that has as its immediate historiographical context the Timurid period.[29]

The chapter opens with a discussion of two conventional elements predating the Timurid dynasty that only sporadically or partially survived into the later period. The first is a list of "the benefits of history." This numerated list includes a short- to medium-length discussion under each "benefit." The convention appears, in modified form, in a variety of Persian chronicles written across the Persianate world. Secondly, following the discussion of the benefits of history, or occasionally preceding it, we sometimes see a "bibliography," or an actual list of works, consisting of specific title and in some cases authors' names, that the chronicler claimed to have consulted in fashioning his narrative or that he considered to be important texts. Historians did not simply replicate in a word-for-word manner this list of benefits or bibliography of books, however. Rather, they modified these sections for a variety of reasons. The chapter then examines genealogies and dream narratives, two conventional elements that appear in many chronicles across the empires. Dynastic genealogies trace the current monarch back to an important religious/legendary figure, and dream narratives focus on the dream or dreams of a dynastic founder or ancestor foretelling the future greatness of a

[29] This was when Bal'ami rewrote Tabari's universal history. See Chapter 4.

particular dynastic king or the entire dynasty. Drawing on my previous research on Safavid genealogies and dream narratives, I compare the Safavid tradition with the Mughal and Ottoman, analyzing these conventions not only in light of historiographical models but also through competing notions of kingship.

Chapter 3, "Historiography and Historians on the Move: The Significance of the Number Twelve," continues our exploration of texts moving across time and place, but in a much more detailed manner, as the focus shifts from a macro to a micro view in order to examine what happens when one historian physically moved across political borders, writing for different dynasties. While Chapter 2 shows how movement across dynasties took place intellectually, as the chroniclers looked beyond dynastic borders to read and cite texts being produced in other parts of the Islamicate world, the movement analyzed in Chapter 3 has less to do with time, as it took place within the lifetime of one specific historian, and more to do with place and space, as he traveled from Khurasan to India. The chapter shows that, in addition to drawing on earlier models, the chroniclers also looked to each other's works or, in this case, their own earlier works as they composed their narratives.

This chapter provides two specific examples of movement across empires. The first, and its centerpiece, consists of a case study of the historian Ghiyas al-Din Khvandamir. Khvandamir wrote one of the earliest Safavid histories, the *Habib al-siyar*, and then moved to India, where he wrote one of the earliest Mughal narratives, the *Qanun-i Humayuni* (941/1534). I show precisely how Khvandamir used a portion of his *Habib al-siyar* dealing with the significance of the number twelve relative to the Shiʿi Imams, and carefully transformed it into a "cosmological" text, incorporating it into his Mughal history written for the emperor Humayun. This analysis also shows how later Mughal writers such as Abu al-Fazl used Khvandamir's *Qanun-i Humayuni* in their own chronicles, thus providing another example of the fluidity of historiographical borders. This chapter employs a method of close textual analysis in order to provide a unique insight into one historian "at work" in the early modern era. Interdynastic movement did not begin and end with Khvandamir. Rather, the next generation of Safavid intellectuals found a welcome home under the Mughals. To demonstrate this point, the chapter concludes by tracing how the descendants of a Safavid chronicler, Mir Yahya Sayfi Qazvini

(d. 962/1555), left Iran for India and came to occupy prominent positions under the Mughals.

Chapter 4, "The First King of the World: Kayumars in Universal Histories," continues to test the strength of imperial boundaries such as those that Khvandamir crossed, but this time the focus is on a *group* of historians writing across empire and across time. How did the chroniclers of the Ottomans, Safavids, Uzbeks, and Mughals narrate one particular story that appears in a large number of universal histories? The universal history was one of the most prevalent genres of early modern Persian historical writing and the most common type of history composed in the early stages of the Ottoman, Safavid, and Mughal dynasties. Are narratives of a Persian heroic figure from the book of kings, the *Shahnamah*, similar in chronicles written under the Ottomans, Safavids, and Mughals, as their authors continued to look to their Timurid or in some cases pre-Timurid models, or did the imperial ideologies of their patrons affect the contents of their accounts?

The chapter addresses such questions by examining the legendary past in universal histories and focusing on accounts of Kayumars, considered the first human or first king in the ancient Persian tradition, in a series of universal histories written under the Ottomans, Safavids, Uzbeks, and Mughals. This chapter makes the point that, while at the end of their universal histories the chroniclers narrated the unique aspects of whatever dynasty they were writing under, they were predominately narrating a shared past that predates the establishment of Islam.

The legend of Kayumars serves as a useful lens through which to test the historiographical boundaries between the Ottoman, Safavid, and Mughal empires. Because of the prevalence of universal history writing in the early stages of the three empires, we have a great deal of source material to use for comparative purposes. The chapter thus devotes some time to establishing the models and the textual relationships between the many chronicles narrating Kayumars. Furthermore, because Kayumars was regarded as a Persian and a king, our chroniclers, particularly those writing under the Ottomans and Mughals, may have had reason to treat his story differently than those historians writing under the Safavids. Chapter 4 demonstrates that our chroniclers did not feel the need to recast the legendary past in a hyperpolitical manner. According to historians writing under the Ottomans,

Safavids, Uzbeks, and Mughals, Kayumars was, generally, the first king of the world. That he was a Persian king did not particularly matter to Ottoman, Uzbek, or Mughal writers. In general, it seems the chroniclers did the best they could, using the libraries and source materials to which they had access.

Universal histories demonstrate a historiographical openness and subtlety in narrating the legendary past that leads us to the main questions that are raised in Chapter 5, "Mirrors, Memorials, and Blended Genres." Did this openness also apply to genre? In other words, what was the nature of movement between genres? How did historians "move" material from another category of text into their own histories? Chapter 5 explores this form of movement by examining how different types of Islamicate literature became incorporated into Persian historiography. Early modern historians drew on a rich variety of Islamicate literatures to compose their narratives, but modern scholarship has not explored this phenomenon. The chapter explores two literary traditions that, while they exist as important stand-alone genres, made their way into Persian histories: mirrors for princes and biographical compendia (*tazkirah*).

We may view certain portions of Persian histories as responses to the genre of literature known as "mirrors for princes." The mirrors for princes literary tradition predates the early modern period, and consists of formal and informal advice literature written to educate a prince or a king on how to conduct himself. The texts are highly normative and draw on the ancient Persian notion of the "circle of justice."[30] Several Persian histories contain a conventional element that describes the qualities of a particular king. Narratives listing the attributes of the Safavid king ʻAbbas I and the Mughal king Akbar (r. 963–1014/1556–1605) reflect the same ideal virtues that a king is *supposed* to possess, as indicated in the mirrors for princes literatures. This convention differs from narratives consisting of more general praise of the king or assertions of the king's virtuousness. Rather, in

[30] Louise Marlow has written extensively on advice literature and mirrors for princes, See, for example, Louise Marlow, "*The Way of Viziers and the Lamp of the Commanders (Minhāj al-wuzarā' wa-sirāj al-umarā)* of Aḥmad al-Iṣfahbadhī and the Literary and Political Culture of Early Fourteenth-Century Iran," in *Writers and Rulers: Perspectives on Their Relationship from Abbasid to Safavid Times*, ed. Beatrice Gurendler and Louise Marlow, 169–193 (Wiesbaden: Reichert, 2004).

the chronicles analyzed in this chapter, we see lists of kingly virtues, where the chronicler names specific virtues and adds a sentence or paragraph elaborating on that particular attribute. While it is not possible to trace direct borrowing or influence, we do find historiographical precedence in, for example, a prominent Mongol-era history, Rashid al-Din Fazl Allah's (ca. 645–718/1247–1318) *Jami' al-tavarikh* ("Compendium of Histories," approx. 699–709/1300–1310) and mirrors for princes works such as Nizam al-Mulk's (ca. 408–485/1018–1092) *Siyasatnamah*.

The chapter then examines the *tazkirah* and its role in Persian histories. Like the mirrors for princes literatures, the biographical compendium forms a genre in its own right that flourished during the Timurid era. Certain Ottoman, Safavid, and Mughal histories contain their own "mini-*tazkirah*" sections. Here I trace the historiographical influences on the mini-*tazkirah*s and show that the Persian historians were not only looking to earlier Timurid histories, which reflected the political situation at the court of Sultan Husayn Mirza Bayqara (r. 875–912/1470–1506), but also writing in response to fellow historians across empires.

Terminology

In this study, I will be using the phrases "Persian historical writing," "Persian historiography," "historical writing in Persian," and "Persian history" interchangeably to refer to historical texts written in the Persian language, regardless of their place of composition or the background of the author. For the historical works themselves, I am using the words and phrases narrative, chronicle, and history interchangeably throughout. There was a tremendous variety of historical output during this period, and I will differentiate between various genres of histories such as universal and dynastic as necessary.

The various historiographical trends and developments discussed in this study do not necessarily fall into neat periodization categories. In other words, the passing of a particular year, decade, or even century does not always correspond with overall changes in the characteristics of historical writing. Periodization does, however, allow us to organize larger blocks of time. In that spirit, I will use the phrase "middle periods" as defined by Marshall Hodgson in his magisterial *Venture of Islam* series to refer to the period of 950–1501. Whereas Hodgson uses the phrase "gunpowder empires" to describe the next period in Islamic history from 1501 to 1800, I will instead use "early modern" in order to acknowledge the fact that this rich period had much more to offer the world than gunpowder alone.[31]

Transliteration Note

This book employs a modified Library of Congress transliteration system in which, except for the bibliography, only technical terms and passages are fully transliterated with diacritical marks. The bibliography contains full transliteration. One further modification is that the Persian letter "zad" will be indicated with a superscript dot above the letter "z" (ż). Other words, such as names and places, will follow the Library of Congress system without diacritical marks. The ayn (ʻ) and hamza (ʼ) will always be indicated. Premodern dates will include the *hijrī* date (AH) followed by the common era (CE) date.

Final Notes

As noted above, I have placed information about the chronicles and chroniclers in the Appendix at the end of this book, so that readers may conveniently refer to the main sources used throughout this study in one place. I have carefully checked and retranslated, revised, or modified, as necessary, all translations of primary sources when such translations are available. In all instances, the first page reference refers to the original text, while the second, marked by "trans.," refers to the translation. Finally, Philip Bockholt's important and groundbreaking scholarship on Khvandamir's *Habib al-siyar* was regretfully unavailable to me when this manuscript was being prepared for submission.

31 Hodgson himself acknowledges that the era he calls the "gunpowder empires" should not simply be defined in terms of gunpowder alone: "Gunpowder was doubtless not the one great decisive factor in the political and social – and ultimately cultural – realignments that occurred in the three generations following 1450; but it played a distinctive role, and perhaps was the most easily identifiable single occasion for them." Hodgson, *The Venture of Islam*, 3: 18.

2 *Continuity and Transformation*
The Timurid Historiographical Legacy

Introduction

Early modern Persian chronicles contain a number of conventional elements or standard sections that can be found in earlier Persian histories. For example, most chronicles open with a preface (*dībāchah/muqaddimah*) that contains certain types of information, such as an overview of the author's past, and a key turn of events that inspired the chronicler to write his history.[1] The purpose of this chapter is to explore the ways in which early modern historians modified, expanded, altered, and interacted with those earlier historiographical elements, contained in their Timurid models, through an analysis of four conventions in select Persian chronicles written across the early modern empires. We will demonstrate, through a close reading of select texts alongside their models, that the inclusion of conventional elements depends, to a very great extent, on the particular model or models that the chronicler used, which were predominantly Timurid texts. In other words, certain information appears in the histories not only because of established convention but also the historiographical models that the chronicler chose to imitate. Furthermore, the popularity of a particular source had a large impact on the survival of a particular element. Before turning to the specific conventions themselves, however, it is first necessary to outline some of the salient features of Timurid historiography due to its impact on later Persian historical writing.

The Timurid Historiographical Legacy

While early modern historians cited and used a number of texts dating back to the earliest period of Islamic history, the chronicles that

[1] For an analysis of this practice, see Quinn, *Historical Writing*, 33–61.

undergo analysis in this chapter reflect and reproduce certain elements found in Timurid sources, in particular Sharaf al-Din 'Ali Yazdi's (d. 858/1454) *Zafarnamah* (839/1435–1436) and Mirkhvand's (837–903/1433 or 4–1498) *Rawzat al-safa* (902/1497). By "Timurid historiographical legacy" is meant those conventional elements that the early modern chroniclers reproduced in writing their histories and, therefore, had a significant impact and influence upon the narratives discussed below.[2]

It is possible to discern which texts early modern historians were utilizing because they very often engaged in a practice of "imitative writing," a technique that predates Timurid historiography. As John E. Woods has demonstrated, late Timurid chroniclers used early Timurid histories and "updated" them in specific ways and for specific reasons while retaining the syntax and style of the earlier text.[3] For example, Woods assesses Sharaf al-Din 'Ali Yazdi's *Zafarnamah* as the best-known representative of early Timurid historiography in Persian, stating that after its composition, it was "widely acclaimed as a model of elegance and style for historical writing in Iran, Central Asia, and India."[4] Yazdi, on his part, primarily used an earlier Timurid history by the same name – Mawlana Nizam al-Din 'Ali Shami's *Zafarnamah* – as a model, which he reworked by removing Chingizid references and replacing them with more "Islamic" ones in order to appeal to evolving Timurid notions of legitimacy.[5] The demands of the genre to conform to certain standards and practices of historical writing and to include conventional elements was strong, because in several instances, we see examples of historians having to

[2] For more on the Timurid legacy in general, see Stephen Frederic Dale, "The Legacy of the Timurids," *Journal of the Royal Asiatic Society* 8 (1998): 43–58. See also Sholeh A. Quinn, "The Timurid Historiographical Legacy: A Comparative Study of Persianate Historical Writing," in *Society and Culture in the Early Modern Middle East: Studies on Iran in the Safavid Period*, ed. Andrew J. Newman, 9–32 (Leiden: Brill, 2003).

[3] John E. Woods, "The Rise of Timurid Historiography," *Journal of Near Eastern Studies* 46 (1987): 81–108.

[4] Woods, "The Rise of Timurid Historiography," 99. İlker Evrim Binbaş provides the most current and detailed analysis of Yazdi's *Zafarnamah* in İlker Evrim Binbaş, *Intellectual Networks in Timurid Iran: Sharaf al-Dīn 'Alī Yazdī and the Islamicate Republic of Letters* (New York: Cambridge University Press, 2016), 217–250. See also Shiro Ando, "Die Timuridische Historiographie II: Šaraf al-Dīn 'Alī Yazdī," *Studia Iranica* 24 (1995): 219–246.

[5] Woods, "The Rise of Timurid Historiography," 98–99, 104–105, 102, 105.

account for or explain why they were deviating from expressing themselves in conventional ways.[6] The most striking example of this phenomenon can be seen in an early modern chronicle from Central Asia: Muhammad Haydar Dughlat's *Tarikh-i Rashidi*, which draws upon Yazdi's *Zafarnamah*.[7]

The Example of the *Tarikh-i Rashidi*

Dughlat's *Tarikh-i Rashidi*, which narrates the story of the Khans of Moghulistan, contains two prefaces (*dībāchah/muqaddimah*) because he divides his history into two books, and each book contains an introduction. Dughlat, who was a maternal cousin of Babur, the first Mughal emperor, wrote Book Two first in 948/1541. This volume covers people, places, and events that he witnessed himself.[8] He then composed Book One devoted to the history of the Khans of Moghulistan, completing it in 952/1546. It has already been demonstrated that in their prefaces, writers generally showcase their best poetry and language, which they use to praise God, the Prophet Muhammad, and the current ruler, and they present this information in a highly conventional way. This unspoken "requirement" to write such a preface apparently caused Dughlat considerable anxiety. In his preface to Book One, Dughlat explains the circumstances that led to his writing, lamenting the fact that no one else had ever written a history of the Mughal khaqans and noting that all that remained was oral history.[9] However, he continues, at the time of his writing, even oral history had been forgotten, and the pressure thus fell on him to write his chronicle:

[6] This bears resemblance to current norms of scholarly writing where, for example, it would be difficult to imagine writing a piece of academic scholarship without proper referencing and citations. If such scholarship does deviate from these standards, authors feel obliged to provide an explanation.

[7] Mirza Haydar Dughlat, *Tarikh-i Rashidi: A History of the Khans of Moghulistan*, trans. and ann. by W. M. Thackston, Sources of Oriental Languages & Literatures 38, 2 vols. (Cambridge: Harvard University Department of Near Eastern Languages and Civilizations, 1996).

[8] Dughlat, *Tarikh-i Rashidi*, trans., vii.

[9] On Dughlat's role as "one who preserved Mongol history," see Anooshahr, *Turkestan*, 118–119. Anooshar states that "Mirza Haydar presented himself and his family as the custodians of the best aspects of Mongol heritage." Anooshahr, *Turkestan*, 118.

As of this date, which is the year 951 [A.D. 1544–1545], there is not a soul left of this group who remembers these stories, and my audacity in this important task is based on necessity, for if I were not so bold, the history of the Moghul khaqans would disappear entirely from the pages of time.[10]

Perhaps as a "preemptive strike" against any potential critics, or as an honest expression of common writer's block, Dughlat next expresses his misgivings about his own writing: "I find that I do not have it within me. I am not capable even of making an introduction and beginning to the book with a praise of God and the Prophet."[11] Instead of continuing along to the best of his ability, his solution was to copy portions from another preface into his own narrative: "Therefore, for auspiciousness and for good luck, I have first quoted verbatim the introduction to Mawlana Sharaf al-Din 'Ali Yazdi's *Zafarnamah*, may God inundate him with forgiveness."[12] And indeed, the beginning of the *Tarikh-i Rashidi* corresponds word for word with the preface to the *Zafarnamah* until the "*ammā' ba'd*" ("now then") marker separating the preamble from the rest of the preface.[13] Dughlat's writing style could also explain why he chose to copy out the preface from the *Zafarnamah*. Wheeler Thackston has evaluated his style as a "simple, unadorned Tajik Persian," noting that "By the standards of his own time, his prose would have been thought shockingly plain."[14]

Dughlat apparently did gain the confidence to write Book One of his *Tarikh-i Rashidi*, but even after the preface, the *Zafarnamah* seems to have loomed heavily on his consciousness. For example, following his explanation of the Chaghatayid Tughluq Timur's (r. 760–764/1359–1363) conversion to Islam, Dughlat states that "as for the history of the khan [i.e., Tughluq Timur], nothing is known among the

10 Dughlat, *Tarikh-i Rashidi*, 4; trans., 3.

11 Dughlat, *Tarikh-i Rashidi*, 4; trans., 3. Chroniclers do not always express humility about their writing abilities in their compositions. In some instances, they boast about their talents and writing abilities. For an example of this convention, see Chapter 3, where Khvandamir brags about his ability to write a history as good as that of Sharaf al-Din 'Ali Yazdi. Iskandar Beg similarly compared his history in a favorable way to Yazdi's *Zafarnamah*. See Quinn, *Historical Writing*, 45.

12 Dughlat, *Tarikh-i Rashidi*, 5; trans., 3.

13 For a discussion of the historiography of Persian prefaces, see Quinn, *Historical Writing*, 33–61.

14 Dughlat, *Tarikh-i Rashidi*, trans., ix.

Moghuls. It is to be found, however, in the *Zafarnamah*, and it is quoted here verbatim."[15] He then proceeds to reproduce entire chapters of the *Zafarnamah* in the first sections of Book One. The portions that he incorporates from the *Zafarnamah* are those concerning two rulers of Moghulistan, Tughluq Timur and Amir Qamar al-Din (r. ca. 767–794/1366–1392), and their various dealings with Timur.

While Yazdi's *Zafarnamah* was Dughlat's most important source, it is not the only text that he cites in the introductions to his chronicle. In the opening portion of Book Two, he provides a discussion that approximates something like a modern day academic "literature review," where he points to a gap in existing knowledge on his topic. He does this by stating that the history of the Moghul khans had received only tangential attention in other historical works and that this coverage was inadequate:

> In what the learned men of Transoxiana, Khurasan, and Iraq have recorded in histories written for their kings and amirs, if the flow of the narrative touches upon the Moghul khaqans they introduce only that much that has to do with the narrative; to what lies beyond that they pay no attention.[16]

Dughlat then cites examples of the histories to which he was alluding, naming the following works: (1) Rashid al-Din Fazl Allah's *Majmu'ah al-tavarikh* (*Jami' al-tavarikh*), (2) Hamd Allah Mustawfi's *Tarikh-i guzidah*, (3) Sharaf al-Din 'Ali Yazdi's *Zafarnamah*, (4) 'Abd al-Razzaq's *Tarikh-i manzum*, and (5) the *Ulus-i arba'ah*. Of these works, the first three are well known and extant, the fourth item is not known, and the final item, a history attributed to Ulugh Beg and abridged as the *Shajarat al-atrak*, is known but not extant.[17] While Thackston equates the *Tarikh-i manzum* with 'Abd al-Razzaq Samarqandi's *Matla'-i Sa'dayn*, aside from the fact that the latter is a well-known Timurid chronicle, there is no evidence that Dughlat was referring to that work, since "*tārīkh-i manẓūm*" means a history in verse, and the

15 Dughlat, *Tarikh-i Rashidi*, 13; trans., 11.
16 Dughlat, *Tarikh-i Rashidi*, 110; trans., 89.
17 For more on the *Ulus-i arba'ah*, see C. A. Storey, *Persian Literature: A Bio-bibliographical Survey*, 3 vols. (London: Luzac & Co., 1927), 1: 272; Binbaş, *Intellectual Networks*, 206, 211–212; Woods, "The Rise of Timurid Historiography," 102; John E. Woods, "Timur's Genealogy," in *Intellectual Studies on Islam: Essays Written in Honor of Martin B. Dickson*, eds. Michel M. Mazzaoui and Vera B. Moreen, 86 (Salt Lake City: University of Utah Press, 1990).

Matla'-i Sa'dayn is prose.[18] Dughlat then repeats his assessment of the inadequacies of these histories, noting their lack of chronology in relation to the Moghul khans: "in every one there are disparate and random mentions of the khans, but the order of things cannot be learned from them."[19]

Finally, Dughlat expresses some concern regarding his own overall methodology and framework for writing his history, which we may read as another response to Timurid historiographical norms and standards. In the introduction to Book Two, he states that he should have employed an approach in which he combines written sources with oral history: "It seems to my feeble mind that I should conjoin what is in written histories with what I have heard in oral accounts of the period after the Moghuls' conversion to Islam and add to it what I myself have witnessed."[20] He rejects this approach, however, noting that he does not have the "talent and ability" to do this: "I have not found it within myself to accomplish this task as it should be."[21] Instead, he decided that it would be

> best to have a trial run in which I recorded the events I witnessed with my own eyes ... for therein will be recorded a good bit of my eventual goal, i.e., the history of the Moghul khans, since most of my own history is intimately tied to them. When this copy, with God's grace, is completed and honored by being viewed mercifully by the discriminating, if it is forgiven and accepted, I will gain confidence. Then I will return to writing the main history (*tārīkh-i aṣl*).[22]

Dughlat's overall relationship to the Timurid historiographical legacy, therefore, is complex. He lists certain Timurid sources by name in order to criticize their limited coverage of the Moghul khans. At the same time, however, he expresses in more than one instance his own lack of self-confidence and ability to write history, in particular his introduction, which by convention should display his best and most elevated writing style. His solution was to reproduce, verbatim, the preface of one of the Timurid histories that he lists as not discussing the Moghul khans

18 Personal communication, John E. Woods, December 19, 2016. *Tarikh-i Rashidi*, 110; trans., 89–90.
19 Dughlat, *Tarikh-i Rashidi*, 110; trans., 90.
20 Dughlat, *Tarikh-i Rashidi*, 110; trans., 90.
21 Dughlat, *Tarikh-i Rashidi*, 110; trans., 90.
22 Dughlat, *Tarikh-i Rashidi*, 111; trans., 90.

adequately: Yazdi's *Zafarnamah*. Other historians created their own ways of addressing the Timurid legacy, which we turn to next.

While writers like Dughlat looked to the Timurid *Zafarnamah* as a model to imitate, not every conventional element that we find in Timurid histories survived into the later period. A number of factors affected this process. These include which model a particular early modern historian imitated in composing his chronicle and the degree to which his own history in turn became a model for later chroniclers. Thus, the choices that our historians made were extremely important in terms of perpetuating certain historiographical conventions. We may better understand this phenomenon by tracing the trajectories of four elements that survived in varying degrees into the early modern period: (1) discussions of the "benefits of history," (2) bibliographies, (3) genealogies, and (4) dream narratives.

The Benefits of History

The practice of a historian listing the advantages of studying history goes back to at least the twelfth century when Ibn Funduq (ca. 490–565/1097–1169) included such a discussion in his *Tarikh-i Bayhaq* (563/1168), a prosopography focusing on the town of Bayhaq, also known as Sabzavar, in Khurasan.[23] This convention survived into the Timurid period when the chronicler Mirkhvand included a similar discussion in his *Rawzat al-safa*. Mirkhvand's version became the model for a small number of early modern chroniclers who chose to include a similar section in their histories. In the preface to his history, Ibn Funduq includes a discursus on the meaning and importance of history. He first places the science (*'ilm*) of history in a group with two other sciences which he considers very important: traditions (*ḥadīth*) and genealogy (*insāb*).[24] He then proceeds to list

[23] See Ibn Funduq, *Tarikh-i Bayhaq*, ed. Ahmad Bahmanyar, 7–17 (Tihran: Mu'assas va Mudir-i Bungah-i Danish, 1317 [1938]). See also Elton Daniel, "The Rise and Development of Persian Historiography," in *Persian Historiography*, ed. Charles Melville, 145–146 (London: I. B. Tauris, 2012); *EIR*, s.v., "Bayhaqī, Ẓahīr al-Dīn," by H. Halm, and C. Edmund Bosworth, "Historical Information from Ibn Funduq's Tarikh-i Bayhaq 563/1167–68," *Iran: Journal of the British Institute of Persian Studies* 48 (2010): 81–106. During this period, *'ilm* did not refer to science in a modern sense, but rather a "field of knowledge." See *EI2*, s.v., "'ilm."

[24] Ibn Funduq, *Tarikh-i Bayhaq*, 3–7.

approximately six benefits or advantages of history, as follows in summary form: (1) History allows one to understand the mistakes that were made in the past, (2) since no one has lived through the entire past, history allows one to understand the events of the past [that one did not witness], (3) the science of history is a subtle and agreeable science; there is nothing better for the eyes and ears, and it is easy to memorize, (4) in a short period, one gains advantages from history that would take many lifetimes to experience, (5) history can be equated with first-hand experience, and (6) one who learns history knows about past events going back to Adam.[25]

Eventually, writing about the benefits of history became a semiconventional, or limited conventional element, and the practice diversified over time. For example, Christopher Markiewicz has distinguished between general lists of the benefits of history such as that of the Timurid historian Hafiz Abru (d. 833/1430), whose account bears some similarity to the *Tarikh-i Bayhaq*, and a more specific debate that took place in the Islamic world in the fifteenth century. In this debate, some five scholars discussed the classification of history as a traditional science and provided extensive discussions on this theme.[26] Here we will focus on historians of the sixteenth century who included benefits of history in their prefaces and also their fifteenth century models, neither of which were part of this particular debate. Of course, even for these chroniclers, writing about the benefits of history was not merely following convention. The very act of including this element in their texts meant that they were simultaneously defending history as a valid field of knowledge.

Between Ibn Funduq's history and the early modern period, a number of chroniclers included benefits of history sections in their narratives. These individuals include Ziya al-Din Barani, whose Delhi Sultanate history, the *Tarikh-i Firuzshahi* (758/1357), includes an account of seven benefits of history.[27] Nearly seventy years later, in

[25] Ibn Funduq, *Tarikh-i Bayhaq*, 7–17.

[26] For an extensive discussion of this debate, see Christopher Markiewicz, *The Crisis of Kingship in Late Medieval Islam: Persian Emigres and the Making of Ottoman Sovereignty* (Cambridge: Cambridge University Press, 2019), 191–239. See also Christopher Markiewicz, "History As Science: The Fifteenth Century Debate in Arabic and Persian," *Journal of Early Modern History* 21 (2017): 216–240; see esp. 222–225.

[27] Blain Auer, "A Translation of the Prolegomena to Żiyāʾ al-Dīn Baranī's Tārīkh-i Fīrūzshāhī," in *Essays in Islamic Philology, History, and Philosophy*, eds.

830/1426–1427, the Timurid historian Hafiz Abru also included in the preface of his universal history, the *Majma' al-tavarikh* (830/ 1426–1427), a discussion of the advantages or benefits of history. Some sixty years after Hafiz Abru wrote, we see an elaboration of the advantages of history in the Aq Qoyunlu historian Khunji-Isfahani's *Tarikh-i 'alam-ara-yi Amini* (ca. 896–897/1490–1491).[28] Thus, by the time the late Timurid historian Mirkhvand composed his *Rawzat al-safa*, providing a section on the benefits of history was already a semiconventional element in Persian prefaces. I have used the term "semiconventional" because not every chronicler included such material in his preface. For example, neither Rashid al-Din's *Jami' al-tavarikh* nor Sharaf al-Din 'Ali Yazdi's *Zafarnamah* includes such a discussion.

Mirkhvand's *Rawzat al-safa*, an extremely important seven-volume late Timurid universal history, composed under the patronage of the famous poet Mir 'Ali Shir Nava'i (844–906/1441–1501), served as the primary model that early modern historians looked to when composing their accounts of the benefits of history.[29] The *Rawzat al-safa* was probably the single most influential Timurid era chronicle for early modern Persianate historiography. Storey/Bregel's biobibliographical survey lists a staggering numbers of nearly 500 surviving manuscripts, attesting to its popularity across time and space.[30] Before demonstrating how, specifically this particular history influenced histories written across empires, we first provide an overview of Mirkhvand's account. Structurally, Mirkhvand's discussion of the benefits of history actually forms part of his preface, and he places it immediately after he lists his table of contents. It is the first in a cluster of three subsections dealing with history and covers the following topics: (1) ten benefits of history, (2) three reasons why governors need history more than other people, and (3) five qualities necessary for a historian. For his benefits of

Alireza Korangy, Wheeler M. Thackston, Roy P. Mottahedeh, and William Granara, 400–418 (Berlin: DeGruyter, 2016).

[28] See, for example, Fazl Allah b. Ruzbihan Khunji-Isfahani, *Tarikh-i 'alam-ara-yi Amini*, ed. J. Woods, abr. Eng. trans. V. Minorsky, rev. and aug. J. Woods, 80–86 (London: Royal Asiatic Society, 1992). See also Markiewicz, *The Crisis of Kingship*, 203–204.

[29] For more information on Mirkhvand and the *Rawzat al-safa*, see Appendix.

[30] See Storey, *Persian Literature*, 1: 92–95; Bregel trans., 1: 361–370. While not every manuscript listed in Storey/Bregel is the entire multivolume work, at least parts of it were copied hundreds of times.

history section, Mirkhvand devotes several sentences to explaining each benefit: (1) In order to become acquainted with affairs of the world, one must read works based on things heard, (2) history promotes cheerfulness and exhilaration, (3) history can be easily studied and remembered, (4) one will acquire the skill of distinguishing between truth and falsehood, (5) one obtains experience by studying history, (6) students of history read opinions of wise men, which are more sound that those of ones contemporaries, (7) the intellect is strengthened by study of history, (8) studying history gives the hope of success at times of calamity, (9) one gains patience and acquiescence to the divine will by studying history, and (10) kings are instructed by history; they are warned by the past and this causes them to behave better.[31]

Three early modern historians took Mirkhvand's "benefits of history" account and used it as the basis for their own explanations of the advantages of history. The fact that they modified Mirkhvand in various ways demonstrates the importance of this Timurid history in the early modern period. These histories are (1) Qasim Beg Hayati Tabrizi's *Tarikh* (961/1554), (2) Husayn Nishapuri Vuqu'i's *Majma' al-akhbar* (1000/1591–1592), and (3) Sharaf Khan Bidlisi's *Sharafnamah* (1005/1596).

Hayati Tabrizi's Tarikh

Until very recently, it would have been possible to state that no Safavid chronicler includes a discussion of the benefits of history in his history, but Kioumars Ghereghlou recently discovered a Safavid historical work long considered lost, namely a history composed by Mawlana Hayati Tabrizi (fl. 961/1554) in 961/1554, covering the Safaviyya Sufi order and the early years of Shah Isma'il.[32] Historians have been

[31] Mirkhvand, *Tarikh-i rawzat al-safa fi sirat al-anbiya va al-muluk va al-khulafa*, 11 vols., ed. Jamshid Kiyan'far (Tehran: Intisharat-i Asatir, 2001). The older standard edition is *Tarikh-i rawzat al-safa*, 7 vols. [ed.] 'Abbas Parviz ([Tehran]: Khayyam, 1338 [1959]), trans. E. Rehatsek as *Rauzat-us-safa or, Garden of Purity*. 3 vols., ed. F. F. Arbuthnot, Oriental Translation Fund, New Series 1 (London: Royal Asiatic Society, 1891), 1: 11–22; trans., 1: 24–33. For a recent discussion of Mirkhvand's benefits of history, see Ali M. Ansari, "Mīrkhwānd and Persian Historiography," *Journal of the Royal Asiatic Society* 26 (2016): 249–259.

[32] Kioumars Ghereghlou provides an introduction and analysis of this chronicle in Kioumars Ghereghlou, "Chronicling a Dynasty on the Make: New Light on the

familiar with this lost work, primarily because Qazi Ahmad Qumi, the first Safavid chronicler to write during the reign of Shah ʻAbbas, names Hayati Tabrizi as a source for his *Khulasat al-tavarikh*.[33] In addition to the valuable information Hayati Tabrizi's history contains on the early Safavid dynasty, he also includes a section on the benefits of history. Ghereghlou correctly notes that Hayati Tabrizi was inspired by Mirkhvand's *Rawzat al-safa* in writing this portion of his chronicle.[34] Hayati Tabrizi's six "virtues" of the science of history bear considerable similarity to those of Mirkhvand not only because of similar themes and subject matter but also because he imitates Mirkhvand in terms of his language. This indicates a close relationship between these two texts.

Hayati Tabrizi does not imitate Mirkhvand in a completely word-for-word manner. Instead, he rather consistently reworks Mirkhvand's account to emphasize the virtues of history in relation to kingship, instead of focusing on the "science" of history itself. Three of Hayati Tabrizi's six virtues of history imitate those of Mirkhvand, the modifications ranging from little to significant. The following example illustrates one instance in which Hayati Tabrizi, in narrating his third virtue of history, imitates Mirkhvand's second benefit with very little deviation:

Rawzat al-safa	Hayati Tabrizi
Second use. – History is a science from which one gains cheerfulness and exhilaration, and wipes off the darkness of misfortune and weariness from the mirror of the mind. The possessor of wisdom knows that the sense of hearing and sight have a higher rank amongst the human senses, such that the sense of sight is delighted by contemplating beautiful pictures and does not become weary. The sense of hearing also does not become weary from listening to narratives and accounts. Indeed, each	Third is such that cheerfulness and exhilaration is gained from the science of history, such that it wipes off the darkness of weariness from the mirror of the mind, and the wise ones have said that the sense of sight has the highest rank amongst the human senses, such that the sense of sight is elated and joyful from seeing beautiful pictures. Hearing also does not become weary from listening to narratives. Rather, hour by hour, his happiness and joyfulness increase. In an account it is related that "the eye is

Early Safavids in Ḥayātī Tabrīzī's History (961/1554)," *Journal of the American Oriental Society* 137 (2017): 805–832.

33 Qazi Ahmad Qumi, *Khulasat al-tavarikh*, 2 vols, ed. Ihsan Ishraqi, 24–26 (Tehran: Danishgah-i Tihran, 1363 [1984]).

34 Ghereghlou, "Chronicling a Dynasty on the Make," 807.

moment his joy and happiness increase. For historical information (*akhbār*) and inquiry (*istikhbār*) is centered in human nature, and the disposition of human beings is formed with it. And in proverbs it is said that "the eye is not satisfied with seeing, nor the ear filled with information (history), nor the earth with rain."[35]

not satisfied with seeing, nor the ear filled with information (history)."[36]

Ānkih, tārīkh ʿilmī ast kih khurramī va bashāshat az vay ḥāṣil āyad va zang-i sha'āmat va malālat az a'īnah-'i khāṭir zadāyad va ṣāḥib-i khirad dānad kih ḥāssah-'i samʿ va baṣar az ḥavās-i insānī martabah-'i ʿulyā dārad chinānchah ḥiss-i baṣar az mulāḥaẓah-'i ṣuvar-i ḥasanah maḥẓūẓ mīshavad va malūl namīgardad. Ḥiss-i samʿ nīz az istimāʿ-i akhbār va āsār malūl namīgardad; balkah har laḥẓah ū rā bahjatī va masarratī mī'afzāyad. Chih akhbār va istikhbār dar jibillat-i basharī markūz ast va ṭibāʿ-i banī ādam bih ān majbūl va dar amsāl vārid kih lā yushbiʿ al-ʿayn min naẓar wa lā al-samʿ min khabar wa la al-arḍ min maṭar.

Ānkih, khurramī va bashāshat az ʿilm-i tārīkh ḥāṣil āyad kih az a'īnah-i khāṭir zang-i malālat zadāyad. Va ḥukamā guftah and kih ḥāssah-i baṣar dar miyān-i ḥavās martabah-'i aʿlá ast, hamchinānchah ḥiss-i baṣar az ru'yat-'i ṣuvar-i khujastah mutalaẕẕiẕ va maḥẓūẓ mīgardad, samʿ nīz az istimāʿ-i akhbār malūl namīgardad, balkah sāʿat-i fasāʿat-i ū rā masarrat va bahjat mī'afzāyad. Dar akhbār āmadah kih lā yushbiʿ al-ʿayn min naẓar wa lā al-samʿ min khabar.

These parallel passages show that Hayati Tabrizi makes two basic changes to Mirkhvand's text. First, he shortens the account, removing Mirkhvand's explicit statements about historical information and inquiry being part of human nature. Second, rather than stating that sight and hearing together are the highest of human senses, he says that sight alone is the loftiest of the senses. While these changes do not suggest a political agenda, Hayati

[35] Mirkhvand, *Rawzat al-safa*, 1: 11–12; trans., 1: 24–25.

[36] Qasim Beg Hayati Tabrizi, *A Chronicle of the Early Safavids and the Reign of Shah Ismāʿīl*, ed. Kioumars Ghereghlou, 25 (New Haven, CT: American Oriental Society, 2019).

Tabrizi's fourth virtue of history contains significant differences in comparison with Mirkhvand's seventh use of history, which he imitates:

Rawzat al-safa	Hayati Tabrizi
Seventh use – Knowledge of the science of history is the reason for the increase of the intellect, and is the cause for the promotion of virtue and the means of integrity of opinion and deliberation. Therefore Barzachumir [Buzurgmihr, Nushiravan's vizier], whose blessed nature was like a preface to the pages of wisdom, has said that the science of history confirms and determines proper opinion, because knowledge of ancient events in sound judgement of successors is a just witness and a virtuous testimony.[37]	Fourth – Knowledge of the conditions of honored sultans is the source of the increase of the intellect and the abundance of heroes, and the integrity of opinion and the knowledge of deliberation. From Barzachumir [Buzurgmihr, Nushiravan's vizier] the wise, it is related that he said that the history of sultans promotes proper opinion, because knowledge of ancient events in sound judgement of successors has a great value.[38]
Ānkih shu'ūr bih 'ilm-i tārīkh sabab-i ziyādatī-i 'aql va vasīlah-'i izdiyād-i fażl va vāsiṭah-'i ṣiḥḥat-i ra'y va tadbīr ast va lihaẕā Būzarjmihr kih ẕāt-i karīmash dībāchah-'i ṣaḥf-i ḥikmat būd, mī'gūyad kih 'ilm-i tārīkh mu'ayyad va mu'ayyan-i r'ay-i ṣavāb ast, chih 'ilm bih aḥvāl-i salaf dar ṣiḥḥat-i ra'y-i khalaf shāhidī 'adl va guvāhī fażl ast.	*Ānkih shu'ūr bih 'aḥvāl-i salāṭīn-i ẕūy al-iḥtirām bā'is̱-i izdiyād-i 'aql va vufūr-i kiyāsat va ṣiḥḥat-i ra'y va iṣābat-i tadbīr ast. Az Būẕarjmihr ḥakīm marvīst kih farmūdah tārīkh-i salāṭīn-i mummid-i r'ay-i ṣavābast, chih 'ilm bih aḥvāl-i salaf dar ṣiḥḥat-i ra'y-i khalaf dakhl-i 'aẓīm dārad.*

Here, Hayati Tabrizi consistently replaces Mirkhvand's notion of the knowledge of the "science of history" (*'ilm-i tārīkh*) with the knowledge of the "conditions of kings" (*aḥvāl-i salāṭīn*). By transforming Mirkhvand's statement that "the science of history confirms and determines proper opinion" into an assertion that "the history of kings promotes proper opinion," Hayati places kingship at the center of his narrative. Hayati Tabrizi makes the same type of change in his sixth virtue of history, which parallels Mirkhvand's ninth benefit of history. In the *Rawzat al-safa*, Mirkhvand explains how the study of history promotes patience and acquiescence, and these qualities can be seen in

37 Mirkhvand, *Rawzat al-safa*, 1: 14; trans., 1: 26.
38 Hayati Tabrizi, *A Chronicle*, 25.

messengers and prophets, who themselves showed patience and resignation in all that befell them. Knowing this, Mirkhvand says, allows one to persevere oneself in the face of "any great calamity."[39] In his history, Hayati Tabrizi again replaces Mirkhvand's notion of the knowledge of events and history (*akhbār va tavārīkh*) with the knowledge of the conditions of kings (*aḥvāl-i salāṭīn*), noting that the patience of kings and their behavior in the face of misfortune inspire one to show patience:

Rawzat al-safa	Hayati Tabrizi
Ninth use – He who is acquainted with the events and histories of the world attains a certain degree of patience and acquiescence, and these two noble virtues are qualities of illustrious and pious men.[40]	Sixth – Anyone who becomes aware of the conditions of kings, becomes cognizant of their patience amidst misfortunes. Without any comparison (resemblance), his level of patience and acquiescence becomes increased.[41]
Ānkih shakhṣī muṭṭaliʿ bar akhbār va tavārīkh buvad bih ḥuṣūl-i martabah-'i ṣabr va riżā fāyiz va bahrahmand shavad va īn dū martabah ashraf-i marātib-i aṣfiyā va atqiyā ast...	*Ānkih har kas kih bar aḥvāl-i salāṭīn iṭṭilāʿ yābad az muṣābarat-i īshān bar makārah vāqif gardad, bi-lā shibh ū rā martabah-'i ṣabr va riżā afzūn shavad...*

Hayati Tabrizi's other three virtues of history are completely different from those of Mirkhvand – the first two emphasize the relationship between the Qur'an and history, and the third focuses on the theme of kingship. In rewriting the Mirkhvand's benefits of history, overall, Hayati Tabrizi places greater importance on the history of kings than on history itself. Historical context helps explain this shift of emphasis. Ghereghlou has explained that while Shah Tahmasb served as the original patron for Hayati Tabrizi's history, eventually he requested that it be dedicated to the shah's sister, Mihin Begum (d. 969/1562), who was Shah Isma'il's oldest daughter. This princess was a "chief superintendent" of *waqf*s (religious endowments). Having dedicated his history to Mihin Begum, Hayati Tabrizi further "recommended her

39 Mirkhvand, *Rawzat al-safa*, 1: 14; trans., 27.
40 Mirkhvand, *Rawzat al-safa*, 1: 14; trans., 27.
41 Hayati Tabrizi, *A Chronicle*, 25.

sister's female associates, or as he put it 'the veiled inhabitants of the nook of intuition,' to study his history and get a good grasp of the life and times of 'their renowned and distinguished ancestry.'"[42] Perhaps, then, as part of his desire to educate the royal women of the harem regarding their family history, as well as to please his original patron, Hayati Tabrizi emphasizes the role of kingship in reworking Mirkhvand's benefits of history discussion.

Despite Hayati Tabrizi's inclusion of this semiconventional element in his chronicle, no other later Safavid history contains a similar discussion. Here, the popularity of certain histories that served as models plays an important role in determining the extent to which a particular convention survived. In other words, even though Qazi Ahmad Qumi made reference to Hayati Tabrizi's history, other later chroniclers, in particular influential ones like Iskandar Beg Munshi, did not.[43] Consequently, Hayati Tabrizi's history was neither very well known nor utilized in a way that would perpetuate this convention into the later Safavid period. Furthermore, most early Safavid chroniclers looked to Khvandamir's *Habib al-siyar* as a model to imitate, and Khvandamir chose not to include a discussion of the benefits of history in his chronicle, despite the fact that Mirkhvand was his grandfather and he imitated the *Rawzat al-safa* in many portions of his history. This, in a sense, closed the historiographical door to this convention surviving into the later Safavid period.

Vuqu'i's Majami' al-akhbar

Despite "benefits of history" elaborations not continuing under Safavid historical writing, the survival of historical conventions did not depend on dynastic boundaries because the next instance of a discussion of the benefits of history appears in a little known Mughal history, Mir Muhammad Sharif Vuqu'i Husayni Nishapuri's (d. 1002/1593–1594) *Majami' al-akhbar*, composed in 1000/1591–1592 during the reign of the Mughal emperor Akbar. The *Majami' al-akhbar* ("compilations of histories") is one of the earliest universal chronicles produced under the Mughals, composed approximately two years after

42 Ghereghlou, "Chronicling a Dynasty on the Make," 807. Hayati Tabrizi, *A Chronicle*, xi–xii.

43 See Quinn, *Historical Writing*, 43; and Qazi Ahmad Qumi, *Khulasat al-tavarikh*, 3.

Vuqu'i entered the court of Akbar in 998/1590. Vuqu'i came from a notable family of sayyids of Nishapur, and his mother was the sister of Shah Tahmasb's assay master.[44] Vuqu'i's history was not very popular, although Vuqu'i himself was well known as a poet and mentioned in other sources from the time.[45] The *Majami' al-akhbar* survives in only one known manuscript copy and does not appear to have been cited by later Mughal chroniclers. Perhaps this is why Vuqu'i includes a discussion of the benefits of history at the beginning of his account.

Vuqu'i's discussion opens with an explanation as to why he chose to discuss the benefits of history in his chronicle:

> It is clear to the wise ones of the world and the learned ones of the age that knowledgeable people have exerted themselves and spent great effort in writing about the benefits of this science. This weak one, too, has written two or three lines in following these wise ones and has tied himself to their harness. And success comes from God, glorified be he.[46]

Vuqu'i follows this by listing seven advantages to the study of history. Briefly summarized, they are as follows: (1) The foundation of history is based on those who have died and passed away, and the remembrance of their death and dying; (2) studying history makes a man wise and knowledgeable about the swiftness of the decline and changing of governments relative to the inconstancy of the world; (3) the most useful experiences are those which a man has gained for himself ... one preserves the treasures of one's own just opinion and sound thinking, observing caution and promoting wisdom; (4) the study of the goodnesses of the conditions of good people and the uglinesses of the actions of bad people has a great effect on the soul; (5) the nobility of this science is such that kings and rulers require it; (6) knowledgeable people know that writing the events of the world from the beginning of the appearance of human beings is customary for the peoples of the world; and (7) stories such as *Kalilah va Dimnah* are all exhortations and moral lessons that are presented in the form of stories and tales.[47]

44 Abd al-Qadir ibn Muluk Shah Badauni, *Muntakhab al-tavarikh*, ed. Mawlavi Ahmad 'Ali Sahib, 3 vols. (Tehran: Anjuman-i Asar va Muvakhir-i Farhangi, 1379 [2000]); trans. as *Muntakhabu't-tawārīkh* by W. H. Lowe, 3 vols. (Delhi: Idarah-i-Adabiyat-i-Delli, 1898), 3: 256–257; trans., 3: 512.

45 For more on Badauni, see Appendix.

46 Vuqu'i, "Majami' al-akhbar," ms. British Library India Office 1758. f. 4a.

47 Vuqu'i, "Majami' al-akhbar," f. 4a–4b.

Of all the "benefits" texts examined here, Vuqu'i's correspond most closely with Mirkhvand's *Rawzat al-safa*.[48] For example, Vuqu'i's third benefit corresponds with Mirkhvand's fifth benefit, which is Mirkhvand's longest and most extensive of all his "benefits of history." Vuqu'i begins with an explanation of three types of intellect that relate to "the intellect acquired by experience" These are (1) "the ability to predict the positive and negative consequences of a matter," (2) "the faculty of distinguishing from the act itself whether it will harm or profit the agent," and (3) "hearing about the events of former times, and the power of ascertaining from them the causes of prosperity and distress, of happiness and calamity."[49] He then says that of the three degrees of experience, the best (most instructive) is that which a man has acquired by participating himself in an event. He continues by expounding on the maxim "A thing is known by study and averted by explanation," saying that studying an event (the first part of the maxim) is the same as participating in it. In this way, a "cheerful and practical narrative of a people" leads an intelligent reader to bring one's own business to a happy issue.[50] In explaining how a thing is "averted by explanation" – the second part of the maxim – he states that the history of "a feeble planning and weak-minded people (*qawmī*)" leads the reader to be put "on his guard" and in doing this, he will "remain unscathed."[51]

In his third benefit, Vuqu'i essentially makes the same points that Mirkhvand does in his fifth benefit though he expresses himself in his own words and in a much shorter and condensed manner. He agrees with Mirkhvand about experience saying, "the most useful experiences are those which a man has gained for himself," and like Mirkhvand, acknowledges that "if there is a reliable account of the past, it is almost like experiencing it yourself."[52] Finally, he also summarizes Mirkhvand's discussion of the maxim "A thing is known by study and averted by explanation" without quoting it. Rather, he acknowledges that through "gathering evidence with a lamp that has been lit by a sound intellect," one observes caution – an allusion to the second part of the maxim – and promotes wisdom, an allusion to the first part of the maxim.[53]

[48] While the *Tarikh-i Firuzshahi* discussed above contains the same seven number of benefits, there is no evidence of imitative writing nor of similarity in terms of content. See Auer, "A Translation of the Prologema," 410–412.

[49] Mikhvand, *Rawzat al-safa*, 1: 12; trans., 1: 25, slightly modified.

[50] Mirkhvand, *Rawzat al-safa*, 1: 12–13; trans., 1: 25, slightly modified.

[51] Mirkhvand, *Rawzat al-safa*, 1: 13; trans., 1: 25–26.

[52] Vuqu'i, "Majami' al-akhbar," f. 4a.

[53] Vuqu'i, "Majami' al-akhbar," f. 4a.

Vuqu'i takes a similar approach in his fifth benefit. Here, Vuqu'i does not imitate Mirkhvand's benefits of history, but rather his account reflects the portion of the *Rawzat al-safa* immediately following the benefits of history. There, Mirkhvand provides three reasons "why governors (*ḥukkām*) ought to be more in need of the craft (*fann*) of history than other people."[54] Mirkhvand's second reason as to why governors need history was the source of Vuqu'i's fifth benefit of history. Mirkhvand explains that when rulers study history, it causes them to act more justly because they learn about ancient kings. Furthermore, he says, when they reflect upon the positive consequences of prior kings' behavior, it brings them pleasure and causes them to want to do better than their predecessors.[55] The full translation of Vuqu'i's fifth benefit is as follows:

> [5] Another: The nobility of this science is such that kings and rulers require it, in relation to the details regarding the true affairs of kingship, which is a divine appointment, and maintain tranquil circumstances for all the subjects, from the peasants to the army, because the concurrence of these different affairs is clear, and the path to justice is one.[56]

In this passage, Vuqu'i's wording is completely different from Mirkhvand's, and he does not engage in any sort of imitative writing. Rather, he condenses Mirkhvand's main points into a few sentences and does so using his own words. Vuqu'i, like Mirkhvand, discusses the relationship between history and kings, pointing to the fact that kings require history for understanding the "true affairs" of kingship and maintaining "tranquil circumstances for all the subjects, from the peasants to the army."[57] Vuqu'i's statement that kingship is a "divine caliphate" (*khilāfat-i ilāhī*) is interesting and probably an allusion to Akbar. Evrim Binbaş has described how the Timurid historian Sharaf al-Din 'Ali Yazdi, whose work was upheld as a model by so many early modern chroniclers, including Khvandamir and Iskandar Beg Munshi, elaborates on this concept in his *Dibachah*, where he distinguishes between a divine caliphate and an "external caliphate (*khilāfat-i ṣūrī*)." In this scheme, kings represented the external caliphate, and prophets, the divine caliphate. Timur was an "external caliph."[58] In invoking the notion

54 Mirkhvand, *Rawzat al-safa*, 1: 15; trans., 1: 28.
55 Mirkhvand, *Rawzat al-safa*, 1: 15–16; trans., 1: 28.
56 Vuqu'i, "Majami' al-akhbar," f. 4a.
57 Vuqu'i, "Majami' al-akhbar," f. 4a.
58 See Binbaş, *Intellectual Networks*, 257. For more information on Yazdi's *Dibachah*, see Binbaş, *Intellectual Networks*, 212–217.

of the divine caliph, Vuquʿi seems to be attributing to the king – in this case Akbar – the same authority as prophets, which was a position that went well beyond Yazdi's formulation.[59] At the same time, Vuquʿi also invokes an older element of Persian kinship: the so-called circle of justice, in which the king was in a circular and interdependent relationship with the army and the peasants, with justice holding the circle together.[60] Here, Vuquʿi says that the just king is one who needs history, and who better to provide that history but Vuquʿi? Thus, the fact that Vuquʿi lightly imitated the *Rawzat al-safa* served to perpetuate that convention into the Mughal empire, where Vuquʿi's account echoed, in a modified form, that text.[61]

Bidlisi's Sharafnamah

We next turn to Sharaf al-Din Bidlisi, ruler of the Kurdish Ruzagi tribe in Bidlis and author of the *Sharafnamah* (1005/1596), a history of the Kurds, who listed the benefits of history in his chronicle. Bidlisi opens his discussion by acknowledging Mirkhvand's *Rawzat al-safa*: "To this effect the author of the history *Rawzat al-safa*, Muhammad b. Khvandshah b. Mahmud, known as Mirkhvand, in the preface to his book, has written that knowing the science of history bears ten benefits."[62] He then proceeds to reproduce a modified version of Mirkhvand's list. For the most part, Bidlisi imitates and modifies the *Rawzat al-safa* by abbreviating and shortening Mirkhvand's list of benefits. More

59 For more on the notion of the *khilāfat-i ilāhī* (divine caliph) in another Mughal chronicle, the *Tabaqat-i Akbari*, see Chapter 5.

60 These ideas will be discussed in greater detail in Chapter 5. For a detailed discussion of the circle of justice, see Linda T. Darling, *A History of Social Justice and Political Power in the Middle East: The Circle of Justice from Mesopotamia to Globalization* (New York: Routledge, 2013).

61 For more parallels between the *Rawzat al-safa* and the *Majamiʿ al-akhbar*, see Chapter 4.

62 Sharaf Khan ibn Shams al-Din Bidlisi, *Sharafnamah*, 2 vols., ed. Vladimir Valiyaminuf Zarnuf (Pitruburgh: Akadamiyah-i Impiraturiyah, 1862), trans. M. R. Izady as *The Sharafnama, or, the History of the Kurdish Nation, 1597* (Costa Mesa, CA: Mazda, 2005), 1: 5; trans., 10–11 (slightly modified).

specifically, he repeats only the first sentence of each benefit. The following example demonstrates this technique:

Rawzat al-safa	*Sharafnamah*
Third use – The art of history, although having many advantages, is easily appropriated, and it is not very troublesome or difficult to acquire that [art] and its foundation is preservation and nothing else; and when someone preserves the events of the past, and becomes occupied in researching it, and spends his time agreeably in following the events, he will sooner be successful in reaching his aims and goals.[63]	Third – Although having advantages, it is easily appropriated; it is not too troublesome or difficult to acquire that [art] and its basis is memory.[64]
Fā'idah-i sivvum ānkih fann-i tārīkh bā vujūd-i kisrat-i favāyid sahl al-m'ākhaz ast va dar istiḥṣāl-i ān ziyādah kuluft va mashaqqatī nīst va mabná-i ān bar ḥifẓ ast va bas va chūn kasī vaqāyi'-i guzashtagān rā muḥāfiẓat namāyad va bih muṭāli'ah-'i ān mashghūl gardad va dar nīl-i āmāl va amānī bih tatabbu'-i awqāt ṣarf kunad, zūdtar bih maṭālib va maqṣūd ḥāfiẓah gardad.	*Sivvum bā vujūd-i favāyid sahl al-m'ākhaz ast va dar istiḥṣāl-i ān chandān kuluft va mashaqqat nīst va mabná-i ān bar quvvat ḥāfiẓah ast.*

Bidlisi similarly replicates the rest of Mirkhvand's benefits of history, albeit with one significant alteration appearing in the sixth benefit. Mirkhvand opens his explanation of the sixth benefit by saying, "He who studies the science of history reads what the wise ones of the world have said about the events that have happened, and it is clear that this type of consultation is superior to consulting with ones contemporaries."[65] He then explains that by studying the past one can partake of the experience of many individuals, thereby preventing calamities and bringing one's own affairs "to a prosperous end."[66] Bidlisi changes this particular

63 Mirkhvand, *Rawzat al-safa*, 1: 12; trans., 1: 25.
64 Bidlisi, *Sharafnamah*, 1: 5; trans., 1: 10.
65 Mirkhvand, *Rawzat al-safa*, 1: 13–14; trans., 1: 26.
66 Mirkhvand, *Rawzat al-safa*, 1: 13; trans., 1: 26.

advantage (*fāyidah*) to state the exact opposite, while still retaining the syntax of Mirkhvand's original, as seen in the following parallel passages:

Rawzat al-safa	*Sharafnamah*
He who studies the science of history reads what the wise ones of the world have said about the events that have happened, and it is clear that this type of consultation is superior to consulting with ones contemporaries.[67]	The one who is learning the science of history, has *no* need to consult the wise ones about the events that take place.[68]
Muta'āmil-i 'ilm-i tārīkh rā dar vāqi'ah-'īkih sānaḥ shavad martabah-i mashvarat bā 'uqalā-yi 'ālam dast dādah bāshad va 'uluv-i martabah-i īn naw mashvarat nisbat bā mushāvirat-i abnā-i 'aṣr ẓāhir ast.	*Ānkih mustahẓar-i 'ilm-i tārīkh dar vāqi'ah'ī kih sānaḥ shavad iḥtiyāj bi-mashvarat-i 'uqalā nadārad.*

It is unclear why Bidlisi uncharacteristically changes the narrative in this way. Aside from scribal error, one reason may be the history of Bidlisi's family's shifting allegiances to the Ottomans (his grandfather) and the Safavids (his father), and his own dealings with both. This experience may have caused him to believe that one cannot trust what past historians have said. It is also possible that earlier historians would have tended to minimize or ignore the history of the Kurds – just as Dughlat objected to Timurid oversights of the history of Moghulistan – which was Bidlisi's main purpose in writing.

This analysis has demonstrated first of all that in reading early modern accounts of the benefits of history, we are actually reading our historians' *responses* to an earlier narrative. All three chroniclers – whether writing under the Safavids, the Mughals, or semiindependently representing the Kurds – engaged in direct dialog with Mirkhvand's *Rawzat al-safa* and produced different responses to that text. Their responses reflect the circumstances under which they wrote. Hayati Tabrizi substituted passages in the *Rawzat al-safa* about history

67 Mirkhvand, *Rawzat al-safa*, 1: 13; trans., 1: 26.
68 Bidlisi, *Sharafnamah*, 6; trans., 1: 10. Emphasis added.

with passages about kingship, thereby educating harem women about their royal ancestry. Vuqu'i used the benefits of history to make his own case to the king for history writing, and Bidlisi showed less trust in what past historians had written than his model, Mirkhvand, due perhaps to his family's uncertain political situation. Interestingly, all three historical works share the common characteristic of being infrequently cited texts written by lesser-known historians. Indeed, two of these three histories – Hayati Tabrizi's and Vuqu'i's – only survive as unique manuscripts, indicating that they were neither well-known nor popular. This may not be a coincidence. By imitating an important and frequently cited Timurid history, these authors anchor their own texts to something their audiences would have recognized. Readers familiar with the *Rawzat al-safa* would hear echos of that work in reading the *Sharafnamah*, Hayati Tabrizi's *Tarikh*, and Vuqu'i's *Majami' al-akhbar*. The actual topic itself, the value of studying history, could also help a less well-known historian gain attention and possibly even patronage by pointing out the benefits – particularly as they pertain to kings – of history writing. This also suggests that historians knew how to manipulate their Timurid historiographical legacy in order to further and legitimize their own interests. However, this conventional element did not survive much beyond these particular texts because better known historians did not choose to include benefits of histories in their own chronicles.

Why it was that the most well-known and popular chroniclers did not include discussions of the benefits of history in their histories is an interesting question but one difficult to answer because explaining historiographical omissions is not as easy as justifying additions to a text. Why, for example, did Khvandamir, who used his grandfather Mirkhvand's history as a model for his *Habib al-siyar*, choose not to include a discussion of the benefits of history? Khvandamir's history was shorter than the *Rawzat al-safa*, and in other portions of his chronicle, he imitates yet condenses Mirkhvand's narrative. However, in omitting the discussion of the benefits of history, he was making a conscious decision. Possible reasons for his and other chroniclers' omission could simply be that there was no need to argue for the importance of doing something that a given chronicler was already doing – namely writing history, especially with royal patronage. For instance, Abu al-Fazl, who was supported by Akbar in writing his *Akbarnamah*, did not need to remind Akbar of the importance of studying history, especially when Akbar himself commissioned the text and held him in high regard.

Presenting an explicit argument in favor of history under these circumstances could render the actual act of writing history seem less important and the chronicler less appreciative. Finally, it could also be the case that discussions of the benefits of history are remnants of an older historiographical tradition that simply fell out of fashion, like a fad or a practice in which fewer and fewer people were engaging.

Bibliographies

Another historiographical convention that survived into the early modern period approximates a modern bibliography. This element usually appears at the very end of a chronicle's preface, following the benefits of history discussion. It consists of a list of historical works that the chronicler states as having consulted or as simply being important works of history. We may view these bibliographies as something approximating a canon of historical works which were either familiar to historians or a list of texts that the historians hoped to read.[69] By including a bibliography, the historian situates himself as a well-read scholar writing within a respected historiographical tradition. Bibliographies thereby help the chronicler legitimize his own history by allowing the reader to view it as the latest in a long line of historical works. Like the benefits of history section, the bibliography can be traced back to Ibn Funduq's *Tarikh-i Bayhaq*, and we see similar examples in the earlier Arabic historiographical tradition.[70] At the very end of his preface, Ibn Funduq provides a list of historical works in a section called "Chapter on a Number of Famous Histories." Here, he mentions some eleven general historical works and their authors, which he follows with a list of approximately 18 authors and titles of local Persian histories (see Table 2.1).[71] As we saw with benefits of history, however, it was the Timurid-era chronicler,

[69] Charles Melville alludes to the conventional nature of bibliographies when he suggests that "such a list by Mīrkhwānd's time was perhaps little more than a formula whereby the author established his place among the ranks of the serious and respectable historians of the past ..." Charles Melville, "From Adam to Abaqa: Qāḍī Baiḍāwī's Rearrangement of History," *Studia Iranica* 30 (2001): 58.

[70] Rosenthal mentions that the ninth-century world history of al-Ya'qubi contains a bibliography. See Franz Rosenthal, *A History of Muslim Historiography*, 2nd revised ed. (Leiden: E. J. Brill, 1968), 132, 134.

[71] Ibn Funduq, *Tarikh-i Bayhaq*, 19–22.

Table 2.1 ***Ibn Funduq's list of "famous" histories***[a]

I. The histories

1. The first person "in Islam" who wrote military campaign narratives (*maghāzī*) and histories was Muhammad b. Ishaq Yasar
2. Wahb bin Munabbah al-Yamani, *Kitab al-Mubtada*. He relies on Jabir bin 'Abd Allah al-Ansari
3. Muhammad bin Jarir al-Tabari, a great history (*tārīkh-i kabīr*)
4. Ibn Muqaffa', *Futuh a'sam* and *Tavarikh al-muluk*
5. Abu 'Ali Miskuwayh Hakim, *Kitab tahzib al-tarikh* and *Kitab tajarub al-umum*
6. *Tawarikh Al Buyah*
7. *Kitab Yamini*
8. Ibn Funduq (on the basis of the Kitab Yamani), *Masharib va ghavarib al-gharayib*
9. Abu al-Hasan Muhammad bin Sulayman, *Mazid al-tarikh*
10. Ibn Tabataba al-'Alavi, *Kitab al-tazhkirah wa al-tabsarah*
11. Khvajah Abu al-Fazl al-Bayhaqi, *Tarikh-i al-i Mahmud* in Persian [plus a discussion of which libraries have this more than a 30-volume work]

II. Enumeration of histories of cities and regions and their authors

1. *Tarikh-i Baghdad*, 10 volumes
2. 'Abbas bin Mas'sab Tarikh-i Marv
3. Ahmad bin Yasar (also a history of Marv)
4. Ma'dani (also a history of Marv)
5. Abu Ishaq Ahmad bin Muhammad bin Yunis al-Bazzaz, *Tarikh-i Herat*
6. Abu Ishaq Ahmad bin Muhammad bin Sa'id al-Haddad, *Tarikh-i Herat*
7. Sa'd bin Jannah, *Tarikh-i Bukhara va Samarqand*
8. al-Sirri bin Dilaviyya, *Tarikh-i Khvarazm*
9. Abu 'Abd Allah Muhammad bin Sa'id, *Tarikh-i Khvarazm*
10. Muhammad bin 'Aqil al-Faqih, *Tarikh-i Balkh*
11. Abu al-Qasim al-Ka'bi al-Balkhi, *Tarikh-i Nishabur* (was burned, the original in the library of the Masjid-i 'aqil)
12. al-Hākim Abu 'Abd Allah Muhammad bin 'Abd Allah bin Hamdawiyya bin Na'im bin al-Hakam al-Hāfiz, 12 vols. *Tarikh-i Nishabur*
13. Imam Abu al-Hasan bin 'Abd al-Ghafir al-Farsi, *Siyaq al-tarikh*, A continuation of (12) above
14. Ahmad al-Ghazi, *Tarikh-i Nishabur* in Persian, 2 vols.
15. Imam 'Ali bin Abi Salih al-Khvari, *Tarikh-i Bayhaq*, a few sections, in Arabic
16. Salami, *Kitab al-Thar*, about the *Tarikh-i Khvar*
17. Salami, *Tarikh-i vilayat-i Khurasan*

[a] Ibn Funduq, *Tarikh-i Bayhaq*, 19–21.

Mirkhvand, whose bibliography or list of famous histories in his *Rawzat al-safa* became the model for a few early modern chroniclers, as we shall explore below.

Khunji-Isfahani's Tarikh-i 'alam-ara-yi Amini

The bibliography convention survived into the fifteenth century in Fazl Allah ibn Ruzbihan Khunji-Isfahani's (860–925/1456–1517) *Tarikh-i 'alam-ara-yi Amini*, an Aq Qoyunlu history of the ruler Ya'qu b. Uzun Hasan (r. 884–896/1479–1490) up to 896/1491 (see Table 2.2).[72] In the introduction to his history, Khunji-Isfahani lists eight different classes (*ṭāyifah*) of historians and provides a number of examples for each category, providing a total of approximately 34 authors and titles. The first such class consists of authors who have written "the history of all the events in the world from Adam to the Seal [i.e. Muhammad] even to the end of the caliphs, and they have related the accounts of the classes (*ṭavā'if*) of prophets and kings and their famous philosophers."[73] Khunji-Isfahani then lists six important historians and historical works as exemplary models for this kind of history: (1) Tabari (224/5–310/839–923) whose work [*Tarikh al-rusul wa al-muluk*] he states some historians have translated into Persian [Bal'ami's *Tarikh*]; (2) Abu al-Faraj ibn al-Jawzi (510–597/1126–1200) [*al-Muntazam*]; (3) Hafiz-i Abru (d. 833/1430) [*Majma' al-tavarikh*]; (4) Rashid al-Din (ca. 645–718/ca. 1247–1318) [*Jami' al-tavarikh*]; (5) the history of Banakati (d. 730/1329–1330) [*Tarikh-i Banakati*]; and (6) the *Tarikh-i guzidah* [Hamd Allah Mustawfi Qazvini (ca. 680–after 740/ca. 1281/1282–after 1339–1340)].[74] Unlike Ibn Funduq, who simply lists his titles, Khunji-Isfahani comments on some of the salient features of these different histories, preferring certain texts over others. For example, Ibn al-Jawzi's history, he says, contains "data on the hadith and the traditionalists," making it "the most perfect work." Rashid al-Din's history (the *Jami' al-tavarikh*), while resembling this class of history, is different due to his method (*uslūb*). Finally, he states that the authors of the *Tarikh-i*

[72] See John E. Woods, *The Aqquyunlu: Clan, Confederation, Empire*, 2nd ed. (Salt Lake City: University of Utah Press, 1999), 220.
[73] Khunji-Isfahani, 87–88; trans., 8–9.
[74] Khunji-Isfahani, 87–88; trans., 8.

Table 2.2 *Bibliography in Khunji-Isfahani's* Tarikh-i 'alam-ara-yi Amini[a]

General histories

1. Tabari (224/5–310/839–923) [*Tarikh al-rusul wa al-muluk*], whose work he states some historians have translated into Persian [Bal'ami's *Tarikh*]
2. Abu al-Faraj ibn al-Jawzi (510–597/1126–1200) [*al-Muntazam*]
3. Hafiz-i Abru (d. 833/1430) [*Tarikh-i guzidah*]
4. Rashid al-Din (ca. 645–718/ca. 1247–1318) [*Jami' al-tavarikh*]
5. The history of Banākati (d. 730/1329–30) [*Tarikh-i Banakati*]
6. The *Tarikh-i guzidah* [Hamd Allah Mustawfi Qazvini (ca. 680–after 740/ ca. 1281–1282–after 1339–1340)]

The lives of Prophets

1. Abu Ishaq Tha'labi, *'Ara'is fi'l-qisas*, and Persian *Qisas al-anbiya'*
2. Wahb b. Munabbih, *Mubtada*
3. Hajari
4. Collectors of Isra'ilite traditions

Collectors of reports on the Prophet

1. Abu 'Abd Allah Muhammad b. Ismail al-Bukhari, *al-Jami' al-Sahih*
2. Said al-Din Kazaruni, trans. Persian by 'Afif al-Din
3. Abu Isa Tirmidhi, *Kitab al-shama'il*
4. Qadi Iyad b. Musa al-Yahsubi, *Kitab al-shifa bi-ta'rif huquq al-Mustafa*
5. Abu al-Faraj b. al-Jawzi, *Kitab al-wafa fi sirat al-Mustafa*
6. Jalal al-Din Suyuti, *Ummudhaj al-labib fi khasa'is al-habib*

Lives of the Prophet's followers

1. Muhammad b. Ishaq, *Maghazi*
2. Ibn Qani, *Mu'jam*
3. Ibn 'Abd al-Aziz, *Isti'ab*
4. Abu Nu'aym al-Isfahani, *Hilyat al-awliya'*

Annalists

1. Ibn al-Athir, *Kamil*
2. Shaykh Imam 'Abd Allah al-Yafi'i al-Yamani, history

Alphabetic dictionaries

1. Ibn Khallikan
2. Safadi

Historians writing on classes of doctors of law and lords of religion

1. Imam Taj al-Din 'Abd al-Wahhab b. 'Ali ibn al-Subki al-Shami, 3 books
2. Asnawi
3. Muhammad b. Isma'il Bukhari
4. Imam Shihab al-Din

5. Abu al-Khayr al-Sakhawi al-Misri (pupil of Shaykh Ibn Hajar)
6. Abu 'Abd al-Rahman Sulami

Histories devoted to particular dynasties

1. 'Ata Malik Juvayni, *Jahan-gusha*
2. Mawlana Sharaf al-Din Fazl Allah Vassaf
3. Imam Abu al-Hasan al-'Utbi (Arabic), historian of Sultan Mahmud
4. Mawlana Mu'in al-Din Yazdi (Persian), *Humayun-nama-yi Mu'ini*
5. Sharaf 'Ali Yazdi, *Zafarnamah*
6. *Tarikh-i Amini*

[a] Khunji-Isfahani, *Tarikh-i 'alam-ara-yi Amini*, 87–88; trans., 8–11.

Banakati and the *Tarikh-i guzidah* are not completely dependable, but he does not explain why.[75]

Mirkhvand's Rawzat al-safa

The next bibliography, in chronological sequence, appears in Mirkhvand's *Rawzat al-safa*, which he composed some six years after Khunji-Isfahani's history. Whereas Ibn Funduq and Khunji-Isfahani divided their bibliographies according to genre, Mirkhvand divided his by language, first registering a number of historical works in Arabic, and then listing Persian histories. He does not provide any comments on the specific titles. Mirkhvand's bibliography is important because it provides the basis for subsequent bibliographies in the early modern period.

The practice of writing bibliographies continued only sporadically into the early modern period. One historian, Muslih al-Din Lari (d. 979/1571–1572), who had ties to the Mughals, Safavids, and Ottomans, included a bibliography in his universal history, the *Mirat al-advar*, which he wrote while living in Ottoman territory and dedicated it to Sultan Selim II's (r. 974–982/1556–1574) grand vizier, Mehmed Sokollu (d. 987/1579). Although he states that his list of histories consists of sources that he consulted in writing his history, he actually simply reproduces the same titles that we find in Mirkhvand's

[75] Khunji-Isfahani, *Tarikh-i 'alam-ara-yi Amini*, 87–88; trans., 8. On Rashid al-Din's historiographical legacy, see Ron Sela, "Rashīd al-Dīn's Historiographical Legacy in the Muslim World," in *Rashīd al-Din, Agent and Mediator of Cultural Exchanges in Ilkhanid Iran*, eds. Anna Akasoy, Charles Burnett, and Ronit Yoeli-Tlalim, 213–222 (London: Warburg Institute, 2013).

Rawzat al-safa.[76] Table 2.3 shows Mirkhvand and Lari's bibliographies in juxtaposition. Lari did not organize his list thematically or by language, but rather in a loose chronological fashion, with some of the earliest histories – such as Tabari's *Tarikh* – at the beginning, and Mongol and Timurid histories at the end. The most striking difference between the two lists is that Mirkhvand ends with the Timurid historian Hafiz Abru, who is the only Timurid era historian that he names. The historian whom he mentions immediately before Hafiz Abru is Rashid al-Din, author of the Mongol world history, the *Jami' al-tavarikh*. Lari, however, inserts four histories that we do not see in the *Rawzat al-safa*. These are the *Tarikh-i Vassaf*, the *Mavahib-i Ilahi* by Mu'in al-Din Yazdi, which Lari describes as a history of the Muzaffarid dynasty,[77] Sharaf al-Din 'Ali Yazdi's *Zafarnamah*, and the *Rawzat al-ahbab*, a history of the lives of the Prophet and his family by Jamal al-Din Muhaddith (Jamal al-Husayni), written at the request of 'Ali Shir Nava'i.[78] Mirkhvand's *Rawzat al-safa* appears as the final item on Lari's list. Lari ends the section by stating that he also used Turkish prose and poetic histories in his account but does not provide the names of any authors or titles.[79] It is clear from this analysis that Lari relies on Mirkhvand for his bibliography. However, his addition of several post-Mongol titles to the end of his list serves the purpose of further legitimizing his own history because his audience would see it as a continuation of a robust post-Mongol/Timurid historiographical tradition that consists of several specifically named, important, and well-known histories.[80] Such a list also betrays a pro-Timurid sentiment, which is highlighted by the fact that he does not include any Ottoman, Safavid, or Mughal histories in his list.[81]

Nizam al-Din Ahmad Bakhshi's Tabaqat-i Akbari

The importance of bibliography in the *Rawzat al-safa* is also reflected in the Mughal chronicle, Nizam al-Din Ahmad Bakhshi's (d. 1003/

76 Muhammad Muslih al-Din Lari, *Mir'at al-advar va mirqat al-akhbar*, ed. Jalil Saghravaniyan (Tehran: Markaz-i Nashr-i Miras-i Maktub, 1393 [2014]), 9–10.
77 See item no. 351 in Storey, *Persian Literature*, 1: 277.
78 See item no. 236 in Storey, *Persian Literature*, 1: 189–191.
79 Lari, *Mir'at al-advar*, 10.
80 Of the four histories listed here, only Vassaf's chronicle dates to the Ilkhanid period. The rest are post-Mongol (Muzaffarid) and Timurid.
81 For more on Lari's anti-Safavid sentiments, see Chapter 5.

Table 2.3 *Mirkhvand and Muslih al-Din Lari's bibliographies (cross-listed)*

Mirkhvand's *Rawzat al-safa*	Lari's *Mir'at al-advar*
[Arab historians]	1. Tarikh-i Muhammad bin Jarir Tabari (4)
1. Imam Muhammad b. Ishaq (13)	2. Tarikh-i kamil, Ibn Athir al-Jazari[b]
2. Imam Wahb ibn Munabih (14)	3. Tarikh-i Tha'labi[c] (14)
3. Imam Waqidi Asma'i[a]	4. Tarikh-i Abi Hanifa-'i Dinavari (15)
4. Muhammad b. Jarir al-Tabari (1)	5. Tarikh al-'alam, Ḥafiz Abi 'Abd Allah Zhahabi[b]
5. Abu 'Abd Allah Muslim b. Qaninah, author of Jami' al-ma'arif[a]	6. Tarikh-i 'Abd Allah bin 'Ali bin Sa'd al-Yafi'i[c] (17)
6. Ahmad b. 'Ali b. A'tham al-Kufi, author of al-Futuh (17)	7. Shahnāmah, Abu al-Qasim Hasan bin 'Ali al-Firdawsi al-Tusi (19)
7. 'Abd Allah b. Muqanna' (20)	8. Tarikh-i Muhammad bin 'Abd Allah Mas'udi (16)
8. Hakim Abu 'Ali Miskawayh (19)	9. Tarikh-i Fakhr al-Din Muhammad bin Abi Dawud Banakati[c] (9)
9. Fakhr al-Din Muhammad b. Abi Dawud	10. Muntazim, Abu al-Faraj ibn al-Jawzi (11)
10. Sulayman al-Banakiti (9)	11. Tarikh-i Shaykh 'Imad al-Din bin Kathir Shami (12)
11. Abu al-Faraj b. Jawzi author of al-Muntazam (10)	12. Tarikh-i Maqdasi (13)
12. 'Imad al-Din b. Kathir al-Shahi [Shami?] (11)	13. Maghazi, Muhammad bin Ishaq (1)
13. Maqdisi (12)	14. [Maghazi] Wahb bin Munabbih (2)
14. Tha'alabi (2)	15. Tarikh, Imam Muhammad bin Isma'il Bukhari[b]
15. Abu Hanifah Dinwari (3)	16. Kubar al-umum, Hamzah bin Husayn Isfahani[b]
16. Muhammad b. 'Abd Allah al-Mas'udi (8)	17. Kitab Futuh, Muhammad bin 'Ali bin I'tham Kufi (6)
17. Imam Kamil 'Abd Allah b. As'ad al-Yamani al-Yafi'i (5)	18. Ma'arif, Abi 'Muhammad Abd Allah bin Muslim bin Qutayba[b]
18. Abu al-Nasr al-'Utbi, author of al-Yamini (long account about him) (23)	19. Kitab-i Abi 'Ali Miskawayh (8)
[Persian historians]	20. Kitab-i Ibn Muqanna' (20)
19. Abu al-Qasim Hasan b. Muhammad b. 'Ali al-Firdawsi al-Tusi (7)	21. Tabaqat-i Fuqaha'-yi Hanifah, Shaykh Majd al-Din Firuzabadi[b]
20. Abu al-Hasan 'Ali b. Shams al-Islam al-Bayhaqi, (24)	

Table 2.3 (*cont.*)

21. Abu al-Husayn Muhammad b. Sulayman, author of Tarikh-i Khusraw (25)	22. Tabaqat-i Shafi'iya, Subki va Usnuvi[b]
22. Khvajah Abu al-Fazl Bayhaqi, compiler of Tarikh-i Al-i Mahmud b. Sibuktagin (26)	23. Kitab-i maqamat-i Yamini, Abi Nasr 'Utbi (18)
23. Abbas ibn Mus'ab (28)	24. Tarikh-i Abi al-Hasan 'Ali bin Shams Bayhaqi (20)
24. Ahmad b. Siyaru (27)	25. Tarikh-i Khusravi, Abi al-Husayn Muhammad bin Sulayman (25)
25. Abu Ishaq Muhammad b. Ahmad b. Yunis al-Bazzaz (29)	26. Jami' al-tavarikh-i al-i Sibuktakin, Abi al-Fazl Bayhaqi (22)
26. Muhammad b. 'Aqil al-Faqih al-Balkhi (30)	27. Tarikh-i Ahmad bin Yasar (24)
27. Abu al-Qasim 'Ali b. Mahmud al-Ka'bi, author of Tarikh-i Hirat va Balkh va Nishapur (31)	28. va 'Abbas bin Mus'ab (23)
28. Abu al-Hasan Muhammad b. 'Abd al-Ghafir al-Farsi, author of Siyaq al-tarikh (33)	29. va Abu Ishaq bin Muhammad bin Musa Bazzaz (25)
29. Sadr al-Din Muhammad b. Hasan al-Nizami, author of Taj al-Ma'asir (34)	30. va Muhammad bin 'Aqil Balkhi (26)
30. Abu 'Abd Allah Minhaj b. Mawdud al-Jurjani, author of Tabaqat-i Nasiri (35)	31. va Abu al-Qasim 'Ali bin Mahmud Ka'bi (27)
31. Kubr al-Din 'Iraqi[a]	32. Jami' al-hikayat, Jamal al-Din Muhammad 'Awfi[c]
32. Abu al-Qasim Muhammad b. 'Ali al-Kashi, author of Zubdat al-tavarikh (36)	33. Bustan al-tavarikh, Abi al-Hasan Muhammad bin 'Abd al-Ghaffar al-Qari (28)
33. Khvajah Abu al-Fazl 'Abd Allah b. Abu Nasr (38)	34. Ma'asir, Sadr al-Din Muhammad bin Hasan al-Bistami (29)
34. Ahmad b. 'Ali al-Mingal, author of Makhzan al-balaghah and Fazayil al-muluk (37&38)	35. Tabaqat [-i Nasiri], 'Abd Allah bin Minhaj al-Jurjani (30)
35. 'Ali al-Din 'Ata al-Malik al-Juvayni, the brother of Sahib Shahid Khvajah Shams al-Din, sahib-i divan, who wrote the Tarikh-i jahan'gushay (39)	36. Zubdat al-tavarikh, Abi al-Qasim Muhammad bin 'Ali al-Kashi (32)
36. Hamd Allah Mustawfi Qazvini, author of the Tarikh-i Guzidah and Nuzhat al-qulub (41)	37. Makhzan al-balagha (34)
	38. Faza'il al-Muluk, Abi al-Fazl 'Abd Allah bin Abi Nasr Ahmad bin 'Ali Mikal (33)
	39. Tarikh-i jahan-gushay, 'Alā al-Dīn Malik Juvayni (35)
	40. Tarikh-i Ibn Khallikān[c]
	41. Tarikh-i guzidah, Hamd Allah Mustawfi Qazvini (36)
	42. Nizam al-tavarikh, Qazi Nāsir al-Din Bayzawi (37)

Table 2.3 (*cont.*)

37. Qazi Nasir al-Din Bayzavi, author of Nizam al-tavarikh (42)	43. Jami', Khvajah Rashid Tabib Vazir (38)
38. Khvajah Rashid Tabib, author of Jami (43)	44. Tarikh-i Mawlana 'Abd Allah Vassaf Shirazi[c]
39. Hafiz Abru (48)	45. Mavahib-i Illahi, mu'alif-i Mawlana Mu'in al-din Yazdi dar akhbar-i Al-i Muzaffar[c]
	46. va Zafarnama mu'alif-i Mawlana Sharaf al-Din 'Ali Yazdi[c]
	47. Rawzat al-aḥbab mu'alif-i sayyid Jamal al-Din Muhaddith[c]
	48. Tarikh-i Hafiz Abru (39)
	49. Rawzat al-safa mu'alif-i Amir Khvand Muvarrikh[c]
	50. And a number of prose and poetic histories which the people of Anatolia (*Rūm*) have written in Turkish

Mirkhvand, *Rawzat al-safa*, 18–22; trans., 31–33; Lari, *Mir'at al-advar*, 9–10.
[a] Title/author unique to Mirkhvand's list.
[b] Pre-Timurid titles unique to Lari's list.
[c] Timurid era title/author unique to Lari's list.

1594) *Tabaqat-i Akbari* (1001/1592–1593), a history of India beginning with the Ghaznavids, continuing through the Sultans of Delhi, and ending with the Mughals and the reign of Akbar. Like Lari, Nizam al-Din appears to use Mirkhvand as a model, but his list (see Table 2.4) demonstrates how early modern chroniclers adapted Timurid historiographical elements for their own purposes. Nizam al-Din's bibliography contains some 28 items.[82] However, unlike his predecessors, the earliest history on Nizam al-Din's list is the *Tarikh-i Yamini*. This

[82] See Nizam al-Din Ahmad Bakhshi, *Tabaqat-i Akbari*, ed. Brajendranath De, 3 vols. (Calcutta: Asiatic Society of Bengal, 1913–1927). Trans. by Brajendranath De and Baini Prashad as *The Ṭabaqāt-i-Akbarī: A History of India from the Early Musalmān Invasions to the Thirty-Eighth Year of the Reign of Akbar*, 3 vols. (Calcutta: Asiatic Society of Bengal, 1927–1939), 1: 3–4; trans., 1: v–vi. For a discussion of this bibliography, see M. Athar Ali, "The Use of Sources in Mughal Historiography," *Journal of the Royal Asiatic Society* 5 (1995): 362–363.

Table 2.4 ***Bibliography in Nizam al-Din's*** **Tabaqat-i Akbari**

1. Tarikh-i Yamani
2. Tarikh-i Zayn al-Akhbar
3. Rawzat al-safa
4. Taj al-ma'asir
5. Tabaqat-i Nasiri
6. Khaza'in al-futuh
7. Tughluqnamah
8. Tarikh-i Firuzshahi by Ziya' Barani
9. Futuhat-i Firuzshahi
10. Tarikh-i Mubarak Shahi
11. Tarikh-i Futuh al-salatin
12. Tarikh-i Mahmud Shahi Mandari
13. Tarikh-i Mahmud Shahi Khurd Mandari
14. Tabaqat-i Mahmud Shahi'i Gazjati
15. Ma'asir-i Mahmud Shahi Gabahrani
16. Tarikh-i Mahmudi
17. Tarikh-i Bahadur Shahi
18. Tarikh-i Bahmani
19. Tarikh-i Nasiri
20. Tarikh-i Muzaffar Shahi
21. Tarikh-i Mirza Haydar [Dughlat]
22. Tarikh-i Kashmir
23. Tarikh-i Sind
24. Tarikh-i Baburi
25. Vaqi'at-i Baburi
26. Tarikh-i Ibrahim Shahi
27. Vaqi'at-i Mushtaqi
28. Vaqi'at-i Hazrat-i Jannat-Ashyani Humayun Padishah

Arabic history of Mahmud of Ghazna, written by Abu Nasr Muhammad b. 'Abd al-Jabbar al-'Utbi (d. 427 or 431/1035–1036 or 1039–1040), is a well-known history that appears in all of the bibliographies examined here.[83] After this item, Nizam al-Din lists the *Zayn al-akhbar*, a Ghaznavid-era universal history, and then Mirkhvand's

[83] See *EIR*, s.v., "ʿOtbi, Abu Naṣr Moḥammad b. ʿAbd-al-Jabbār," by Ali Anooshahr. Nizam al-Din, *Tabaqat-i Akbari*, 1: 3–4; trans., 1: v–vi.

Rawzat al-safa. The remaining items are all historical sources from the Delhi Sultanate and other ruling dynasties in India.[84] If we use this bibliography as a historiographical trajectory, for Nizam al-Din, significant historical writing begins with the Ghaznavids, makes a brief stop in the Timurid period, and then continues directly to India, ending with the Mughals. Rather than build upon histories dating back to the earliest sources, Nizam al-Din's bibliography mirrors the scope of his history. In this way, Nizam al-Din positions the Mughal Empire, bibliographically and politically, as a continuation of the Ghazanavids rather than as a continuation of the Timurids.

While historians spanning from Ibn Funduq to Mirkhvand were interested in showing their audiences the histories they claimed to be familiar with and used in their works, like "benefits of history," this historiographical practice continued only sporadically into the later period with the Mughal chronicle, *Tabaqat-i Akbari*, being the latest chronicle discussed here to contain a bibliography. The importance of Mirkhvand's *Rawzat al-safa* as a transitional historiographical text cannot be overemphasized. His chronicle contains certain elements that, by his time of writing, had become either conventional or semi-conventional. However, as in the case of the "benefits of history" section, in the early modern period, the practice of including bibliographies had fallen into disuse. Why was this the case? Initially, perhaps, including a bibliography could be seen as a way in which the chronicler legitimized himself as a historian to potential patrons by demonstrating that he was well read and familiar with a fairly impressive number of historical works. In the same way that discussing the benefits of history could convince a potential patron of the importance of history writing, so too could showing knowledge of older historical works. By the time of the Ottomans, Safavids, and Mughals, however, such knowledge could have been assumed for those chroniclers who were secure in their positions and already had loyal patrons. And for those historians who were not looking to Mirkhvand as a model, or who were writing contemporary or near-contemporary dynastic histories, as opposed to universal histories, including a bibliography of earlier historical works may not have been a historiographical priority. Thus, while bibliographies did not have the same impact on later historical writing as genealogies and dream

84 Nizam al-Din Ahmad, 1: 3–4; trans., 1: v–vi.

narratives, they demonstrate the fact that the Timurid historiographical legacy was neither uniform nor straightforward, but rather complex and varied, and that not every convention survived into the later period. Other aspects of the Timurid tradition, however, continued to suit their historiographical purposes, such as genealogy, to which we now turn.

Genealogies

Including the genealogy of a significant historical figure forms another semiconventional feature of early modern Persian historiography. In comparison with benefits of history and bibliography sections, genealogy was a much more popular convention for the early modern chroniclers. The genre of genealogy has had a close relationship with historical writing in the Islamicate tradition.[85] In Persian historiography of the early Islamic era, interest in genealogy manifests itself most clearly in universal histories, where chroniclers elaborated on the genealogies of a wide variety of individuals, such as biblical prophets, Islamic caliphs, and Iran's kings, including pre-Islamic and legendary rulers.

The emphasis on genealogy during the Timurid era has its roots in the Mongol Ilkhanid period. In particular, the historian and minister Rashid al-Din, in a number of historical works including his celebrated world history, the *Jami' al-tavarikh* and his lesser known genealogical work, the *Shu'ab-i panjganah*, outlined the genealogy of Chingiz Khan (r. 603–624/1206–1227) in a family tree that incorporated both his ancestors and his descendants. Other historians of Timur (771–807/1370–1405), particularly Sharaf al-Din 'Ali Yazdi, presented Timur's genealogy in their chronicles, as they initially sought to emphasize his common ancestry with Chingiz Khan and trace his descent back to the Islamo-biblical Adam. They did this as part of a larger project of legitimizing Timur's rule.[86]

[85] See Rosenthal, *A History of Muslim Historiography*, 95–100; Fred Donner, *Narratives of Islamic Origin: The Beginnings of Islamic Historical Writing* (Princeton, NJ: Darwin Press, 1998), 104–111.

[86] Subsequently, a Timurid historian, Hafiz Abru, produced an "updated" version of the *Shu'ab-i panjganah* entitled the *Mu'izz al-ansab*. These genealogical works are analyzed and discussed in Woods, "Timur's Genealogy," 85–125; Binbaş, *Intellectual Networks*, 208–209; and Sholeh A. Quinn, "The *Mu'izz al-*

Genealogy continued to have an important place in early modern chronicles as historians traced ruling dynastic family trees back to a number of important figures such as Oghuz Khan, Chingiz Khan, Timur, the Imam Musa al-Kazim (128–183/745–799), and Adam. Within the genre of universal chronicle, genealogies often formed significant portions of a text and, along with biography, were integral parts of the narrative. However, in addition to these lengthy discussions in the main sections of the chronicles, many early modern histories also contain a single genealogy of the current ruler in the opening prefatory sections of their histories.[87] This shorter genealogy and/or genealogical discussion became a common semiconventional element in early modern historiography. What follows is an analysis of this historiographical convention in select historical works.

Safavid Genealogies

In Safavid histories, nearly all chroniclers include at least one family tree of the Safavids in the opening sections of their histories. Without describing in an in-depth manner the problems associated with various versions of the Safavid genealogy, it is nevertheless important to note that beginning with the two earliest Safavid chronicles, the Safavid genealogy tracing the descent of Shaykh Safi al-Din, the founder of the Safaviyyah Sufi order, back to Musa al-Kazim, the seventh Imam of the Twelver Shiʿah, appears in nearly every Safavid history in almost the exact same form.[88] The two earliest chronicles are Sadr al-Din Sultan Ibrahim Amini Haravi's (882–894/1447/1448–1535) *Futuhat-i shahi*

Ansab and *Shu'ab-i Panjganah* as Sources for the Chaghatayid Period of History: A Comparative Analysis," *Central Asiatic Journal* 33 (1990): 229–253. Other stand-alone genealogies in the form of scrolls and family trees were produced in the Timurid period. See İlker Evrim Binbaş, "Structure and Function of the Genealogical Tree in Islamic Historiography (1200–1500)," in *Horizons of the World. Festschrift for İsenbike Togan*, eds. İlker Evrim Binbaş and Nurten Kılıç-Schubel, 465–544 (Istanbul: Ithaki, 2011). Genealogies were also inscribed on royal seals. See Annabel Teh Gallop, "The Genealogical Seal of the Mughal Emperors of India," *Journal of the Royal Asiatic Society* 9 (1999): 77–140.

87 Rosenthal notes that "The histories of later rulers of Bedouin origin, such as the various Turk rulers and the Mongols, usually contained some ethnic-genealogical introduction and proceeded then according to the ordinary biographical scheme." Rosenthal, *A History of Muslim Historiography*, 97.

88 See Quinn, *Historical Writing*, 83–86.

(commissioned 926/1519–1520) and Khvandamir's *Habib al-siyar*. The initial impetus for including Shaykh Safi's genealogy was most likely due to Ibrahim Amini and Khvandamir's reliance on the *Safvat al-safa*, the fourteenth-century hagiography of Shaykh Safi for their accounts of the Safaviyya Sufi order. In the beginning portions of this text, Ibn Ishaq includes a genealogy of Shaykh Safi. This genealogy underwent certain modifications, such that by the time of Ibrahim Amini and Khvandamir's writing, it indicated Shaykh Safi as a descendant of the Prophet Muhammad via Musa al-Kazim. In tracing their genealogy back to the Shi'i imams, the Safavids used their alleged Imami Shi'i descent to legitimize their rule and transform Iran into a Shi'i state.[89]

While the Safavids were not drawing on a Timurid historiographical tradition for their Safavid genealogies, it is interesting to note that claims to sayyidship were not unique to the Safavids. Woods and Binbaş have pointed to a genealogical inscription in Timur's tomb, the "Gur-i Amir," which states that Alan Qo'a, an important ancestor common to Chingiz Khan and Timur, was impregnated by a ray of light. This inscription equates Alan Qo'a with the Virgin Mary and the ray of light with the Imam 'Ali. Woods has suggested that the inscription reconciles "Mongol and Semitic traditions after the definitive conversion of the Mongol conquerors to Islam in the second half of the fourteenth/eighth century," and at the same time connects Timur to "the two most powerful notions of dynastic legitimacy in post-'Abbasid, late Mongol Iran and Central Asia."[90] Binbaş further suggests that as Chingizid legitimacy and prestige began to lose its power, 'Alid legitimacy filled the void. This in turn helped create a new "template" for Timurid authority, one that combined Chingizid and Shi'i elements.[91]

Genealogy in the Tarikh-i Rashidi

The Khans of Moghulistan were descendants of Chingiz Khan via his son Chaghatay (r. 624–639/1227–1241), making them true

89 For a recent study on the Safavid 'Alid genealogy, see Kazuo Morimoto, "The Earliest 'Alid Genealogy for the Safavids: New Evidence for the Pre-dynastic Claim to *Sayyid* Status," *Iranian Studies* 43 (2010): 447–469.

90 Woods, "Timur's Genealogy," 88.

91 Binbaş, *Intellectual Networks*, 278, 282–284.

Chingizids. However, we have already established Dughlat's reliance on Timurid historiography, particularly Yazdi's *Zafarnamah*, in the introduction to his history. This point becomes important in understanding how Mirza Haydar Dughlat, himself a descendant of Chingiz Khan's son Chaghatay, presents the genealogy of his ancestor Tughluq Timur, the first of the "Khans of Moghulistan" to convert to Islam. He places the genealogy at the beginning of Book One of his history. Tughluq Temur, who lived in the fourteenth century, ruled the eastern portion of the Chaghatayid khanate, which came to be known as "Moghulistan."[92] This genealogy traces Tughluq Timur's ancestry via Chaghatay back to the Mongol ancestor Alan Qo'a. However, Dughlat does not highlight Chingiz Khan's name in the family tree nor does he emphasize Chaghatay. Rather, immediately after the genealogy, he imitates the Timurid historian Sharaf al-Din 'Ali Yazdi's description of Alan Qo'a, which compares her to the Virgin Mary, and points to the "immaculate conception" of Bodhonchar Khan, Chingiz Khan and Timur's ancestor.[93] Dughlat thus emphasizes a version of the Mongol genealogy as mediated through a specific Timurid history. His account is as follows:

> According to the *Zafarnamah*: 'A light and illumination (*nūr va rawshanī*) entered into her mouth, and she became pregnant, just as Mary the daughter of Amran became pregnant by Gabriel's touch, without the intermediary of a father. Neither of these is beyond God's power. "If you hear the story of Mary, you will incline to Alan Qoa."[94]

Dughlat then explains that his reason for going into this discussion was to note that Bodhonchar Khan, the son of Alan Qo'a and the "light and illumination," "was born of his mother without [a] father."[95] He adds that Alan Qoa Kürklüq's lineage "as recorded in all histories, goes back to Japheth, son of Noah."[96]

The text by Yazdi that Dughlat actually refers to and imitates is commonly referred to as the *Muqaddimah*. Binbaş notes that this universal history, which opens with genealogies of Chingiz Khan and Timur, was

92 See Dughlat, *Tarikh-i Rashidi*, viii.
93 *Tarikh-i Rashidi*, 8; trans., 6. See also Woods, "Timur's Genealogy," 86–88.
94 *Tarikh-i Rashidi*, 8; trans., 6. Translation slightly modified.
95 *Tarikh-i Rashidi*, 8; trans., 6.
96 Dughlat, *Tarikh-i Rashidi*, 8; trans., 6. For more on Japheth in Yazdi's *Muqaddimah*, see Binbaş, *Intellectual Networks*, 209–212.

often bound with Yazdi's most well-known work, the *Zafarnamah*, even though it was not the formal preface to this history. This could explain Dughlat's referring to this work as the *Zafarnamah*. Furthermore, Dughlat was writing at a time when the *Muqaddimah* was becoming a more popular text.[97] Dughlat's extending the family tree back to Japheth, son of the biblical Noah, also reflects the universal history portion of Yazdi's *Muqaddimah*. While the *Muqaddimah* traces Timur's genealogy all the way back to the biblical-Qur'anic Adam, Dughlat traces it back to Japheth, who was depicted as a common ancestor to Timur and Chingiz Khan.[98]

Genealogy in Mughal Chronicles

Like the Safavids and the Khans of Moghulistan, the Mughals also promoted their genealogy, which appears in a number of Mughal historical works. The Mughals traced their ancestry back to Timur and, beyond that, to the Islamic-biblical first man, Adam.[99]

Genealogy in Qandahari's Tarikh-i Akbari

The earliest Mughal chronicle to contain a genealogical section is Muhammad Arif Qandahari's *Tarikh-i Akbari* (998/1580), a history of Akbar's reign, preceded by a brief account of Humayun's reign. Historiographically, Qandahari, who served as tutor to the young prince Akbar, appears to have realized that, by convention, he needed to discuss Akbar's genealogy somewhere in the preliminary portions of his chronicle. One of the histories he mentions in his preface, the *Tarikh-i al-i Muzaffar*, contains a genealogy of Mubariz al-Din Muhammad ibn Muzaffar, second founder of the Muzaffarid dynasty. Qandahari, therefore, would have known of the genealogy in the *Tarikh-i al-i Muzaffar*. He also quotes a poem from Sharaf al-Din

97 Binbaş, *Intellectual Networks*, 201–212.

98 For Timur's full genealogy in the *Muqaddimah*, see Sharaf al-Din 'Ali Yazdi, *Zafarnamah*, eds. Sa'id Mir Muhammad Sadiq, 'Abd al-Husayn Nava'i (Tehran: Kitabkhanah, Muzah va Markaz-i Asnad-i Majlis-i Shura-yi Islami, 1387 [2008]), 224.

99 For an overview of the significance of genealogy in the Mughal period, see Lisa Balabanlilar, *Imperial Identity in the Mughal Empire: Memory and Dynastic Politics in Early Modern South and Central Asia* (London: I. B. Tauris, 2012), 37–70.

'Ali Yazdi toward the end of his preface and, thus, was also familiar with at least some of Yazdi's writings.

The *Tarikh-i Akbari* does not present a "traditional" generation-by-generation genealogy of Akbar. Rather, in his introductory section to the *Tarikh-i Akbari*, Qandahari includes a general discussion of certain aspects of Akbar's genealogy and distinguishes four major aspects of his ancestry. First, he notes that Akbar's genealogy goes back to the "*ṣāḥib qirān*" (Timur). He then states that Akbar descended "through his mother from Shaykh al-Islam Zhindah Pil ('collosal elephant'), Ahmad al-Jami [Ahmad-i Jam]." Ahmad-i Jam (440–536/1049–1141) was an important eleventh-century Sufi who wrote numerous treatises. His descendants became respected and influential figures. One of them married Humayun and was Akbar's mother.[100] After noting Akbar's maternal ancestry, Qandahari continues to say that even though he could not provide a detailed account of Akbar's [paternal] genealogy, "the emperor's ancestors right up to Hazrat Adam himself have all been either kings or symbols of kings."[101] Qandahari's final point elaborates on Akbar's being a seventh generation descendant of Timur.[102] This was an important matter to Qandahari and formed the nucleus of his genealogical discourse. Here, he elaborates on the significance of the "mystery" of the number seven, associating it with a variety of natural and religious phenomena. In this way, he connects genealogy to number symbolism, thereby linking Akbar's Timurid descent to ancient cosmological assumptions about the universe and Quranic symbols.[103]

That Qandahari chose to emphasize the numerical aspect of Akbar's genealogy should not come as a surprise. As Matthew Melvin-Koushki has pointed out, the sixteenth-century Islamic world was one in which the occult sciences (*'ulūm-i gharībah*) flourished. The occult sciences combined with Sufism and sacral power, or *wilāyah*, to form one of the

100 *EIR*, s.v., "Ahmad-e Jām," by Heshmad Moayyad.

101 Hajji Muhammad 'Arif Qandahari, *Tarikh-i Akbari: ma'ruf bih tarikh-i Qandahari*, ed. Hajji Sayyid Mu'in al-Din Nadavi, Sayyid Azhar 'Ali Dihlavi, Imtiyaz 'Ali 'Arshi, 8 (Rampur: Hindustan Printing va Raks, 1382 (1962)); translated by Tasneem Ahmad as *Tarikh-i Akbari* (Delhi: Pragati Publications, 1993), 14.

102 Qandahari, *Tarikh-i Akbari*, 8; trans., 14.

103 Qandahari, *Tarikh-i Akbari*, 8–9; trans., 14–15. On number symbolism, see Annemarie Schimmel, *The Mystery of Numbers* (New York: Oxford University Press, 1993).

ways of accessing power.[104] While the most popular of the occult sciences appear to be geomancy, astrology, and lettrism, we may add the sciences of numbers, or numerology, to this equation. In the Islamicate world, number mysticism or numerology can be traced back to tenth-century texts authored by a group known as the "Ikhwan al-safa" or "brethren of purity."[105] Their texts emphasized the numbers seven and twelve. It should, therefore, also not be surprising that Qandahari emphasizes the number seven in his account and, as we will see in the next chapter, Khvandamir focuses on the number twelve.

Qandahari's seven cosmological associations with the number seven, which he does not count as he lists them, are as follows: (1) God made the sky (*āsmān*) in seven layers, (2) the existence of seven planets, (3) seven seas (*daryā*) are divided into (4) seven regions (*haft aqālīm*), (5) seven metals are obtained from the earth, (6) there are seven days, and (7) seven parts/organs (*i'żā*) in the human body.[106] Qandahari also lists approximately seven religious associations with the number seven: (1) the Qur'an was revealed in seven dialects, (2) there are seven Qira'ats, or readings, of the Qur'an, (3) there are seven verses (*āyāt*) in the *Surah-i Fatihah*, (4) pilgrims run seven times between Safa and Marwah, (5) circumambulate the Kaaba seven times, (6) in the dream of the King/Pharaoh of Egypt (Walid-i Riyan) and Joseph's (Yusuf's) interpretation of it, seven fat cows are devoured by seven lean and lank cows, and (7) [in the same dream] there are seven green and flourishing bunches while seven are dry.[107] Qandahari ends the section by stating that his overall purpose for elaborating on the number seven is "to say that by this calculation an analogy must be made, and that the graciousness of the blessed quintessence of his holiness *khāqān* Akbar is a manifestation (*maẓhar*) of infinite favor."[108]

Qandahari's explication of the number seven lays out two heptadic schemata. The first set of "sevens" presents a macrocosmic to microcosmic schema of the universe. Qandahari begins at the highest macro-

104 Matt Melvin-Koushki, "Early Modern Islamicate Empire: New Forms of Religiopolitical Legitimacy," in *The Wiley-Blackwell History of Islam*, eds. Armando Salvatore, Roberto Tottoli, and Babak Rahimi, 353–354 (Malden, MA: Wiley-Blackwell, 2017).
105 Schimmel, *Mystery of Numbers*, 19.
106 Qandahari, *Tarikh-i Akbari*, 9; trans., 14–15.
107 Qandahari, *Tarikh-i Akbari*, 9; trans., 14–15.
108 Qandahari, *Tarikh-i Akbari*, 9; trans., 14–15. This translation is my own.

level: the seven-layered sky or heavens. He then works his way down or into the earth, ending with the most microlevel: the interior of the human body. The second heptadic schema is Quranic/Islamic. Here, Qandahari begins his associations with aspects of the Qur'an itself, then moves to Islamic pilgrimage rituals, and ends with a biblically rooted Qur'anic dream account. Akbar, then, in light of his Timurid ancestry, had superior connections to the cosmos, beginning with the heavens and ending with his body. He also had superior connections to the Islamic faith in relation to its ideals as enshrined in the Qur'an, its practices as in the pilgrimage, and, finally, in relation to dream interpretation.

Qandahari completed his history in 988/1580, one year after an imperial decree claimed Akbar the jurisprudent (*mujtahid*) of the age.[109] This was also two years before Akbar commissioned the *Tarikh-i alfi*, or "millenial history," a chronicle that proclaimed Akbar as renewer or *mujaddid*, that figure prophesized on the basis of a *ḥadīth* who would revive God's religion at the beginning of every century. Azfar Moin notes that Akbar's designation as the *mujaddid* for the second millennium carried with it a messianic and sacred significance.[110] While Qandahari does not refer to Akbar as a "renewer," he certainly portrays the monarch as a sacred king because, through the cosmic and Qur'anic significance of his genealogy, he reflected what Moin calls a "highly embodied notion of sacrality," and at the same time, he held the highest authority in terms of Islam.[111]

Genealogy in the Akbarnamah

Another Mughal historian from the time of Akbar, Abu al-Fazl 'Allami, also includes a detailed version of Akbar's genealogy in his celebrated *Akbarnamah*. Akbar commissioned Abu al-Fazl to write an official history of the Mughal dynasty from its origins, which he continued working on until his death in 1011/1602.[112] The Mughal king made certain that Abu al-Fazl had at his disposal a considerable

109 See Moin, *Millennial Sovereign*, 139.
110 Moin, *Millennial Sovereign*, 133–134.
111 See Moin, *Millennial Sovereign*, 135.
112 *EIR*, s.v., "Akbar-nāma," by R. M. Eaton.

amount of chancellory and other information in order for him to write his history.[113]

Abu al-Fazl's rendition of Akbar's genealogy has roots in the Timurid period in general and in Yazdi's *Muqaddimah* in particular. At the beginning of his *Akbarnamah*, Abu al-Fazl first presents the Mughal genealogy, then provides a brief biography of each individual whom he mentions. Although Akbar was not a direct descendant of Chingiz Khan, Abu al-Fazl nevertheless includes Chingiz Khan's name and a brief summary as part of another branch of the family tree. Abu al-Fazl places genealogical information in several portions of his *Akbarnamah*, most notably in a section on dreams and, later, in a separate chapter devoted entirely to Akbar's ancestry. Here, we will present an overview of the first thirteen chapters of the *Akbarnamah*, which along with the preface are all introductory in nature. We will then discuss the specific chapter devoted to Akbar's ancestry. The genealogical information contained in Abu al-Fazl's chapter on dreams will be covered in the section below on dream narratives.

In the opening chapters of the *Akbarnamah*, Abu al-Fazl situates Akbar within numerous cosmological contexts.[114] He devotes chapter one to the various auspicious events that accompanied Akbar's birth, including several dream narratives, at least one of which also relates to genealogy. The second chapter narrates the birth and naming of Akbar. In doing this, Abu al-Fazl connects Akbar's name via *abjad* (letter/number) calculations to the word *āftāb*, or sun, and further analyzes the name according to the elemental categories of fire, air, earth, and water associated with each letter in Akbar's name. Chapters three through eight present different versions of Akbar's horoscope according to the calculations of Greek astrolabes, Indian astrologers, the astrologer 'Azud al-Dawlah Amir Fath Allah Shirazi. The chapters then include an explanation of the actual horoscopal judgements, a horoscope by Mawlana Ilyas of Ardabil, and an explanation of the

113 Harbans Mukhia, *Historians and Historiography during the Reign of Akbar* (New Delhi: Vikas Pub. House, 1976), 66–72.

114 Ruby Lal has noted that in the *Akbarnamah*, "Akbar did not need to draw on any vital connection; he who was divinely ordained did not require legitimacy." Ruby Lal, "Settled, Sacred and All-Powerful: Making of New Genealogies and Traditions of Empire under Akbar," *Economic and Political Weekly*, 36(11) (Mar. 17–23, 2001): 942.

difference between the Greek and Indian horoscopes. Chapter nine consists of Akbar's "nurses and cherishers," chapter ten, an account of Akbar's arrival to Humayun's camp after his birth, chapter eleven, a chronogram providing the date of Akbar's birth, and finally, chapter twelve, an account of Akbar's ancestors. Abu al-Fazl, thus, presents Akbar's genealogy after an extensive and detailed discussion where he firmly situates Akbar's destiny and auspiciousness in the world of dreams, the lettrist universe, the heavens as understood and interpreted in multiple astrological traditions, and, finally, the women who nursed him. Like Qandahari's explanation of the significance of the number seven, which moved from a macrocosmic to a microcosmic universal scheme, Abu al-Fazl places Akbar first within the heavens and cosmos through dreams and horoscopes, and then shifts to the earth and finally Akbar's body as it was physically born after generations of ancestors and nourished by wet nurses.[115]

It is within this context that we may understand Akbar's genealogy in the *Akbarnamah*. Abu al-Fazl not only traces Akbar's ancestry to Timur, but also – like Dughlat did for Tughluq Temur – extends it back to the biblical Adam, via Alan Qoa and a number of biblical figures.[116] He furthermore invokes Jain and Brahma notions of cycles of time and alludes to Akbar as the fulfillment of certain beliefs within each of these traditions, thereby broadening the Mughals' legitimizing ideology.[117] Abu al-Fazl follows this chapter with three chapters in which he provides a brief biography of each of the ancestors on his list and then begins his narrative of the Mughal kings, starting with Babur. The *Akbarnamah*'s genealogy connection to Yazdi's *Zafarnamah* will be discussed in relation to the dream narratives, which we turn to next.

Dream Narratives

Accounts of a ruler or important figure having a significant dream of future greatness appear in Persian texts dating as early as the Buyid

115 For more details on this, see Corinne Lefevre, "In the Name of the Fathers: Mughal Genealogical Strategies from Bābur to Shāh Jahān," *Religions of South Asia* 5 (2011): 409–442.

116 Abu al-Fazl, *Akbarnamah*, ed. and trans. Wheeler Thackston as *The History of Akbar* (Cambridge and London: Harvard University Press, 2015), 1: 176–267.

117 Abu al-Fazl, *Akbarnamah*, 1: 93–105. Audrey Truschke discusses the Sanskrit influence in Mughal sources in Truschke, *Culture of Encounters*.

period.[118] Various scholars have discussed the significance of such texts, especially in terms of their political import, as the chroniclers express contemporary notions of political legitimacy by elaborating or rewriting the dream's interpretation and its significance.[119] Early modern dream narratives incorporate specific elements to the point of their becoming a recurring theme: an important individual, usually a dynastic founder, dreams of some sort of natural phenomenon, whether a star, a tree, or a light, which becomes world encompassing. An important figure, usually a holy man or a close family member, interprets the dream as an auspicious future event, such as the rule of a particular king, conversion to Islam, or world domination. Such dream accounts appear at the beginning sections of Ottoman, Safavid, and Mughal histories. The practice of including a dream narrative associated with a dynastic founding father became popular during the early modern period. Beginning with Ashikpashazadah's Ottoman Turkish account of Osman Ghazi's dream, two significant dreams of Shaykh Safi, founder of the Safaviyyah Sufi order, a dream fortelling the conversion of Tughluq Temur of Moghulistan, and a dream foretelling the rule of the Mughal Akbar, all attest to dream narratives becoming a semiconventional element in early modern historiography. In the case of this particular element, only one chronicler, the Mughal historian Abu al-Fazl, directly responded to a Timurid historical work. In the other examples presented here, dream narratives were derived from different historiographical traditions. However, the fact that they all occupy a structural position at the beginning of the chronicles, and contain similar elements, does not reflect Timurid practice, but rather something new in the early modern period. We begin with Ottoman dream narratives which, while fewer in number than their Safavid and

[118] There has been considerable scholarly interest in dreams and their role and function in Islamicate societies and texts. For a general overview, see Nile Green, "The Religious and Cultural Role of Dreams and Visions in Islam," *Journal of the Royal Asiatic Society* 3 (2003): 287–313; Mimi Hanaoka, "Visions of Muhammad in Bukhara and Tabaristan: Dreams and Their Uses in Persian Local Histories," *Iranian Studies* 47 (2014): 289–303; Ahmet Tunç Şen, "A Mirror for Princes, a Fiction for Readers: The Habnâme of Veysî and Dream Narratives in Ottoman Turkish Literature," *Journal of Turkish Literature* 8 (2011): 41–65.

[119] See, for instance, Roy Mottahedeh, *Loyalty and Leadership in an Early Islamic Society* (Princeton, NJ: Princeton University Press, 1980), 69, 71, and Cemal Kafadar, *Between Two Worlds: The Construction of the Ottoman State* (Berkeley: University of California Press, 1995), 132–133.

Mughal counterparts, provide elements which make for important comparisons across empires.

Ottoman Dream Narratives

The earliest and perhaps best-known dream narrative appears in an early Ottoman Turkish chronicle, Ashikpashazadah's *Tarikh-i al-i Osman*. In this fifteenth-century history, Osman (r. 680–724/ 1281–1324), the Ottoman dynastic founder, dreamt that a moon came out of the breast of a holy shaykh, Edebali, and then entered his own breast.[120] Subsequently, Osman saw a tree sprouting from his navel. The tree's shadow encompassed the entire world. Surrounding the tree were streams, gardens, and fountains, from which people drank, watered gardens, and "caused fountains to flow."[121] Osman woke up from his dream and approached the shaykh, asking him to interpret the dream. The shaykh agreed, and told Osman that the dream meant that sovereignty was granted to Osman and his descendants. He also granted his daughter's hand in marriage to Osman.[122]

After Ashikpashazadah, the dream narrative continued to appear in nearly every Ottoman chronicle covering Ottoman origins.[123] This particular dream narrative, however, not only appears in Ottoman language chronicles but also in at least one Persian history of the Ottoman Empire, namely Idris Bidlisi's (d. 926/1520) *Hasht Bihisht*,

[120] For more on Shaykh Edebali, see Jonathan Brack, "Was Ede Bali a Wafā'ī Shaykh? Sufis, Sayyids and Genealogical Creativity in the Early Ottoman World," in *Islamic Literature and Intellectual Life in Fourteenth- and Fifteenth-Century Anatolia*, eds. A. C. S. Peacock and Sara Nur Yıldız, 333–360 (Würzburg: Ergon Verlag in Kommission, 2016). See also Halil Inalcik, "How to Read 'Ashik Pasha-zade's History," in *Studies in Ottoman History in Honour of Professor V. L. Ménage*, eds. Colin Heywood and Colin Imber, 139–156 (Istanbul: Isis Press, 1994).

[121] Aşikpaşazade, *Die altosmanische Chronik des 'asikpasazade*, ed. F. Giese (Leipzig, 1929), 6–35; trans. Robert Dankoff as "From 'Ashiqpashazada's History of the House of 'Osman," ed. and ann. By John E. Woods, TMS [photocopy].

[122] Aşikpaşazade, *Die altosmanische Chronik*.

[123] "Later chroniclers had a number of variants to report, all of which predicted future glory and conquest." Gottfried Hagen, "Dreaming 'Osmāns: Of History and Meaning," in *Dreams and Visions in Islamic Societies*, eds. Özgen Felek and Alexander D. Knysh, 99–122 (Albany: State University of New York Press, 2012), 114.

a chronicle completed in 908/1502.[124] Idris Bidlisi's account of Osman's dream contains many of the same elements that we see in Ashikpashazadah's account. Idris Bidlisi recounts, for example, how while in Shaykh Edebali's guest house, Osman Ghazi dreamt of a moon coming out of Shaykh Edebali's breast and entering his own. At the same time, a large tree grew out of his navel, and it was full of leaves, branches, and fruit. In the environs of the tree were tall mountains, rivers, and streams, which provided water for gardens, orchards, and plants. Like Ashikpasazadah, Idris Bidlisi also notes that Osman recounted the dream to Shaykh Edebali, who interpreted it to mean that sovereignty belonged to Osman and his descendants.

In addition to repeating these similar aspects of the dream narrative, Idris Bidlisi adds a number of details that do not appear in Ashikpashazadeh's account. Two such additions stand out as particularly interesting and significant. The first of these is that in Idris Bidlisi's account, Osman dreams that in place of one of the green leaves in the tree was a jeweled sword resplendent like a shining star. He saw that several times the rays of its shining blade motioned towards Constantinople. Edebali interpreted the sword as a clear sign of the conquest of Constantinople at the hand and by the blade of one of the offspring of the Ottoman family (*khāndān*), and that land, Edebali stated, would be brightened by the flashing of the sword through the light of faith and the message of "verily I am the sword."[125] Idris Bidlisi's adding this element to the dream, and writing after the conquest of Constantinople, reflects an attempt to legitimize the Ottoman sultans in light of this successful campaign.

The second interesting addition that Idris Bidlisi makes is to the interpretation of the tree, which he elaborates on by associating it with the rulership of the world (*sulṭānī-i ʿālam*) and the throne of kingship (*shāhanshāhī*). In this respect he also says that the descendants of the shaykh, presumably as a result of the union of Osman with Edebali's daughter, would all become the "manifestations of both religious and worldly authority" (*maẓhar-i khilāfat-i dīnī va dunyavī*) and would all become the sultans of both external and spiritual dominion (*mulk-i*

124 All references here are to Idris Bidlisi, "Hasht Bihisht," ms. Ayasofia 3541–3918, f. 26b–27b. I have also consulted ms. Nurosmaniye 3209–3919, f. 35a–37a.

125 Idris Bidlisi, "Hasht bihisht," f. 27a.

ṣūrī va ma'navī).[126] Here, it is important to note that Idris Bidlisi is saying that the Ottoman sultans would hold two types of authority, both an external and an internal or spiritual dominion, very similar to Vuqu'i's statement discussed above that kingship was a divine caliphate (*khilāfat-i ilāhī*). This again represents a departure from the earlier Timurid notion that kings were only external caliphs and is a later addition that we do not see in the original Ashikpashazadah accout. Bidlisi ends the narrative of Osman's dream and its interpretation by comparing it to Joseph's dream, citing the following Quranic passage: "This is the interpretation of my earlier dream. My lord has verily made it come true" (Q 12:100).[127]

Safavid Dream Narratives

Safavid historiography contains an extensive tradition of narrating dreams. The two earliest Safavid chronicles, Ibrahim Amini's *Futuhat-i shahi* and Khvandamir's *Habib al-siyar*, contain dream narratives of Shaykh Safi al-Din. Both writers cite the fourteenth-century hagiography of Shaykhi Safi, the *Safvat al-safa*, as their source. Structurally, these dream narratives do not appear at the beginning of the histories because neither the *Futuhat-i shahi* nor the *Habib al-siyar* are proper "dynastic" chronicles. The *Futuhat-i shahi* narrates the story of creation, the genealogy of Muhammad, and the history of the Shi'i imams before covering the Safaviyya sufi order and the rise of Shah Isma'il. Khvandamir, in his *Habib al-siyar*, focuses on the Safavids in the final portion of his fully fledged universal chronicle. It was not until the Safavid chroniclers started writing *dynastic* histories, relying primarily on the *Habib al-siyar* for the early Safavid period, that dream narratives came to occupy a structural position at the beginning of the chronicle.[128]

In the Safavid dynastic chronicle tradition, the dream narratives appear after the preface, and within accounts of Shaykh Safi al-Din. In one dream narratives drawn from the *Safvat al-safa*, chroniclers describe how Shaykhi Safi saw himself on a mountaintop wearing a hat and a sword tied to his waist. When he removed the hat, a sun

[126] Idris Bidlisi, "Hasht bihisht," f. 27a.
[127] Idris Bidlisi, "Hasht bihisht," f. 27a.
[128] See Quinn, *Historical Writing*, 24–28.

shined from his head, shedding light upon the world. He was unable, however, to draw the sword. Shaykh Safi's spiritual teacher, Shaykh Zahid, interpreted the sun as representing the "light of sainthood" and the sword the "mandate of sovereignty." Early Safavid chroniclers such as Ibrahim Amini, author of the *Futuhat-i shahi*, and Khvandamir, would rewrite the dream interpretation by adding their own explanations, stating that the dual modes of authority – temporal and spiritual – represented by the sword and the sun, would not be fulfilled until the appearance of Shah Isma'il, who uprooted oppression and innovation through the sword of war, "by whose flashing blade people must perish or embrace the true faith."[129] Regardless of the modifications made to the dream accounts, every Safavid history that covers the life of Shaykh Safi al-Din includes a version of at least one dream narrative, thus making dream texts a fully conventional element in Safavid historiography, like accounts of Osman Ghazi in Ottoman historiography.[130]

Interestingly, the dream narratives of Shaykh Safi and Osman Ghazi follow similar patterns of transformation and rewriting. In Ashikpashazadah's version, Osman Ghazi's dream contains no reference to a sword. That element is introduced later and appears in Idris Bidlisi's account. Similarly, in the Safavid case, while the sword appears in the earliest version of the dream, the early chroniclers associate the significance of the sword with the reign of Shah Isma'il. The later recensions of the Ottoman and Safavid dreams contain other striking similarities, such as the assertion that Osman Ghazi and Shaykh Safi/Shah Isma'il had both religious and temporal power. Finally, the motifs of light and the sword appear in each dream, both of which are interpreted by a holy shaykh. While it is not possible to

[129] Quinn, *Historical Writing*, 63–76.

[130] Of course, dream narratives appear elsewhere in numerous Safavid chronicles and other sources. For a discussion of Shah Tahmasb's dreams in his own autobiography, see Kathryn Babayan, *Mystics, Monarchs, and Messiahs: Cultural Landscapes of Early Modern Iran* (Cambridge, MA: Harvard University Press, 2002), 309–325. For a full overview of dream narratives in the Safavid period, see Nuzhat Ahmadi, *Ru'ya va siyasat dar 'asr-i Safavi* (Tehran: Nashr-i Tarikh-i Iran, 1388 [2009]). For an analysis of dream narratives in late Safavid chronicles, see Sholeh A. Quinn, "The Dreams of Shaykh Safi al-Din in Late Safavid Chronicles," in *Dreaming Across Boundaries: The Interpretation of Dreams in Islamic Lands*, ed. Louise Marlow, 221–234 (Cambridge, MA: Harvard University Press, 2008).

trace direct historiographical connections between the Ottoman and Safavid dream narratives, their presence in the chronicle traditions indicate how prevalent dream narratives were at the time.

Dream Narratives in the Tarikh-i Rashidi

Like his Ottoman and Safavid fellow historians, Dughlat includes a dream narrative at the beginning of his *Tarikh-i Rashidi*. He follows his introduction to Book One with a section entitled "The Beginning of the Tarikh-i Rashidi," where he presents a brief overview of the moment of creation, and quotes from Hujwiri's *Kashf al-mahjub*, an important early work on Sufism, as a prelude to explaining Tughluq Timur's conversion to Islam. He follows this discussion with a dream narrative, using the dream to explain how Tughluq Timur converted to Islam. Dughlat viewed this conversion as an extremely important event in the history of Moghulistan, stating in his introduction that one of the three reasons why he begins his history with Tughluq Timur is that "of the Moghul khans it was he who converted to Islam, and after him the Moghuls' necks were freed of the yoke of heathenism, and by the grace of Islam, like all other peoples, they entered among the Muslim peoples."[131] Dughlat, thus, views Tughluq Timur as a sort of "founding father" of Moghulistan, a figure not unlike his neighboring fourteenth-century counterparts, Osman and Safi al-Din.[132]

In the opening sections of the *Tarikh-i Rashidi*, Dughlat describes how a Sufi shaykh named Jamal al-Din related his dream to his son Mawlana Arshad al-Din, as follows:

"I had a dream," he said, "in which I was holding atop a hill a lamp by which all the lands of the east were illuminated. After that, Tughlugh-Temur Khan came to me in Aksu and spoke (as has already been mentioned). Since I will not have the chance during my life time, you be ready. When that young man becomes khan, go to him. He may keep his promise and convert

[131] Dughlat, *Tarikh-i Rashidi*, 5; trans., 4.
[132] The fact that Tughluq Timur was installed as ruler by Dughlat's ancestor, Amir Bulaji Dughlat, may have also played a part in Dughlat's emphasizing Tughluq Timur. Ali Anooshahr points to another of Dughlat's ancestor, Amir Tulak, as the individual who "supported the conversion of Tughlugh Temür to Islam." Dughlat and his family, therefore, played an important role in bolstering Mongol rule in Moghulistan. Anooshahr, *Turkestan*, 119.

to Islam, and this felicity, by which a population will be enlightened, will be due to your endeavor."[133]

Dughlat continues by stating that the shaykh's dream came true and Tughluq Timur did indeed meet the shaykh's son, just as he predicted, and converted to Islam. Dughlat does not cite any written texts as he does elsewhere in his history for this dream narrative. However, several motifs in this account bear resemblance to Ottoman and Safavid dream narratives. For example, the motif of a world-illuminating light as a portent of a future significant event related to a future ruler is similar to the world-encompassing tree in Osman Ghazi's dream, which foretold the greatness of the Ottoman house. Similarly, the lamp in Jamal al-Din's dream resembles the light featured in the dreams of Shaykh Safi al-Din. The theme of light, this time in the form of stars, continues into the Mughal historiographical tradition.

Mughal Dream Narratives

Among Mughal chronicles, Abu al-Fazl's *Akbarnamah* is the only history that directly responds to a Timurid dream narrative. The first chapter of the *Akbarnamah* contains seven dream narratives foretelling the appearance and future greatness of Akbar. The seventh of these dreams has considerable historiographical significance because Abu al-Fazl names an earlier Timurid history, Sharaf al-Din 'Ali Yazdi's *Zafarnamah*, in his dream narrative. More specifically, Abu al-Fazl's dream narrative has its origins in the *muqaddimah* of Yazdi's *Zafarnamah*, not the *Zafarnamah* itself. There, Yazdi explains how a Timurid ancestor, Qachulay, dreamed of his twin brother Qabul having four stars rising from his breast. The last star filled the world with light. Qachulay subsequently dreamed of seven stars and then an eighth that rose from his breast. His father interpreted these dreams as signaling the greatness of Chingiz Khan, a fourth generation descendant of Qabul, and Timur, who was an eighth generation descendant of Qachulay.[134]

At least two Persian histories composed before the *Akbarnamah*, namely Mirkhvand's *Rawzat al-safa* and Khvandamir's *Habib al-siyar*, also contain narratives of Qachulay's dreams. However, neither

[133] Dughlat, *Tarikh-i Rashidi*, 12; trans., 10.
[134] Woods, "Timur's Genealogy," 91.

Mirkhvand nor Khvandamir explicitly cite their sources. Mirkhvand imitates Yazdi nearly word for word in his account, and Khvandamir directly imitates either Mirkhvand or Yazdi. As for Abu al-Fazl, his account makes direct mention of Qachulay's dream in the *Zafarnamah*. Assuming that his audience was already familiar with the details of the dream itself, for he does not fully recount it, Abu al-Fazl simply states that

> It is well known to insightful scholars that Mawlana Sharaf al-Din 'Ali Yazdi included an account of Qachulai Bahadur's interpretation of it as a portent of H. M. Sahib-Qiran [Timur], and he interpreted the eighth bright star that illumined the world and arose from Qachulai Bahadur's loins as H. M. Sahib-Qirani, who is H.I.M.'s [Akbar] ancestor in the eighth degree.[135]

Abu al-Fazl continues to say that Yazdi's interpretation was an outward or superficial (*ẓāhir*) interpretation, and that the eighth star, a world-encompassing light, in reality represented Akbar. The reason for this is that the seven stars presumably representing the generations between Qachulay and Timur were "not graced with the crown of world rule."[136] In other words, Timur's ancestors going back to Qachulay were not powerful enough rulers to be equated with "stars." The seven stars, he continues, actually represent "seven exalted monarchs," implying the seven individuals that genealogically connected Akbar to Timur. Abu al-Fazl then elaborates on the notion of Akbar's light as a light of justice and a "manifestation of the perfection of divine might" that "sheds light upon the inner and outer world." He ends the account by saying that "the truth of this is not hidden from those who search for the reality of things."[137]

Abu al-Fazl's retelling the story of Qachulay's dream demonstrates first of all the strength of the Timurid past and of Timur's position in the Mughal period. The dream and its interpretation could not be ignored, but was rather something to be refashioned, reimagined, and revived. In his account, Abu al-Fazl decenters Timur and places the textual spotlight on Akbar. In saying that Yazdi's interpretation was superficial, Abu al-Fazl does not discount Yazdi completely, but

135 Abu al-Fazl, *Akbarnamah*, 1: 56–57.
136 Abu al-Fazl, *Akbarnamah*, 1: 56–57.
137 Abu al-Fazl, *Akbarnamah*, 1: 56–57.

rather renders his narrative incomplete and superficial in comparison with his own interpretation of the dream as deep and representative of an inner dimension or reality. Historiographically, Abu al-Fazl's approach does not differ greatly from that of Khvandamir or Ibrahim Amini, who recounted the story of Shaykh Safi's dream, but then added their own "true" interpretation, thereby allowing the dream to portend the appearance of Shah Isma'il rather than the greatness of Shaykh Safi. Abu al-Fazl contrasts his interpretation of the dream as one that is deep and representative of an inner dimension or reality, with Yazdi's interpretation as incomplete and superficial.

With his deft reworking of Yazdi's narrative, in which he does not completely delegitimize the account, Abu al-Fazl is able to provide a complete description of Qachulay's dream later in the *Akbarnamah*, in his account of Akbar's ancestors. There, in his account of Qachulay, he imitates Yazdi's *Muqaddimah* nearly word for word. In contrast with his earlier discussion of Qachulay, Abu al-Fazl does not repeat his earlier criticism of Yazdi's interpretation of the seven stars "incorrectly" alluding to Timur, but rather keeps the dream's interpretation intact. Furthermore, Abu al-Fazl clarifies the dream narrative by adding an extra discussion not found in Yazdi's *Muqaddimah*, explaining that Akbar's ancestors, from Adam to Tumanay Khan, held both absolute and independent sovereignty and some also held spiritual authority. He states that because "divine wisdom ... was waiting for the time of the birth of H.I.M. [Akbar]," it did not make Qachulay king, but rather clothed him

> in the rainment of deputyship in order to gather together and make him appreciate the value of worthy service so that all states of this condition might be experienced by this exalted line and all such degrees might be assembled in H.I.M.[138]

In this way, Abu al-Fazl explains away the fact that Qachulay did immediately succeed his father, but rather his brother Qabul did, while Qachulay served as "commander-in-chief, tactician, general, and wielder of the sword."[139] Ultimately, the world had to wait for Akbar to become the ideal king.

[138] Abu al-Fazl, *Akbarnamah*, 1: 230–231.
[139] Abu al-Fazl, *Akbarnamah*, 1: 230–231.

Conclusion

Early modern historians, regardless of which dynasty they were writing for, inherited a powerful historiographical tradition, one that supplied them with imitative models containing the general themes through which they could promote their dynasty's ideology and legitimate right to rule. Whether in discussions of the benefits of history, bibliographies, genealogies of dynastic founders, or dream narratives, the historians refashioned Timurid and pre-Timurid texts in different ways, discontinuing or limiting some elements while at the same time adding new strands reflecting changes the Islamic world experienced in the early modern age. It is important to note that while these historians tapped into a historiographical tradition that looked to Timurid dynastic and cultural practices as ideals worthy of literary emulation, not every early modern chronicler shared their interests.[140] Nevertheless, they represent an important and substantial part of the overall Persianate historiographical landscape. Although distinct political units were in control of various portions of the early modern empires, the historians writing under the Ottomans, Safavids, and Mughals spoke in a cultural language that transcended political boundaries and was broadly understood.

[140] For example, the Safavid historian Hasan Beg Rumlu, author of the *Ahsan al-tavarikh*, did not include many of the historiographical elements discussed here in his chronicle. See Quinn, *Historical Writing*, 42–43.

3 *Historiography and Historians on the Move*

The Significance of the Number Twelve

Introduction

Having established some of the salient features of the Timurid historiographical legacy, we now examine, through a close reading of texts, how that legacy moved across empires. The process of early modern historians inheriting and elaborating on the Timurid historiographical legacy was not a static process. Intellectuals writing in Persian had more opportunity to find patronage and support for their work by looking beyond the borders of the empire in which they resided. We find the most extensively documented example of this kind of movement with the poets who left Safavid Iran for Mughal India. The traditional explanation for the poets moving to India – that they were fleeing religious persecution – has been superseded by other explanations: for example, that they went to India in search of patronage and better financial reward, due to an overabundance of poets in Safavid Persia, or due to the Safavid kings' negative attitudes toward poetry.[1] Although their numbers were not as high as the poets, historians, at times with all or part of their families, also moved to India and influenced the historiography of multiple ruling dynasties. The concept of the poet "on the move," then, does not depict such an individual choosing to leave Iran due to simply the desire for a change of scenery or feeling the impulse to move for the sake of moving. Rather, the same sorts of political and economic factors that led the poets to move must have similarly led historians and other scholars to migrate to India, where their skills and talents found them employment and where they

[1] See Losensky, *Welcoming Fighānī*, 140–142, and Sunil Sharma, *Mughal Arcadia: Persian Literature in an Indian Court* (Cambridge, MA: Harvard University Press, 2017), 20. See also Nobuaki Kondo, "Making a Persianate Society: Literati Migration to Mughal India," in *Crossing the Boundaries: Asians and Africans on the Move: Proceedings of the Papers Presented at Consortium for Asian and African Studies (CAAS) 7th International Conference*, Tokyo University of Foreign Studies, October 22–23, 2016, 67–73.

contributed to creating the intellectual underpinnings and justification for the Mughal Empire. Such was the case with the chronicler Khvandamir, who wrote for multiple dynasties, and the descendants of Mir Yahya Sayfi Qazvini, who left Safavid Iran and rose to prominence under the Mughals.

The first historian to make such a move was Khvandamir, who not only settled in Mughal territory, but also ended up writing for the Mughals. Other early modern historians followed suit. In this chapter, we will examine "historiographical movement" by analyzing the similarities and differences in related sections of the *Habib al-siyar*, a historical work that Khvandamir wrote under the Safavids, and the *Qanun-i Humayuni*, which he wrote for the Mughals. Doing so allows us to gain a better understanding of the origins of Persianate historiography in the early modern period. Such a comparative analysis also provides insight regarding the relationship between empires that were politically divided but, historiographically speaking, part of a cultural whole.

While this analysis is limited to one historian and his movement between two empires, the Safavid and Mughal, the purpose here is to demonstrate the benefits of engaging in very close reading of two related texts. The nature of such highly detailed analysis makes it necessary to limit the scope of this case study to one historiographical example and one study of an entire family's movement from Safavid to Mughal territory. Such an approach, however, could just as easily be applied to similarly related texts written by historians writing, for example, under the Mughals and the Ottomans, or the Ottomans and the Safavids.

When the historian Khvandamir traveled to India, he found himself in the company of Babur, founder of the Mughal dynasty. Having already enjoyed a long and distinguished career in Herat and elsewhere before arriving in India, Khvandamir was received with great respect and appreciation. After Babur's death, he proceeded to write, for Babur's successor Humayun, the *Qanun-i Humayun*, his last historical composition and the first history of the new dynasty, with the exception of Babur's own autobiography.

A Historian on the Move

Khvandamir represents the first generation of Safavid/Mughal historiographical interactions because he was the first individual who wrote history for both dynasties. Khvandamir's story, however, is not one of simply moving from Safavid territory to Mughal territory. Before leaving Iran for India, he composed a number of texts in multiple genres including history, biography, politics, and something approximating mirrors for princes, a genre of normative advice literature written for rulers. Furthermore, he wrote for at least five different patrons who represented several different ruling dynasties and groups in the turbulent late fifteenth and early sixteenth centuries, as seen in Table 3.1.[2]

Khvandamir left Herat for Qandahar in 933/1527, three years after the death of Shah Isma'il, and just one year after Babur had established himself as the Mughal emperor. On the Safavid side, Shah Tahmasb had not yet gained control over the Qizilbash, who were engaged in internal warfare, yet still wielded power at the Safavid capital court in Qazvin.[3] Khvandamir remained in Qandahar until 934/1528, when he left for India. The circumstances of his departure are unclear. M. Hidayat Hosain states that this was "probably due to his disagreement with the successor of Shah Ismail [Shah Tahmasb] or to some internal political troubles, concerning which history is silent."[4] Khvandamir's family ties help explain why he would have felt welcome in Mughal territory. His father, Khvajah Humam al-Din Muhammad, was minister to Sultan Mahmud, second son of Timurid ruler Sultan Abu Sa'id (r. 855–873/1451–1469). Sultan Mahmud's brother and Abu Said's sixth son was Mirza Umar Shaykh, who was Babur's father.[5] In other words, Khvandamir's father served as minister to

[2] See *EI2,* s.v., "Khwandamir"; by H. Beveridge and J. T. P. de Bruijn; Khvandamir, *Makarim al-Akhlaq*, ed. T. Gandjeï, ix–xi (London: E. J. W. Gibb Memorial Trust, 1979).

[3] Rula Jurdi Abisaab, *Converting Persia: Religion and Power in the Safavid Empire* (London: I. B. Tauris, 2004), 14–15; Martin B. Dickson, "Sháh Ṭahmásb and the Úzbeks: The Duel for Khurásán with 'Ubayd Khán (930–946/1524–1540)" (Ph. D. diss., Princeton University, 1958); Gregory Aldous, "Qizilbash Tribalism and Royal Authority in Early Safavid Iran, 1524–1534" (Ph.D. diss., University of Wisconsin, Madison, 2013).

[4] M. Hidayat Hosain, "Preface," to Khvandamir, *Qanun-i-Humayuni*, ed. M. Hidayat Hosain, xiv (Calcutta: The Royal Asiatic Society of Bengal, 1940). Hereafter cited as Hosain, "Preface."

[5] Hosain, "Preface," i. M. Hidayat Hosain suggests that Khvandamir "had to" leave Herat "probably due to his disagreement with the successor of Shāh Ismā'īl or to some internal political troubles, concerning which history is silent," but he provides no evidence for this statement. See Hosain, "Preface," xiv.

Table 3.1 *Khvandamir's compositions*

Title	Date of composition	Patron	Description
1. *Ma'asir al-muluk*	Before 903/1498	'Ali Shir Nava'i (Timurid)	Collection of political maxims
2. *Khulasat al-akhbar fi bayan ahwal al-akhyar*	905/1499–1500	'Ali Shir Nava'i (Timurid)	Concise world history
3. *Makarim al-akhlaq*	906/1501	'Ali Shir Nava'i (Timurid)	Panegyric biography of 'Ali Shir Nava'i
4. *Dastur al-vuzara*	915/1509–1510	Khvajah Kamal al-Din Mahmud, vizier/minister of Sultan Husayn Bayqara (Timurid) (Uzbeks in power)[a]	Biographies of famous ministers
5. *Namah-yi nami* correspondence (*insha'*)	925/1519	?	A work of model
6. *Muntakhabat-i Tarikh-i Vassaf*	?	?	Mentioned in the preface of the *Habib al-siyar* as one of the author's works, seems not to have survived
7. *Habib al-siyar*	930/1524	Dedicated initially to Ghiyas al-Din Amir Muhammad ibn Amir Yusuf Husayni, one of the notables of Herat, and then to Karim al-Din Habib Allah, a Safavid governor (Safavid)	Universal history
8. *Qanun-i Humayuni*	941/1534	Humayun (Mughal)	Institutions, ordinances, and building projects of Humayun

[a] See Colin Mitchell, *The Practice of Politics in Safavid Iran: Power, Religion, and Rhetoric* (London: I. B. Tauris, 2009).

Babur's uncle. Khvandamir's family and Babur's family were thus very well known to each other, and in going to India, Khvandamir would have found himself among old family friends, albeit in a new geographical setting.

At the time of Khvandamir's arrival in India in 934/1528, he was prominent enough for Babur to have mentioned him at least twice in his memoirs/autobiography, the *Baburnamah*. Here, Babur records the first instance in which Khvandamir met him. Under his entry for 4 Muharram 935/19 September 1528, Babur lists the daily arrivals to his court on 3 and 4 Muharram. He notes that a certain ʻAskari had arrived on 3 Muharram 935 (Friday 18 September 1528), and on 4 Muharram 935 (Saturday 19 September 1528), and notes that "Khvandamir the historian, Mawlana Shihab the enigmatist, and Mir Ibrahim the dulcimer player, a relative of Yunus Ali, all of whom had long ago left Herat wishing to enroll in my service, came and paid homage."[6] The second time Babur mentions Khvandamir was after his successful Bengal expedition in 935/1529, in which Khvandamir had accompanied him.[7] Afterward, when Babur was in pursuit of the Afghan Shaykh Bayazid Farmuli, he camped "beside the Gomati one kos from Maing." Babur explains how, at around noon, he "indulged in some *maʻjūn*" and summoned some friends, including Khvandamir, to join the party, issuing the invitation in the form of a poem: "[Turki] Shaykh [Zayn], Mulla Shihab, and Khwandamir: come all three, or two, or one."[8] Khvandamir presumably accepted the invitation, and the gathering took place on 1 Shawwal 935/Tuesday 7 June 1529.

Khvandamir and Humayun

After Babur's death, Khvandamir entered the service of Babur's son and successor, Humayun. He wrote his *Qanun-i Humayuni* at

[6] Babur, *Baburnama*, trans. Wheeler Thackston (New York: Modern Library, 2002), 412; trans. Annette Beveridge (London: Luzac, 1922), 605.

[7] See Hosain, "Preface," xv. An extensive analysis of Babur and the *Baburnamah* can be found in Stephen F. Dale, *The Garden of Eight Paradises: Bābur and the Culture of Empire in Central Asia, Afghanistan and India (1483–1530)* (Leiden: Brill, 2004).

[8] *Maʻjun* is what Dale refers to as a "drug-laced confection." For more on Babur's use of alcohol and drugs, see Dale, *The Garden of Eight Paradises*, 36–38. Babur, *Baburnama*, trans. Wheeler Thackston, 455; Babur, *Baburnama*, trans. Annette Beveridge, 683.

Humayun's request and finished it in 940/1534, some four years after Humayun succeeded the throne (at the age of 25, in 937/1530).[9] Although at least four historical works have survived that cover the reign of Humayun, the *Qanun-i Humayuni* is the earliest history among those that were composed during Humayun's own lifetime. The other three, Jawhar Aftabchi's *Tazkirat al-vaqi'at*, Bayazid Bayat's *Tarikh-i Humayun*, and Gulbadan Begum's *Humayunnamah*, were written at the command of Akbar in order to assist the great chronicler Abu al-Fazl in compiling his *Akbarnamah*.[10] Humayun, like Babur, held Khvandamir in high esteem, and gave him the title of chief chronicler (*amīr al-akhbār*) the same year that he became king. Khvandamir describes this event in the *Qanun-i Humayuni*: "On the day of the grand feast, the generous king conferred newly created ranks on some of the Persian and Turkish (*tāzīk va turk*) learned and the nobles ... and the author of these pages received the title of chief chronicler (*amīr al-akhbār*)."[11]

Khvandamir, thus, became an important figure in Humayun's retinue, and his family continued to enjoy royal favor even after his death. One of his sons, who must have been born shortly before or after Khvandamir's passing, was apparently "brought up from his infancy by the emperor Akbar and attained the rank of seven hundred."[12] Akbar himself gave that son the title "Sayyid 'Abd Allah Khan," and he participated in military and diplomatic missions for the king. For example, during the ninth year of his reign, Akbar ordered Sayyid 'Abd Allah Khan to join a group of other officers in pursuit of 'Abd Allah

[9] Hosain, "Preface," xxxiv. See also Storey, *Persian Literature*, 1: 536–539.

[10] See Hosain, "Preface," v. For an early translation and edition of Gulbadan Begum's *Humayunnamah*, see Gul-Badan Begum, *Humayun-nama, The History of Humayun*, trans. Annette S. Beveridge (New Delhi: Goodword Boks, 2002). For recent translations and editions of these memoirs, see *Three Memoirs of Homayun*, trans. Wheeler M. Thackston (Costa Mesa, CA: Mazda Publishers, 2009).

[11] Khvandamir, *Ma'asir al-muluk bi zamimah-i khatima-'i khulasat al-akhbar va qanun-i Humayuni*, ed. Mir Hashim Muhaddis, 276–277 ([Tehran]: Mu'assasah-'i Khadamat-i Farhangi-i Rasa, 1372 [1993]). Hereafter cited as *Qanun-i Humayuni*. Trans. Baini Prashad (Kolkata: The Asiatic Society, 1940), 42.

[12] Hosain, "Preface," xvii. The ranking refers to the *mansabdari* system which "placed all officers of the empire in a single hierarchy with numerical ranks that represented the number of troops they were required to support." Streusand, *Islamic Gunpowder Empires*, 218.

Khan, the Uzbek leader, who had fled to Gujrat. During his thirty-first year as king, Akbar sent Sayyid 'Abd Allah Khan to Qasim Khan, the governor of Kashmir. According to Abu al-Fazl, Qasim Khan was "the son of Mirza Dost's sister, who was an old servant of the Timurids" and had supervised the construction of the Agra Fort. Upon being appointed commander of Agra, Qasim Khan was under orders to conquer Kashmir, which he did. Sayyid 'Abd Allah Khan presumably went to Kashmir to assist in this operation.[13] In Akbar's thirty-fourth regnal year, he was killed by a number of Kashmiris.[14] While Sayyid 'Abd Allah Khan did not engage in historical writing, his brother Amir Mahmud, who had remained in Safavid territory when his father and brother went to India, wrote a continuation of his father's chronicle.[15] Amir Mahmud completed his history in 957/1550.

Khvandamir's *Qanun-i Humayuni*

Khvandamir's *Qanun-i Humayuni* consists of an introduction, seven chapters, and a concluding poem. The chapters cover the following topics: (1) praise of the king, (2) Humayun's ordering his society, (3) Humayun's entertaining style, (4) Humayun's crown and his dress, (5) the buildings that Humayun erected, (6) some of the festivals that he instituted, and (7) a few further practices. In terms of genre, the *Qanun-i Humayuni* is not so much a work of history as a sort of summary of Humayun's achievements, or a "normative, but – as of its

13 Abu al-Fazl ibn Mubarak, *Ain-i Akbari*, ed. H. Blochmann, 2 vols. (Calcutta: Asiatic Society of Bengal, 1877); trans. H. Blochmann as *The Ain-i-Akbari*, 3 vols. (Calcutta: Royal Asiatic Society, 1873), trans., 1: 380 (Blochmann notes).

14 For more information on Sayyid 'Abd Allah Khan, see Abu al-Fazl, *Ain-i Akbari*, 1: 465; Shah Navaz Khan Awrangabadi and 'Abd al-Hayy ibn Shahnavaz, *Ma'asir al-umara'*, eds. 'Abd al-Rahim and Mirza Ashraf 'Ali, 3 vols., 2: 401 (Calcutta: Asiatic Society, 1888–1891); trans. H. Beveridge as *The Maāthir-ul-umarā Being Biographies of the Muḥammadan and Hindu Officers of the Timurid Sovereigns of India from 1500 to about 1780 A.D.* (Calcutta: Asiatic Society, 1952), 1: 80–81; Adam Jacobs, "Sunni and Shi'i Perceptions, Boundaries and Affiliations in Late Timurid and Early Safawid Persia: An Examination of Historical and Quasi-Historical Narratives" (Ph.D. diss., University of London, School of Oriental and African Studies, 1999), 109; Charles Rieu, *Catalog of the Persian Manuscripts in the British Museum*, vol. 1 (London: British Museum, 1879), 96–97; Hosain, "Preface," xvii.

15 Amir Mahmud, *Iran dar ruzgar-i Shah Isma'il va Shah Tahmasb Safavi*, ed. Ghulam Riza Tabataba'i (Tehran: Bunyad-i Mawqufat-i Duktur Mahmud Afshar, 1370 [1991]).

writing – unfulfilled, vision of imperial power."[16] The historiographical antecedents for compositions such as this include Rashid al-Din's account of Ghazan Khan's attributes and accomplishments in his *Jami' al-tavarikh*, and Khvandamir's own *Makarim al-akhlaq*, a panegyric tribute to his distinguished patron, the poet and courtier Mir 'Ali Shir Nava'i, which he composed some 32 years earlier.[17] Significant portions of the *Makarim al-akhlaq* focus on Nava'i's personal qualities, with entire chapters devoted to virtues such as his humility, generosity, compassionate disposition, and wisdom – a feature we do not find in the *Qanun-i Humayuni*. Other chapters of the *Makarim al-akhlaq*, however, such as those describing the construction projects that Nava'i sponsored, and the mosques built and restored under his charge, bear resemblance to some of the themes in the *Qanun-i Humayuni*.

In his introduction to the *Qanun-i Humayuni*, which follows many of the same conventional patterns as other Persianate texts, Khvandamir introduces himself and notes that important kings and rulers had historians in their service chronicling their accomplishments.[18] In a passage reminiscent of the bibliographies described in Chapter 2, he invokes a number of earlier historians and poets, including 'Utbi and 'Unsuri, both of whom wrote for Mahmud of Ghazna (r. 388–421/998–1030), and Mu'izzi (ca. 440–519/21/1048/1049–1125/1127) and Anvari, who wrote for Sultan Sanjar (r. 490–552/1097–1157): "For example, the eulogistic pages of 'Utbi and 'Unsuri narrate and preserve the glories of Mahmud while the

16 Munis D. Faruqui, *The Princes of the Mughal Empire, 1504–1719* (Cambridge: Cambridge University Press, 2012), 62. For more on the *Qanun-i Humayuni*, see Stephan Conermann, *Historiographie als Sinnstiftung: Ind-persische Geschichtsschreibung während der Mogulzeit (932–1118/1516–1707)* (Weisbaden: Reichert Verlag, 2002), 154–159. See also Eva Orthmann, "Ideology and State-Building: Humāyūn's Search for Legitimacy in a Hindu-Muslim Environment," in *Religious Interactions in Mughal India*, eds. Vasudha Dalmia and Munis D. Faruqui, 3–29 (New Delhi: Oxford University Press, 2014).

17 See Sholeh A. Quinn, "Through the Looking Glass: Kingly Virtues in Safavid and Mughal Historiography," *Journal of Persianate Studies* (2010): 143–155. The influence of this genre on early modern historiography will be discussed in greater detail in Chapter 5. For more on 'Ali Shir Nava'i and his relationship with Sultan Husayn Bayqara, see Maria Eva Subtelny, "'Alī Shīr Navā'ī: Bakhshī and Beg," *Harvard Ukranian Studies* 3–4 (1979–1980): 797–807.

18 On conventional elements in prefaces, see Quinn, *Historical Writing*, 33–61.

matchless compositions (*qaṣā'id*) of Mu'izzi and Anvari record in detail the gallant deeds of Sanjar."[19] He repeats Anvari and 'Utbi's names in a poem, and ends by mentioning Sharaf al-Din 'Ali Yazdi:

Who would remember Hakim Anvari
Had he not composed the epic about Sanjar and his deeds
'Utbi by recording praises of Mahmud,
Fully realized his objective
Sharaf became famous in the world
For he wrote in praise of Timur Gurgan.[20]

In writing these lines, Khvandamir positions himself and his *Qanun-i Humayuni* among earlier Ghaznavid historians and poets and an important Timurid historian and history. Khvandamir then states that Humayun commissioned him to compose the *Qanun-i Humayuni* and even told him what to write about. In doing so, he repeats the alleged words that Humayun spoke in issuing the command:

It is right and proper that the inventions of my auspicious mind and the discoveries of my erudite understanding should be chronicled in the proper order of their announcement and currency, so that the light of these happy works may eternally shine near and far in the pages (of the history) of the world.[21]

Khvandamir apparently planned to write further histories and hoped for Humayun's support in these endeavors. This theme of expected patronage appears in the final poem (*masnavī*) which constitutes the conclusion of the *Qanun-i Humayuni*. Here, Khvandamir boasts that if Humayun supported him, he would "sing poems (in praise of) your prosperity."[22] In expressing such hopes, he compares his poetical abilities to those of Firdawsi and Anvari (whom he mentioned in his introduction), and his historiographical skills to Sharaf al-Din 'Ali Yazdi's *Zafarnamah*. His repeated reference to the *Zafarnamah* indicates the importance of that text:

By writing your chronicles, O prosperous Monarch
I may fill the skirts of the world with pearls.
Like Firdawsi and Anvari,

19 Khvandamir, *Qanun-i Humayuni*, 255; trans., 12.
20 Khvandamir, *Qanun-i Humayuni*, 255; trans., 12.
21 Khvandamir, *Qanun-i Humayuni*, 255–256; trans., 14–15.
22 Khvandamir, *Qanun-i Humayuni*, 306; trans., 83.

I may also renew the dress of poetry
Provided your order is issued, [as]
Without [your] order it cannot be undertaken.
I may write such an enticing *Zafarnamah*
That its love may make people restless.
The beauty of its arrangement should deprive the heart of its senses
It may humiliate the eloquence of Sharaf.[23]

Given the contents of the *Qanun-i Humayuni*, we may view it in one sense as a sort of practice run or showpiece – a fairly short portfolio-like text, consisting of some 60 pages in the 1993 edition – in which Khvandamir displays to Humayun in an abbreviated form what he is capable of writing for him. In making the case for his future project, Khvandamir points to his own social position and his training:

I also am of noble birth and have acquired learning and the propriety of conduct:
Hereditary virtues and acquired knowledge.
Therefore, I hope, O Lord of the crown,
that I may win further patronage.[24]

Khvandamir never did win further patronage, for he died approximately a year after writing the *Qanun-i Humayuni*. This happened when he accompanied Humayun in his Gujarat campaign against Bahadur Shah (r. 932–943/1526–1537), the Sultan of Gujarat, in 1534.[25] Khvandamir, who was approximately 59 years old by then, contracted dysentery along the way, and died sometime after that.[26] The historian Firishtah states that his remains were taken to Delhi, and he was buried next to the tomb of the Sufi Nizam al-Din al-Awliya and the poet Amir Khusraw.[27]

Khvandamir's writing and travels serve to bridge at least two historiographical traditions. By using his grandfather Mirkhvand's

[23] Khvandamir, *Qanun-i Humayuni*, 306; trans., 83. Translation slightly modified. Anooshahr analyzes this passage in Anooshahr, *Turkestan*, 159.
[24] Khvandamir, *Qanun-i Humayuni*, 307; trans., 83–84. See also Anooshahr, *Turkestan*, 158–159.
[25] Hosain, "Preface," xv.
[26] Hosain, "Preface," xvi. See also Muhammad Qasim Hindu Shah Astarabadi Firishtah, *Tarikh-i Firishtah*, ed. Muhammad Riza Nasiri, 2 vols. (Tehran: Anjuman-i Asar va Mafakhir-i Farhangi, 1387 [2008]), 2: 69; trans. John Briggs as *History of the Rise of the Mahomedan Power in India*, 4 vols. (Calcutta: R. Cambray & Co., 1909), 2: 69; trans., 2: 81.
[27] Firishtah, *Tarikh-i Firishtah*, 2: 69; trans., 2: 81.

Rawzat al-safa as a model for his *Habib al-siyar*, he ensured that the late Timurid historiographical tradition would survive into the Safavid period. Indeed, we may trace the historiographical genealogies of many later Safavid chronicles back to Khvandamir, sometimes via his son Amir Mahmud.[28] Khvandamir took that tradition with him to India, by which time he was a seasoned writer who commanded a great deal of respect. He was much admired by two Mughal kings and at least one later chronicler, as Abu al-Fazl included some portions of the *Qanun-i Humayuni* in his *Akbarnamah*, as we will discuss below.[29]

The *Qanun-i Humayuni* and the Significance of the Number Twelve

One way to understand in a more in-depth manner the way in which early Safavid and early Mughal historiographies became connected is through examining how Khvandamir transferred his writings from Safavid Iran to Mughal India. In composing a particular section of the *Qanun-i Humayuni*, Khvandamir took a portion of his *Habib al-siyar* and rewrote it in ways that we will explain below. The analysis here will demonstrate how Khvandamir engaged in the rewriting process and how he "double-bridged" the historiographical traditions to which he was connected. This discussion will also serve as a historiographical and methodological reminder as to why we should be aware – to the greatest extent possible – of our sources' sources.

In the second chapter of the *Qanun-i Humayuni*, Khvandamir provides an account of how Humayun reorganized Mughal society, describing how he divided the officers of state into three groups or classes: (1) the people of government (*ahl-i dawlat*), who were "his brothers and other relatives, his officers (*'umarā'*), his ministers (viziers) and his soldiers"; (2) the people of happiness (*ahl-i sa'ādat*), consisting of "holy persons, great shaykhs, the respectable sayyids, the learned men, the qadis of Islam, the band of philosophers and poets, the judges, the nobles and worthy people"; and (3) the people of

[28] See Quinn, *Historical Writing*. For a recent study of the *Habib al-siyar*, see Shahzad Bashir, "A Perso-Islamic Universal Chronicle in Its Historical Context: Ghiyāṣ al-Dīn Khwāndamīr's *Ḥabīb al-siyar*," in *History and Religion*, eds. Jörg Rüpke, Susanne Rau, and Bernd-Christian Otto, 209–225 (Berlin: Walter de Gruyter, 2015).

[29] Hosain, "Preface," xv.

pleasure (*ahl-i murād*), consisting of "those who possessed beauty and elegance, those who were young and handsome, also clever musicians and sweet singers."[30] Humayun presented a designated leader of each group with a golden arrow, symbolic of "the arrow of his design" reaching "the target of success." That individual was responsible for ordering the affairs of his group unless or until he neglected his responsibilities.[31] Humayun divided the three groups, *ahl-i dawlat*, *ahl-i sa'ādat*, and *ahl-i murād* into twelve more subclasses, each receiving an arrow of a particular grade of gold. The twelve classes/arrows range from the king and his intimates at the highest levels to porters and camel drivers at the lowest levels. The full range of classes are as follows: "(12) the emperor, (11) the relatives, brothers, and other sultans who serve the emperor, (10) the greatest of shaykhs, the prophet's family and men of knowledge, and the People of Felicity, (9) the great nobles, (8) the emperor's personal servants and officers who hold rank, (7) (non-rank-holding) officers in general, (6) clan leaders and elders, (5) unique young men of ability, (4) special servants, (3) young hunters, (2) servants in waiting, (1) porters, camel drivers, etc."[32] Azfar Moin explains how this organizational scheme should be understood as a "ritual display of kingship," one that had a "formal, cosmological shape."[33] Moin also suggests that while Khvandamir cast Humayun in the mold of a "universal Islamic" and Persian king, Shattari Sufis also influenced his imperial formulations.[34]

Khvandamir concludes his discussion of Humayun's social structuring by explaining the significance of the number twelve in connection with the twelve classes, stating that twelve "is the number of digits on which the regulation of most worldly affairs, and of every momentous business has been ordained since the creation of the world to the

30 Khvandamir, *Qanun-i Humayuni*, 264–265; trans., 25–26.

31 Khvandamir, *Qanun-i Humayuni*, 265–266; trans., 28.

32 Khvandamir, *Qanun-i Humayuni*, 268–269; trans., 31–32. Here I am using a slightly modified translation from Moin, *Millennial Sovereign*, 118.

33 Moin, *Millennial Sovereign*, 111. For more on Humayun and cosmology, see Ali Anooshahr, "Science at the Court of the Cosmocrat: Mughal India, 1531–56," *The Indian Economic and Social Review* 54 (2017): 295–316.

34 For a discussion on the Shattari brothers, see Moin, *Millennial Sovereign*, 97–110. It is interesting to note that the notion of society being organized according to classes of people was thought to have originated with the pre-Islamic Persian king Ardashir and the legendary Persian king Jamshid. See Louise Marlow, *Hierarchy and Egalitarianism in Islamic Thought* (Cambridge: Cambridge University Press, 1997), 66–90.

present time."[35] He then proceeds to give five explanations for the significance of the number twelve, in the following order:

(1) The eighth celestial sphere (*falak*) is divided into twelve signs of the zodiac; the sun, moon, stars, and seven planets rotate through the signs of the zodiac, and the calculation of months and years are based on this.
(2) When day and night are at an equilibrium, each has twelve hours.
(3) There were twelve tribes of Israel, or sons of Jacob.
(4) Muhammad appointed from amongst his friends twelve people as his agents on the night of ʿAqaba, and there were twelve Imams.[36]
(5) The number of letters in each half of the testimony of faith (*shahādah*) is twelve ("there is no God but God" [*lā Ilāha illā Allāh*] and "Muhammad is the messenger of God" [*Muḥammad rasūl Allāh*]).[37]

Historiographical Background

While Humayun was the central focus and primary audience for Khvandamir's *Qanun-i Humayuni*, a closer examination of this passage shows that Khvandamir did not compose it from scratch for this work. In order to understand the historiographical background of this text, we must first turn to two earlier texts: (1) Mirkhvand's *Rawzat al-safa* and (2) Khvandamir's earlier composition, his *Habib al-siyar*. As noted above in Chapter 2, Khvandamir modeled his universal history, the *Habib al-siyar*, on his grandfather Mirkhvand's *Rawzat al-safa*, often imitating it and using it as the basis for his overall organizational scheme. Mirkhvand divides the *Rawzat al-safa* into an introduction and six chapters or portions (*qism*), as follows: (1) the beginning of creation and stories of the prophets and the events of the Iranian kings and ancient philosophers, (2) the circumstances and conquests of the Prophet and the events related to the Rashidun caliphs, (3) the circumstances of the twelve Imams and the Umayyad and Abbasid caliphs,

35 Khvandamir, *Qanun-i Humayuni*, 269; trans., 32.
36 The night of ʿAqaba refers to the episode in 622 in which Muhammad requested that twelve people be appointed to propagate his religion in Medina. See *EI2*, s. v., "al-Madina," by R. B. Winder.
37 Khvandamir, *Qanun-i Humayuni*, 269–271; trans., 32–34. For a recently analysis of this passage, see Moin, *Millennial Sovereign*, 118.

(4) dynasties of Iranian kings during the Abbasid caliphs, (5) the history of Chingiz Khan and the Ilkhanid Mongols in Iran, and (6) Amir Timur and his descendants. Although the main divisions of Khvandamir's *Habib al-siyar* differ slightly from the *Rawzat al-safa*, the sequence is the same. Khvandamir's first chapter includes subsections on (a) prophets and sages, (b) pre-Islamic kings of Persia and Arabia, (c) Muhammad, and (d) the first four caliphs. The second section covers (a) the twelve Imams, (b) the Umayyads, (c) the Abbasids, and (d) dynasties contemporary to the 'Abbasids.[38] Mirkhvand opens his chapter on the twelve Imams by narrating the story of the second Imam of the Twelver Shi'a, Imam Hasan. He had already discussed the first Imam, 'Ali b. Abi Talib, in the previous chapter about the Rashidun caliphs. There, 'Ali appears in the narrative as the fourth "rightly guided" caliph.

Khvandamir's account of the twelve Imams contains both similarities and differences in comparison with his grandfather's *Rawzat al-safa*. Like Mirkhvand, he too ends his chapter prior to the one on the twelve Imams with an account of 'Ali as the fourth of the Rashidun caliphs.[39] Unlike his grandfather, however, his next chapter on the twelve Imams does not immediately start with an account of the second Imam Hasan. Rather, he inserts two introductory sections, one entitled "the noble characteristics and virtues of the Bani Hashim," and the second, "an account regarding the restriction of the Imams to the number twelve, according to the hadith of the best of humanity (*khayr al-bashar* [Muhammad]) and the sayings of the learned 'ulama, peace be upon the prophet and his family until the day of judgement."[40]

Scholars have noted that Khvandamir actually held considerable sympathy for the first three caliphs. He also sympathized with Zayd b. Zayn al-'Abidin, the founder of the Zaydi line of Shi'is. The latter is not surprising given Khvandamir's own Zaydi background. Adam Jacobs has placed Khvandamir's writings in the context of his personal sympathies and concluded that despite his apparent sympathy for the first three caliphs [and others?], he "promotes a variety of Shi'i beliefs

[38] Storey, *Persian Literature*, 1: 104.

[39] See Jacobs, "Sunni and Shi'i Perceptions," 151.

[40] Khvandamir, *Tarikh-i habib al-siyar*, 4 vols., ed. Jalal al-Din Huma'i ([Tehran]: Kitabkhanah-'i Khayyam, 1333 [1954]), trans. Wheeler Thackston as Habibu's-siyar, 2 vols. (Cambridge: Harvard University Department of Near Eastern Languages and Civilizations, 1994), 2: 5–8.

and rituals in the *Habib al-siyar* that are noticeably absent in both his pre-Safavid and Mughal works. This would suggest that they were included merely to gratify the Safawids."[41] Such attitudes also reflect the notion of "confessional ambiguity" as discussed by Woods and others.[42] By adding these two "new" sections, Khvandamir highlights the importance of the twelve Imams in terms of their family lineage and their number. Khvandamir's second section consists of a series of reasons that he puts forth as to why there were twelve (as opposed to any other number) Imams, whereby he explains the significance of the number twelve.

Khvandamir was not the first to offer an explanation for the number twelve. The celebrated historian and minister to the Ilkhanid Mongol rulers, Rashid al-Din, included an analysis of twelve in an exposition that he wrote about numbers (*risālah-i 'adad*). This appears in the final treatise of his *Latayif al-haqayiq*, which itself is the fourth book of his collected treatises. The *Risalah-i 'adad*, which Rashid al-Din wrote in 708/1308, includes nine sections (*favā'id*) discussing the special attributes and the superiority of the number twelve to other numbers in a highly philosophical manner. The final section of this treatise has the subheading "The attributes of the number twelve" (*khvāṣṣ-i 'adad-i davāzdah*).

In his treatise on the attributes of the number twelve, Rashid al-Din states that however extensively the erudite scholars had expounded on the significance of this number, there were still other attributes that had been forgotten, and he would therefore point these out at the end of his treatise. He lists the twelve following characteristics: (1) the offspring (*absāṭ*) [of Jacob] were twelve, (2) the leaders (*nuqabā*) of the children of Israel were twelve, (3) the leaders (*nuqabā*) that the prophet chose from among the Helpers (*anṣār*) were twelve, (4) the Imams of the

41 Jacobs, "Sunni and Shi'i Perceptions," 158.

42 On the notion of "confessional ambiguity," Woods states that "it is no exaggeration to say that the prevailing religious winds during this period were popular, Shi'i, and 'Alid, even in circles nominally Sunni. This confessional ambiguity may be seen in many facets of life in the central Islamic lands before the rise of the Safavids." Woods, *The Aqquyunlu*, 4. See also Judith Pfeiffer, "Confessional Ambiguity vs. Confessional Polarization: Politics and the Negotiation of Religious Boundaries in the Ilkhanate," in *Politics, Patronage and the Transmission of Knowledge in 13th–15th Century Tabriz*, ed. Judith Pfeiffer, 129–168 (Leiden: Brill, 2014); and Binbaş, *Intellectual Networks*, 196, 283.

People of the House (*ahl-i bayt*) were twelve, (5) the letters of "there is no God except God" are twelve, (6) the letters of "Muhammad is the messenger of God" are twelve, (7) the [zodiac] constellations of the sky are twelve, (8) the hours in the day are twelve, (9) the hours of the night are twelve, (10) the year has twelve months, (11) modes (*pardah*): there are twelve musical modes, and (12) the Chinese and the Mongols have fixed their years and day and hours at twelve.[43] While this treatise provides a historiographical precedent rather than a model for Khvandamir, who looked to other sources for imitation, its existence points to an earlier intellectual milieu that led to the kind of composition that we see in Rashid al-Din and Khvandamir.

Khvandamir begins his discussion on the number twelve in his *Habib al-siyar* by citing approximately seven hadith foretelling the appearance of twelve successors after the prophet.[44] He then presents a list of six reasons why there were twelve Imams. In doing so, he names his sources, providing us with a direct historiographical link: Shaykh Mufid's *Kitab al-irshad* and 'Ali b. 'Isa al-Irbili's (d. 692/1293) *Kashf al-ghumma fi ma'rifat al-a'imma*. The *Kitab al-irshad* is an important treatise on Shi'ism, and it forms a major repository of information about and biographies of the Twelver Shi'i Imams. Al-Irbili was a Shi'i apologist who, for his account as to why there were twelve Imams, imitates nearly word for word the work of a certain "ibn Talha," who was Kamal al-Din Muhammad b. Talha al-'Adawi al-Nisibini, author of the *Matalib al-su'ul fi manaqib āl al-rasul*.[45] Al-Nisibini was a Shafi'i scholar who served as vizier to al-Malik al-Sa'id, one of the Mardin-based Artukid rulers. He was one of a group of Sunni scholars who "supported the Imami belief that the Twelfth Imam was the Expected Mahdi."[46] He composed his treatise in 650/1252 in order to support "the imamate of the Twelve Imams

43 I am grateful to Judith Pfeiffer for bringing this text to my attention. See Rashid al-Din, *Latayif al-Haqayiq*, ed. Hashim Rajabzadah, 2 vols., 2: 894–895 (Tehran: Markaz-i Pazhuhashi-i Miras-i Maktub, 1394 [2015]). For a discussion of the dating of the treatise, see 1: lii, where the internal date is set to 30 Rabi' I, 708/25 September 1308.

44 Khvandamir, *Habib al-siyar*, 2: 6–7.

45 al-Nasibi, Muhammad ibn Ṭalhah Abu Salim, *Matalib al-su'ul fi manaqib al al-rasul*, ed. 'Abd al-Aziz Tabataba'i (Beirut: Mu'assasat al-Balaghah, 1999). See *EI2*, s.v., "al-Mahdi," by W. Madelung. He is perhaps more commonly known as al-Nisibini and will be referred to by this name throughout this book.

46 *EI2*, "al-Mahdi."

and answered Sunni objections to the belief that the Twelfth Imam was the Mahdi."[47]

Why Twelve?

For his account of the significance of the number twelve, Khvandamir draws exclusively from al-Irbili. A general summary of al-Irbili and al-Nisibini's reasons as to why the number twelve is significant as follows:

(1) Each of the two phrases of the testimony of faith (*shahādah*) contains twelve letters and therefore the imamate has twelve Imams.
(2) The leaders of the tribes of Moses were twelve people, and on the night of 'Aqaba Muhammad had appointed twelve people among the "helpers" (*anṣār*) as chiefs and, therefore, the number of Imams was twelve.
(3) The children of Jacob were divided into twelve tribes and, therefore, there were correspondingly twelve Imams.
(4) When day and night are at an equilibrium, each has twelve hours, and similarly, there are twelve Imams.
(5) There are twelve zodiac signs and twelve Imams.
(6) There were twelve generations between Muhammad and the Quraysh ancestor Nazr, and twelve generations between Muhammad and the "Lord of the [eschatological] age" (*ṣāḥib al-zamān*).[48]

[47] *EI2*, "al-Mahdi." For some information on al-Irbili and al-Nisibini, see *EI2*, "al-Mahdi." Al-Nisibini was part of a group of Sunni writers who accepted the notion that the twelfth Imam and the Mahdi were one and the same.

[48] Khvandamir, *Habib al-siyar*, 2: 7–8. Al-Nasibi, *Matalib al-su'ul*, 43–44. 'Ali b. 'Isa al-Irbili, *Kashf al-ghumma fi ma'rifat al-a'imma*, 3 vols. (Beirut: Dar al-adwa', 1985), 1: 56. It is interesting to note that Rashid al-Din repeats all but one of the explanations we find in al-Irbili and al-Nisibini, and these cover his first nine explanations. He does not mention the number of generations between Muhammad and Nazr and between Muhammad and the "lord of the age" (*ṣāḥib al-zamān*). Rashid al-Din's last three explanations – the twelve months in a year, the twelve modes of music, and the Chinese and Mongol calendars – are unique to his account. This suggests that al-Nisibini, al-Irbili, and Rashid al-Din all inhabited a common intellectual milieu. There are no instances of imitative writing when we compare Rashid al-Din to the accounts discussed here.

The parallel passages in Khvandamir's two works tell us something about the relationship between Safavid and Mughal historiography in their earliest stages, for if we closely compare them, several interesting differences become apparent. The *Habib al-siyar* preserves the order of the items in the *Kashf al-ghumma*, beginning with those reasons why twelve is a significant number most closely associated with Twelver Shi'ism, the Qur'an, or the Bible, and ending with the more cosmological reasons, with the exception of his final point. For his *Qanun-i Humayuni*, Khvandamir reverses the order of the items in the *Habib al-siyar*, starting with the cosmological reasons and ending with the Qur'anic or Biblical ones.[49] Secondly, in the *Qanun-i Humayuni*, Khvandamir completely eliminates the sixth and final item appearing in the *Habib al-siyar*, regarding the imamate and the number of generations between the Prophet Muhammad and the Quraysh ancestor Nazr.

The parallel passages below indicate how Khvandamir engaged in imitative writing. In general, Khvandamir makes two broad types of changes to al-Irbili's text, beyond translating it from Arabic into Persian. First, he removes all allusions and references to a future eschatological or messianic event in connection with the twelve Imams.[50] In other words, while the Imams still hold a central place in his discourse on the number twelve, he carefully rewords al-Irbili's narrative and hints that the messianic event has already taken place, presumably in the form of Shah Isma'il. Khvandamir then rewrites the *Habib al-siyar*, making a second set of changes in order to render it suitable for his *Qanun-i Humayuni*. In addition to reversing the order of the actual items and removing the sixth explanation, he strips all of the imamological explanations and allusions to twelver Shi'ism that appear in the *Habib al-siyar* and the *Kashf al-ghumma*.

[49] Eva Orthmann has noted that for Khvandamir, "the cosmological explanation is the most important one." See Eva Orthmann, "Court Culture and Cosmology in the Mughal Empire: Humāyūn and the Foundations of the *dīn-i ilāhī*," in *Court Cultures in the Muslim World: Seventh to Nineteenth Centuries*, eds. Albrecht Fuess and Jan-Peter Hartung, 206 (London: Routledge, 2011).

[50] It should be remembered that here, in every instance Khvandamir is described as imitating al-Irbili, this passage actually goes back to al-Nisibini.

The following analyses provide a very close reading of each reason why the number twelve is important according to al-Irbili's text in the first column and Khvandamir's reworking of al-Irbili for his *Habib al-siyar* in the second column. The final column shows how Khvandamir rewrote the *Habib al-siyar* for the *Qanun-i Humayuni.*

The First Reason

Kashf al-ghumma	*Habib al-siyar*	*Qanun-i Humayuni*
The first reason: In which it is mentioned something as is related to letters and numbers, as it is said, faith (*īmān*) and submission (*islām*) are based upon the two phrases of "there is no God but God" [and] "Muhammad is the Messenger of God" (*la illāha illā Allāh Muḥammad rasūl Allāh*) and each one of these two foundations (bases) consist of twelve letters. And the imamate is a branch of faith, so it thus follows that the Messianic Ariser (*qā'im*) comes from twelve Imams.[51]	First: The Islamic religion is based on two excellent phrases: "there is no God but God" [and] "Muhammad is the Messenger of God" (*la illāha illā Allāh Muḥammad rasūl Allāh*), and each of the two phrases, to which the source of faith is connected, contains twelve letters. Thus the matter of the imamate, which is among the branches of faith, is connected to twelve Imams.[52]	Five: Each half of the letters of the profession of faith (*shahādah*) is computed at twelve letters.[53]

For the first reason explaining the significance of the number twelve, when we compare the first two passages, we see that Khvandamir essentially reproduced al-Irbili's account, rendering it almost word for word into Persian. He did make one significant change to the text in regard to the word *qā'im* (Messianic Ariser). Whereas al-Irbili connects the imamate to

51 al-Irbili, *Kashf al-ghumma*, 1: 55. 52 Khvandamir, *Habib al-siyar*, 2: 8.
53 Khvandamir, *Qanun-i Humayuni*, 270; trans., 34.

three elements – faith (*al-īman*), the *qā'im*, and the twelve Imams – Khvandamir has it that the imamate is connected to faith and the twelve Imams, but not the *qā'im*, because he removes that portion of the passage found in the *Kashf al-ghumma*. Khvandamir most likely made this change deliberately, in order to avoid references to a future messianic figure, because presumably the term had messianic connotations that he wanted to avoid. For his *Qanun-i Humayuni*, Khvandamir provides this reason as the fifth and final item, thus making it the least important. In this explanation, he simplifies the text in the *Habib al-siyar*, providing only one short sentence about the *shahādah* containing twelve letters in each half.

The Second Reason

Al-Irbili's second explanation relates two separate instances of the number twelve – one from the Qur'an and the other from early Islamic history: (1) there were twelve leaders from among the children of Israel/tribes of Moses, and (2) Muhammad appointed twelve leaders from among the helpers (*anṣār*) to act as chiefs. These two explanations serve as another reason why there were twelve Imams.

Kashf al-ghumma	*Habib al-siyar*	*Qanun-i Humayuni*
The second reason: God revealed in his mighty book, "God took compact with the children of Israel, and we raised up from them twelve leaders" (Q 5:12). He thus made the number of the leaders/uprisers (*qā'imīn*) in that matter twelve. Similarly, the number of the Messianic Ariser (*qā'imīn*) Imams are the same. And when the Messenger of God, peace be upon him and his family,	2. According to the noble verse [of the Qur'an], "God took compact with the Children of Israel; and We raised up from among them twelve leaders" [Q 5:12]. The leaders of the tribe of Moses were twelve people and the prophet – may the blessings of God be upon him – also in the night of 'Aqaba had appointed twelve people among the "helpers" (*anṣār*) as chiefs, therefore the	4. The Best of Mankind (i.e., Muhammad) appointed out of his friends twelve people as his leaders on the night of 'Aqaba, and the number of the chaste Imams was twelve. (*Habib al-siyar* #2) 3. The tribes of Israel, that is the sons of Jacob (*Habib al-siyar* #3), were twelve in number, as the holy words indicate (Q 7:159–160 and Q 5:13). Also, the commentators and reliable authorities

commissioned the "helpers" (*anṣār*) on the night of Aqabat, he said "bring to me from amongst you twelve leaders, just as the leaders (*nuqabā*) of the children of Israel," and thus it happened in a corresponding manner and with the same number [twelve].[54]	number of Imams were also fixed at the same number.[55]	have established the number of leaders of the tribes of Moses to be twelve (*Habib al-siyar* #2).[56]

In these passages, the most significant change that Khvandamir made to the *Kashf al-ghumma* was to remove every instance of the word *qā'imīn* (messianic arisers) from the narrative. While al-Irbili uses the term in connection with both the leaders of the "children of Israel" and the twelve Imams, Khvandamir uses another Arabic word, *nuqabā*, in referring to the leaders of the twelve tribes of Moses, and he uses the word imams (*a'imma*) without the word *al-qā'imīn* when mentioning the twelve Imams. This change is consistent with the one he made in his first reason, and serves to remove the messianic associations from the Imams.

For the *Qanun-i Humayuni*, Khvandamir rearranges and recombines the second and third reasons from the *Habib al-siyar*, transforming them into the third and fourth reasons. His third reason basically repeats the same information as the second and third reasons in the *Habib al-siyar*, but he omits all reference to the Imams. His fourth reason, however, is different. There, he makes the only specific reference in his entire account to the imams, stating that the number of the chaste Imams was twelve, and lists it as merely one of two reasons – along with the twelve leaders that Muhammad appointed on the night of 'Aqaba – as to why the number twelve was important.

54 al-Irbili, *Khashf al-ghumma*, 1: 55.
55 Khvandamir, *Habib al-siyar*, 2: 8.
56 Khvandamir, *Qanun-i Humayuni*, 270; trans., 33.

The Third Reason

Kashf al-ghumma	*Habib al-siyar*	*Qanun-i Humayuni*
The third reason: God the Exalted has said, 'Of the people of Moses there is a nation (*umma*) who guide by the truth, and by it act with justice. And we divided them up into twelve tribes, nations" (Q 7:159–160). Thus, he made the offspring guiding them to truth [God] according to this number, as similarly were the Imams.[57]	3. The offspring (*absāṭ*), in other words, the children of Jacob, upon him be peace, according to the [Qur'anic] verse, "Of the people of Moses there is a nation who guide by the truth, and by it act with justice. And we cut them up into twelve tribes, nations" (Q 7:159–160), were twelve, therefore it is apt that the number of guiding Imams of the truth from the pure Mustawfiyan family (*'itrat*) should be corresponding to them [i.e. the children of Jacob].[58]	4. The Best of Mankind (i.e. Muhammad) appointed out of his friends twelve people as his leaders on the night of 'Aqba, and the number of the chaste Imams was twelve (*Habib al-siyar* #2). 3. The tribes of Israel, that is the sons of Jacob (*Habib al-siyar* #3), were twelve in number, as the holy words indicate (Q 7:159–160 and Q 5:13). Also, the commentators and reliable authorities have established the number of leaders of the tribes of Moses to be twelve (*Habib al-siyar* #2).[59]

In these passage, Khvandamir repeats the same Qur'anic verse that we see in the *Kashf al-ghumma* for his *Habib al-siyar*. He then makes two significant changes to the narrative. First, he adds clarification by identifying the "offspring" mentioned toward the end of al-Irbili's account as the "children of Jacob." Second, he expands on the Imams. Whereas al-Irbili simply states that the number of the Imams was the same as the twelve tribes of the people of Moses, Khvandamir describes them as the "guiding Imams of the truth from the pure Mustawfiyan family." While Khvandamir may have made the first

[57] al-Irbili, *Kashf al-ghumma*, 1: 55. [58] Khvandamir, *Habib al-siyar*, 2: 8.
[59] Khvandamir, *Qanun-i Humayuni*, 270; trans., 33.

change for the purposes of clarification, he could have had other reasons for identifying the "offspring" mentioned toward the end of al-Irbili's account as the children of Israel. By highlighting both the genealogical descent of the "children of Moses" as descendants of Abraham, and then emphasizing the Imams as members of the "pure Mustawfiyan family," he draws parallels between the twelve tribes and the twelve Imams on the basis of their respective genealogies. Furthermore, since the word "Mustawfiyan" could mean both "chosen" and "descendant of Muhammad," in drawing attention to the Imami genealogy and its being "chosen," Khvandamir could also be indirectly acknowledging the genealogy of the Safavid family, in particular its current king, Shah Isma'il. This would act as a subtle reminder to his audience that the Safavid king was claiming descent from the Imams and was similarly chosen. In contrast to the additions Khvandamir made to his *Habib al-siyar*, for the *Qanun-i Humayuni*, he shortens the explanation, simply stating that there were twelve tribes of Israel who were sons of Jacob. And as in his other explanations, he removes all references to the twelve Imams.

The Fourth Reason

The fourth reason in the *Kashf al-ghumma* regarding the importance of the number twelve moves away from Qur'anic and Biblical explanations and emphasizes the role of time in relation to the number twelve:

Kashf al-ghumma	*Habib al-siyar*	*Qanun-i Humayuni*
The fourth reason: The affairs of the world are dependent on their regulations, because their occurrences are differentiated by time, [which] is an expression of night and day, and each one of them [night and day] is, [in] a condition of equilibrium, specified to	Fourth: The order of some of the affairs are necessitated by time, and time is an expression of the hours of night and day, and each one of night and day in a condition of equilibrium is twelve hours. And by way of this analogy the affairs of the people of the	Also (second): The order of some of the affairs of the world are necessitated by time; and time is an expression of the hours of night and day and each one of night and day in a condition of equilibrium, an allusion of which is the first [day] of the season of

twelve hours. And the affairs of the world are [similarly] dependent upon the Imams, upon them be peace, and their guidance, and thus their number was made to be likewise [i.e., twelve].[60]	world are due to the existence of the just Imam (*imām-i ʿādil*). In addition to this, their number [the Imams] was also restricted to twelve.[61]	spring and the beginning of autumn, is restricted to twelve hours, and according to the text, "the number of months in the sight of God is twelve [in a year]" Q 9: 36.[62]

In his *Habib al-siyar*, Khvandamir repeats the information found in al-Irbili about time, noting that when the world is at equilibrium, there are twelve hours in both day and night. Like al-Irbili, he draws a parallel between the twelve hour time period regulating worldly affairs and the twelve Imams. However, he changes the narrative to say that people's affairs depended not on the Imams, as al-Irbili stated, but on the "just Imam," the *imām-i ʿādil*. Khvandamir's changes to al-Irbili's fourth reason are consistent with his rewriting of al-Irbili's third reason. Here, his addition of the phrase "just Imam" likely refers to Shah Isma'il, at least indirectly, and positions Shah Isma'il in this passage as the lord and master of time, reminding one of the messianic title "Lord of the time" or "Lord of the age" (*ṣāḥib al-zamān*), which Khvandamir uses in his sixth explanation. As the phrase *imām-i ʿādil* does not appear in the *Kashf al-ghumma*, Khvandamir deliberately added it. According to Andrew Newman, Shah Isma'il had become familiar with the notion of the "just Imam" during his stay in Lahijan, before assuming the throne. Later, he used the concept in order to claim that he was the returned (twelfth) Imam.[63] Newman has also pointed to a mosque in Isfahan upon which a firman was inscribed, in 1505, referring to Shah Isma'il as the "just Imam."[64] Use of this term

[60] al-Irbili, *Kashf al-ghumma*, 1: 55–56.
[61] Khvandamir, *Habib al-siyar*, 2: 8.
[62] Khvandamir, *Qanun-i Humayuni*, 269; trans., 33.
[63] For more on the notion of the just Imam, see Andrew J. Newman, *The Formative Period of Twelver Shīʿism: Ḥadīth as Discourse between Qum and Baghdad* (Richmond, Surrey: Curzon, 2000), 183, and Andrew J. Newman, *Safavid Iran: Rebirth of a Persian Empire* (London: I. B. Tauris, 2006), 14.
[64] See Andrew J. Newman, "The Myth of the Clerical Migration to Safawid Iran: Arab Shiite Opposition to ʿAli al-Karakī and Safawid Shiism," *Die Welt des Islams* 33 (1993): 70–71, esp. n. 13.

was approved by al-Karaki, the twelver Shi'i cleric who became influential in Safavid Iran during the reign of Shah Isma'il.

In transforming the text for his *Qanun-i Humayuni*, Khvandamir repeats the idea that day and night both consist of twelve hours when in equilibrium. As in the other explanations in the *Qanun-i Humayuni*, he removes all references to the twelve Imams. However, perhaps in an attempt to fill the gap, he elaborates on the idea of a day in equilibrium by stating that the two days in which the hours of day and night are the same are the first day of spring and the first day of autumn (the vernal and autumnal equinoxes). Khvandamir ends by adding a Qur'anic passage stating that there are twelve months in a year. In this way, he adds a very general religious justification for this reason.

The Fifth Reason

Al-Irbili and Khvandamir's fifth reason also relates to astronomical phenomena:

Kashf al-ghumma	*Habib al-siyar*	*Qanun-i Humayuni*
The fifth reason: He said it is because of its clear beauty and its fixed lights and its arrangement that the light of the imamate guides the hearts and the minds to traverse the path of truth (*ḥaqq*), just as the light of the sun and the moon guides the vision of the people to traverse the path, as it is the location of these two guiding lights of guidance for those who follow the twelve signs of the zodiac. And the location of the second	Fifth: Insomuch as the rays of the moon and the sun are a guide for people's vision in traversing the path of perception (feeling), [similarly] the lights of the imamate also act as a guide for the hearts and minds in traversing the path of guidance and the way of piety, and just as the location (*maḥal*) of the light of the sun and the moon are the twelve signs of the zodiac, the place of the forms of the light of the imamate are	First: because the eighth celestial sphere is divided into twelve signs of the zodiac, and the direction of the revolutions (*ḥarakāt*) of the sun, the moon, and the rest of the stars, and the seven planets is contingent on those signs of the zodiac, and the calculations of the months and years by those means take on the quality of clarity, and the light of the truth (*ṣidq*) of this matter (*sukhan*) shines as the passage of days and

guiding light is for insights, and it is the light of the imamate of the twelve Imams. Note: and it appears in the hadith of the prophet that the earth and what is upon it is being carried by the fish and in this is a subtle sign and a noble wisdom and the final pace of that light is the fish, and it is the final sign of the zodiac, and it is bearing the heavy weight of all existence, and [similarly] the final location of the twelfth light is the light of the imamate which upholds the gravitas of the peace-bringer for all religions, who is the Mahdi, upon him be peace.[65]	[similarly] from the twelve Imams.[66]	months upon the face of humanity.[67]

In these parallel passages, Khvandamir, in the *Habib al-siyar*, juxtaposes the sun and the moon in relation to the zodiac with the guiding light of the twelve Imams, just as al-Irbili does. The sun and the moon provide actual light that guides people, and the Imams similarly guide people in providing insight and spiritual direction. Both authors also draw a connection between the sun and the moon being a light in relation to the twelve signs of the zodiac and the light of the imamate coming from the twelve Imams. The biggest change Khvandamir makes to the narrative has to do with the hadith regarding the earth being carried by a fish. While al-Irbili makes a parallel between the fish being the twelfth sign of the zodiac and the Mahdi being the twelfth

[65] al-Irbili, *Kashf al-ghumma*, 1: 55–56. [66] Khvandamir, *Habib al-siyar*, 2: 8.
[67] Khvandamir, *Qanun-i Humayuni*, 269; trans., 33.

Imam, Khvandamir chooses not to repeat this passage at all. In making this omission, Khvandamir may have attempted to streamline his narrative. But he may have also wanted to avoid underlining the figure of the Mahdi in his narrative. As he was writing during the reign of Shah Isma'il, alluding to the eschatology of a future Mahdi figure would in a sense replace the authority of the partly realized eschatology of the contemporary Shah Isma'il.[68] Although for his fourth reason Khvandamir introduced into his *Habib al-siyar* a reference to the just Imam (*imām-i 'ādil*) as an allusion to Shah Isma'il, in this instance he removes mention of the Mahdi. These two historiographical changes are similar in the sense that they are both part of Khvandamir's attempt to focus indirectly on Shah Isma'il.

For his *Qanun-i Humayuni*, the primary overall change that Khvandamir made was to remove the entire discussion about the twelve Imams. He then fills the gap by developing the cosmological discussion about the twelve signs of the zodiac, stating that the months and years were calculated through them.

While the discussion of the number twelve in each of these texts is relatively brief, its implications are significant. The passages in the *Qanun-i Humayuni* appear as Khvandamir's own words, but they rest on passages that he originally wrote in his *Habib al-siyar*, which he then rewrote for the Mughal emperor Humayun, removing the Twelver Shi'i references and changing the order of the items. The passages in the *Habib al-siyar* in turn have as their basis the text of a thirteenth-century Shi'i treatise written by a Shafi'i scholar. Khvandamir reworded that text to remove future messianic associations for his *Habib al-siyar*. Through deft historical rewriting, Khvandamir transforms allusions to a legitimate Shi'i messianic king (Isma'il) into references to a legitimate cosmic king (Humayun).

In terms of Khvandamir's access to sources, for writing his *Qanun-i Humayuni*, he certainly had a copy of his *Habib al-siyar*, which he revised while in India – and probably copies of his earlier writings or notes as well – and employing a method similar to modern practices of cutting, pasting, and then modifying a narrative from one piece of writing into another, decided to do this for his *Qanun-i Humayuni*. In this way, he saved himself time by repurposing something he had previously composed. Khvandamir thus brought at least one element

68 Newman, *Safavid Iran*, 14.

of a history which he wrote under Safavid patronage into one that he wrote for the Mughals.

Khvandamir in Later Mughal Historiography

The historiographical borrowing and refashioning of Khvandamir's writings did not end with his death, however, for portions of the *Qanun-i Humayuni* became incorporated into the later Mughal historiographical tradition through Abu al-Fazl's *Akbarnamah*. We know a great deal about the process by which this history came into being, with Abu al-Fazl engaging in what we might call oral history research, conducting interviews with various individuals who were associated with the king. Furthermore, Akbar himself issued an order that those who remembered his father and grandfather – Humayun and Babur respectively – should write down their memories of them, three of which have survived today.[69]

Chapter 61 of the *Akbarnamah* consists of an account of Humayun and a "description of some of his remarkable inventions and regulations." Abu al-Fazl reproduces nearly word-for-word the information from Khvandamir's *Qanun-i Humayuni* describing how Humayun organized Mughal society into three groups, the three golden arrows representing the three divisions, and his arrangement of the three groups into twelve classes.[70] Abu al-Fazl even mentions Khvandamir's *Qanun-i Humayuni* in the chapter: "Mir Khwandamir the historian has stated in his *Qanun-i-Humayuni*: 'During the time of my attachment to the retinue, the Arrow of Felicity was held autonomously by the most learned Maulana Muhammad Farghali.'"[71] Interestingly, Abu al-Fazl chose not to reproduce Khvandamir's discussion of the number twelve. While Khvandamir, as described above, conscientiously disassociated his *Qanun-i Humayuni* narrative on the

[69] See Taymiya R. Zaman, "Instructive Memory: An Analysis of Auto/Biographical Writing in Early Mughal India," *Journal of the Economic and Social History of the Orient* 54 (2011): 682–683. Baini Prashad, in the introduction to his English translation of the *Qanun-i Humayuni*, states that "Abul Fadl's *Akbarnama* appears to have been modelled on Khwandamir's style, and where the former has included entire passages or summaries from the latter's work it is almost impossible to differentiate between the compositions of the two authors." *Qanun-i Humayuni*, trans., vii.

[70] Abu al-Fazl, *Akbarnamah,* 2: 480–489.

[71] Abu al-Fazl, *Akbarnamah*, 2: 484–485.

number twelve from Shi'ism, he still mentioned the twelve Imams in his text. Abu al-Fazl, who sought to raise Akbar above sectarian politics, may have found it easier to remove the discussion of twelve altogether from his narrative.[72]

Full Circle

The theme of twelve being a significant number appears in other sources of early modern Persianate historiography. Approximately 200 years after Rashid al-Din, the Ottoman historian Mustafa Ali composed his *Cami'ül-kemalat*, a treatise on the significance of the number twelve, in 994/1584.[73] In this treatise, Mustafa Ali predicted that Sultan Murad III (r. 982–1003/1574–1595), for whom he wrote the text, would live to the age of 120 (he died at age 49). Other significances of the number twelve in this treatise include Murad's being the twelfth king of the Ottoman house, the prophet's birthday on the twelfth of Rabi' I, and Muhammad Mahdi as the twelfth Imam.[74] Writing under the Safavids in 1007/1598–1599, some 15 years after Mustafa Ali's *Cami'ül kemalat*, in the preface to his *Futuhat-i Humayun*, a chronicle narrating Shah 'Abbas's Khurasan campaign against the Uzbeks, Siyaqi Nizam attempted to connect Shah 'Abbas to the number twelve. In doing so, he states that the following phrases each contain twelve letters: (1) There is no God but God (*lā Ilāha illā Allāh*); (2) Muhammad is the Messenger of God (*Muḥammad rasūl Allah*); (3) 'Ali ibn Abi Talib; (4) Shah 'Abbas Husayni; and (5) Supreme Lord of the Fortunate Conjunction (*ṣāḥibqirān-i a'lá*). This is all part of Siyaqi Nizam's attempt to connect Shah 'Abbas to Timur and to twelver Shi'ism.[75] While there was no direct borrowing in this instance, the example suggests that the practice of discussing the significance of the number twelve was still alive at this time.

More Historians on the Move

Khvandamir was not the only historian on the move. Indeed, other chroniclers such as Sharaf al-Din Bidlisi, whose benefits of history

[72] *EIR*, s.v., "Abu'l Fażl 'Allāmī," by R. M. Eaton.
[73] Fleischer, *Bureaucrat and Intellectual*, 111.
[74] I am grateful to Tunç Şen for bringing these details to my attention.
[75] For a more detailed discussion of this chronicle, see Quinn, *Historical Writing*, 46–53.

account was discussed in the previous chapter, and Muslih al-Din Lari, whose universal history will be analyzed in the next chapter, similarly wrote for multiple dynasties. But movement was not confined to isolated individuals who crossed dynastic lines in the search for patronage and support. In other instances, with perhaps more far-reaching consequences, multiple members of a family left a particular territory and settled down in another, producing offspring who became prominent intellectuals in their new home. Such was the case with the family of Mir Yahya Sayfi Qazvini. Sayfi Qazvini is best known as author of the Shah Tahmasb era universal history, the *Lubb al-tavarikh*, which he composed in 945/1542. His descendants, however, rose to prominence under the Mughals. They included two sons, two grandsons, and one great-grandson. Of these individuals, at least four, including Sayfi Qazvini himself, were known for their literary compositions.[76] Sayfi Qazvini's enemies were apparently jealous of his favored position with Shah Tahmasb, and therefore "turned the Shah against him saying that Sayfi Qazvini and his son Mir 'Abdul Latif were Sunnis, and the leaders of the Sunnis of Qazvin."[77] Consequently, Shah Tahmasb ordered that Sayfi Qazvini and Mir 'Abd al-Latif be imprisoned in Isfahan. Sayfi Qazvini eventually died in prison in 962/1555. His sons, however, Mir 'Abd al-Latif and Mir 'Ala al-Dawlah, known as "Kami," both went to India.[78] No doubt if Sayfi Qazvini had not been imprisoned he would have joined them. Shah Navaz Khan Awrangabadi (d. 1171/1758), in his *Ma'asir al-umara'*, explains how Mir 'Abd al-Latif ended up in Mughal territory, having heard the news from his brother that he was about to be arrested and taken to Isfahan:

> But Mir 'Abd al-Latif on receipt of the news at once fled to Gilan, and later on at the invitation of Humayun went to India. Humayun, however, had died before his arrival, and the Mir reached India with his sons and grandsons in the beginning of Akbar's reign. He was graciously and kindly

[76] Mir Yahya Qazvini himself wrote the *Lubb al-tavarikh* in Iran in 945/1542.

[77] See Shah Navaz Khan Awrangabadi and 'Abd al-Hayy ibn Shahnavaz, *Ma'asir al-umara'*, 3: 813; trans., 2: 381–382. This information is repeated by Blochmann in Abu al-Fazl, *Ain-i Akbari*, trans., 1: 496–499 and *The History of India as Told by Its Own Historians*, eds. H. M. Elliot and John Dowson, 8 vols. (London: Trübner and Co., 1867–1877), 4: 293–297. Translation slightly modified.

[78] Awrangabadi, *Ma'asir al-umara'*, 3: 813–814; trans., 2: 382. See also Blochmann and summary notes in Abu al-Fazl, *Ain-i Akbari*, trans., 496–499.

received, and in the second year was exalted with the appointment of Akbar's tutor.[79]

The Qazvini family, though persecuted in Iran for their allegedly Sunni beliefs, is represented in the Mughal sources as religiously moderate and enjoying the patronage of the Mughal court, as we have seen with Badauni's account above. Abu al-Fazl, in a passage perhaps trying to cast Mir 'Abd al-Latif in line with Akbar's universal religious stance, states that

> The mir was outstanding for his learning the fluency of his tongue, the assurance of his heart, and other noble qualities. Because of his lack of fanaticism and the expansiveness of his mind, in India he was accused of being a Shiite, while in Persia he was labeled a Sunni. Since he conducted himself in a manner of universal peace (*sulḥ-i kull*), the exaggerators (*ghāliyān*) of every sect reviled him.[80]

Sayfi Qazvini's second son and Mir 'Abd al-Latif's younger brother and foster-son, Mir 'Ala al-Dawlah, was in Azerbaijan at the time of his father's arrest. He too eventually made his way to India, where he composed, using the pen name "Kami," the *Nafa'is al-ma'asir*, a biographical compendium (*tazkirah*) that he dedicated to Akbar.[81]

Each of these two brothers had sons who continued to write under the Mughals. Mir 'Abd al-Latif's son, Mir Ghiyas al-Din 'Ali "Naqib Khan," accompanied his father to India and served under both Akbar and Jahangir.[82] According to the author of the *Ma'asir al-umara'*,

79 Awrangabadi, *Ma'asir al-umara'*, 3: 813–814; trans., 2: 382. Translation slightly modified. See also Blochmann notes and summary in Abu al-Fazl, *Ain-i Akbari*, trans., 496–497.

80 Abu al-Fazl, *Akbarnamah*, 3: 60–61, trans. slightly modified. In an interesting reference in the *Ain-i Akbari*, Blochmann states, without citing his sources, that Mir 'Abd al-Latif "was the first that taught Akbar the principle of *çulh i kul* [*sulh-i kull*], 'peace with all,' the Persian term which Abu al-Fazl so often uses to describe Akbar's policy of toleration." See Abu al-Fazl, *A'in-i Akbari*, trans. H. Blochmann, 1: 497, note 2.

81 Badauni uses this biographical compendium for information on poets who lived during See Badauni, *Muntakhab al-tavarikh*, 3: 119; trans., 3: 239. For the *Nafa'is al-ma'asir* see, Storey, *Persian Literature*, 2: 800–802.

82 For more information on Naqib Khan, see Reyaz Ahmad Khan, "Naqib Khan: Secretary to Emperors Akbar and Jahangir," *Proceedings of the Indian History Congress* 74 (2013): 240–244. For background on Naqib Khan's participation in translating the *Razmnamah*, see Audrey Truschke, "The Mughal *Book of War*: A Persian Translation of the Sanskrit *Mahabharata*," *Comparative Studies of South Asia, Africa and the Middle East* 31 (2011): 507–508.

Naqib Khan was exceptionally well versed in the knowledge of Hadith, travels, and chronicles. His historical knowledge was unequalled. it is stated that he had learnt the seven volumes of *Rawzat al-safa* by heart, and was also skilled in geometry.[83]

The Mughal emperor Jahangir corroborates the fact that Naqib Khan had an outstanding memory, writing in his own memoirs about it and about Naqib Khan's connection to his family:

At the beginning of his reign [my father] took lessons with him, and for this reason he addressed him as *ākhūnd* [master]. In the science of history and the proper reading of men's names he is without equal. Today there is no historian like him in all the world. He has the entire history of the world from creation till today on the tip of his tongue. Such a memory only God can give to a person.[84]

Naqib Khan's knowledge of history was, thus, certainly known to Akbar and Jahangir and helps explain why he was the most important of the first group of seven historians that Akbar commissioned to write the *Tarikh-i Alfi*, along with Badauni, Mir Fath Allah Shirazi, and others.[85]

Later, Jahangir writes about Naqib Khan's death, stating that

On the same day [Thursday 1 Khurdad] I was told that Naqib Khan had passed away. He was a Sayfi sayyid and originally from Qazvin. The tomb of his father, Mir 'Abd al-Latif, is also in Ajmer. Two months before he died, his wife, for whom he had the utmost affection, had a fever for twelve days and tasted the bitter dregs of death. I ordered him buried beside his wife who had been laid to rest in the blessed khwaja's shrine.[86]

83 See Shah Navaz Khan Awrangabadi and 'Abd al-Hayy ibn Shahnavaz, *Ma'asir al- umara'*, 3: 813–815; trans, 2: 381.

84 Jahangir, *Jahangirnamah: tuzuk-i Jahangiri*, ed. Muhammad Hashim ([Tehran]: Intisharat-i Bunyad-i Farhang-i Iran, 1359 [1980]), 17; trans. Wheeler M. Thackston as *The Jahangirnama: Memoirs of Jahangir, Emperor of India* (New York: Freer Gallery of Art, 1999), 34. Translation slightly modified.

85 Ali Anooshahr, "Dialogism and Territoriality in a Mughal History of the Islamic Millennium," *Journal of the Economic and Social History of the Orient* 55 (2012): 224.

86 *Jahangirnamah*, 150; trans., 160. Translation slightly modified. According to Henry Beveridge, Naqib Khan is also mentioned by the Jesuit priest Du Jarric as disputing with the Catholic priests before Jahangir. See *The Tuzuk-i Jahangiri; or, Memoirs of Jahangir*, trans. Alexander Rogers, ed. Henry Beveridge (London: Royal Asiatic Society, 1909–1914), 28. Naqib Khan is also mentioned in the *Ain-i Akbari*, trans., 496–498.

The author of the *Ma'asir al-umara'* does not go into these details; he merely states that Mir 'Abd al-Latif was a "wise and learned man ... but later he became insane and died."[87] Finally, Mir 'Ala al-Dawla Kami's son was a poet named Mir Yahya Husayni Sayfi who is mentioned in his father's *Nafa'is al-ma'asir*. Other members of Sayfi Qazvini's extended family lived in the Mughal Empire and some, like Naqib Khan's son Mir 'Abd al-Latif, ran into problems with the emperor Jahangir.

Conclusion

This chapter has demonstrated that historiographical boundaries did not conform to political lines that divided early modern empires. As they moved from empire to empire, early modern chroniclers took with them the Timurid historiographical legacy that they inherited and rewrote to suit their political purposes. When understood in this light, Khvandamir's life and writings showcase a historian on the move – one who did not appear to have any qualms about rewriting and repurposing something that he wrote in one context for another. The analyses of Khvandamir's account on the number twelve demonstrate how deftly – sometimes by changing just a single word or removing a short phrase – he negotiated the task of writing for different patrons associated with different dynasties and empires. A text justifying the twelve imams but modified to accommodate the claims of Shah Isma'il became, as Khvandamir wrote across empires, part of Humayun's project of constructing a model of kingship based on cosmological principles, with the number twelve connected first and foremost with celestial phenomena such as the zodiac. In this way, the late Timurid historiographical tradition that Khvandamir incorporated into his Safavid chronicle the *Habib al-siyar* and then took with him from Iran to India survived into the later Safavid and Mughal periods.

Khvandamir's rewriting of his own history and his life as a historian on the move seems to suggest a Persianate historiographical tradition that occupied a fluid, flexible, and easily modified cultural space. Khvandamir was certainly not the last historian on the move. Rather, many individuals took Timurid historiographical principles across a

[87] Shahnavaz Khan Awrangabadi and 'Abd al-Hayy ibn Shahnavaz, *Ma'asir al-umara*, 3: 813–815; trans., 2: 381.

very broad geographical region and helped perpetuate Persian as a historiographical lingua franca in the early modern era. The trajectory of Sayfi Qazvini's family helps us understand how this happened. The historiographical interconnectedness that Khvandamir and other historians on the move represent is reflected in one of the most important genres of historical writing: the universal chronicle. In the next chapter, we examine this genre in order to uncover further elements of early modern Persian historiography.

4 The First King of the World

Kayumars in Universal Histories

Introduction: A Brief Overview of Early Modern Universal Histories

Universal history was a popular genre during the time of the Ottomans, Safavids, and Mughals. We may view such works as the culmination of two earlier syntheses. The first occurred in the mid-eighth century, when the Abbasid secretary Ibn al-Muqaffaʿ (ca. 103–139/ca. 721/757) translated a number of pre-Islamic Persian works containing historical or legendary material into Arabic. This corpus included a "book of kings" (*kwadāy-nāmag*). Later ninth-century historians such as Ibn Qutayba (213–276/828–889) and Abu Hanifa Dinvari (d. ca. 281–290/894–903) made use of this material in their own compositions. The second synthesis occurred when the Samanid ruler Mansur ibn Nuh (r. 350–69/961–976) commissioned Abu ʿAli Balʿami to compose a "translation" of Abu Jaʿfar Muhammad b. Tabari's celebrated Arabic history of prophets and kings, the *Tarikh al-rusul wa al-muluk*.[1]

From their origins in the mid-ninth century, universal histories encompassed a variety of chronological schemes. Most often, however, such texts narrate the history of the world from creation until the chronicler's own time period, thereby encompassing the pre- and post-Islamic period. The pre-Islamic period includes the history of biblical prophets and kings. Universal histories also often incorporate the history of Greece, India, Arabia, China, and Persia as part of the pre-Islamic tradition, although considerable variation exists in terms of including these regions.[2]

[1] *EIR*, s.v., "Historiography iii. Early Islamic Period," by Elton L. Daniel.

[2] See Rosenthal, *A History of Muslim Historiography*, 133–150; Chase F. Robinson, *Islamic Historiography* (Cambridge: Cambridge University Press, 2003), 136.

Writing about the historiography of universal chronicles, Hayrettin Yücesoy outlines their evolution into the post-'Abbasid age. Initially composed to "create a master historical narrative for the community and the caliphate," and eventually drawing on sources such as the Qur'an, biographies of Muhammad (*sīra*), and stories of the prophets (*qiṣaṣ al-anbiyā'*), these texts were developed and diversified over time, yet still retained an emphasis on narrating the history of the entire Muslim community as part of a humanity that traced its genealogy back to a single family, as opposed to favoring one particular sect over another.[3] Chase F. Robinson further notes that universal historians made "the history of the pre-Islamic world conform to the Islamic model of politics and history" and "located Muhammad and his polity in a succession of monotheistic events."[4] The genre of universal history was not only recognized by scholars today; indeed, the category of universal history was recognized as a distinct genre by Khunji-Isfahani in the introduction to his *Tarikh-i 'alam-ara-yi Amini*, as discussed above in Chapter 2. The two earliest Persian language histories composed in the Ottoman Empire were universal histories: Shukr Allah Rumi's (778–894/1375/1376–1488/1489) *Bahjat al-tavarikh* (855/1451) and Muslih al-Din Lari's (d. 979/1572) *Mir'at al-advar* (974/1566). Not only did the Ottomans produce universal histories, but they also had considerable interest in universal histories composed in earlier centuries. In her analysis of 'Arif's 965/1558 *Anbiyanamah*, the title of the first of five volumes of his Ottoman universal history known as the *Shahnamah-yi al-i Osman*, Fatma Sinem Eryılmaz points to a relatively large number of universal histories in the Topkapı Palace Museum manuscript library. These include six volumes of Tabari's famous history (*Tarikh*), three copies of Rashid al-Din's *Jami' al-tavarikh*, nine copies of Mirkhvand's *Rawzat al-safa*, two of which were copied before or during the sixteenth century, two copies of Shukr Allah's *Bahjat al-tavarikh*, and one copy of al-Bukhari's *Tavarikh-i 'alam*.[5] All

[3] Hayrettin Yücesoy, "Ancient Imperial Heritage and Islamic Universal Historiography: al-Dīnawarī's Secular Perspective," *Journal of Global History* 2 (2007): 135–155.

[4] Robinson, *Islamic Historiography*, 135.

[5] Fatma Sinem Eryılmaz, "From Adam to Süleyman: Visual Representations of Authority in 'Ārif's *Shāhnāma-yi Āl-i 'Osmān*," in *Writing History at the Ottoman Court: Editing the Past, Fashioning the Future*, eds. H. Erdem Çıpa and Emine Fetvacı, 116 (Bloomington: Indiana University Press, 2013).

Table 4.1 ***The earliest chronicles written under the Safavids***

1. Amini, *Futuhat-i shahi*, commissioned 926/1520	Semiuniversal
2. Khvandamir, *Habib al-siyar*, 930/1524	Universal
3. Qazvini, *Lubb al-tavarikh*, 948/1542	Universal
4. Amir Mahmud, *Zayl-i habib al-siyar*, 957/1550	Dynastic, but seen as continuation of *Habib*
5. Ghaffari, *Nusakh-i jahan-ara*, 971/ 1563–1564	Universal
6. Abdi Beg Shirazi, *Takmilat al-akhbar*, 977/1570	Universal
7. Hasan Beg Rumlu, *Ahsan al-tavarikh*, 985/1577	Universal, earlier volumes have not survived
8. Qazi Ahmad, *Khulasat al-tavarikh*, 999/1590–1591	Universal, earlier volumes have not survived

of this suggests, Eryılmaz says, "a marked interest in universal histories and literature on the stories of the prophets."[6] She notes that this shows how "religious and political histories were conceived as integral parts of the same story of human civilization."[7]

The *Anbiyanamah*'s encompassing the history of Iran's mythical pre-Islamic kings was not an exceptional case, for we see a similar interest in the Safavid Empire, where universal histories were the predominant type of chronicle written until the reign of Shah 'Abbas I. As Table 4.1 indicates, only two out of the first seven prose histories written during the Safavid period are dynastic chronicles: Ibrahim Amini's *Futuhat-i shahi* and Amir Mahmud's *Zayl-i habib al-siyar*. However, Ibrahim Amini's *Futuhat-i shahi*, while emphasizing Shah Isma'il and his ancestors, is not a fully-fledged dynastic history as his history begins with an account of the life of the Prophet Muhammad. Furthermore, the *Zayl-i habib al-siyar* purports to be a continuation of Khvandamir's universal history, the *Habib al-siyar*, and was written by Khvandamir's son, Amir Mahmud.

The Mughals also had considerable interest in writing universal history; the earliest universal history was Ibrahim ibn Jarir's *Tarikh-i*

6 Eryılmaz, "From Adam to Süleyman," 116.
7 Eryılmaz, "From Adam to Süleyman," 116.

Ibrahimi or *Tarikh-i Humayuni* (956/957/1549/1550), composed during the reign of Humayun. During the reign of Akbar, several scholars compiled, upon Akbar's command, the *Tarikh-i alfi* (997/1588–1589), an extensive universal history beginning with the death of the prophet. Then, in the late sixteenth and early seventeenth century, Mir Muhammad Sharif Vuquʿi Husayni Nishapuri (d. 1002/1593–1594) and Tahir Muhammad Sabzavari composed the *Majamiʿ al-akhbar* (1000/1591–1592) and the *Rawzat al-tahirin* (1014/1605–1606), respectively. While the period of Akbar witnessed the composition of numerous dynastic histories, chroniclers still composed universal histories during his reign and later.

Despite the proliferation of universal histories composed in the early modern period, we still do not know a great deal about many aspects of their composition, and many questions remain unanswered. For example, what methodologies did historians use in composing them? How did they rewrite the distant, mythical, or legendary past? How might competing imperial ideologies have influenced their work? This chapter will attempt to address these questions by focusing on one case study: accounts of the mythical first Persian king, Kayumars. Through a close reading and analysis of a number of Persian chronicles written under the Ottomans, Safavids, Shaybani Uzbeks, and Mughals, we will demonstrate that the early modern historians did indeed rewrite aspects of the distant past, basing their accounts on earlier models and often employing the same imitative writing methods that have been outlined in Chapters 2 and 3. However, they did so often with great subtlety and not always for polemical reasons. Furthermore, the political boundaries separating the early modern chroniclers were not as strong as the open cultural pathways that connected them to each other, for they showed familiarity with earlier histories written across the Islamic world.

The chronicles discussed in this chapter are uneven in terms of how many correspond with each of the early modern dynasties. Table 4.2 lists each chronicle and its corresponding dynasty.[8] While there are only two Ottoman chronicles and one written under the Shaybani Uzbeks, it is still important to include them because these authors

[8] I have not listed the earlier models that many of the early modern chroniclers used in their accounts. These will be discussed at the appropriate point in the chapter.

Table 4.2 *Chapter 4 chronicles*

Ottoman	Safavid	Shaybani Uzbek	Mughal/Deccan
1. Shukr Allah, *Bahjat al-tavarikh*, 855/1451 2. Lari, *Mir'at al-advar*, 974/1566	1. Khvandamir, *Habib al-siyar*, 930/1524 2. Sayfi Qazvini, *Lubb al-tavarikh*, 948/1542 3. Ghaffari, *Nusakh-i jahan-ara*, 972/1564–1565	1. Mas'udi b. 'Usman Kuhistani, sometime between 947–959/1540–1551 *Tarikh-i Abu al-Khayr Khani*	1. Ibrahim bin Hariri, *Tarikh-i Ibrahimi*, 956/957/1549/1550 2. Qubad al-Husayni, *Tarikh-i Ilchi-yi Nizamshah*, 970/1562–1563 3. Vuqu'i, *Majami' al-akhbar*, 1000/1591–1592 4. Sabzavari, *Rawzat al-tahirin*, 1014/1605–1606

made use of sources either written outside of Ottoman and Uzbek territory or that predate the Ottomans and Uzbeks altogether.

Kayumars: The Mythical First Persian King

A thorough and comprehensive examination of all universal chronicles written during this period is far beyond the scope of this chapter. Therefore, here we shall focus on how the universal histories treat one particular figure from the pre-Islamic period: Kayumars. There are many reasons why analyzing accounts of Kayumars is an effective means of addressing the issues raised above. First of all, Kayumars figures significantly in all of the universal histories examined here.[9] In the context of Iran's mythical pre-Islamic past, Kayumars was often considered the first human and the first king in a dynasty of eleven

[9] The *Tarikh-i alfi* is one significant exception.

mythical "*pīshdādī*" Persian kings. He was also an important heroic figure in Zoroastrianism.[10] Kayumars's position as the first *Persian* king and in some cases the first human, frequently equated with Adam, provides an interesting case study through which we may understand how the Ottomans and the Mughals, who traced their ancestry back to biblical prophets via either Japheth or Esau, treated the same figure, and allows us to detect evidence of dynastic barriers in early modern Persian historiography.[11] Furthermore, while nearly all universal histories include accounts of Kayumars, his mythical persona could provide our chroniclers with space to improvise, retell, expand, and elaborate on his story.

The most spectacular example of how Kayumars was reimagined in the early modern period appears in Persian painting, the famous illustrated *Shahnamah* of Shah Tahmasb. In this manuscript, the painting by Sultan Muhammad referred to as "The Court of Kayumars" accounts for one of the most important and central illustrations in the book.[12] He thus held an important position in the early modern period, at least as far as the Safavids were concerned. The following analyses will not comprehensively survey every account of Kayumars produced in the early modern era. Indeed, Sven Hartman, writing in 1956, brought together a large number of pre-Islamic and Islamic-era accounts of Kayumars, providing French translations for the relevant

10 *EIR*, s.v., "Gayōmart," by Mansour Shaki. For an analysis of Kayumars in pre-Islamic sources, see Sven S. Hartman, *Gayōmart: Etude sure le Syncretisme dans l'ancien Iran* (Uppsala: Almqvist & Wiksells Boktryckeri AB, 1953), 1–129. See also Arthur Christenson, *Les types du Premier Homme et du Premier Roi. Ie partie: Gajomard, Masyayet Masyānay, Hosang et Taxmoraw* (Stockholm: 1917); IIe partie: Jim (Leiden, 1934), Archives d'Etudes Orientales, 14: 1–2.

11 For more on Japheth in Ottoman sources, see Ferenc Csirkés, "'Chaghatay Oration, Ottoman Eloquence, Qizilbash Rhetoric': Turkic Literature in Ṣafavid Persia" (Ph.D. diss., University of Chicago, 2016), 36–72. See also Hiroyuki Ogasawara, "The Biblical Origin of the Ottoman Dynasty in the 15th and 16th Century," *Bulletin of the Society for Near Eastern Studies in Japan* 51 (2008): 110–139.

12 There is considerable scholarship on the *Shahnamah* of Shah Tahmasb. See, for example, Martin B. Dickson and Stuart Cary Welch, *The Houghton Shahnameh*, 2 vols. (Cambridge, MA: Harvard University Press, 1981); Sheila R. Canby, *The Shahnama of Shah Tahmasp: The Persian Book of Kings* (New York: The Metropolitan Museum of Art, 2015); and Robert Hillenbrand, "The Iconography of the *Shāh-nāma-yi Shāhī*," in *Safavid Persia*, ed. Charles Melville, 53–78 (London: I. B. Tauris, 1996).

passages and reproducing the Persian and Arabic originals. Even given the some thirty six accounts that he examines for the Islamic period, he only provides information for two of the texts analyzed below and does not establish the historiographical relationships between the historical works that he lists.[13] This chapter seeks to supplement and extend Hartman's approach by focusing on aspects of the narratives where significant imitation and rewriting took place, or instances in which the intertextual relationships provide insights regarding the questions posed above.

Kayumars in Early Universal Histories

In order to understand the historiographical context of early modern accounts of Kayumars, it is necessary to provide a brief overview of the narrative in early sources. Kayumars appears in the earliest Islamic universal histories, beginning with Abu Jaʿfar Muhammad ibn Jarir al-Tabari's (224–310/839–923) tenth-century Arabic *Tarikh al-rusul wa al-muluk*, an important and highly influential chronicle. In this work, Tabari, a gifted scholar who came from the Caspian Sea region of Tabaristan but eventually settled in Baghdad, incorporates his accounts of Persian mythical kings into his chronology of biblical figures, placing the story of Kayumars in a section covering the period from the biblical creation of the world to the time of the flood of Noah, following his discussion of Cain and Abel. Elton Daniel has suggested that this was part of Tabari's overall project of blending the Iranian historical tradition with the biblical, through "identifying a figure from one tradition with that in the other or by comparative chronology."[14]

Tabari opens his account by explaining Kayumars's ancestry. Rather than present one definitive version, he lists four:

(1) Most Persian scholars assume that Jayumart is Adam.[15]

[13] Hartman, *Gayōmart.*

[14] Daniel, "The Rise and Development of Persian Historiography," 155.

[15] Recent scholarship has focused on this early historiographical tradition and discussed and analyzed the relationship between Adam and Kayumars in early sources such as Tabari and Bal'ami. Ghazzal Dabiri suggests that Tabari's inclusion of this particular genealogy "gave the Iranians a competitive genealogy by which to establish their equality with the Arabs, who placed a high value on genealogies and tribal lineages." Ghazzal Dabiri, "The *Shahnama*: Between the Samanids and the Ghaznavids," *Iranian Studies* 43 (2010): 13–28; See also

(2) Some say he is the son of Adam by Eve.
(3) Others have many diverse statements about him but it is too much to go into it here, and not the purpose of this book.
(4) Non-Persian scholars disagree with Persian scholars, and they say he is Adam in name, but disagree as to the identity. They say he is Gomer (ʿAmir) b. Japheth (Yafis) b. Noah (Nuh).

While scholars disagree on these points, Tabari says, everyone agrees on Kayumars's position as the "father of the non-Arab Persians."[16] It appears that already by the time of Tabari's writing, considerable disagreement had surfaced regarding Kayumars's identity and genealogy. In an almost exasperated tone and perhaps in order to preempt any criticism, Tabari stresses the fact that he does not want to enter disputes over an individual's genealogy, and that such discussions fell outside his purpose in writing:

> The discussion of the different views on the pedigree of a given king is not the kind of subject for which we have undertaken the composition of the book. If we do mention something of the sort, it is to identify someone mentioned by us for those unacquainted with him. (I repeat:) The discussion of differing opinions on (a person's) pedigree is not something intended in this book of ours.[17]

Tabari refers to Kayumars as a "long-lived lord" (*muʿammara sayyida*) who lived in the mountains of Tabaristan "and ruled there and in Fārs."[18] He then explains that Kayumars

> built for himself cities and castles and populated them and made them prosperous. He also assembled weapons and established a cavalry. At the end of his life, he became a tyrant. He took the name of Adam and said: If someone calls me by any other name, I shall cut off his hand. He married thirty women who gave him many offspring.[19]

Ghazzal Dabiri, "Historiography and the Sho'ubiya Movement," *Journal of Persianate Studies* 6 (2013): 216–234; and William F. McCants, *Founding Gods, Inventing Nations: Conquest and Culture Myths from Antiquity to Islam* (Princeton, NJ: Princeton University Press, 2012).

16 Abu Jaʿfar Muhammad b. Ḥarīr al-Tabari, *Tarikh al-rusul wa al-muluk*, ed. M. J. de Goeje (Leiden: Brill, 1879–1901), 1: 147; trans. Franz Rosenthal as *The History of al-Ṭabarī*, vol. 1 (Albany: State University of New York Press, 1989), 318–319.

17 Tabari, *Tarikh*, 1: 147; trans., 1: 318.

18 Tabari, *Tarikh*, 1: 147; trans., 1: 318.

19 Tabari, *Tarikh*, 1: 147–148; trans., 1: 318–319.

Tabari ends his discussion of Kayumars by returning to questions of genealogy. He states that Kayumars's son and daughter, Mārī and Māriyānah, respectively, were the ancestors of kings, and again notes that no one doubts that Kayumars was "the father of the non-Arab Persians." The only disagreement was whether or not he was Adam.[20]

Although a number of universal chroniclers cite Tabari as a source or mention his history in their narratives, they instead seem to be drawing either directly on a Persian history related to Tabari, the history (*tārīkh*) of Abu ʿAli Muhammad Amirak Balʿami (d. between 382–387/992–997), or on other intermediary chroniclers who themselves drew on Balʿami. Balʿami wrote the earliest Islamic era history in the Persian language. His history was long regarded as a translation of Tabari's universal chronicle, but more recently and more accurately, scholars describe the text as a reinterpretation or a transformation of Tabari, or even an independent work.[21] The complex circumstances and motivations that led Balʿami to embark on his "translation" can only be briefly summarized here. The project started when the Samanid ruler Mansur b. Nuh (r. 350–365/961–976) commissioned Balʿami to translate and make specific changes to Tabari's history. In a recent study on Kayumars in Balʿami's *Tarikh*, Maria Subtelny summarizes the scholarly opinions on the history, noting that the text formed part of a process of "Islamization" and the promotion of a Sunni perspective on the part of the Samanids.[22] Together with two other early Persian-Samanid-sponsored "translations," namely Tabari's Qur'an commentary (*tafsīr*) and the *Kitab al-sawad*, a Hanafite doctrinal exposition, the

[20] Tabari, *Tarikh*, 1: 147–148; trans., 1: 318–319. Full diacritics added for clarification.

[21] See Daniel, "The Rise and Development of Persian Historiography," 110; Andrew Peacock, *Mediaeval Islamic Historiography and Political Legitimacy: Balʿamī's* Tārīkhnāma (London: Routledge, 2007), 4–6.

[22] Maria Subtelny, "Between Persian Legend and Samanid Orthodoxy: Accounts about Gayumarth in Balʿami's *Tarikhnama*," in *Ferdowsi, the Mongols and the History of Iran: Art, literature and Culture from Early Islam to Qajar Persia*, eds. Robert Hillenbrand, A. C. S. Peacock, and Firuza Abdullaeva, 34 (London: I. B. Tauris, 2013). On the Islamization process, see D. G. Tor, "The Islamisation of Iranian Kingly Ideals in the Persianate Fürstenspiegel," *Iran* 49 (2011): 115–122.

Samanids appeared intent on promoting a Hanafite Islamic perspective on the Qur'an and religious doctrine, and also a particular perspective on Iran's pre-Islamic past, one that had coopted Iran's Zoroastrian past, which at the time of Bal'ami's writing was no longer considered a threat.[23] At the same time, however, Subtelny, drawing on the scholarship of Julie Meisami, acknowledges that both the Iranian and Islamic historiographical traditions "co-existed and were being forged simultaneously in the eastern Islamic world under the Samanids."[24] As Elton Daniel has noted, the Samanid project enjoyed great success, as evidenced by the many surviving manuscripts – more than 160 – of Bal'ami's history.[25]

While Bal'ami bases his account on Tabari, he also draws on a great deal of additional and supplementary material, rendering his account of Kayumars much longer and more extensive than Tabari's. Subtelny states that his sources include "Persians/Iranians (*'ajam*), Zoroastrians (*gabrān, mughān*), the common people of Balkh (*'āmmah-i Balkh*), the doctors of Islam (*'ulamā-yi Islām*), and historians (*'ulamā-yi akhbār*)." She also states that Bal'ami cites written texts such as histories of the ancient Persian kings, the Sasanian *Khudaynamah*, and Ibn al-Muqaffa'.[26] For his account of Kayumars, Bal'ami neither attempts to reconcile the many anecdotes and events he relates nor tries to blend them into a single narrative. Rather, he presents the material as a collection of stories.

Bal'ami, like Tabari, identifies Kayumars at the beginning of his account, but he provides many more theories about his ancestry than Tabari, suggesting that he did not share Tabari's distaste for matters of genealogy and identity. He presents the following variations:

(1) Groups of Persians say that he is the one they call Adam, and people descended from him.

[23] Subtelny, "Between Persian Legend and Samanid Orthodoxy," 34–35.
[24] Subtelny, "Between Persian Legend and Samanid Orthodoxy," 34. See also Julie Scott Meisami, "The Past in Service of the Present: Two Views of History in Medieval Persia," *Poetics Today* 14 (1993): 250–251.
[25] Elton L. Daniel, "Manuscripts and Editions of Bal'ami's 'Tarjamah-i Tārīkh-i Ṭabarī,'" *Journal of the Royal Asiatic Society of Great Britain and Ireland* 2 (1990): 286–288.
[26] See Subtelny, "Between Persian Legend and Samanid Orthodoxy," 36. See also Hartman, *Gayōmart*, 131–132.

(2) And they call him the "Mud/Earth King" (*gilshāh*), because he was created from clay/mud (*gil*) and ruled over the earth (*gil*).
(3) A group of scholars of history say that he is the grandson of Adam.
(4) A group of Persians say that his children were Mashi and Mashayah, who were plants (*giyāh*) and they grew out of the ground in human form, like today, and then God granted them a spirit
(5) After Adam, Seth (Shis) succeeded, and then Enosh (Anush) b. Seth, then Kenan (Qinan) b. Enosh (Anush), then Kayumars.
(6) And the scholars of Islam say that he (Kayumars) was one of the children of Ham.[27]

At the end of his account, Bal'ami adds two more alternatives:

(7) One group says he was a messenger (*payghambar*) and called him "first created" (*pīshdād*).[28]
(8) A group of Eastern leaders say he was among the offspring of Mahalalel (Mahabil) b. Kenan (Qinan).[29]

After the genealogical information, Bal'ami narrates approximately eight anecdotes about Kayumars: (1) the story of the death of Hushang (Kayumars's son) and the omen of the owl; (2) several related stories involving a rooster symbolizing, as Subtelny notes, the Zoroastrian deity Surush;[30] (3) the etymology of the city of Balkh and an explanation of why its residents were so happy; (4) the story of a woman turning to stone; (5) how Kayumars became king; (6) the death of Siyamak, who was Kayumars's son (or grandson); (7) Hushang and the lion; and (8) Kayumars teaching the arts of weaving and sewing to the world. Subtelny concludes that Bal'ami included these various stories, drawn from Zoroastrian legend, "as relics of a confused pre-Islamic past that had been superseded, thanks to the Samanids, by a clearly formulated, unambiguous Hanafite-Muslim present."[31] In

[27] Abu Muhammad b. Muhammad Bal'ami, *Tarikh-i Bal'ami*, eds. Muhammad Taqi Bahar and Muhammad Parvin Gunabadi (Tehran: Zavvar, 1379 [1990]), 75–76.
[28] I am using Subtelny's suggested translation for this term. For a discussion on the meaning of *pishdad*, see Subtelny, "Between Persian Legend and Samanid Orthodoxy," 44, n. 68.
[29] Bal'ami, *Tarikh-i Bal'ami*, 86. See also Hartman, *Gayōmart*, 131–132; XV.
[30] Subtelny, "Between Persian Legend and Samanid Orthodoxy," 39–40.
[31] Subtelny, "Between Persian Legend and Samanid Orthodoxy," 41.

Table 4.3 ***General organizational scheme of Shukr Allah's* Bahjat al-tavarikh**

Chapter (*bāb*) 1: On the creation of the world
Chapter 2: The prophets
Chapter 3: Muhammad's genealogy
Chapter 4: The life of Muhammad
Chapter 5: The Prophet's wives and children and their names
Chapter 6: The forerunners of the companions of the Prophet
Chapter 7: His companions
Chapter 8: The imams
Chapter 9: Shaykhs and famous ones (includes Sufi masters)
Chapter 10: The Greek philosophers
Chapter 11: Kayanid kings
Chapter 12: Umayyads, 'Abbasids, and 'Alavis
Chapter 13: The Ottomans

other words, by the time of Bal'ami's writing, inclusion of the Zoroastrian material did not pose any sort of threat to the Samanid project and could be used for purposes such as entertainment, edification, and preserving the past. Historiographically speaking, it is important to note that the anecdotes in Bal'ami, not Tabari, served as the building blocks that subsequent generations of universal chroniclers used to construct their own narratives of Kayumars.

Kayumars in the Earliest Ottoman Chronicle in Persian

The first Persian universal history from the middle/early modern periods is Mawlana Shukr Allah Rumi's *Bahjat al-tavarikh*, the scope of which goes up to 855/1451.[32] Shukr Allah, whose history was the earliest universal history in Persian to be written under the Ottomans, engaged in diplomatic activity for Sultan Murad II, divides his history into a total of thirteen chapters, with the final chapter devoted to the Ottomans. These are indicated in Table 4.3. His chapter on the

[32] For more information on Shukr Allah and the *Bahjat al-tavarikh*, see Appendix. For Shukr Allah's dates, see Sara Nur Yildiz, "Ottoman Historical Writing in Persian, 1400–1600," in *Persian Historiography*, ed. Charles Melville, 443 (London: I. B. Tauris, 2012).

Ottomans is brief and forms less than 5 percent of the entire chronicle.[33]

Shukr Allah opens his discussion of Kayumars in the same way as Bal'ami, by stating that there is much disagreement over Kayumars's identity, and like Bal'ami, he presents a number of theories regarding Kayumars's lineage. Shukr Allah's list, however, differs significantly:

(1) Some Arab historians say that he is among the descendants of Cain (Qabil).
(2) Some Persians say that Kayumars was created out of the dust just like Adam "the pure one," without mother or father, and some say that just like a plant, he grew out from the ground (Bal'ami #2).
(3) Some Persians say that Kayumars was the son of Enosh (Anush) b. Seth (Shis).
(4) Some say that he is among the sons of Mahalalel (Mihla'il) b. Kenan (Qinan) (Bal'ami #8).
(5) Some say he is among the descendants of that Adam who was created before Adam "the pure one." This, however, is an error, because the time between that Adam and this Adam "the pure one" was 150,000 years, and it was never the case that Adam could have lived that long.[34]
(6) The Greeks say that Kayumars is the same as Seth (Shis), and this is also a weak statement.
(7) Some of the Persians say that Kayumars is the son of that Seth (Shis) (Bal'ami #3).
(8) Some say that he is Adam the pure one (Bal'ami #1).
(9) The clerics (*'ulama'*) of the people of Islam say that Kayumars is among the descendants of Jan b. Jan, and lived to the time of Seth (Shis).[35]

Of these nine versions of Kayumars's genealogy, only four are the same as in Bal'ami. Furthermore, five of the nine genealogies attempt to

[33] The section on the Ottomans numbers approximately 14 folios out of approximately 305.

[34] There is a Shi'i hadith saying that there have been multiple Adams separated by large periods of time. Shukr Allah may be drawing on this and related traditions. Dr. Stephen Lambden, personal communication, January 7, 2015.

[35] Shukr Allah, "Bahjat al-tavarikh," MS. Istanbul Süleymaniye Kütüphanesi Ayasofia 2990 f. 193a–194b. Jan b. Jan was considered the last of the 72 kings (Solomon) who ruled the jinn. For more on Shukr Allah's account on Kayumars in the *Bahjat al-tavarikh*, see Hartman, *Gayōmart*, 202–207 and LXI–LXV.

connect Kayumars to Adam and his early descendants, particularly through his son Seth. While Shukr Allah's specific sources for Kayumars's genealogy are still unclear, he references Persians, Greeks, and the religious scholars (*'ulamā'*). He does not appear to imitate any specific earlier universal history for this portion of his account.

While there are significant differences between Bal'ami and Shukr Allah in terms of Kayumars's identity, Shukr Allah provides a lengthy narrative filled with anecdotes about Kayumars, and this section bears much similarity to Bal'ami's history. Although the only source that Shukr Allah specifically names is Tabari, we will show in the following section that Shukr Allah was in reality imitating Bal'ami.

Kingmaking in Bal'ami's Tarikh *and Shukhr Allah's* Bahjat al-tavarikh

One of the most important instances of Shukr Allah rewriting Bal'ami's history appears in his account of how Kayumars became king. For this portion of his history, Shukr Allah relies on Bal'ami's history, but recasts that narrative in interesting ways. Because of the close relationship between the two histories, it is necessary to explain in considerable detail how Bal'ami narrated this episode, in order to understand how Shukr Allah changed the account.

Bal'ami begins his narrative on how Kayumars became king by noting that Kayumars was the first king in the world.[36] He then explains the circumstances under which this happened. According to Bal'ami, Kayumars became king by going to every city and proclaiming his kingship, telling people that "God, exalted and glorified be he, has made me your king. Do not sin, for if God, exalted and glorified be he, would have forgiven someone's sins, he would have forgiven Adam's sins."[37] Bal'ami then states that Kayumars was the first person among the children of Adam to deliver a sermon (*khuṭbah*), and explains that when he did so, Kenan, a biblical patriarch who was the grandson of Seth – himself considered the third son of Adam – and son of Enosh, was present. In the following passage, Kayumars orders Kenan to recognize him as king and explains to him that whereas he

[36] "*Va nukhustīn pādishāh andar jahān ū būd.*" Bal'ami, *Tarikh-i Bal'ami*, 75.
[37] Bal'ami, *Tarikh-i Bal'ami*, 82.

(Kenan) had the authority to appoint his successor (*khalīfat*), God made Kayumars the king:

And in that group was the leader Kenan (Qinan). He [Kayumars] said, "You are your father's vicegerent/successor (*khalīfat*) over this people; be a vicegerant (*khalīfat*), and with your [own] hand, make anyone you want to be *your* successor (*khalīfat*), and recognize my kingship (*marā bi-pādishāhī bi-shinās*), for God – may he be exalted – has made me your king (*pādishāh*). I will not forgive anyone who sins."[38]

Bal'ami adds that he found a copy of that first address (*khuṭbah*) that Kayumars delivered and reproduces its contents:

And this was the address (*khuṭbah*) that I found in Arabic; I do not know if he [Kayumars] said it in Arabic or in Persian (*pārsī*) or in Syriac: "Praise be to God, who bestowed upon us his generosity and encompassed us with his kindness and chose us for his religion (*dīn*), so may he be praised for his beneficence and thanked for his blessings which he bestowed upon his prophets through his mercy and the receiving of his forgiveness. And may all be servants before God."[39]

After delivering the *khuṭbah*, Bal'ami explains that everyone accepted Kayumars and told him they were at his service. Kayumars replied to them, saying, "Accept advice and wisdom from anyone who gives it. Do not look at the person, look at the value of their words, and see the truth wherever it resides, so that God will be your protector from difficulties."[40] After this, the people accepted Kayumars' advice. Bal'ami ends the story by saying "That day the name of kingship fell upon him [Kayumars]."[41]

In these passages, Bal'ami makes a number of important points reflecting notions of kingship and authority at his time of writing. Most notably, Bal'ami distinguishes between the biblical Kenan's position as a successor or vicegerent, who had the authority to appoint his own successor, and Kayumars, who as king, was appointed by God. On the basis of that divine appointment, Kayumars had the authority to order Kenan to recognize him as king. Here, Bal'ami's account articulates the notion of separate yet interdependent spheres for prophetic and kingly authority that appears in a late Sasanian normative

38 Bal'amī, *Tarikh-i Bal'ami*, 82–83. Emphasis added.
39 Bal'ami, *Tarikh-i Bal'ami*, 83.
40 Bal'ami, *Tarikh-i Bal'ami*, 83.
41 Bal'ami, *Tarikh-i Bal'ami*, 83.

text, the *Ahd-i Ardashir*, or Testament of Ardashir, where we read, "Know that kingship and religion are twins; one cannot exist without the other, for religion is the foundation of royalty and the king is the defender of religion."[42] This formulation would appear most famously some 500 years after the composition of the *Ahd-i Ardashir*, in al-Ghazali's (450–505/1058–1111) *Nasihat al-muluk*, where he presented a version of this saying: "The quality which kings most need is correct religion, because kingship and religion are like brothers."[43]

Bal'ami's narrative on Kayumars also confirms the notion that one of his purposes in writing was not necessarily Persianization, but rather Islamization, or to spread and consolidate Islam. In this respect, Bal'ami makes Kayumars a proto-Muslim, if his sources had not already done so. In other words, Bal'ami Islamicizes Kayumars or interprets him from an Islamic point of view.[44] At the same time, we also see the tension between what Ghazzal Dabiri describes as "the strained coexistence between the Iranian and Islamic ideas of kingship," as histories such as Bal'ami's "sought to reconcile the Islamic narrative with that of the conquered peoples into a cohesive and inclusive universal history."[45] This is borne out by the description of Kayumars delivering the first *khuṭbah*, an allegedly proto-Islamic "sermon" or "address," in which he proclaims God's religion (*dīn*), which we may assume to be Islam, or proto-Islam. Furthermore, Kayumars urges his people to accept "truth," again – presumably the truth of Islam – according to the value of the words, not the person uttering those words. That Bal'ami had Kayumars, the first mythical Persian king, deliver this message certainly would have helped make Islam acceptable not only to those reading or hearing his history but to those who were hearing the message of Islam delivered by a diverse range of presumably imperfect individuals at the time of Bal'ami's writing.

42 Quoted in Parvaneh Pourshariati, *Decline and Fall of the Sasanian Empire: The Sasanian-Parthian Confederacy and the Arab Conquest of Iran* (London: I. B. Tauris, 2008), 324; Pourshariati provides a detailed analysis of this concept in her important monograph, 324–327.

43 Al-Ghazali, *Nasihat al-muluk*, ed. Jalal al-Din Huma'i (Tehran: Kitabkhanah-i Tihran, 1938), 51; trans. F. R. C. Begley as *Ghazālī's Book of Counsel for Kings (Naṣīhat al-mulūk)*. London: Oxford University Press, 1964, 59. Translation slightly modified. This text will be discussed further below.

44 The Islamization of pre-Islamic Persian kings eventually became a common historiographical practice. For a discussion of this process, see Tor, "The Islamisation of Iranian Kingly Ideals," 115–122.

45 Dabiri, "The *Shahnama*: Between the Samanids and the Ghaznavids," 18–19.

Turning now to the *Bahjat al-tavarikh*, Shukr Allah's account of Kayumars's becoming king departs from Bal'ami in some significant ways. Bal'ami emphasizes the fact that Kayumars delivered the first *khuṭbah* by stressing this point both at the beginning of his narrative of Kayumars's encounter with Kenan and through repeating the text of the *khuṭbah* itself. Shukr Allah, however, completely removes all references in his account of Kayumars delivering the *khuṭbah*. Instead, he only describes the encounter that Kayumars had with Kenan, and in doing this, Kayumars is no longer the figure who was spreading and promoting the religion through sermonizing.

In his actual passage related to Kayumars becoming king, rather than Kayumars ordering Kenan to recognize him as king, as Bal'ami narrates, Shukr Allah states that Kayumars *asks* Kenan to make him king through his power as vicegerent (*khalīfah*). In writing his passage, Shukr Allah very clearly imitates Bal'ami, as seen in the parallel passages below:

Bal'ami *Tarikh*	Shukr Allah *Bahjat al-tavarikh*
And in that group the leader was Kenan. He [Kayumars] said, "You are your father's vicegerent/successor (*khalīfat*) over this people; be a vicegerant (*khalīfat*), and with your [own] hand, make anyone you want to be your successor (*khalīfat*), and recognize my kingship (*marā bi-pādishāhī bi-shinās*), for God–may he be exalted–has made me your king (*pādishāh*)."	And Kenan son of Enosh son of Seth was present. He [Kayumars] said "Oh Kenan, you are Seth's vicegerent (*khalīfah*). Be a vicegerent (*khalīfah*) and establish me as king." Kenan chose (appointed) him to be king.[46]
va andar gurūh mihtar Qīnān būd, guft: 'khalīfat-i pidarī barīn gurūh bar khalīfat bāsh, va az dast-i [khvīsh] har ki-rā khvāhī khalīfat kun, va marā bi-pādishāhī bi-shinās, kih marā khudā-yi ta'alá bar shumā padishāh kardast.	*va Qīnān bin Ānūsh bin Shīs ḥāẓir būd guft yā Qīnān taw khalīfah-'i Shīsī bāz khalīfah bāsh va marā bi-pādishāhī muqarar dār; Qīnān vay rā bi-pādishāhī gumāsht.*

[46] Shukr Allah, "Bahjat al-tavarikh," ms. f. 194b.

Historical context could help explain the different emphases in each account. As noted above, Bal'ami Islamicizes Kayumars and proto-distinguishes between caliphal and kingly authority, making kingship a divine appointment. This reflects notions of kingship and authority at the time of the Samanids that can be traced at least as far back as the late Sasanian period, when the author of the *Ahd-i Ardashir* stated that kingship and religion were like twin brothers. It is interesting to note that in one portion of his *Nasihat al-muluk*, al-Ghazali echoes this portion of the *Ahd-i Ardashir*, when he provides an account of Kayumars. Here, al-Ghazali contrasts Kayumars's authority with the Islamo-Biblical figure Seth. As D. G. Tor has noted, in al-Ghazali's account, Adam, whom he considered the first Muslim prophet, entrusted two of his sons, Seth and Kayumars, with distinct responsibilities:

> It is related in the (Persian) traditions that Adam, on whom be peace, had many sons. From their number he chose two, Seth and Kayumars, to whom he gave forty of the Great Books, by which they were to work. Then he charged Seth with the preservation of religion and (affairs of) the next world, and Kayumars with the affairs of this world and the kingship.[47]

Al-Ghazali seems here to echo Bal'ami's formulation, in which Kenan (son of Seth, rather than Seth himself) and Kayumars have separate spheres of authority.

We may assume that al-Ghazali was drawing on earlier accounts in making this particular distinction between Seth and Kayumars and their roles and responsibilities. Shukr Allah's account more closely follows a later perspective, one which renders kingly authority as submissive to religious authority, a position similar to Seljuq or Mamluk notions of kingship and most famously articulated by the Shafi'i jurist al-Mawardi (364–450/974–1058) in his *Ahkam al-sultaniyya*.[48] In his *Ihya 'ulum al-din*, al-Ghazali states that rulers who held political power gave their loyalty to the caliph: "The function of government in the various lands is carried out by means of sultans, who owe allegiance to the caliphate. Government in these days is a consequence solely of political power, and whosoever he may be to

[47] Al-Ghazali, *Nasihat al-muluk*, trans., 47–48, slightly modified. Begley notes that this passage only appears in the Arabic version of the *Nasihat al-muluk*. Tor, "The Islamisation of Iranian Kingly Ideals," 118.

[48] For a discussion of al-Mawardi, see Darling, *A History of Social Justice*, 77–79.

whom the possessor of military power gives his allegiance, that person is the caliph."[49] While the passage by Shukr Allah quoted here is too brief to draw definitive conclusions, that he chose to rewrite Bal'ami in this way suggests that he was cognizant of the fact that notions of caliphal and kingly authority had changed significantly since Bal'ami's time and chose to rewrite the passage to make it conform to more current standards.

The Earliest Safavid Account of Kayumars

Writing some sixty-five years after Shukr Allah, Khvandamir was the first Safavid chronicler to relate the story of Kayumars. The account appears in Volume One, Part Two of his *Habib al-siyar*, in a chapter devoted to Iran's pre-Islamic kings.[50] As a universal history, the *Habib al-siyar* mostly focuses on the pre-Safavid period, with only some seven percent of the text devoted to the Safavids. Table 4.4 indicates the organizational scheme of the *Habib al-siyar* in comparison with the *Rawzat al-safa*. In order to understand Khvandamir's account of Kayumars, we must read it alongside two other texts that he imitates: Mirkhvand's *Rawzat al-safa*, and Khvandamir's own *Ma'asir al-muluk* (before 903/1498), which consists of chapters devoted to the writings and sayings of pre-Islamic kings and sages, followed by narratives of the Islamic dynasties. While Khvandamir uses both of these sources for his narrative on Kayumars, his primary model was his grandfather's *Rawzat al-safa*.

Khvandamir's *Habib al-siyar* and the *Rawzat al-safa*

Like other earlier universal historians, Khvandamir opens his account of Kayumars by discussing different versions of his ancestry. Imitating the *Rawzat al-safa*, he presents five different possibilities. However, only three out of five of his explanations for Kayumars's ancestry are the same as the *Rawzat al-safa*:

[49] Quoted in Woods, *The Aqquyunlu*, 4.

[50] Khvandamir's organizational and chronological schemes are analyzed in Shahzad Bashir, "On Islamic Time: Rethinking Chronology in the Historiography of Muslim Societies," *History and Theory* 53 (2014): 532–535.

Rawzat al-safa	*Habib al-siyar*
1. Some historians stated that Kayumars was the eldest son of Adam, and al-Ghazali's *Nasihat al-muluk* supports this option.[51] (*Habib* #1)	1. Some historians said Kayumars was the eldest son of Adam. (*Rawzat* #1)
2. Some say that Umim b. Laud b. Aram (Arim) b. Shem (Sam) b. Noah (Nuh) was originally known as Kayumars. (*Habib* #3)	2. Another group believed that Kenan (Qinan) b. Enosh (Anush) b. Seth (Shis) b. Adam was called Kayumars.
3. According to the author of the *Ghunyah*, Kayumars was one of the sons of Japheth (Yafis) b. Noah (Nuh), and called Gomer ('Amir) by the Arabs and Kayumars by the Persians.[52]	3. According to the Magis, he was synonymous with Adam, and his title (*laqab*) was "Gilshah" (Mud/Earth King). (*Rawzat* #5)
4. According to the Persians, when Kayumars was invested with absolute power, he ordained that anyone who called him anything but Adam should be beheaded. However, this opinion differs from most writers, who state that the khans of Turkistan are of the lineage of Japheth (Yafis), but not the kings of Fars, who are	4. Umim b. Laud b. Aram (Arim) b. Shem (Sam) b. Noah (Nuh) was called Kayumars, as was stated in the *Rawzat al-safa*. (*Rawzat* #2)

51 The passage in the *Nasihat al-muluk* is as follows: "It is related in the (Persian) traditions that Adam, on whom be peace, had many sons. From their number he chose two, Seth and Kayūmarth, to whom he gave forty of the Great Books, by which they were to work." al-Ghazali, *Nasihat al-muluk*, 42; trans., 47. On al-Ghazali's political formulation, see Said Arjomand, "Perso-Indian Statecraft, Greek Political Science and the Muslim Idea of Government," *International Sociology* 16 (2001): 455–473.

52 The translator of the *Rawzat al-safa* states that this is a Persian work of al-Ghazali's, but does not cite his source for this information. I have not been able to trace this source. None of the texts that Hartman studied contain this particular version of Kayumars's genealogy with reference to a work entitled "Ghunyah." There are, however, a number of sources that equate Kayumars with Gomer, thus making this particular version of Kayumars's genealogy part of the Islamic Arabic literary tradition going back to Tabari. The earliest chroniclers writing in Persian to include this particular formulation are Bayzavi in his *Nizam al-tavarikh* and Rashid al-Din in his *Jami' al-tavarikh*. See Hartman, *Gayōmart*, 156, 159.

acknowledged to be descendants of Kayumars.	
5. Finally, the Magi believe that Kayumars is synonymous with Adam, and also called Gilshah (Mud/Earth King), because in that time, there was nothing to rule over except for earth. (*Habib* #3)[53]	5. Finally, the best possibility is that he was the son of Shem (Sam).[54]

Table 4.4 ***General organizational scheme of the*** **Rawzat al-safa** ***and the*** **Habib al-siyar**

Rawzat al-safa	*Habib al-siyar*
1. Creation of the world to Yazdigird	I. Pre-Islamic kings and sages, Muhammad, and the Rashidun caliphs
2. Muhammad and the first four caliphs	1. Pre-Islamic prophets and Greek sages
3. The Twelve Imams, the Umayyads and the Abbasids	2. Persian and Arab kings
4. Kings contemporary to the Abbasids	3. Muhammad
5. Chingiz Khan and the rule of his descendants in Iran and Turan	4. Rashidun caliphs
6. Timur and his descendants to the death of Sultan Abu Sa'id (873/1469)	II. The 12 Imams, the Umayyads, the Abbasids, and the kings around the world contemporary to the Abbasids
7. Sultan Husayn and his sons to 929/1522–1523	5. The twelve imams
8. Khatimah (conclusion)	6. The Umayyads
	7. The Abbasids
	8. Kings contemporary to the Abbasids
	III. Kings and queens after the Abbasids
	9. Khans of Turkestan, Chingiz Khan and his descendants around the world
	10. Kings around the world contemporary to Chingiz Khan
	11. Timur and his descendants to the present day
	12. Shah Ismail
	Khatimah (conclusion)

53 Mirkhvand, *Rawzat al-safa*, 1: 569–570.
54 Khvandamir, *Habib al-siyar*, 1: 175.

The two possible ancestries for Kayumars in the *Rawzat al-safa* that Khvandamir "removes" include one that references a work he calls the *Ghunyah*, stating that Kayumars was a son of Japheth. The second alternative that Khvandamir omits is one where Mirkhvand notes two different opinions about Kayumars, one from Persians, who said that Kayumars demanded that everyone call him Adam, and another that distinguished the Khans of Turkistan as descendants of Japheth and the kings of Fars as descendants of Kayumars. In the place of these two explanations, Khvandamir inserts one that equates Kayumars with Kenan, and another, which he considers the best explanation, that equates Kayumars with the son of Shem.[55] In doing this, Khvandamir essentially removes the two associations of Kayumars with Japheth that Mirkhvand presented and replaces them with Kayumars as a descendant of Adam through Kenan and as a son of Shem. Khvandamir may have done this because Japheth was traditionally considered the ancestor of the Turks, while Shem the ancestor of the Persians. Indeed, in stating that the best possibility for Kayumars's ancestry was that he was the son of Shem, Khvandamir "Persianizes" Kayumars's ancestry.

For the rest of his narrative on Kayumars, Khvandamir imitates his sources to varying degrees. In some instances, he reproduces earlier texts word for word, with little to no deviation from the original. On other occasions, he makes deliberate alterations to his model text, for reasons we shall discuss below. Finally, he also engages in the historiography of omission, that is, at certain points he chooses not to include details from his earlier sources. Here we shall provide examples of all three of these practices, beginning with one instance in which Khvandamir faithfully reproduces the earlier narratives he imitates with very little change.

The passage below describes how Kayumars's son asks his father what the best attribute to possess is. Kayumars names two: worshipping God and abstinence from cruelty. This answer led his son to retreat to Mount Damavand and spend his time in worshipping God. The anecdote originates in the *Rawzat al-safa*. Khvandamir imitates that passage for his *Ma'asir al-muluk*, and then reproduces the same

55 For a discussion of Kayumars's ancestry in Khvandamir, see Shahzad Bashir, "A Perso-Islamic Universal Chronicle," 220.

Ma'asir al-muluk text verbatim in his *Habib al-siyar*. The parallel passages below demonstrate the relationship between the three texts:

Rawzat al-safa	*Ma'asir al-muluk*	*Habib al-siyar*
One day he asked Kayumars which was the best of all pursuits. He answered, "Abstinence from cruelty and the worship of the great and glorious God." The son said, "What is abstinence from cruelty and worshipping God" He said "Abstinence from cruelty depends on separation from humanity, and worshipping is based on seclusion and solitude."[56]	One day he asked his father, "which is the best human attribute?" Kayumars answered, "abstinence from cruelty and serving the exalted lord." That knowledgeable youth thought to himself and said "abstinence from cruelty depends on separation and serving is based on seclusion and solitude."[57]	One day he asked his father, "which is the best human attribute?" Kayumars answered, "abstinence from cruelty and serving the exalted lord." That knowledgeable youth thought to himself and said "abstinence from cruelty depends on separation and serving is based on seclusion and solitude."[58]
Rūzī az Kayūmars̱ pursīd kih 'az kārhā chih bihtar?' Javāb dād kih 'kam āzārī va parastīdan-i khudā-yi 'izz va jall.' Pisar guft kih 'kam āzārī va parastīdan-i khudā bih chih chīz ast?' Guft kih 'bī-āzārī mutrattib bar judā'ī ast az khalq; va parastash mawqūf bar vaḥdat va tanhā'ī.	*Rūzī az pidar pursīd kih 'bihtarīn ṣifat-i basharī kudām ast? Javab dād kih 'kam āzārī va 'ibādat-i ḥaẕrat-i bārī.' (Ān) javān-i nuktah-dān bā khūd ta'āmul namūdah guft 'kam āzārī mutrattib bar judā'ī ast va 'ibādat mawqūf bar vaḥdat va tanhā'ī.'*	*Rūzī az pidar pursīd kih 'bihtarīn ṣifat-i basharī kudām ast? Javab dād kih 'kam āzārī va 'ibādat-i ḥaẕrat-i bārī.' (Ān) javān-i nuktah-dān bā khūd ta'āmul kardah guft 'kam āzārī mutrattib bar judā'ī ast va 'ibādat mawqūf bar vaḥdat va tanhā'ī.'*

We have already demonstrated in Chapter 3 that part of Khvandamir's method of historical writing was to repurpose texts he had written in one context for another. Unlike his extensive reworking of the significance of the number seven passage as described above in

56 Mirkhvand, *Rawzat al-safa*, 2: 570.
57 Khvandamir, *Ma'asir al-muluk*, 21.
58 Khvandamir, *Habib al-siyar*, 1: 175.

Chapter 3, here he made only slight and inconsequential changes to the *Ma'asir al-muluk* narrative.

While in many cases Khvandamir faithfully reproduces the *Rawzat al-safa* text, he did not refrain from rewriting his grandfather's narrative when he felt it appropriate to do so. One striking example of this practice appears in a passage referring to Magis, or Zoroastrian priests. In this instance, Khvandamir removes an anti-Zoroastrian statement made by Mirkhvand and replaces it with a neutral sentence. The passage appears in an anecdote describing how a son of Kayumars was killed by demons.[59] This anecdote can be traced back to Bal'ami. According to Mirkhvand's *Rawzat al-safa*, when Kayumars discovered his son, he began lamenting, and at this moment, God revealed a well at the top of the mountain, where Kayumars buried his son and lit a fire at the mouth of the well. Mirkhvand then notes that this story was familiar to the Magi, and says, "Respecting this well and the fire, the Magi have many traditions, so opposite and contradictory to common sense, as to be rejected by every intelligent mind."[60] The original account in Bal'ami goes so far as to state that the Magi believe that Kayumars himself built the hole in the mountain and the fire is Kayumars, who is keeping the demons (*dīv*) away from his son.[61] Like Mirkhvand, Khvandamir similarly says that God brought forth a well in which Kayumars buried his son and lit a fire. However, he directly responds to Mirkhvand's negative comment about Magi beliefs by replacing it with a specific example of one such belief, which he does not criticize:

Rawzat al-safa	*Habib al-siyar*
He kindled a great fire at its mouth. Respecting this well and the fire, the Magi have many traditions, so opposite and contradictory to common sense, as to be rejected by every intelligent mind.[62]	He kindled a great fire at its mouth. Some Magis believe that from that day until the end, every day ten to fifteen times a fire rises from that well and then goes down.[63]

59 For more on Zoroastrians in the Safavid period, see Kioumars Ghereghlou, "On the Margins of Minority Life: Zoroastrians and the State in Safavid Iran," *Bulletin of the School of Oriental and African Studies* 80 (2017): 45–71.
60 Mirkhvand, *Rawzat al-safa*, 1: 571; trans., 55.
61 Bal'ami, *Tarikh-i Bal'ami*, 77.
62 Mirkhvand, *Rawzat al-safa*, 2: 571.
63 Khvandamir, *Habib al-siyar*, 1: 176.

Bar sar-i ān chāh ātashī buland bar afrūkht, va majūs dar qiṣṣah-i ātash va chāh kharāfāt-i bisyār dārand kih ṭab'-i salīm az qabūl-i ān abā mīnamāyand.	*Bar sar-i ān ātashī buland bar afrūkht va ba'ẓī majūsiyān rā 'aqīdah ānast kih az ān rūz bāz tā ghāyat har rūzah dah pānzdah nawbat ātash az ān'chāh zabānah mīzanad va bāz bi-chāh furū mī'nashīnad.*

Here, Khvandamir may have not wanted to make negative statements about Zoroastrian beliefs in light of Shah Isma'i's rather positive relations with Zoroastrians during his 910/1504–1505 invasion of Yazd, after which he occupied the city.[64]

Knowing that Khvandamir based most of his Kayumars narrative on the *Rawzat al-safa* allows us to understand at which points he omitted details from his grandfather's work. In some instances, the omissions are as important as the changes and additions. It is noteworthy that in two cases, Khvandamir chose to remove discussions related to kingship. The first omission is a discussion about Kayumars becoming king. He describes how, before Kayumars became king, the world was full of disorder, violence, and oppression, until a group of "wise men and nobles" decided that the universe was like a human body and its affairs would best be guided by a just king who would establish peace and tranquility.[65] Mirkhvand ends this passage by stating that Kayumars was essentially nominated or elected king, a description that bears more similarity to the *Bahjat al-tavarikh* than Bal'ami's history:

> After duly resorting to divine and human counsels, the lot of selection fell on Kayūmars. And as soon as he had confirmed, by oath, his assent to the conditions proposed by the nobles of the realm and the heads of religion, the crown of kingship was placed on his head and he was seated on the throne of the sultanate.[66]

64 See Ghereghlou, "On the Margins of Minority Life," 54–56.

65 Mirkhvand, *Rawzat al-safa*, 2:569; trans., 47–49.

66 Mirkhvand, *Rawzat al-safa*, 2:569. Translation is my own. The published translation is as follows: "After duly resorting to divine and human counsels, the lot of election fell on Kaiomars: and as soon as he had ratified, by oath, his assent to the conditions proposed by the nobles of the realm and the heads of religion, his auspicious brow was encircled with the royal diadem, and he was seated on the imperial throne." Trans., 49.

> *Ba'd as istikhārah va istishārah qur'ah-'i ikhtiyār bih nām-i Kayūmars uftād va ū chūn paymān-i ahl-i mulk va millat rā dar bāb-i muṭāva'at bih īmān mu'akad gardānīdah tāj-i shāhī bar sar nahād va bar sarīr-i salṭanat mutamakin gasht.*

Khvandamir completely omits this opening account from his narrative, thereby leaving ambiguous the means by which Kayumars became king. Khvandamir may have made this omission because of length, for it seems that he shortened the discrete stories of Kayumars by removing the longer philosophizing explanations that Mirkhvand supplies, thereby streamlining the narrative. The *Rawzat al-safa* is nearly three times as long as the *Habib al-siyar*, and part of Khvandamir's overall writing process was to shorten the *Rawzat al-safa* as he imitated it. However, Khvandamir also had choices to make in terms of what portions of the *Rawzat al-safa* narrative he should omit. In this instance, writing at a time of political upheaval, and not too long before he left Iran for the Mughal court of Humayun in India, Khvandamir may have wanted to play it safe by not commenting on how someone who was universally recognized as the first Persian king came to power, or the very large impact he had on the world.

In another example of omission, Khvandamir chose not to include a passage in which Mirkhvand talks about the significance of Kayumars's justice; he says that "through the influence of his equity the sheep and the wolf were like siblings, and the lion and the deer went (together) to watch over the desert."[67] This statement echoes a passage in Isaiah 11:6 which states that "The wolf also shall dwell with the lamb, and the leopard shall lie down with the kid; and the calf and the young lion and the fatling together; and a little child shall lead them." This biblical passage provided the inspiration for a series of later Mughal paintings of the emperor Jahangir, in which he is represented in a Mughal allegorical painting as "shooting poverty" while standing on a globe of the world, and inside the globe are depicted a lion and a lamb. Another painting shows him embracing Shah 'Abbas while both monarchs are standing on a globe also showing a lion and a lamb lying together.[68] Here, Khvandamir may have chosen not to

67 Mirkhvand, *Rawzat al-safa*, 1: 570; trans., 51.

68 See Jasper C. van Putten, "Jahangir Heroically Killing Poverty: Pictorial Sources and Pictorial Tradition in Mughal Allegory and Portraiture," in *The Meeting Place of British Middle East Studies: Emerging Scholars, Emergent Research and Approaches*, eds. Amanda Philips and Refqa Abu-Remaileh, 99–120 (Newcastle upon Tyne: Cambridge Scholars Publishing, 2009).

include this description of Kayumars because of the eschatological connotations of Isaiah 11:6.[69] The actual text that Mirkhvand evokes suggests Kayumars was the primordial initiator and sustainer of peaceful relationships among diverse peoples. As was the case with the concept of the just Imam (*imām-i ʻādil*) discussed in Chapter 3, such designations were, at least informally, the purview of Shah Isma'il himself. In summary, for his account of Kayumars, Khvandamir rewrote the *Rawzat al-safa* and his own *Ma'asir al-muluk*, making his *Habib al-siyar* account conform to the political climate in which he was writing.

A Central Asian Universal History

Mas'udi b. 'Usman Kuhistani composed the only universal history written under the Uzbeks of Transoxiana examined in this study, the *Tarikh-i Abu al-Khayr Khani*. That we do not know very much about Kuhistani's life or career makes it difficult to understand what texts he had access to, and he does not name any of his sources for his composition. Nevertheless, three main elements stand out in Kuhistani's narrative on Kayumars. The first is that he probably had access to Khvandamir's *Habib al-siyar* and seems to have used that text as one of his models. The second is his extensive use of Firdawsi's *Shahnamah*, a reliance that is greater than any of the other chronicles examined in this chapter. A third unique feature of the *Tarikh-i Abu al-Khayr Khani* includes Kuhistani's not elaborating extensively on Kayumars's genealogy; he only refers to him as the son of Adam and mentions that he was known as "Gilshah" (Mud/Earth King).

That Kuhistani relied on the *Habib al-siyar* for his *Tarikh-i Abu al-Khayr Khani* can be seen from the following parallel passages, drawn from the very first sentence in each account about Kayumars:

Habib al-siyar	*Tarikh-i Abu al-Khayr Khani*
As for the "first created ones," with Kayumars they were 10 individuals, and the period of their kingship,	[The first category: the "first created ones,"] and they were 11 persons, and the period of their kingship was

[69] Interestingly, Khvandamir makes a similar reference in relation to Humayun in his *Qanun-i Humayuni*, where he describes Humayun's justice, stating that Humayun's justice was such that the deer slept freely with the leopard under the shadow of his justice. Khvandamir, *Qanun-i humayuni*, 253.

according to the words of Hamzah bin Husayn Isfahani is 2470 years and according to the account of Bahram Shah bin Muradshah, 2734 years, and according to the narrative of Ḥamd Allah Mustawfi, 2450 years. And the first person of this type of human who became in charge of governing the people of the world is Kayumars.[70]	2485 years. The first person to whom the names of sultanate and kingship became attached was Kayumars son of Adam.[71]
Ammā pīshdādiyān bā Kayūmars dah nafar būdand va muddat-i pādishāhī-i īshān bi-qawl-i Ḥamzah bin Ḥusayn Iṣfahānī dū hizār va chahār ṣad va haftād sāl ast va bi rivāyat-i Bahrām Shāh bin Murādshāh dū hizār va haftṣad va sī va chahār sāl va bi-ʿaqīdah-i Ḥamd Allah Mustawfī dū hizār va chahār ṣad va panjāh sāl va nukhustīn kasī as nawʿ-i insān kih mutaṣaddī-i iyālat-i jahāniyān gasht Kayūmars ast.	*[ṭabaqah-i avval pīshdādiyān] va īshān yāzdah tan and muddat-i pādishāhī-i īshān dū hizār va chahār ṣad va hashtād va panj sāl būd avval kasī kih ism-i salṭanat va pādishāhī barū iṭṭilāq gardāndah Kayūmars ibn Ādam būd.*

Although we see enough similar phrasing and wording in these two passages to suggest that Kuhistani was imitating Khvandamir, the striking difference between these two passages is that Kuhistani removes all the different possibilities for the total number of years that the "*pishdadi*" kings ruled, as well as the sources that Khvandamir cites, and comes up with a unique total number that we do not see in any of the chronicles consulted in this chapter. It is possible that Kuhistani, whose account is much shorter than Khvandamir's, wanted to present a sort of composite number representing the different variations in the *Habib al-siyar* without having to list all the different historians and their numbers as Khvandamir does. In this way, Kuhistani streamlines his narrative.

70 Khvandamir, *Habib al-siyar*, 1: 175.
71 Kuhistani, "Tarikh-i Abu al-Khayr Khani," ms. British Library ADD 23513, f. 78a.

Another feature of Kuhistani's historiographical style is that not only does he rewrite and imitate Khvandamir's prose narrative, but also one of his poems. Kuhistani includes a poem at the same structural positon as a poem the *Habib al-siyar*, which he rewrites in a lightly imitative fashion, reproducing the general meaning of the poem, including some of the same words and phrases, but changing the poem. Khvandamir's poem actually appears originally in the *Rawzat al-safa* and a number of chroniclers reproduce it. However, here, Kuhistani does something that none of the other chroniclers do: he rewrites the poem. The poem emphasizes the point that both chroniclers make about Kayumars being the first king of the world:

Habib al-siyar	*Tarikh-i Abu al-Khayr Khani*
The first ruler who conquered the world The leader of the crown-holders (kings) was Kayumars.[72]	The first lord of the crown and of rank Kayumars was the king across the world.[73]
Nukhustīn khidīvī kih kishvar gushūd	*Nukhustīn khudāvand-i dīhīm va gāh*
Sar-i tājdārān Kayūmars būd	*Kayūmars bi-dawr-i jahān pādishah*

After the poem, Kuhistani stops imitating the *Habib al-siyar*, and instead reproduces a fairly large number of passages from Firdawsi's *Shahnamah* account of Kayumars, including some eighteen-and-a-half rhyming couplets. Kuhistani does not rely solely on the *Shahnamah* for his verses; approximately thirteen rhyming couplets cannot be found in Firdawsi's work and should be considered, unless or until another model can be found, as original to Kuhistani. Kuhistani, then, seems to have been particularly interested in displaying his poetic abilities, whether through rewriting the poem of a prominent historian or through interspersing his own compositions in the midst of quoting from Firdawsi.[74]

72 Khvandamir, *Habib al-siyar* 1: 175.
73 Kuhistani, "Tarikh-i Abu al-Khayr Khani," f. 78a.
74 Kuhistani was of course not alone in his use of the *Shahnamah*, as will be demonstrated below. Earlier middle period prose writers, particularly authors of mirrors for princes literature also made use of the *Shahnamah*. See Nasrin Askari, *The Medieval Reception of the Shāhnāma as a Mirror for Princes* (Leiden: Brill, 2016), 171–228.

Why would he include so many passages from the *Shahnamah* in his narrative? Kuhistani included a great deal of *Shahnamah* material throughout his chronicle, so the section on Kayumars is not necessarily unique.[75] Jaimee Comstock-Skipp has explained the reason for the Shaybani Uzbeks' interest in the *Shahnamah*, and noted that in histories such as the *Tarikh-i Abu al-Khayr Khani* look to the Ilkhanid past in order to forge a new Mongol identity and illustrated such historical works accordingly.[76] The Shaybani Uzbeks were interested in illustrated *Shahnamahs*, finding visual inspiration from texts such as the Ilkhanid *Great Mongol Shahnamah* and even illustrated copies of Rashid al-Din's *Jami' al-tavarikh*. Episodes in the *Shahnamah*, such as the story where Firaydun the king divided his territory between his three sons, giving Transoxiana (Turan) to his middle son Tur and the Iranian heartland to his youngest son Iraj, and Iraj getting killed by his oldest brothers, provided "obvious counterparts to the formation of sixteenth-century Safavid and Shaybanid territorial domains."[77] By invoking the *Shahnamah*, then, the Uzbeks could identify or correlate their own territory with Firdawsi's Turan. This could explain why Kuhistani chose to forego imitating Khvandamir in much of his narrative and instead rely upon Firdawsi.

Two Shah Tahmasb-Era Universal Histories

The reign of the Safavid Shah Tahmasb witnessed the composition of a number of universal histories. These texts differ from the *Habib al-siyar* in the sense that they are much shorter, and their pre-Safavid sections devote only a few sentences to Kayumars. There are a number of reasons why this may be the case. As the Safavid dynasty was establishing itself, we see the Safavid portion of the universal histories becoming lengthier, while the pre-Safavid portions became shorter. Later, by the time of Shah 'Abbas, dynastic history, along with the regnal history – or aspects of the regnal history – of Shah 'Abbas himself would replace universal history as the most popular genres.[78] But at this time, we see the transition from universal to dynastic and

75 Rieu, *Catalog of Persian Manuscripts in the British Museum*, 1: 102–103.

76 Jaimee K. Comstock-Skipp, "Heroes of Legend, Heroes of History: Militant Manuscripts of the Shaybani Uzbeks in Transoxiana," forthcoming, 6.

77 Comstock-Skipp, "Heroes of Legend," 10.

78 See Quinn, *Historical Writing*, 24–28.

Table 4.5 ***General organizational scheme of the*** **Lubb al-tavarikh**

Qism (section) 1: The Prophet Muhammad and the Imams
fasl (chapter) 1: Muhammad
fasl 2: The Imams
Qism II: Pre-Islamic kings
fasl 1: Pishdadiyan
fasl 2: Kayanids
fasl 3: The party kings
fasl 4: Sasanians
Qism III: Groups who reigned after Islam
maqalah (discourse) 1: A group who reigned after the prophet
maqalah 2: Umayyads
maqalah 3: Abbasids
Babs (divisions) 1–6: (1) The Sultans who ruled at the time of the 'Abbasids, (2) the Mongols, (3) the kings who ruled after the Mongols, (4) the Timurids, (5) the Turks, (6) the Uzbeks
Qism IV: The Safavids

regnal history occurring. Mir Yahya Sayfi Qazvini's *Lubb al-tavarikh* and Ghaffari's *Nusakh-i jahan-ara* reflect this historiographical shift.

Sayfi Qazvini's Lubb al-tavarikh

Sayfi Qazvini's table of contents divides his history into four main chapters, with the fourth and final chapter devoted to the Safavids. Overall, the Safavid portion of his history takes up some 12 percent of his chronicle (see Table 4.5). Sayfi Qazvini's brief account of Kayumars provides only two versions of Kayumars's identity. He says that (1) some historians call him Adam, and (2) some consider him to be the offspring (*nasl*) of Shem (Sam) b. Noah (Nuh), and Qazi Bayzavi in his *Nizam al-tavarikh* prefers this option. Sayfi Qazvini ends by stating that God knows which version is correct.[79] The rest of his narrative, in its entirety, is as follows:

According to all accounts, before him [Kayumars] there was no king. His place was in caves and he used to wear animal skins. At the end of his life he

[79] Yahya ibn 'Abd al-Latif Husayni Qazvini, *Lubb al-tavarikh*, ed. Mir Hashim Muhaddis (Tehran: Anjuman-i Asar va Mafakhir-i Farhangi, 1386 [2007]), 46.

constructed buildings and made homes and the cities came forth from that. Kayumars lived 1000 years but reigned for 30 years. Among his works are Istakr-Fars and Damavand and Balkh.[80]

While Sayfi Qazvini's referencing Nasir al-Din Bayzavi's *Nizam al-tavarikh* (ca. 674/1275–1276) – a short Mongol-era universal history and the prolific author's only Persian work – at the beginning of his narrative suggests that Bayzavi was his main source; in reality, Sayfi Qazvini imitates in an almost word-for-word manner an intermediary and unnamed source, the universal history of a fellow Qazvini from the Mongol era, Hamd Allah Mustawfi Qazvini's (ca. 680–ca. 744/ca. 1281–ca. 1344) *Tarikh-i guzidah*.[81] Mustawfi Qazvini composed his history in 730/1329–1330 and dedicated it to Khvajah Ghiyas al-Din Muhammad, son and successor to the famous Ilkhanid vizier and scholar, Rashid al-Din.[82] The following parallel passages demonstrate where Sayfi Qazvini obtained his information from and the relationship between these two texts. The excerpt from the *Tarikh-i guzidah* is not reproduced in its entirety. The portion represented by ellipses [. . .] will be discussed below:

Mustawfi Qazvini *Tarikh-i guzidah*	Sayfi Qazvini *Lubb al-tavarikh*
However, according to all accounts, before him [Kayumars] there was no king. He lived in caverns and he would wear the skin of animals. At the end of his life he built buildings and constructed houses; villages and cities came forth from those . . . Kayumars was a thousand years old, but he was king for 30, after killing the demons (*dīvs*). Among his works are Istakhr in Fars and Damavand and Balkh.[83]	According to all accounts, before him [Kayumars] there were no monarchs. He lived in caverns and he would wear the skin of animals. At the end of his life he built buildings and constructed houses, and cities came forth from those. Kayumars lived 1000 years, but reigned for 30 years. Among the works of his are Istakhr in Fars and Damavand and Balkh.[84]

80 Qazvini, *Lubb al-tavarikh*, 46.
81 For an account of Bayzavi's narrative on Kayumars, see Hartman, *Gayōmart*, 156–158; XXX–XXXII.
82 Qazvini, *Lubb al-tavarikh*, 46.
83 Hamd Allah Mustawfi Qazvini, *Tarikh-i guzidah*, ed. 'Abd al-Husayn Nava'i (Tehran: Mu'assasah-i Amir Kabir, 1339 [1960]), 75–76.
84 Qazvini, *Lubb al-tavarikh*, 46.

Ammā bi-hamah qawlī, pīsh az ū shāh nabūd. Maqām-i ū dar ghārhā būdī va pūst-i ḥayvānāt pūshīdī. Dar ākhar-i ʻumr ʻimārāt sākht va khānah kard, dīh va shahr az ān paydā gasht … Az ās̲ārash Iṣṭakhr-i Fārs va Damāvand va Balkh ast.	*Bih hamah qawl pīsh az ū pādishāh nabūdah. Maqām-i ū dar ghārhā būdah va pūst-i ḥayvānāt pūshīdī. Dar ākhar-i ʻumr ʻimārāt sākht va khānah kard va shahr az ān paydā gasht. Az ās̲ār-i ū baʻẓī az Iṣṭakhr-i Fārs va Damāvand va Balkh ast.*

These passages demonstrate that despite the popularity of both Mirkhvand's *Rawzat al-safa* and Khvandamir's *Habib al-siyar*, Sayfi Qazvini looks to an earlier universal history written in his home town of Qazvin as a model to imitate. Sayfi Qazvini could have made this choice because the *Tarikh-i guzidah* was of a length that approximated Sayfi Qazvini's own history. Another possibility is that Sayfi Qazvini relied on those sources that were available to him, and the work of a fellow Qazvini could have been more accessible than, say, the *Rawzat al-safa* or the *Habib al-siyar*.

The portion of the *Tarikh-i guzidah* that Sayfi Qazvini chose to remove says something about his historiographical priorities. The parallel passages quoted above are nearly word-for-word identical, with two exceptions. The first is that he eliminates the short phrase "after killing the demons (*dīv*s)," thereby omitting any reference to these mythological creatures from his narrative. The second omission consists of this portion from the *Tarikh-i guzidah*:

He had a son named Siyamak and according to another account [Siyamak was] his grandson. The divs at that time were not hidden from humans and they were governed by human beings. For that reason, Siyamak fortified against the divs, and the divs killed him. Kayumars sorrowed in separation from him, until Hushang the son of Siyamak, and according to one account, the son of Farvāk bin Siyamak grew up. Grandfather and grandson together went to fight the divs, and they killed the leader of the divs, as they wanted to revenge Siyamak.

Kayumars when he became ruler of the world
He first created a place inside the mountain
He came forth from the mountain crowned and enthroned
Wearing leopard skin along with his people
He was king and ruled well for 30 years
He was like a fixed sun to the world

(Firdawsi, *Shahnamah*)
And according to one account, they say that he did not call himself king (*pādishāh*).[85]

Mustawfi Qazvini is the second chronicler examined here who quotes directly from the *Shahnamah*. Charles Melville has shown that early Timurid chroniclers, particularly Sharaf al-Din ʻAli Yazdi, either emulated or incorporated the *Shahnamah* into his *Zafarnamah*, thereby acknowledging the influence of the great epic poem on Timurid historiography and on dynastic legitimacy.[86] This practice did not originate with the Timurids, as Melville notes the importance of the *Shahnamah* in Ravandi's *Rahat al-sudur* and Juvayni's *Tarikh-i jahangusha*.[87] It is significant that Sayfi Qazvini chose to omit this particular passage in his narrative on Kayumars, because in doing so, he removed the more legendary and mythical elements from his account. The mischievous demons and the heroic Kayumars who slayed the demon leader in revenge for his son's murder are gone, and so too is the passage quoted from the *Shahnamah*. Sayfi Qazvini has retained the least legendary elements in the story. Why? In his *Encyclopedia Iranica* entry on Sayfi Ghazvini, Kioumars Ghereghlou states that

> Sayfi's narrative rests on a solid chronological foundation, a feature that makes it the precursor of annalistic historiography in Safavid Iran as exemplified in the works of such late 16th-century historians as Aḥmad Ḡaffāri Qazvini, Ḥasan Rumlu, and Aḥmad Ḥosayni Qomi.[88]

We may perhaps, then, view the *Lubb al-tavarikh* as something of a transitional text between the early Safavid universal histories that contain a great deal of legendary material and the more sober annalistic and dynastic chronicles and histories of a single ruler that were so

85 Mustawfi Qazvini, *Tarikh-i Guzidah*, 75–76.
86 Charles Melville, "ʻAli Yazdi and the *Shāhnāme*," in *International Shāhnāme Conference the Second Millennium*, ed. Forogh Hashbeiky (Uppsala: Acta Universitatis Upsaliensis, 2015), 128. For more on the *Shahnamah* in Timurid sources, see Michele Bernardini has discussed the role of the *Shahnamah* in Timurid sources. See Michele Bernardini, "The *Shahnama* in Timurid Historiography," in *Shahnama Studies III: The Reception of the Shahnama*, eds. Gabrielle van den Berg and Charles Melville, 155–172 (Leiden: Brill, 2018).
87 Melville, "ʻAli Yazdi and the *Shāhnāme*," 126.
88 *EIR*, s.v., "Sayfi Qazvini," by Kioumars Ghereghlou.

prevalent in the later Safavid period. The *Nusakh-i jahan-ara* takes these tendencies even further.

Qazi Ahmad Ghaffari's Nusakh-i jahan-ara *(*Tarikh-i jahan-ara*)*

Qazi Ahmad Ghaffari (d. 975/1567–1568), who came from a learned family in Qazvin, wrote the last universal history, the *Nusakh-i jahan-ara* (974/1564–1565) under the Safavids until the post-Shah ʻAbbas period. In a sense, his narrative represents the final "moment" of universal history writing under the Safavids, and it thus should not come as a surprise that his account of Kayumars consists of only one sentence:

> Kayumars bin Awlad bin Umim bin Aram bin Arfashah bin Sam (Shem) bin Nuh (Noah), upon him be peace, was titled Gil Shah, meaning the viceregent (*valī*) of mud/earth. His reign was 30 years. Istakhr and Fars and Damavand were amongst the cities he established.[89]

In this account, we find just one genealogy for Kayumars, his title, the length of his reign, which is a plausible number as opposed to a mythical extra-human period of time, and the name of the cities he allegedly built.

The rest of the "first created" (*pīshdādī*) kings receive similarly abbreviated treatment, whereas the Safavid portion of the history takes up approximately one fifth of the chronicle. By the time of Ghaffari's writing, then, historiographical interest was clearly shifting away from universal history. The next history written under the Safavids was the *Futuhat-i humayun*, a history covering the first twelve years of Shah ʻAbbas's reign.[90] The Safavids would not produce another universal history until after the death of Shah ʻAbbas.[91]

It is interesting to note that at the same time that narratives of Kayumars were reduced to just one sentence in the *Nusakh-i jahan-ara*; in another genre, Kayumars spectacularly occupied the center stage. As noted above, a famous illustrated *Shahnamah* produced

89 Qazi Ahmad Ghaffari Qazvini Kashani, *Tarikh-i jahan-ara*, ed. Hasan Naraqi (Tehran: Kitab'furushi-i Hafiz, 1342 [1963]), 28.

90 Only one portion of this history has survived.

91 See Storey, *Persian Literature*, 1: 130–131, for descriptions of Kamal Khan b. Jalal Munajjim's *Zubdat al-tavarikh* and Muhammad Yusuf Valah's *Khuld-i barin*.

during the reign of Shah Tahmasb contained a painting of Kayumars by Sultan Muhammad, who was one of several artists who worked on the project. According to Sultan Muhammad's fellow artist Dust Muhammad, when the other artists saw this painting, they "hung their heads in shame."[92] In his analysis of illustrated histories in the Safavid period, Charles Melville suggests what might account for this disparity, noting that "illustrations of the rise of Islam" migrated "from the latter 'universal history' to works specifically devoted to that subject, most notable in the *Qisas al-anbiya* (stories of the Prophets) genre."[93] It could similarly follow that pre-Islamic Persian history "migrated" to *Shahnamah* production at the same time that dynastic historiography was eclipsing universal history writing.[94]

The Influence of Mirkhvand's *Rawzat al-safa* on Three Universal Histories

Ibrahim ibn Hariri's Tarikh-i Ibrahimi

The earliest historical work written under the Mughals was Babur's own autobiography, the *Baburnamah*, and several of his royal descendants followed suit in writing their own memoirs. The *Baburnamah* set a historiographical precedent of sorts, whereby the composition of a number of autobiographical works inspired by this text followed. For example, Akbar ordered a number of family members and friends write their own memoirs so that Abu al-Fazl could use them in his *Akbarnamah* for accounts of Babur and Humayun.[95] Subsequently, the Mughal emperor Jahangir also wrote his autobiography, and thus the genre became more popular than under the Ottomans or the

92 Stuart Cary Welch, *The Shah-nameh of Shah Tahmasp* (New York: The Metropolitan Museum of Art, 1972). On the afterlife of this manuscript, see Üner Rüstem, "The Afterlife of a Royal Gift: The Ottoman Inserts of the Shāhnāma-i shāhī," *Muqaranas* 29 (2012): 245–337.

93 Charles Melville, "The Illustration of History in Safavid Manuscript Painting," in *New Perspectives on Safavid Iran: Empire and Society*, ed. Colin P. Mitchell, 171 (London: Routledge, 2014).

94 This does not, of course, suggest that the Safavids lacked "world consciousness," as Sanjay Subrahmanyam has cautioned us to remember, but that reasons for changes in historiographical emphases are complex and multidimensional. See Sanjay Subrahmanyam, "On World Historians in the Sixteenth Century," *Representations* 91 (2005): 45.

95 See Zaman, "Instructive Memory," 682.

Safavids, and also enjoyed a certain legitimacy due to the resources and energy devoted to producing such memoirs, with assistance from the Mughal monarchs themselves.[96] While this did not preclude the production of other types of history, it may explain why we see the first instance of universal history writing comparatively late, with Ibrahim bin Hariri (or Jariri)'s *Tarikh-i Ibrahimi* or *Tarikh-i Humayuni*, a little-known or utilized universal history composed in 956 or 957/1549 or 1550.

In some ways, Ibrahim's account of Kayumars echoes the accounts of Mirkhvand and Khvandamir, but it is considerably shorter than either of these earlier histories. Ibrahim offers three alternative versions of Kayumars's genealogy, saying that he was either:

(1) The oldest offspring of Adam
(2) Mim b. Laud b. Aram b. Shem (Sam) b. Noah (Nuh)
or
(3) The son of Shem (Sam) b. Noah (Nuh)[97]

Noticeably absent from this list is the genealogical claim that equated Kayumars with Adam, so common to nearly all the chronicles examined here. Furthermore, it seems the case that over time, chroniclers showed less interest in establishing Kayumars's identity at all, presenting fewer possible ancestries for Kayumars. Ibrahim may have chosen not to equate Kayumars with Adam because other Mughal chronicles such as Abu al-Fazl in his *Akbarnamah* traced Akbar's genealogy back to Adam. After the genealogical discussion, Ibrahim references Qazi Bayzavi in stating that Kayumars built Istakhr and Damavand, and according to some, he also built Balkh. Ibrahim adds one anecdote explaining how Balkh received its name. He also notes that Kayumars introduced inventions and practices such as bridles, saddles, riding, and spinning and said that he reigned for either 30 or 40 years and lived for 1,000 years.[98] He ends his narrative with an account of one of Kayumars's sayings.[99] Ibrahim's inclusion of this maxim is unique in the early modern universal histories discussed here. Only one earlier author, Sharaf al-Din Fazl

[96] Zaman argues "that auto/biographical writing, which threads through several genres, is central to the historiography of early Mughal India." Zaman, "Instructive Memory," 677.

[97] Ibrahim bin Hariri, "Tarikh-i Ibrahimi," ms. British Library India Office ISL 1874, f. 32a. Here after cited as "Tarikh-i Ibrahimi."

[98] "Tarikh-i Ibrahimi," f. 32b. [99] "Tarikh-i Ibrahimi," f. 32b.

Allah Husayni Qazvini (d. 740/1339), ends the Kayumars account in his *al-Mu'jam fi asar muluk al-a'jam* (684/1258) with four Arabic maxims ascribed to Kayumars.[100] Khvandamir reproduces two of these in his *Ma'asir al-muluk*. Ibrahim includes only one such saying, but it is in Persian, and not a translation of the Arabic maxims, so unless an earlier source containing this poem is found, we must consider this a unique addition to the narrative. Ibrahim states that

> Among his sayings is "Retesting someone who is already educated, and scratching the forehead of a fierce lion with the nail of friendship, and freeing enemies after their being in shackles is the work of crazy people."[101]

Ibrahim was not, however, the only chronicler who included this saying. The author of the *Tarikh-i ilchi-yi Nizam Shah* did the same, and we next turn to that text.

Qubad al-Husayni's Tarikh-i ilchi-yi Nizam Shah *(970/1562–1563)*

Khvurshah b. Qubad al-Husayni's (d. 972/1564–1565) account of Kayumars in his *Tarikh-i ilchi-yi Nizam Shah*, a universal history written by Burhan Nizam Shah I's (r. 914–961/1508–1553) ambassador to the court of Shah Tahmasb, primarily imitates the *Rawzat al-safa*, as evidenced by the following parallel passages describing how Kayumars became king:

Rawzat al-safa	*Tarikh-i Ilchi-yi Nizam Shah*
When he had ratified, by oath, his assent to the conditions proposed by the people of the kingdom and the heads of the state, he was seated on the throne of the sultanate.[102]	When he had ratified his assent to the conditions proposed by the nobles of the kingdom and the heads of the state, he placed the kingly crown upon his brow and sat on the throne of kingship.[103]
Chūn paymān-i ahl-i mulk va millat rā dar bāb-i [muṭāva'at] bih īmān	*Chūn ū paymān-i a'yān-i mulk va millat rā bi-īmān mu'kad gardānīd tāj-i*

[100] Sharaf al-Din Fazl Allah Husayni Qazvini, *al-Mu'jam fi asar muluk al-a'jam*, ed. Ahmad Futuhi'nasab (Tehran: Anjuman-i asar va mafakhir-i farhangi, 2005), 89.

[101] Khvurshah ibn Qubad al-Husayni, "Tarikh-i ilchi-yi Nizam Shah," ms. British Library ADD 23513, f. 14b.

[102] Mirkhvand, *Rawzat al-safa*, 1: 569; trans., 49.

[103] Qubad al-Husayni, "Tarikh-i ilchi-yi Nizam Shah," f. 13b.

mu'kad gardānīdah tāj-i shāhī bar sar nahād va bar sarīr-i saltanat mutamakin gasht.	*khusravī bar farq-i humāyūn nahād va bar masnad-i shāhī bi-nishast.*

Qubad al-Husayni reproduces in condensed form a number of the same anecdotes about Kayumars from the *Rawzat al-safa*, thereby streamlining his narrative. Qubad al-Husayni's account gives us pause to consider the phenomenon of imitative writing via an intermediary source and cautions that chroniclers many not actually be imitating the source that they name. Such is the case with Qubad al-Husayni's mentioning the *Tarikh-i mu'jam* and the *Nizam al-tavarikh*.[104] Although he specifically names these sources, in reality he is imitating the *Rawzat al-safa*:

Rawzat-i safa	*Tarikh-i ilchi-yi Nizam Shah*
And it becomes thus apparent from the *Tarikh-i mu'jam* and the *Nizam al-tavarikh* that the name of the son of Kayumars—who was killed by the hand of the demons (*dīvs*) at Mount Damavand—was Siyamak. And from the history of Hafiz Abru it becomes thus understood that when Kayumars was finished with building Balkh, he ordered some of his children to settle in that region [and] he returned to Istakhr.[105]	In histories it is presented that that son who was killed by the hand of the demons (*dīvs*)was named Siyamak, and this understanding is mentioned in the histories of the *Mu'jam* and the *Nizam al-tavarikh*. However, Hafiz Abru in his own history has said that after completing the history of Balkh, God gave him a son and he named him Siyamak.[106]
Va az Tārīkh-i mu'jam *va* Niẓām al-tavārīkh *chinān ma'lūm mīshavad*	*Dar tavārīkh āmadah kih ān pisar kih bi-dast-i dīvān kushtah shud ū rā*

104 The *Tarikh-i mu'jam*, or *al-Mu'jam fi athar muluk al-'ajam* is by Sharaf al-Din Fazl Allah Husayni Qazvini, who wrote during the reign of the Atabak ruler Nusrat al-Din Ahmad b. Yusuf Shah (r. 695 or 696–730 or 733/1295 or 1296–1329 or 1333). See Storey, *Persian Literature*, I: 243. See also Hartman, *Gayōmart*, 160–183. The *Nizam al-tavarikh* (ca. 674/1275) is a well-known Mongol history by Qazi Bayzavi. Melville has written extensively on the historiography of this chronicle. See Charles Melville, "From Adam to Abaqa: Qāḍī Baiḍāwī's Rearrangement of History," *Studia Iranica* 30 (2001): 67–86; and Charles Melville, "From Adam to Abaqa: Qāḍī Baiḍāwī's Rearrangement of History (Part II)," *Studia Iranica* 36 (2007): 7–64.

105 Mirkhvand, *Rawzat al-safa*, 1: 573; trans., 61.

106 Qubad al-Husayni, "Tarikh-i ilchi-yi Nizam Shah," f. 14a.

kih nām-i pisar-i Kayūmars kih bar dast-i dīvān bih kūh-i Damāvand kushtah shud Siyāmak būd. Va az tārīkh-i Ḥāfiẓ Abrū chinān mafhūm mī'gardad kih chūn Kayūmars az banā-yi Balkh fārigh shud ba'ẓī az awlād-i khūd rā dar ān diyār bih tavaṭṭun amr farmūdah khūd bih jānib-i Iṣṭakhr mu'āvvadat namūd.

Siyāmak nām būd va īn ma'nī dar tavārīkh-i Mu'jam *va* Niẓām al-tavārīkh *zikr raftah ammā Ḥāfiẓ Abrū dar tavārīkh-i khūd āvardah kih Kayūmars rā ba'd az ittimām-i shahr-i Balkh khudā-yi ṭa'lá farzandī bi-ū dād nām-i ū Siyāmak guẕasht.*

While Qubad al-Husayni's primary model is the *Rawzat al-safa*, there is some evidence suggesting that he might have been familiar with Ibrahim's history. This is due to his quoting, at the end of his account, the same maxim found at the end of the *Tarikh-i Ibrahimi*: "Retesting someone who is already educated, and scratching the forehead of a fierce lion with the nail of friendship, and freeing enemies after their being in shackles, is the work of crazy people." None of the other chronicles examined here include this particular detail, suggesting that al-Husayni may have had access to the *Tarikh-i Ibrahimi* while he was in the Mughal empire. As we know very little about the author of the *Tarikh-i Ibrahimi*, we cannot place him definitively within the orbit of Qubad al-Husayni. However, until another source for this saying of Kayumars is found, we must assume that Qubad al-Husayni relied on the *Tarikh-i Ibrahimi* for this portion of his chronicle.

Muhammad Muslih al-Din Lari's (d. 979/1572) Mir'at al-advar va mirqat al-akhbar

Muslih al-Din Lari was, like Khvandamir, a historian on the move. Among Lari's writings is the *Mirat al-advar*, an extensive universal history ending in 974/1566. Certain portions of the *Mirat al-advar* suggest that Lari was familiar with and relied on Mirkhvand's *Rawzat al-safa*, which by the time of Lari's writing, as noted above, was well known in the Ottoman empire and had even been translated into Ottoman Turkish some sixteen years before Lari composed his history.

Like Ibrahim, Lari opens his account of Kayumars with three variants of Kayumars's ancestry. These are not the same genealogies that we see in Ibrahim's history. Lari's first identification is that "most say he is the son of Shem (Sam)," but only two of the universal chronicles examined here make this point: Qazvini's *Lubb al-tavarikh* and Khvandamir's *Habib al-siyar*. The other two reference specific texts or historians: al-Ghazali's *Nasihat al-muluk* and Qazi Bayzavi:

(1) Most say he is the son of Shem (Sam).
(2) Al-Ghazali in the *Nasayih al-muluk*, says he is the brother of Seth (Shis).
(3) Qazi Bayzavi says he is descended from Noah, because according to historians, at the time of Manuchihr, Abraham had appeared, and from him to Kayumars, to the Persians, is 1,200 years, and from the time of Moses to the time of the flood the same [amount of] time.[107]

Conspicuously absent from Lari's account, like that of Ibrahim, is any mention of Kayumars being equated with Adam. This omission seems to diminish Kayumars's position in ancient mythical history. In removing this particular identification for Kayumars, Lari might be maintaining the pristine Islamic status of the first man, Adam, and thereby downgrading Kayumars's identity in this respect.

Despite not equating Kayumars with Adam, Lari does assert that Kayumars was divinely assisted in assuming the throne. His account of Kayumars becoming king states that

> When Kayumars adorned the throne of kingship with divine assistance, [both] jinn and humans were subdued by his heroic power and submitted to his authority ... [he] was distinguished and distinct by [his] perfect conduct, a beautiful image and excellent majesty. And the generality of people and jinn (*'ām-i thaqalayn*) turned their faces every day to his glorious court, and with obedience to his commands, lifted up their heads in exaltation.[108]

In this passage, Kayumars was not appointed by a religious figure, as we saw in the *Bahjat al-tavarikh*, nor was he nominated by nobles of the land, as narrated in the *Rawzat al-safa*. The only power that caused him to become king was divine power.

Lari's account is consistent with Sayfi Qazvini in terms of its brevity, making it similar to the Safavid universal histories written under Shah Tahmasb. He gives a short sketch of Kayumars's accomplishments, noting that he built Balkh and was responsible for saddles, bridles,

[107] Lari, *Mir'at al-advar*, 33. [108] Lari, *Mir'at al-advar*, 33–34.

riding, and weaving. Lari says Kayumars's son was called Siyamak, who was killed by *jinn*, and explains that Kayumars mourned his death and asked God for revenge. Lari ends his account by noting that different historians had estimated the length of his reign to be anywhere between 30 and 1,000 years.[109]

While the *Mir'at al-advar* lacks the detail that we see in earlier narratives like the *Rawzat al-safa* and the *Habib al-siyar*, Lari seems to be alluding to the stories in them, thereby demonstrating his familiarity with the earlier historiographical tradition. The most interesting example of this appears in the story of Kayumars and the death of his son, whom Mirkhvand and Khvandamir do not name. In the *Rawzat al-safa* and *Habib al-siyar*, we read that when Kayumars's son died, he buried him in a well at the top of a mountain, and then lit a fire at the mouth of the well. This is the same passage analyzed above, where Khvandamir removes the negative reference to the Magi from his *Rawzat al-safa*-based account. Lari does not mention any of these specifics, except he does state that the son's name was Siyamak. However, he makes a subtle allusion to that fire in his description of Kayumars's sorrow and anger over his son's death, suggesting that he was familiar with the *Rawzat al-safa* and the *Habib al-siyar*, when he says: "Kayumars, from the intensity of his horror, threw the fire of anger into the heap of hope."[110] Lari then quotes four couplets (*bayt*) from Jami's *Haft awrang*. The first couplet continues with the theme of fire:

> The sigh of the universe was set alight
> From the effects of this heart-burning story[111]

Lari's use of fire imagery at the same point in the narrative where Mirkhvand and Khvandamir stated that Kayumars building an actual fire cannot be a coincidence. Rather, he seems to be improvising on a theme or story by using the imagery in the story in an abstract manner, while simultaneously quoting a popular poem at his time of writing, Mawlana 'Abd al-Rahman Jami's (817–898/1414–1492) *Haft awrang*.

[109] Lari, *Mir'at al-advar*, 34. [110] Lari, *Mir'at al-advar*, 34.
[111] Lari, *Mir'at al-advar*, 34.

Lari's including the poetry of Jami provides an interesting insight into the popularity of certain texts in the sixteenth century. Indeed, Jami's *Haft awrang*, a collection of seven *masnavis*, occupied a special position in Persianate circles at the time of Lari's writing. Some ten years prior to Lari's completing the *Mir'at al-advar*, the Safavid prince Sultan Ibrahim (946–984/1540–1577) had commissioned a luxurious copy of Jami's *Haft awrang*. The project took some nine years to complete, with numerous artists and calligraphers contributing to it.[112] In addition to this specific manuscript, the poem was extremely popular in nonroyal circles.[113] Lari quotes from a specific poem (*masnavī*) within the *Haft awrang*, the *Khiradnamah-i Iskandari*, or "Alexander's Book of Wisdom." The portion of the poem that he cites is from the death of Alexander. In reproducing these lines, Lari indirectly associates Kayumars with Alexander the Great, a figure who was considered both a prophet and a king of great magnitude in the Islamic tradition.[114] However, he does so in an extremely indirect way. Overall, Lari's account is unique in quoting from Jami and in his indirect allusions to the *Rawzat al-safa* and *Habib al-siyar*.

Two Mughal Universal Chronicles

We have already encountered Mughal universal history writing with the *Tarikh-i Ibrahimi*, a chronicle which echoed, in terms of its Kayumars section, the *Rawzat al-safa* and the *Habib al-siyar*. Two more Mughal chroniclers from the time of Akbar composed universal histories. These texts differ from their Safavid counterparts in the sense that, although they are brief, they include stories about Kayumars that we see in much earlier Timurid and pre-Timurid sources, and introduce new details to the narrative.

112 Mariana Shreve Simpson, *Sultan Ibrahim Mirza's* Haft Awrang: *A Princely Manuscript from Sixteenth-Century Iran* (New Haven, CT: Yale University Press, 1997), 13.

113 Shreve Simpson, *Sultan Ibrahim*, 27, n. 45.

114 For a discussion of Alexander in the *Khiradnamah-i Iskandari*, see Minoo S. Southgate, "Portrait of Alexander in Persian Alexander-Romances of the Islamic Era," *Journal of the American Oriental Society* 97 (1977): 279, 282–283.

Vuqu'i's Majami al-akhbar

Vuqu'i's *Majami al-akhbar* contains a unique combination of accounts of Kayumars. While his narrative follows a similar structure to earlier narratives by opening with Kayumars's genealogy, including some familiar details, he introduces a number of elements that do not appear in any other source examined here.

Vuqu'i presents four versions of Kayumars's genealogy: (1) some consider him to be the offspring of Shem (Sam) b. Noah (Nuh), (2) and they also call him the son of Elam (Lam) b. Shem (Sam) b. Noah (Nuh); (3) some consider him to be the brother of Seth, and (4) a group of the Magi consider him Adam because he was the first king among the kings of the world.[115] We find three of these variations in the *Rawzat al-safa/Habib al-siyar* tradition, but his statement that some consider Kayumars the brother of Seth only appears in Muslih al-Din Lari's *Mir'at al-advar*.

Vuqu'i's treatment of Kayumars is relatively short. Like many historians before him, he states that Kayumars was the first king (*pādishāh*) of the world, whose name in Syriac means living speech (*ḥay nāṭiq*), a detail that can be traced back to Bal'ami's *Tarikh*. He goes on to state that Kayumars would roam naked around the world, and he named whatever he saw in the mountains and desert. He also defeated the enemies of the biblical Cain. He wore the skin of animals, and engaged in building and agriculture. Then, in a passage that lightly imitates Mirkhvand's *Rawzat al-safa*, Vuqu'i highlights Kayumars's justice:

Rawzat al-safa	*Majami' al-akhbar*
Through the influence of his equity, the magnet ceased to attract iron and the amber refrained from oppressing the straw.[116]	During his era of justice, the magnet and the amber refrained from controlling (*taṣarruf*) iron and straw.[117]
ū miqnātīs az sar-i jaẕb-i āhan dar guẕasht va kāhrubā dast-i ta'arruż az dāman-i kāh kūtāh gardānīd.	*Dar 'ahd-i 'adl-i ū miqnātīs va kāhrubā dast-i taṣarruf az āhan va kāh kūtāh kardand.*

[115] Vuqu'i, "Majami' al-akhbar," f. 29a.
[116] Mirkhvand, *Rawzat al-safa*, lithography (Bombay, n.p., 1261 [1845]), 205.
[117] Vuqu'i, "Majami' al-akhbar," f. 29b.

According to Vuqu'i, Kayumars worshipped one God, and when he finished his work with the world, he made his home in mountains and caves.

In terms of Kayumars's descendants, Vuqu'i states that he had a son named Mashi, and when Mashi grew up, he had a son named Siyamak, who himself had a son called Farud, who was Hushang's father. These three individuals (Mashi, Siyamak, and Farud) died during Kayumars's reign, which lasted for thirty years. When Kayumars died, his son Hushang became his successor. This narrative of Kayumars's descendants, which makes Hushang Kayumars's great great grandson, is also unique. Vuqu'i ends his account by noting the sayings that are inscribed around his pulpit (*minbar*). These sayings are as follows:

> Too much joy (*nishāt*) makes the soul (*nafs*) proud (*maghrūr*) and excessive happiness (*farraḥ*) destroys the heart.
>
> And sorrow is an opportunity from which is born the removal of bitterness.
>
> Prosperity (*na'mat*) is a branch that with the hand of gratitude becomes fresh (*tāzah*) and fruitful (*barūmand*).[118]

Here, Vuqu'i adds moral imperatives that warn against excess happiness, that celebrate the benefits of sorrow, and that remind one of the importance of gratitude. Whether Vuqu'i was reflecting on his own life, or sending a message to a potential patron, is unclear. Whatever the case, he seems to have felt he had the intellectual and creative space to innovate in his account of Kayumars. Finally, while Vuqu'i's description of the sayings inscribed on Kayumars's pulpit does not appear in any earlier text, it is interesting to note that he places this information at the end of the narrative, in the same structural position where other chroniclers included sayings or maxims of Kayumars.

Reviving an Earlier Tradition: Sabzavari's *Rawzat al-tahirin*

Tahir Muhammad Sabzavari's treatment of Kayumars in his *Rawzat al-tahirin* (1014/1605–1606) is unique in the way that he explains where he obtained his information about the pre-Islamic Persian kings. Apparently, the Mughal emperor Akbar had requested a certain Mawlana Taqi al-Din Muhammad Shushtari to "extract" from

[118] Vuqu'i, "Majami' al-akhbar," f. 29b.

Firdawsi's *Shahnamah* the portion from the beginning of the Persian kings to the end of Kaykhusraw.[119] Shushtari, however, was so grieved over the death of Akbar that he stopped working on the text and asked his friend, Sabzavari, to complete the project, which he did.[120] Indeed, in the beginning of his discussion of pre-Islamic Persian kings, Sabzavari relates this state of affairs and presents a brief account of the circumstances under which Firdawsi came to write his *Shahnamah*, reproducing a number of lines from this poem. This would make it appear that Sabzavari based his account of Kayumars on the *Shahnamah* itself. Such is not the case, however. Sabzavari in fact reproduces a poem from the *Rawzat al-safa*, indicating that he is using this text as his model:

Rawzat al-safa	*Rawzat al-tahirin*
As soon as he ratified by oath his assent to the conditions proposed by the nobles of the realm and the heads of religion, his auspicious brow was encircled with the royal diadem and he was seated on the imperial throne.	The first person who was fixed upon the throne of authority was Kayumars, such as the poet says
The first khediv [ruler] who conquered the world For those who wore the crown was Kayumars.[121]	The first khediv [ruler] who conquered the world For those who wore the crown was Kayumars.[122]

In terms of genealogy, Sabzavari calls him Kayumars b. Laud b. Umim b. Aram b. Arfakhshad (Arpakhshad) b. Shem (Sam) b. Noah (Nuh). This genealogy bears some resemblance to Kayumars's genealogy in the *Rawzat al-safa*. He also states that Kayumars is known as the father of humanity (*abū al-bashar*), that

119 See Rieu, *Catalogue of the Persian Manuscripts*.
120 See Rieu, *Catalogue of the Persian Manuscripts*, 1: 119, and Vuqu'i, "Majami' al-akhbar," f. 15b. For a discussion of the *Rawzat al-tahirin* in relation to the writing of world history, see Subrahmanyam, "On World Historians."
121 Mirkhvand, *Rawzat al-safa*, 569; trans., 49.
122 Tahir Muhammad Sabzavari, "Rawżat al-ṭāhirīn," ms. Oxford Bodleian Elliot 314, f. 16b. The poem transliterated is as follows: "*Nukhustīn khidīvī kih kishvar gushūd/sar-i tājdārān Kayumars būd.*"

some historians call him the son of Shem (Sam) b. Noah (Nuh), an ancestry that echoes the *Habib al-siyar*, and in the Syriac language, someone who is an orator (*shakhs-i sukhan-gūy*) is called Kayumars. Notably missing from his account is a statement that equates Kayumars with Adam.

Unlike the Safavid universal historians writing after Mirkhvand and Khvandamir, who sought to remove the legendary elements from their Kayumars narratives, Sabzavari revives a number of stories from the *Rawzat al-safa* that we do not see in other later chronicles. For example, he repeats the legend telling how Kayumars encountered an owl that screeched in his ear on his way to visit his son. He took this to be a bad omen when he discovered that the demons had killed him. He also mentions that the demons killed Kayumars's son Siyamak, who took revenge upon them by killing many of them.[123]

The last two Mughal universal histories discussed here and written under Akbar's reign differ strikingly from their Safavid counterparts. While the Safavid chroniclers Sayfi Qazvini and Ghaffari continued the process of de-mythologizing and shortening the story of Kayumars, Vuquʿi and Sabzavari looked back to the late Timurid *Rawzat al-safa* tradition and in the case of Sabzavari, the *Shahnamah*, when composing their accounts. Their histories also include unique details, suggesting that they had the creative space to innovate in their narratives.

Conclusion

This chapter has demonstrated that universal histories contain a variety of perspectives regarding Kayumars, in terms of his identity and the story of his elevation to kingship. There is no single narrative version that is common to every history, and our historians drew on a range of sources for their information. The choices they made in terms of their sources depended on factors such as regional loyalty and access, as in the case of Qazvini in the *Lubb al-tavarikh*, or family loyalty, as with Khvandamir and the *Habib al-siyar*. We also demonstrated that many chroniclers looked to the *Rawzat al-safa* as a model source, and chroniclers writing under Akbar's reign did not de-mythologize accounts of Kayumars like their Safavid counterparts. In many instances, chroniclers engaged in intertextual dialog as they

[123] Sabzavari, *Rawzat al-tahirin*, f. 17a.

updated, responded to, and modified their models. Being aware of their historiographical choices is the only way that we can understand how they modified their accounts of Kayumars, and by extension, other figures and events. For example, without knowing that Shukr Allah chose to imitate Balami, we would not know how he significantly changed the narrative of how Kayumars became king. Without knowing that Sayfi Qazvini imitated Mustawfi Qazvini, we would not know that he removed the more legendary aspects of Kayumars's life, perhaps in an attempt to focus on other aspects of historiography, such as chronology and dynastic history.

The very existence of Persian universal chronicles in the Ottoman, Safavid, and Mughal empires says something about their popularity and importance. In composing their histories, our chroniclers are drawing on an extensive body of historical material that had evolved for several hundred years. When read together comparatively and across empires, their narratives more closely represent variations on a theme, rather than separate and independent historiographical strands. Less polemical in nature than their dynastic chronicle cousins, they suggest the centrality to the Ottomans, Safavids, Shaybani Uzbeks, and Mughals, of a shared past.

5 Mirrors, Memorials, and Blended Genres

Introduction

The histories examined in Chapter 4 all fall under the category of universal history. Their authors often engaged in imitative writing as they rewrote accounts of Kayumars, the first Persian king. Rather than composing polemic accounts reflective of imperial political agendas, chroniclers composed their narratives of Kayumars by rewriting earlier narratives in often subtle and discreet ways. The political boundaries between empires were not as strong as the popularity of an early chronicle such as the *Rawzat al-safa*, which was utilized by a number of chroniclers across empires. Often, the chroniclers blended earlier narratives as they added their own distinct voices to their accounts. The sort of blending and re-creating discussed in connection with Kayumars was not the only way that chroniclers engaged in creative acts of historical writing. They also blended and combined the genres themselves, drawing on vast and rich Islamicate literatures to compose their narratives. For example, a Safavid chronicle such as Iskandar Beg Munshi's *Tarikh-i 'alam-ara-yi 'Abbasi*, while appearing as a "dynastic history," contains a brief introductory section on the ancestors of the Prophet, an element common to universal histories. He also includes a list of Shah 'Abbas's virtues at the beginning of his chronicle, and inserts, at various points, biographical sketches. Similarly, in a reverse example, Sam Mirza's (923–974/1527–1566/1567) *Tuhfah-i Sami* (ca. 957/1550) is predominantly a biographical compendium of poets (*tazkirah*), but it also contains a historical section on Shah Isma'il and the dynastic kings contemporary to him.[1]

This chapter will explore the ways in which two different types of Islamicate texts became incorporated into early modern Persianate historiography. Specifically, we will focus on two literary genres: one known as "mirrors for princes" and another, biographical compendia

[1] Sam Mirza Safavi, *Tuhfah-i Sami*, ed. Vahid Dastgirdi (Tehran: Armaghan, [1936]), 6.

(*tazkirahs*). While these two literatures exist as important stand-alone genres, by the early modern period, they made their way into some of the most important and influential Persian histories. Becoming familiar with the process of how the chroniclers blended genres allows us to read and utilize the histories in a more critical fashion. For example, reading lists of kingly virtues in Persian histories through a "mirrors for princes" lens helps us understand how and why the chroniclers chose to include the specific information that they included in their histories. And understanding how and why *tazkirahs* found a place in historical writing demonstrates how chroniclers used different genres to further their political and ideological agendas.

The Sources

As we have seen in previous chapters, the number of sources analyzed in relation to the dynasty under which they were written is uneven. In the first part of this chapter, the approach used is similar to that of Chapter 3, where two specific chronicles are analyzed in light of potential models or earlier influential texts. This discussion is limited to two sources, one Mughal and one Safavid, because none of the Persian Ottoman histories contain a section similar to those studied here. The texts are: (1) Muhammad Arif Qandahari's *Tarikh-i Akbari* (988/1580), and (2) Iskandar Beg Munshi's *Tarikh-i ʻalam-ara-yi ʻAbbasi* (1038/1629).

For the second part of this chapter, which examines the incorporation of *tazkirah* material into historical chronicles, I analyze seven chronicles, including one Ottoman, one Central Asian, two Safavid, and three Mughal histories. The reason for the larger number of Mughal sources and only one Ottoman or Central Asian source is due to the fact that these are the chroniclers who include *tazkirah* material in their histories: (1) Khvandamir, *Habib al-siyar*, (2) Dughlat, *Tarikh-i Rashidi*, (3) Lari, *Mir'at al-advar*, (4) Abu al-Fazl, *Akbarnamah*, (5) Nizam al-Din Bakhshi, *Tabaqat-i Akbari*, (6) Badauni, *Muntakhab al-tavarikh*, and (7) Iskandar Beg Munshi, *Tarikh-i ʻalam-ara-yi ʻAbbasi*.

Mirrors for Princes and Lists of Kingly Virtues

Our exploration of how mirrors for princes literature impacted early modern historical writing begins with "lists of kingly virtues." Safavid and Mughal chroniclers portray their kings in ways that reflect contemporary currents of political and religious legitimacies. How the chroniclers actually accomplish this depends largely on their backgrounds and areas of expertise. In general, however, they employ a number of narrative techniques throughout their chronicles, placing special emphasis on kingship in the all-important introductory sections of their accounts. In these portions of the histories, we find information that sheds much light on significant topics such as politics, religion, and kingship. These themes find expression in conventions – some of which are described in Chapter 2 – such as royal genealogies, dream narratives, myths of dynastic origin, horoscopes, and "lists of kingly virtues." Through analyzing "lists of kingly virtues," not only do we learn something about the nature of early modern Islamicate kingship but also we gain insight as to why the chronological portions of the chronicles contain certain types of information. In other words, there appears to be a correlation between the lists of kingly virtues and the contents of the rest of the chronicle. Here, we will first explore the historiographical background for lists of kingly virtues, and then analyze the relationship between those lists and rest of the history.

Kingly Virtues in the *Tarikh-i Akbari* and the *Tarikh-i 'alam-ara-yi 'Abbasi*

As the Ottoman, Safavid, and Mughal empires expanded and became increasingly powerful, their rulers made competing claims to universal rule. They attempted to distinguish themselves from their rivals and at the same time provide a suitable response to the claims being put forward by their counterparts. This is reflected in the historiography of the period. By the time of 'Abbas and Akbar, dynastic history was becoming the favored type of chronicle. At the same time, a new element appeared at the beginning of two Safavid and Mughal court chronicles – one which highlights the qualities and attributes of the king: Qandahari's *Tarikh-i Akbari* and Iskandar Beg Munshi's *Tarikh-i 'alam-ara-yi 'Abbasi.*

Qandahari devotes all of chapter six of his *Tarikh-i Akbari*, which follows immediately after his account of Akbar's coronation, to the virtues and deeds of his king. He does this, he says, because

> though, while describing his accession, some of the merits and good deeds of His majesty have already been narrated briefly, it however seems proper to mention further (of them), by this most humble beggar, the observer of these lines, of the incidents that happened day to day as a result of his laudable character, and praiseworthy deeds and auspicious actions undertaken by him. In short, a drop out of the ocean might be brought so that the world would be able to know and feel sure that its mention is not a mere formality.[2]

With this statement, Qandahari holds up Akbar as not only a king by virtue of his descent, but as someone whose character matches his position and rank. They number roughly thirty-four short entries (*fiqrahs*) that mostly consist of one or two sentences, although some are as long as half a page. Sometimes Qandahari provides a simple general statement or description of a particular characteristic, and in other instances he gives specific examples to back up his more general claims. For example, one of Akbar's attributes is that "he is a builder who dressed or adorned in a manner worth of pride, the buildings."[3] Qandahari follows this with specific examples of such buildings, mentioning "the great edifices in Fatehabad Sikri, and very strong and lasting forts of red stone in the capital city of Agra and the city of Lahore with burnt-bricks, as also in many other towns of Hindustan."[4]

Iskandar Beg Munshi organizes his chronicle into three treatises/books (*saḥīfah*). Book One, completed in 1025/1616, consists of twelve discourses (*maqālah*) and forms the introductory section of the chronicle. The first discourse is by far the longest. Here, Iskandar Beg presents Shah 'Abbas's genealogy and a brief account of his ancestors going back to the origins of the Safavid Sufi order. He follows this with accounts of the reigns of preceding Safavid kings, starting with Isma'il I and ending with Sultan Muhammad Khudabandah (r. 985–995/1578–1587). Discourses two to twelve are each devoted to one kingly virtue of Shah 'Abbas, and are much shorter. Finally, Books Two and Three, completed in 1038/1629, contain the chronological narrative of 'Abbas's rule.

2 Qandahari, *Tarikh-i Akbari*, 2 and 18; trans., 51.
3 Qandahari, *Tarikh-i Akbari*, 42; trans., 60.
4 Qandahari, *Tarikh-i Akbari*, 42; trans., 60–61.

Iskandar Beg explicitly states at the end of the first discourse why he decided to include this list of kingly virtues and place it at the beginning of his chronicle:

Readers who have studied Book I will have a foretaste of what is to come and will gain some idea of Shah 'Abbas's powers of innovation, his abilities as a ruler, and his other outstanding qualities, which enabled him with God's help to achieve such mighty victories, to improve the possibilities of advancement on the part of the officers of state, and to order the affairs of his people in such a way that both territory seizing sultans and masters of opinion (*ra'y*) and deliberation (*tadbīr*) will make this record their exemplar.[5]

By telling his audience how they should contextualize the information they read in Books Two and Three, Iskandar Beg provides a theoretical introduction or framework for his actual narrative of Shah 'Abbas's reign and suggests how to approach the chronological portion of his history. He also suggests that Shah 'Abbas was a model for both kings and clerics.

Shah 'Abbas's eleven kingly virtues according to Iskandar Beg are as follows: (1) his piety (*tavajjuh va istighrāq*), (2) his judgment, divinely given wisdom, and excellence of policies (*ra'y va dānish-i khudādād va ḥusn-i tadbīr*), which are in conformity with the Divine Will, (3) his being the "Lord of the Auspicious Conjunction" (*ṣāḥib-qirān*), (4) his justice (*'adl*), concern for security of the roads (*amniyat-i ṭuruq*) and welfare of his subjects (*ṭarqiyah-yi ḥāl-i 'ubbād*), (5) his authority and despotic behavior (*nafād-i amr-i qahhārī*), (6) his policy and administration (*ā'īn-i jahāndārī va farmānravā'ī*), (7) his simplicity of life (*darvīsh-nahādī*), lack of ceremony (*bī-takallufīhā*), and contrary qualities, (8) his concern for the rights (*ḥuqūq*) of his servants, and his not laying hands on their possessions, (9) his breadth of vision, knowledge of world affairs and classes of society (*ta'āruf-i aḥvāl-i 'ālam va ṭabaqāt-i 'umam*), (10) his public works and building achievements (*'imārāt*), and (11) his battles and victories (*muḥārabāt va futūḥāt*).

In terms of the basic features of this list, like those listed in the *Tarikh-i Akbari*, the amount of space devoted to each virtue varies. In this case, each entry ranges anywhere between approximately one

[5] Iskandar Beg, *'Alam-ara-yi 'Abbasi*, ed. Iraj Afshar, 2nd ed. 2 vols. (Tehran: Amir Kabir, 1350 [1971]), trans. Roger Savory as *The History of Shah 'Abbas the Great*, 2 vols. (Boulder, CO: Westview Press, 1978), 373; trans., 514, slightly modified.

half to six pages, with most about one and a half page long in the printed editions of the text. Under each general item, Iskandar Beg explains how Shah ʻAbbas reflects a particular attribute by providing specific examples. For example, in the eleventh discourse, which discusses his construction projects, Iskandar Beg refers either to the buildings that Shah ʻAbbas had erected or the improvements he made to the existing ones. Thus, he describes how in Ardabil, Shah ʻAbbas restored the tomb of Shaykh Zahid Gilani, Shaykh Safi's Sufi teacher, and how he put a gold railing around the dais on the shrine of Shaykh Jabra'il, another important Safavid Sufi ancestor. Iskandar Beg lists as new building projects the congregational mosque and the bridge of forty arches in Isfahan, a caravanserai in Qazvin, a public bath in Kashan, and many others, totaling approximately sixty-five improvements and new constructions.[6]

Historiographical Precedents: Rashid al-Din's Jami al-tavarikh *and Amini's* Tarikh-i ʻalam-ara-yi Amini

Regardless of the disparity of the numbers of kingly attributes that each chronicler lists, we may place them into seven general categories: (1) personal virtues, (2) military power, (3) good fortune, (4) justice, (5) traditional kingly activities, (6) construction, and (7) wealth. These similarities raise questions about the historiographical relationships between the two texts. It is not inconceivable that Iskandar Beg could have been familiar with Qandahari's history even though he does not refer to it by name, and he does mention another Mughal history – the *Akbarnamah* – in his chronicle, which suggests that he had some knowledge of the Mughal historiographical tradition. However, the *Tarikh-i Akbari* does not appear to have been a very popular history, judging by the few existing manuscripts of the text.[7] A more plausible explanation for the similarities would be that both chroniclers were independently looking to past examples. At least two histories predating the Safavid and Mughal periods may have influenced both chronicles: Rashid al-Din's *Jamiʻ al-tavarikh* and Khunji-Isfahani's *Tarikh-i ʻalam-ara-yi Amini*. Although we see no evidence of direct borrowing or imitative writing, these two sources provide examples of

[6] Iskandar Beg, *ʻAlam-ara-yi ʻAbbasi*, 1110–1111; trans., 535–538.
[7] See Storey, *Persian Literature*, 1: 541, where only two manuscripts are listed.

historiographical precedents, indicating that neither Qandahari nor Iskandar Beg were completely innovative in providing lists of kingly virtues in their chronicles.

Rashid al-Din completed his famous and extensive world history, the *Jami' al-tavarikh* "compendium of histories," in ca. 710/1310–1311. He composed it for Ghazan Khan (r. 694–713/1295–1304), the seventh Mongol Il-Khanid ruler. Ghazan initially asked Rashid al-Din to write an ancestral history of the Mongols, which he did, but Ghazan's brother and successor, Oljeitu (r. 704–716/1304–1316), requested that Rashid al-Din extend the work to embrace a history of "all the peoples with whom the Mongols had come into contact."[8] At the end of the chronological account of Ghazan Khan's reign, Rashid al-Din includes an extensive section consisting of some forty stories (*ḥikāyat*). These all relate to Ghazan's "conduct and character, monuments of his justice and beneficence, charity and piety, [and] the pronouncements and orders he gave for the benefit of all people."[9] Far more extensive than either Iskandar Beg or Qandahari's lists, and indeed constituting more than half the section on Ghazan Khan, the forty "stories" read more like a resume of Ghazan's reforms rather than a list of his "virtues."

Khunji-Isfahani was familiar with the *Jami' al-tavarikh*, for Rashid al-Din is one of the historians he lists in his various categories of classes of historians.[10] While Khunji-Isfahani does not mention any mirrors for princes texts in the *Tarikh-i 'alam-ara-yi Amini*, he wrote a political treatise entitled the *Suluk al-muluk*, itself a mirrors for princes, thereby indicating that he was thoroughly familiar with the genre. Khunji-Isfahani's *Tarikh-i 'alam-ara-yi Amini* contains a list of eight chapters (*bāb*), each devoted to one of Sultan Ya'qub's virtues, as follows: (1) he is a noble descendant of Bayandur and thus like a sweet sugar cane, (2) he possesses a sun-like appearance veiled by the screen of modesty, (3) he is brave, (4) he is generous, (5) he is merciful and forgiving, (6) he is

[8] *EI2*, s.v., "Rashid al-Din," by D. O. Morgan.
[9] Rashid al-Din Fazlallah Hamadani, *Jami' al-tavarikh*, ed. Bahman Karimi (Tehran: Iqbal, 1338 [1959]), trans. Wheeler Thackston as *Rashiduddin Fazlullah's Jame 'u't-tawarikh: Compendium of Chronicles: A History of the Mongols*, 3 vols. (Cambridge, MA: Harvard University Department of Near Eastern Languages and Civilizations, 1998), 964; trans., 663. I am grateful to Charles Melville from bringing this to my attention.
[10] Khunji-Isfahani, *Tarikh-i 'alam-ara-yi Amini*, 87–88; trans., 8.

just, (7) he abounds in knowledge and has a mild nature, and (8) his religious beliefs are strict and he enforces the *shari'ah*. Taverns have been closed.[11]

Many of the virtues in the *Jami' al-tavarikh* and the *Tarikh-i 'alam-ara-yi Amini* also appear in Qandahari and Iskandar Beg's histories. For example, Rashid al-Din points out that Ghazan Khan had an interest in keeping the roads safe, instituting punishments for highway robbers and thieves, and installing highway patrols to police the roads.[12] Similarly, Iskandar Beg tells us that Shah 'Abbas "called for the principal highway robbers in each province to be identified, and he then set about eliminating this class of people."[13] In another instance, Rashid al-Din stresses Ghazan Khan's bravery in battle, calling him an "enraged lion," a "roaring lion," and a "lion-hearted champion."[14] Khunji-Isfahani emphasizes Ya'qub Khan's bravery in battle and his strength, stating that he is stronger than the pre-Islamic hero Rustam.[15] Qandahari may be recalling one of these histories when he states that Akbar "is such a destroyer of armies, that whether it is battlefield or an assembly of festivities, when he has to oppose the enemy or adorn a festive occasion, he has proved his prowess as well as his generosity and mercy to the kings of the world."[16] Similarly, Iskandar Beg says that since he [Shah 'Abbas] "has always turned to God for help, his reign has been crowned by victories, and success has attended him from his accession up to the present day."[17]

As a final example, Rashid al-Din states that Ghazan Khan exhibited great piety, forbidding wine in his empire and giving the order that "anyone who comes drunk into cities and marketplaces will be arrested, stripped naked, and tied to a tree in the middle of the market so that people can pass by and revile him."[18] In a very similar vein, according to Khunji-Isfahani, Ya'qub Khan strictly enforced the *shari'ah*, displayed steadfastness in his religious beliefs, and closed the taverns: "Taverns under the miserable Qara Qoyunlu have now been

[11] Khunji-Isfahani, *Tarikh-i 'alam-ara-yi Amini*, 40–50; trans., 19.
[12] Rashid al-Din, *Jami' al-tavarikh*, 1050–1053; trans., 718–720.
[13] Iskandar Beg, *'Alam-ara-yi 'Abbasi*, 1104; trans., 523.
[14] Rashid al-Din, *Jami' al-tavarikh*, 987; trans., 678.
[15] Khunji-Isfahani, *Tarikh-i 'alam-ara-yi Amini*, 19; trans., 42–43.
[16] Qandahari, *Tarikh-i Akbari*, 37; trans., 55.
[17] Iskandar Beg, *'Alam-ara-yi 'Abbasi*, 539; trans., 1112.
[18] Rashid al-Din, *Jami' al-tavarikh*, 1087; trans., 743.

closed by the storm of royal anger."[19] Echoing Rashid al-Din and Khunji-Isfahani, Qandahari tells us that Akbar "is such a paragon of justice that he has purified the whole country from the dirt and sin of drinking and adultery."[20]

Through the Looking Glass: Responding to Mirrors for Princes

As outlined above, the *Jami' al-tavarikh* and *Tarikh-i 'alam-ara-yi Amini* provide historiographical precedents in that they include "lists of kingly virtues." These two texts represent a chronicle tradition with which Iskandar Beg and Qandahari were familiar. However, the lists were also informed by another genre of Islamicate writing, namely "mirrors for princes" literatures. Texts of this genre generally describe an ideal king by listing the qualities that a good king should possess, and providing various kinds of advice – from practical to abstract – to a real or theoretical king. Historians treat this material as normative because it describes the qualities a perfect king should have rather than attributes that an actual king does have. Given this context, we may understand the historians' lists as a response to the mirrors for princes.

Nizam al-Mulk's Siyasatnamah

In order to analyze our sources in this context, we begin with an overview of one of the most well-known "mirrors" texts: Nizam al-Mulk's *Siyasatnamah* ("book of government"). It is important to state at the outset that while the *Siyasatnamah* did not serve as a direct model for the two chronicles under discussion here, its significance lies in the general themes it covers and how it describes an "ideal king," which bears similarity to a number of other well-known Persian advice literature texts. We may view the *Siyasatnamah* as representative of a genre of texts that inform, in a general way, the "lists of kingly virtues" in Qandahari and Iskandar Beg's histories.

The *Siyasatnamah* was written in 484/1091 by Nizam al-Mulk, a minister under the Saljuq sultans Alp Arslan (r. 455–465/1063–1072) and Malikshah (r. 465–485/1072–1092). Nizam al-Mulk states in his

19 Khunji-Isfahani, *Tarikh-i 'alam-ara-yi Amini*, 49; trans., 19.
20 Qandahari, *Tarikh-i Akbari*, 55; trans., 37.

introduction that Malik Shah had ordered him and several other individuals to

> consider whether there is in our age and time anything out of order either in the divan, the court, the royal palace or the audience-hall – anything whose principles are not being observed by us or are unknown to us; whether there are any functions which kings before us have performed and we are not fulfilling: consider further what have been the laws and customs of past kings, make a digest of them and present them for our judgment.[21]

Nizam al-Mulk then boasts that the only treatise that Malik Shah found acceptable was Nizam al-Mulk's own. Next, he outlines his *Siyasatnamah*, which consists of some fifty chapters, with most devoted to a single kingly duty or responsibility. In the *Siyasatnamah*, Nizam al-Mulk holds up Malikshah as the ideal king who is handsome, of good disposition, brave, manly, skilled in horsemanship and the use of arms, accomplished in the arts, of sound faith, engaged in prayer and fasting, respectful of religious authorities, and generous in giving alms and helping the poor.[22] He proceeds to dispense advice to the king, explaining in thirty six successive chapters how a good king is one who, after having been chosen by God, promotes the security of his subjects, accepts his good fortune and uses it to select capable ministers and officers, and promotes building projects such as canals, bridges, fortifications, new towns, and lofty and magnificent buildings.[23] The examples that Nizam al-Mulk provides for kings who achieved these tasks come from the pre-Islamic or early Islamic past.

[21] Nizam al-Mulk, *Siyasatnamah*, ed. ʿAta Allah Tadayyun (Tehran: Intisharat-i Tihran, 1373 [1994]), trans. Hubert Darke as *The Book of Government or Rules for Kings* (London: Routledge and Paul, 1960), 43; trans., 1.

[22] Nizam al-Mulk, *Siyasatnamah*, 47–48; trans., 10–11.

[23] Nizam al-Mulk, *Siyasatnamah*, 46–48; trans., 9–11. Marta Simidchieva categorizes the kingly virtues that Nizam al-Mulk outlines into three groups, the first being "autocratic supremacy and unchallenged political control over a state," the second a "group of virtues, which makes the rightful ruler a capable manager and steward of his domain," and the third group being "personal accomplishments and distinctions, which are not given to all kings, and therefore are not essential to the royal office." Marta Simidchieva, "Kingship and Legitimacy in Niẓam al-Mulk's *Siyāsatnāma*, Fifth/Eleventh Century," in *Writers and Rulers: Perspectives on their Relationship from Abbasid to Safavid Times*, eds. Beatrice Gruendler and Louise Marlow, 104–105 (Wiesbaden: Reichert Verlag, 2004).

The mirrors for princes literature was very popular in the early modern period. Linda Darling has noted that "when he Persianized the administration in 1575, Akbar included in his new curriculum for bureaucrats a number of Middle Eastern works where the idea of the circle of justice was expressed, including Nasir al-Din Tusi's ... *Akhlaq-i Nasiri* (Nasirean Ethics) and Khwandamir's history." She concludes that Mughal administrators and bureaucrats would have been quite familiar with the mirrors genre.[24] It is possible, then, that historians such as Qandahari may have desired somehow to incorporate this new syllabus, or at least demonstrate their knowledge of it in their chronicles.

In light of this, it is important to note that for nearly each of the normative qualities of a good king that Nizam al-Mulk outlines, Iskandar Beg and Qandahari provide specific, nonnormative examples from the lives of Shah 'Abbas and Akbar. It seems as though these two chroniclers are holding up the mirror for princes before their own king and seeing him in the reflection. For example, as noted above, the *Siyasatnamah's* Malik Shah is skilled in horsemanship. Correspondingly, Qandahari's Akbar is a good horse rider and a master polo player: "[Entry (*Fiqrah*) 8] He is such a mighty horse rider that in the field of art and manner in which he sits his horse and in the skill of chaugan [polo], he takes away prize from the renowned horsemen and wrestlers of the world."[25] Nizam al-Mulk's Malik Shah displays "sound faith and true belief, devotion to the worship of God and the practice of such virtuous deeds as praying in the night."[26] According to Iskandar Beg, Shah 'Abbas, "when he prayed, he was so absorbed in his devotions that he appeared to have left his material body."[27] Nizam al-Mulk states that the king should send out spies and use them for the good of the country and the people: "Spies must constantly go out to the limits of the kingdom in the guise of merchants, travelers, Sufis, pedlars (of medicines), and mendicants, and bring back reports of everything they hear."[28] Almost as if writing in

[24] Linda T. Darling, "'Do Justice, Do Justice, for That Is Paradise': Middle Eastern Advice for Indian Muslim Rulers," *Comparative Studies of South Asia, Africa and the Middle East* 22 (2002): 8. See also Darling, *A History of Social Justice*.
[25] Qandahari, *Tarikh-i Akbari*, 36–37; trans., 54.
[26] Nizam al-Mulk, *Siyasatnamah*, 48; trans., 11.
[27] Iskandar Beg, *'Alam-ara-yi 'Abbasi*, 1099; trans., 515.
[28] Nizam al-Mulk, *Siyasatnamah*, 90; trans., 78.

response, Qandahari tells us that Akbar "is such an expert in espionage that he keeps 4,000 foot-runners ... They are on His Majesty's service day and night so that news and reports reach regularly everyday from all sides of the world."[29] Similarly, Shah 'Abbas "knows in minute details what is going on in Iran and also in the world outside. He has a well-developed intelligence system, with the result that no one, even if he is sitting at home with his family, can express opinions which should not be expressed without running the risk of their being reported to the Shah."[30]

Each chronicler, then, fits his own king's virtues into a mirrors for princes framework, which he then uses to articulate agendas that were specific to the dynasty for which he was writing. For example, in addition to stating that Shah 'Abbas prayed ardently, in his fifth discourse, devoted to the king's justice, Iskandar Beg describes both the shah's religious devotion and his justice, explaining that Shi'is in the empire received a tax break during the fasting month of Ramadan:

Second, all *dīvān* levies were waived for all Shi'ites throughout the empire during the month of Ramadan. The total revenues for one month, which according to the computation of the *dīvān* officials amounted to some twenty thousand *toman*, were given to the people as alms. The object was that they should be free from demands for taxes during this blessed month, which is a time to be devoted to the service and worship of God.[31]

As Said Arjomand explains, "With some eclecticism, Quranic verses, including the 'authority verse,' are also on occasion adduced to enjoin obedience to kings. Conversely, the primary ethical obligation of the king is to rule with justice and to eliminate oppression."[32] In this passage, then, Iskandar Beg portrays 'Abbas not only as a just and pious king through his reading the Qur'an, but also as a specifically

[29] Nizam al-Mulk, *Siyasatnamah*, 43–44, trans., 62.
[30] Iskandar Beg, *'Alam-ara-yi 'Abbasi*, 1109; trans., 533.
[31] Iskandar Beg, *'Alam-ara-yi 'Abbasi*, 1104; trans., 523. Translation slightly modified.
[32] Said Arjomand, *The Shadow of God and the Hidden Imam: Religion, Political Order, and Societal Change in Shi'ite Iran from the Beginning to 1890* (Chicago: University of Chicago Press, 1984), 181. On the notion of justice in mirrors for princes literature, see Erik Ohlander, "Enacting Justice, Ensuring Salvation: The Trope of the 'Just Ruler' in Some Medieval Islamic Mirrors for Princes," *The Muslim World* 99 (2009): 237–252.

Shiʿi king who makes special provisions for the Shiʿis living in his empire.

Qandahari similarly emphasized how Akbar read the Qur'an and was, therefore, a pious king. At the same time, however, he makes reference to Akbar's ecumenical openness when he describes him as the "shelter or patron of all the high qualities":

When he is free from the affairs of state and administration, on Thursday night he invites men of all classes and of high rank and convenes an assembly in the house of worship (*ʿibādat-khānah*) and makes them sit in four-rows … *sayyids*, nobles, men of letters, scholars and righteous persons of all sects and beliefs, engage in debate or discussion. Thus they discuss religious beliefs (*ʿaqā'id-i sharīʿah*) and rules of reason (*qavāʿid-i ʿaqliyah*) and every one of them is given prizes in cash and kind and is made happy. During these debates whenever acute and knotty problems crop up, His Majesty puts them on the right path … the time, which is spent in discussing learned topics, scholarly problems and reading the *Quran*, which is a source of removing sorrow and misfortune.[33]

This description refers to a period in Akbar's reign when he sponsored religious debates as part of his ecumenical activities. Qandahari portrays Akbar as the individual who settles religious debates and solves religious problems, placing him above scholars and other religious experts.

The Seventeenth Year

In order to determine more closely the relationship between the lists of kingly virtues in the chronicle introductions and the information in the later annalistic sections of the narratives, what follows is a detailed analysis of the seventeenth regnal year of each king, Akbar and Abbas. By their seventeenth year on the throne, both kings had had time to establish their rule, address initial challenges, and embark on their own policies and projects. "Entry 28" for Akbar started in late Safar 981/ June 1573. The chapter focuses on the emperor's embarking toward and the conquest of Gujarat. ʿAbbas's seventeenth regnal year, the year of the Hare, began in 1011/1603 when he was engaged in the reconquest of Tabriz and Azerbaijan. Although both narratives emphasize military campaigns, many of the details surrounding the campaigns

[33] Qandahari, *Tarikh-i Akbari*, 40–41; tr. 58–49, trans. slightly modified.

and the way each chronicler frames and explains the episodes reflect the norms described in his list of kingly virtues.

The Seventeenth Year in the Tarikh-i Akbari

Qandahari's narrative under Entry (*fiqrah*) 28 covers a number of Akbar's activities, many of which relate directly to the military expedition, but a number of others that do not. These include accounts of Akbar hunting, his receiving gifts from various visiting officials who presented themselves to the court, and his dispensing of justice. Qandahari opens his account by stating that Akbar left Fatehpur Sikri in late Safar 981/June 1573 in order to visit the shrine of the Sufi saint Shaykh Muin al-Din Chishti (536–633/1141–1236).[34] But before describing the king's visit to the shrine, Qandahari states that on the way, he issued a decree (*farmān*) ordering that his men engage in a hunt for lions and tigers – a traditional kingly activity.[35] Qandahari tells us that it was the beginning of monsoon season and as such, the weather was cool and the ground was covered in grass and flowers. Akbar hunted a great deal, so much so that "the hunting ground looked blood red like a ruby of Badakhshan."[36] The narrative of the brief hunting episode centered on Akbar's confronting a lion "before whom even the tiger of the jungle bends his head like a cat."[37] Akbar proceeded to bring it down with his lance and kill it.[38] Qandahari's inclusion of this information, which in general emphasizes one of the traditional activities associated with kingship – hunting – also corresponds with two of the kingly virtues that he lists earlier in his chronicle. In the ninth entry, Qandahari states that Akbar "is fond of games when he is full of delight in the forest. When he is engaged in hunting lions or stags and in releasing birds to fly, he exhibits great interest in gratifying hearts of hunters."[39] Similarly, in Entry 32, Qandahari states that "The lion-hearted king occasionally diverts his full attention towards chase and hunt of tiger, of dreadful attacking power and sharp

[34] Qandahari *Tarikh-i Akbari*, 155–156; trans., 190.
[35] Qandahari, *Tarikh-i Akbari*, 156; trans., 190.
[36] Qandahari, *Tarikh-i Akbari*, 156; trans., 190.
[37] Qandahari, *Tarikh-i Akbari*, 156; trans., 190. Translation slightly modified.
[38] Qandahari, *Tarikh-i Akbari*, 156; trans., 190.
[39] Qandahari, *Tarikh-i Akbari*, 37; trans., 54–55

claws, which is called 'chita' (leopard) in Hindi language."[40] Thus, not only does the fact that he went hunting make Akbar appear kingly, but by elevating hunting to a kingly "virtue" earlier in his chronicle, we can understand why Qandahari included this information in his account of the Gujarat campaign.

The predominant kingly attribute as reflected in the mirrors for princes literature is justice. Implicit in the literature is the idea of the "circle of justice." Drawing from ancient Persian notions of kingship, the circle of justice expresses the idea that justice is maintained as follows: the sovereign depends on soldiers, who depend on wealth, which depends on the subjects, who depend on the sovereign for justice. Qandahari stresses Akbar's justice in at least two places in his list of Akbar's virtues, stating that "He has won respect and obedience of the people by his justice and liberality; they are submissive while his sword is active," and "By the force of his justice, tyranny and injustice have fled a hundred stages away into the forest of non-existence."[41] In the *Tarikh-i Akbari*, Qandahari describes how Akbar arrived in Baroach and heard that the former administrator of Baroach, a certain Chingiz Khan, had been killed by Jajjar Khan Habshi, one of the Gujarati amirs, for no reason. The mother of Chingiz Khan came and complained about Jajjar Khan. On the basis of her complaint, a date was set at which time Akbar would issue judgment on Jajjar Khan. Qandahari states that Akbar considered the case and ordered that Jajjar Khan be punished by being crushed under the feet of an elephant.[42]

Upon initial examination, the murder of Chingiz Khan by Jajjar Khan Habshi might appear an insignificant episode in the account of the subjugation of Gujarat. Certainly many were killed in the battle itself and hundreds of people sought out Akbar on a daily basis. Qandahari's highlighting this episode makes better sense if we place it in the context of the kingly quality of justice. In other words, Qandahari chose to include this story because of his overall framework, which presents Akbar as a just king.

In terms of the actual military conquest of Gujarat, the central episode in this campaign was the Mughal attack on the fort at Surat.

[40] Qandahari, *Tarikh-i Akbari*, 48; trans., 67. Translation slightly modified.
[41] Qandahari, *Tarikh-i Akbari*, 36; trans., 54.
[42] Qandahari, *Tarikh-i Akbari*, 172; trans., 199–200.

According to Qandahari, the fort of Surat "was one of the most famous forts of Guajarat and its strength could be easily estimated."[43] Akbar successfully captured the fort, as Qandahari describes in considerable detail. Fortresses – including their construction, destruction, protection, and attack – play a large part in Mughal and Safavid chronicles. Not surprisingly, one of Qandahari's longest entries in his list of Akbar's virtues discusses fortresses. Here, he describes the strength of Akbar's fortifications: "He is the world-taker, the depth of the moat of his forts and strongholds reach the earth's centre . . ."[44] As a specific example of the general statement he made at the beginning of his chronicle, Qandahari continues by noting that Akbar managed to capture heavily guarded fortresses until "in short, the forts of the cities of Hindustan were conquered and held firmly."[45]

The Seventeenth Year in the Tarikh-i 'alam-ara-yi 'Abbasi

Turning now to Shah 'Abbas, in the year of the Hare, the seventeenth year of his reign (1011–1012/1602–1604), the Safavid monarch embarked upon the conquest of Tabriz and Azerbaijan. This campaign included the capture of forts in Nakhjavan and Yerevan. While the retaking of Tabriz was the central event of this year, Iskandar Beg, like Qandahari, intersperses his narrative with points that directly reflect his list of kingly virtues. For example, one of the points that Iskandar Beg makes in this chapter is that Shah 'Abbas had access to very good intelligence information, and this intelligence helped him with the conquest of Tabriz and the other military goals he had at the time. Thus, Iskandar Beg Munshi states that Shah Abbas heard about the size of the Ottoman army in Tabriz from his "efficient intelligence service."[46] And later in the same chapter, he notes that before taking the fortress in Nakhjavan, the king sent someone to gather intelligence about Ottoman forces there.[47] These details correspond with Iskandar Beg's the tenth discourse, which lists Shah Abbas's awareness of world affairs as one of his qualities:

[43] Qandahari. *Tarikh-i Akbari*, 163–164; trans., 194–195.
[44] Qandahari, *Tarikh-i Akbari*, 41–42; trans., 60.
[45] Qandahari, *Tarikh-i Akbari*, 42; trans., 60.
[46] Iskandar Beg, *'Alam-ara-yi 'Abbasi*, 640; trans., 831.
[47] Iskandar Beg, *'Alam-ara-yi 'Abbasi*, 643; trans., 833.

> He [Shah 'Abbas] knows in minute details what is going on in Iran and also in the world outside. He has a well-developed intelligence system, with the result that no one, even if he is sitting at home with his family, can express opinions which should not be expressed without running the risk of their being reported to the Shah.[48]

Another point that Iskandar Beg emphasizes in his entry for this year is the king's good luck, or auspicious rule. For example, before deciding to capture Tabriz, we learn that Shah 'Abbas's "intuition told him that now is the time to strike, and since his intuition in affairs of state had always proved reliable, his advisers concurred."[49] After that, he ordered Munajjim Yazdi, his court astrologer, to choose the specific auspicious moment to set out.[50] Later, during the year in question, an embassy from Akbar arrived, bringing the gift of a scabbard, a coat of mail, and other costly jewels. Iskandar Beg specifically states that among the gifts was a sword, and this particular gift, "coming from a descendant of Timur, was seen as a happy augury of Shah's ultimate victory in Azerbaijan and Shirvan."[51] Both of these episodes in the *Tarikh-i 'alam-ara-yi 'Abbasi* connect to Iskandar Beg's fourth discourse in his list of Shah 'Abbas's virtues, devoted to the king's good fortune. There, he states that Shah 'Abbas was the true "lord of the auspicious conjunction" (*ṣāḥib-qirān*), despite the fact that many previous monarchs had received this title.[52] The implication is that the good fortune that the Mughals claimed transferred to Shah 'Abbas through the gift of a sword from the Timurid Mughals. Thus, Iskandar Beg's emphasis on this particular gift from Akbar serves as further evidence of Shah 'Abbas's position as the "true" *sāḥib-qirān*.

[48] Iskandar Beg, *'Alam-ara-yi 'Abbasi*, 1109; trans., 533.

[49] Iskandar Beg, *'Alam-ara-yi 'Abbasi*, 637–638; trans., 828.

[50] Iskandar Beg, *'Alam-ara-yi 'Abbasi*, 637–638; trans., 828. Jalal al-Din Munajjim Yazdi was the author of an important chronicle of Shah 'Abbas. See Mulla Jalal al-Din Munajjim Yazdi, *Tarikh-i 'Abbasi ya ruznamah-'i Mulla Jalal*, ed. Sayf Allah Vahid Niya ([Tehran]: Intisharat-i Vahid, 1366 [1987]). For information on Munajjim Yazdi and his descendants, see 'Ali Asghar Mossadegh, "La Famille Monajjem Yazdi," in "Notes sur des Historiographes de l'Epoque Safavide," by Jean Calmard, 'Ali Asghar Mossadegh and M. Bastani Parizi, 125–129, *Studia Iranica* 16 (1987): 123–135.

[51] Iskandar Beg, *'Alam-ara-yi 'Abbasi*, 647; trans., 837.

[52] Iskandar Beg, *'Alam-ara-yi 'Abbasi*, 1102; trans., 519. For a recent study on the history of this title, see Naindeep Singh Chan, "Lord of the Auspicious Conjunction: Origins of the *Ṣāḥib-Qirān*," *Iran and the Caucasus* 13 (2009): 93–110.

One persistent element in both chronicles, and indeed in many chronicles of this era, is the practice of the chronicler listing names of individuals that the king appointed to various offices and positions. This information usually appears toward the end of a particular year's entry or at the end of the description of a military victory. For example, at the end of his entry for Shah 'Abbas's seventeenth year, Iskandar Beg's last statement was that "Mirza 'Ali Dawlatabadi was dismissed from his office of comptroller of finance (*mostowfī al-mamālek*) and was replaced by Mo'ezzā Ebrāhīmā Shirāzī, who the previous year had accused the royal secretariat of certain malpractices."[53] We can better understand why Iskandar Beg includes this information when we look to discourse number seven, which deals with the king's policy making and administrative talents. Here, Iskandar Beg states that Shah 'Abbas was a great administrator and that he particularly "tightened up provincial administration ... Any emir or noble who was awarded a provincial governorship, or who was charged with the security of the highways, received his office on the understanding that he discharge his duties in a proper manner."[54]

Keeping in mind that Iskandar Beg and Qandahari were the first chroniclers writing under the Safavids and Mughals, respectively, to include lists of kingly virtues in their texts, the question arises as to why the chroniclers might, at this point in time, choose to innovate in this way. The reigns of the Safavid and Mughal monarchs, 'Abbas and Akbar, represent something new in terms of historiography. The *Tarikh-i 'alam-ara-yi 'Abbasi*, for example, is an elaborate history that departs from traditional universal histories or straightforward dynastic chronicles. In his chronicle, Iskandar Beg Munshi weaves together a number of different historiographical elements. Organizing Book One of his history into twelve "discourses," and using the virtues of Shah 'Abbas as a way to frame the rest of his history, does not follow a traditional annalistic organizational scheme. He may have done this because Mughal chroniclers, at the same time, were influenced by concepts such as Ibn al-'Arabi's "perfect man" (*insān-i kāmil*), casting

53 Iskandar Beg, *'Alam-ara-yi 'Abbasi*, 651; trans., 841. Translation slightly modified.

54 Iskandar Beg, *'Alam-ara-yi 'Abbasi*, 1106; trans., 527.

him as a combination of the perfect man and the perfect ruler.[55] Iskandar Beg could not have been unaware of such representations. Indeed, he shows familiarity with the *Akbarnamah* in his history and refers to it by name.[56]

Conclusion

Lists of kingly virtues appear as an important item in the overall political agenda that Safavid and Mughal chroniclers sought to advance – an agenda that seems to plays itself out in the remaining chronological portions of the chronicles. We are now able to view the type of information appearing in those sections in a new light. It makes sense, for example, that Iskandar Beg would end his *Tarikh-i ʻalam-ara-yi ʻAbbasi* with a list of the ministers that ʻAbbas appointed, when we remember that mirrors for princes literature emphasizes the importance of choosing ministers. Iskandar Beg's careful description of the shah's building of Isfahan appears in his chronicle for a reason because good kings were supposed to build important cities and impressive buildings.[57] Qandahari emphasizes Akbar's numerous military victories because good kings should display bravery and enjoy victory in battle, as Nizam al-Mulk stated. Reading the chronicles in light of the mirrors for princes literature makes the seemingly arbitrary pools of names, dates, and places from which historians extract "facts" take on a more deliberate form than previously thought and reveals more about the nature of Persianate historiography.

This discussion has focused on two chronicles containing explicit "lists of kingly virtues" and shown the connection between particular virtues and specific information in the annalistic portion of the chronicles. The approach taken here, however, does not need to be confined to these two histories or to other chronicles that may contain lists of

55 Douglas E. Streusand, *The Formation of the Mughal Empire* (Delhi: Oxford University Press, 1989), 132. For a discussion of Ibn al-ʻArabi's influence on Mughal historiography, see Moin, *Millennial Sovereign*, 159–161.

56 See Iskandar Beg Munshi, *ʻAlam-ara-yi ʻAbbasi*, I: 98; trans., I: 162.

57 For a comparative account of the building of Isfahan in Fazli Isfahani's *Afzal al-tavarikh* and Iskandar Beg Munshi's *ʻAlam-ara-yi ʻAbbasi*, see Charles Melville, "New Light on Shah ʻAbbas and the Construction of Isfahan," *Muqarnas* 33 (2016): 155–175.

kingly virtues. Rather, the analyses of the seventeenth year of the kings Akbar's and Abbas's reigns in the *Tarikh-i Akbari* and the *Tarikh-i 'alam-ara-yi 'Abbasi*, respectively, suggest that we may begin to understand why certain information appears in the annalistic sections of the chronicles in the first place, and further help us understand why chroniclers chose to include the particular information that they did in their narratives.

History As Memorial: *Tazkirah* in Early Modern Persianate Chronicles

"Mirrors for princes" literature was not the only genre that informed early modern chroniclers. They also brought into their narratives information from biographical compendia (*taẕkirah*). We may broadly define *tazkirah* as literary biographical anthologies, most commonly in the form of poets and poetical works, although the genre also encompassed other categories such as the lives of saints and the lives of artists and calligraphers.[58] Although Khunji-Isfahani never uses the word *tazkirah* in his outline of the different classes of historians, many of his categories encompass biographical compendia of one form or another, including writers of the lives of prophets, authors of the lives of the Prophet's followers, alphabetic dictionaries of celebrities of this community [of Muslims] from among the great famous sultans, and historians who wrote on classes of doctors of law and prominent religious figures.[59]

Here we will analyze a select group of broadly related post-Timurid chronicles containing *tazkirah* material and explore some of the

[58] For general background and information on *tazkirah*, see *EI2*, "tadhkira." For an example of a tazkirah of saints' lives, see Farid al-Din 'Attar, *Kitab-i tazkirat al-awliya*, ed. Muhammad Qazvini (Tehran: Intisharat-i Markazi, [1957]), trans. by Paul Losensky as *Farid ad-Din 'Attār's Memorial of God's Friends: Lives and Sayings of Sufis* (New York: Paulist Press, 2009). The *Gulistan-i hunar* is a well-known Safavid era *tazkirah* of painters and calligraphers by Qazi Ahmad Qumi. See Qazi Ahmad Qumi, *Gulistan-i hunar*, ed. Ahmad Suhayli Khvansari ([Tehran]: Intisharat-i Bunyad va Farhang-i Iran, n.d). Trans. by V. Minorsky as *Calligraphers and Painters*, with an Introduction by B. N. Zakhoder, Freer Gallery of Art Occasional Papers, vol. 3, no. 2 (Washington, DC: Smithsonian Institution, 1959).

[59] Khunji, 87–88; trans., 8–9.

reasons why certain historians chose to include biographical material in their chronicles, and how the historiographical tradition fits into the picture.

Origins and Development of the Convention

As Paul Losensky has noted, the practice of including *tazkirah*-style biographies in Persian histories predates the Safavid era. The practice goes at least as far back as Hamd Allah Mustawfi Qazvini's Mongol era chronicle, the *Tarikh-i guzidah*, composed in 1330.[60] Melville has observed that this practice has its origins with "the merging of biographical records (or necrologies) with annals in the works of the Arabic chroniclers, who mention the deaths of important figures at the end of each year, or from the example of writers such as Hamze of Isfahan (ca. 961)."[61] In general, the historian narrates the reign of a particular ruler (or dynasty), and at the end of that subsection he adds a collection of minibiographies devoted to a number of individuals from certain social groups. The most common focus of the stand-alone *tazkirah* consists of poets and religious figures, but early modern chroniclers also included biographies of military commanders, viziers, painters and calligraphers, philosophers and physicians, musicians, and others, in various combinations.

In the post-Timurid period, Khvandamir was the first historian to include biographical entries into his *Habib al-siyar*.[62] At the end of his narrative sections on certain rulers, Khvandamir provides short biographies of poets, viziers, and others who were alive or who died during that ruler's time. Table 5.1 indicates, starting with the Mongols, the rulers to whom Khvandamir attached such biographies.

Khvandamir's source for this information was quite likely Mirkhvand's *Rawzat al-safa*. It is important to remember that in addition to imitating the *Rawzat al-safa*, Khvandamir also wrote its seventh volume, devoted to Sultan Husayn Bayqara and his sons, and

[60] Paul E. Losensky, "Biographical Writing: Tadhkere and Manâqeb," in *Persian Prose, A History of Persian Literature*, vol. 5, forthcoming, 19.

[61] Charles Melville, "The Historian at Work," in *Persian Historiography*, ed. Charles Melville, 61–62 (London: I. B. Tauris, 2012).

[62] See Jacobs, "Sunni and Shi'i Perceptions," 114.

Table 5.1 ***Biographies in the*** **Habib al-siyar**

Ruler
[*Mongols*]
Hulagu
Abaqa
Arghun
Ghazan
Oljeitu
Abu Sa'id
Amir Shaykh Hasan Chubani
[*Mamluks*]
Bunduqdar [Baybars I]
Sayf al-Din Qala'un
Al-Nasir
[*Muzaffarids*]
Amir Muhammad Muzaffar
Shah Shuja'
[*Karts*]
Malik Ghiyas al-Din Kart
Malik Mu'izz al-Din Husayn Kart
[*Timurids*]
Timur
Shahrukh
Ulugh Beg
Sultan Abu Said
Sultan Husayn Mirza (Bayqara)
Babur
[*Aq Qoyunlu/Safavid*]
Aq Qoyunlu/Shah Isma'il combined

composed the conclusion (*khātimah*).[63] However, the *Rawzat al-safa* only includes biographical notices for one ruler, the Timurid Sultan Husayn Bayqara, and it is likely that Khvandamir wrote this section himself. This would explain why we see word-for-word similarity in the corresponding biographical accounts in the *Rawzat al-safa* and the *Habib al-siyar*, and why they appear in the same structural position in

[63] See *EI2*, s.v. "Mirkhwand," by A. Beveridge [Beatrice Forbes Manz]. Volume seven continues to 929/1522–1523, and Khvandamir completed the conclusion (*khātimah*) sometime after 907/1502.

both chronicles. The following example, taken from the entries for a certain Ghiyas al-Din Afzal b. Sayyid Hasan, demonstrates the close relationship between the two texts:

Rawzat al-safa	*Habib al-siyar*
Sayyid Ghiyas al-Din Afzal son of Sayyid Hasan, in excelling in learning and [legal] knowledge, was exceptional and superior to most of the sayyids of holy Mashhad. For many years he carried out the necessities of the position of shaykh al-islam and important legal matter.	Sayyid Ghiyas al-Din Afzal son of Sayyid Hasan, in excelling in learning and [legal] knowledge, was exceptional and superior to most of the sayyids of holy Mashhad. For many years in that province he carried out the necessities of the position of shaykh al-islam and legal decrees.
Sayyid Ghiyās al-Dīn Afżal bin Sayyid Ḥasan bih mazīd-i ʿilm va faqāhat az aks̱ar-i sādāt-i Mashhad-i muqaddasah mumtāz va mustas̱ná būd. Sālhā-yi farāvān bih lavāzim-i manṣib-i shaykh al-islāmī va fayṣal-i muhimāt-i sharʿiyah iqdām mī'namūd.[64]	*Sayyid Ghiyās al-Dīn Afżal bin Sayyid Ḥasan bi-mazīd-i ʿilm va faqāhat az aks̱ar-i sādāt-i Mashhad-i muqaddasah mumtāz va mustas̱ná būd va sālhā-yi farāvān dar ānvilāyat bi-lavāzim-i manṣib-i shaykh al-islāmī va fayṣal-i qażāyā'-i sharʿiyah iqdām mī'farmūd.*[65]

For the rest of his biographical entries, Khvandamir had to rely on texts other than the *Rawzat al-safa*. He occasionally names these sources, which are a combination of historical works and *tazkirahs* (see Table 5.2). For example, in Khvandamir's Mongol sections, he cites Hamd Allah Mustawfi Qazvini's *Tarikh-i guzidah* and ʿAbd al-Rahman Jami's *Nafahat al-uns*; for the Chupanids, ʿAbd Allah ibn Asad Yafiʿi's *Mirat al-janan* [referred to as "Imam Yafiʿi's history"]; for the Mamluks, the *Tashih al-masabih*; for the Muzaffarids, Mirkhvand's *Rawzat al-safa* and the *Nafahat al-uns*; for the Karts, the *Rawzat al-safa*; and finally, for the Timurids, the *Nafahat al-uns*, the *Rawzat al-safa*, ʿAbd al-Razzaq Samarqandi's *Matlaʿ-i saʿdayn*, Sharaf al-Din ʿAli Yazdi's *Zafarnamah*, and ʿAli Shir Nava'i's *Majalis al-nafa'is*.

A direct or indirect relationship exists between the *Habib al-siyar* and the sources that Khvandamir names, even though he might have

64 Mirkvand, *Rawzat al-safa*, 11: 5941.
65 Khvandamir, *Habib al-siyar*, 4:334; trans., 2: 517.

Table 5.2 ***Named sources in the biographical sections of the* Habib al-siyar**

Mongols	Qazvini's *Tarikh-i Guzidah*
Chubanids	Jami's *Nafahat al-uns*
Mamluks	Yafi'i's *Mirat al-janan*
Muzaffarids	*Tashih al-masabih*
Karts	*Rawzat al-safa*
Timurids	*Nafahat al-uns*
	Rawzat al-safa
	Samarqandi's *Matla'-i sa'dayn*
	Sharaf al-Din 'Ali Yazdi's *Zafarnamah*
	'Ali Shir Nava'i's *Majalis al-nafa'is*

been imitating an intermediate, unnamed text. For example, in the following entry for Sadr al-Din Savaji, a scholar during the reign of Hulagu Khan, Khvandamir cites Qazvini's *Tarikh-i guzidah*, and imitates that history, adding more details to his own entry:

Tarikh-i guzidah	*Habib al-siyar*
Sadr al-Din Savaji, in mind and intellect, was peerless, to the extent that he could memorize the equivalent of a quire of writing having read it only once. Among his poetical writings is a superb *qasida* on prosody and rhyme.[66]	Another of the learned of Hulagu's time was Sadr al-Din Savaji, who was known for his keen mind and excellent memory and for his knowledge of metrics and prosody. It is recorded in the *Tarikh-i guzidah* that Sadr al-Din could memorize the equivalent of a quire of writing having read it only once. He lived in Damascus during Hulagu Khan's time, and he was executed on a charge of sorcery. Among his poetical compositions is a superb *qasida* on prosody and rhyme.[67]
Ṣadr al-Dīn Sāvajī dar z̲ihn va z̲akā' 'adīm al-mis̲āl būd tā bi-martabah'ī kih kitābī c̄hand juzv bi-yak	*Va dīgarī az jumlah-i fuẓalā-'i zamān-i Hūlākū Khān Ṣadr al-Dīn Sāvajī ast va ū bi-ḥiddat-i z̲ihn-i salīm vujūdat-i*

66 Mustawfi Qazvini, *Tarikh-i guzidah*, 695–696.
67 Khvandamir, *Habib al-siyar*, 3: 108; trans., 1: 61.

khvāndan yād mīgirift. Qaṣīdah-i ḥusnā dar 'ilm-i 'arūẓ va qavāfī az taṣānīf-i ūst. Bi-'ahd-i Hulākū Khān bi-tuhmat-i siḥr shahīd shud.

ṭab'-i mustaqīm va vufūrat-i ḥāfiẓah va vuqūf bar 'ilm-i 'arūẓ va qāfiyah ittiṣāf dāsht. Va dar Tārīkh-i guzīdah masṭūr ast kih Ṣadr al-Dīn muvāzī-yi yakjuzv kitābat rā bi-yak khvāndan yād mīgirift va dar zamān-i Hulākū Khān dar Shām muqayyim būd bi-siḥr mutahim gashtah sharbat-i shahādat chashīd. Qaṣīdah-i ḥusnā dar 'ilm-i 'arūẓ va qavāfī az jumlah-'i manẓūmāt-i ūst.

There are several historiographical explanations as to why Khvandamir may have added this *tazkirah* information for the different dynasties that he discusses. The first is stylistic or genre-based. The genre of poetical *tazkirahs* had become very popular in the Timurid period.[68] Furthermore, we know that Khvandamir was familiar with biographical compendia and contributed to the genre himself, because in 915/1509–1510 he composed the *Dastur al-vuzara*, a *tazkirah* biographical compendium devoted to viziers from the period of the Umayyads until Sultan Husayn Bayqara (r. 873-911/1470–1506).[69] The second has to do with the preservation of knowledge in the premodern and early-modern era. Through imitating earlier texts, chroniclers both preserved and carried forward knowledge of the past. Thus, many historians incorporated large portions of multiple earlier histories into their own narratives, often imitating them word-for-word. In this way, Khvandamir's history was not only a continuation of his grandfather's *Rawzat al-safa*, because he brought forward the narrative to include the life of Shah Isma'il, but also an expansion of it, in the sense that he went back and filled in the pre-Safavid sections with biographies that do not appear in the *Rawzat al-safa*.

Beyond matters of style and the preservation of knowledge, politics may also have played a role in Khvandamir's biographical additions. If we examine the number of biographies that Khvandamir included for

68 See Losensky, "Biographical Writing," 10.

69 This work was dedicated to Khvajah Kamal al-Din Mahmud, vizier of Sultan Husayn. Khvandamir, *Dastur al-vuzara'*, ed. Sa'id Nafisi (Tehran: Iqbal, 1317 [1938]).

each ruler beginning with the Mongols (see Table 5.3), we see that they are fairly consistent for the pre-Timurid period. In other words, for various pre-Timurid rulers, Khvandamir lists approximately seven to ten individuals. There are a few "outliers" to this general rule: one Muzaffarid ruler, Amir Muhammad Muzaffar, has only two individuals listed after his section, and one Kart ruler, Malik Ghiyas al-Din Kart, has only one.[70] In contrast to these small numbers, the Mamluk ruler Sultan al-Nasir (r. 693–694/1293–1294; 698–708/1299–1309) has some twenty individuals listed in chronological sequence, a format that differs from Khvandamir's other *tazkirah* sections.[71]

Khvandamir dramatically increased the number of biographies for the Timurid rulers. Beginning with Timur himself, Khvandamir includes some twenty-two notices and adds the names of three additional chess players without including their biographies. For Timur's son Shahrukh (r. 807–850/1405–1447), Khvandamir lists forty-nine individuals and – for the first time in his narrative – organizes the biographies into categories, listing four *ṣadr*s, four viziers, and forty-one sayyids, shaykhs, and learned men. These categories of biographies seem to be listed in order of importance, beginning with the most significant category of *ṣadr*s and ending with the least important, the sayyids, shaykhs, and learned men. Ulugh Beg, another of Timur's sons (r. 850–853/1447–1449), and Abu al-Qasim Babur – Timur's grandson and Shahrukh's son (r. 853–861/1449–1457) – receive a total of fourteen uncategorized biographies each. Sultan Abu Sa'id (b. Sultan Muhammad b. Miranshah b. Timur; r. 855–873/1451–1469) has twenty-five names associated with his reign. However, the Timurid who receives more biographies under his name than any other ruler by far is Sultan Husayn Mirza Bayqara, Timur's great great grandson via his son Umar Shaykh. The entries consist of fourteen *ṣadr*s, ten viziers, and eighty-eight sayyids, leaders, shaykhs, clerics (*'ulama'*), and other learned individuals. This is nearly twice as many entries as we see under Shahrukh or the combined section on Aq Qoyunlu rulers and Shah Isma'il, which all together contains fifty-nine biographies.

What, then, accounts for the large number of biographies associated with Sultan Husayn Bayqara? In real life, Sultan Husayn surrounded himself with poets and artists, partly to increase the prestige of his

[70] Khvandamir, *Habib al-siyar*, 3: 379; trans., 1: 219–220.
[71] Khvandamir, *Habib al-siyar*, 3: 264–266; trans., 1: 152–153.

Table 5.3 ***Number of biographies by ruler in Khvandamir's*** **Habib al-siyar**

Ruler	Number of biographies
[*Mongols*]	
Hulagu	8
Abaqa	14
Arghun	6
Ghazan	6
Oljeitu	8
Abu Sa'id	11 (incl. Shaykh Safi)
Amir Shaykh Hasan Chubani	5
[*Mamluks*]	
Bunduqdar [Baybars I]	5
Sayf al-Din Qala'un	6
Al-Nasir	20 (year by year)
[*Muzaffarids*]	
Amir Muhammad Muzaffar	2
Shah Shuja'	3
[*Karts*]	
Malik Ghiyas al-Din Kart	1
Malik Mu'izz al-Din Husayn Kart	7
[*Timurids*]	
Timur	22 (plus three named chess players)
Shahrukh Mirza	49 (4 comptrollers, 4 viziers, and 41 sayyids, shaykhs, and learned men)
Mirza Ulugh Beg Kuragan	14
Mirza Abu al-Qasim Babur	14
Mirza Shah Mahmud	0
Mirza Sultan Ibrahim	0
Mirza Sultan Abu Sa'id Kuragan	25
Sultan Husayn Mirza (Bayqara)	112 (14 comptrollers, 10 viziers, and 88 sayyids, naqibs, shaykhs, and ulama)
[*Aq Qoyunlu/Safavid*]	
Aq Qoyunlu/Shah Isma'il combined	59

court and to bolster his political legitimacy.[72] Mirkhvand and Khvandamir appear to have done the same thing for Sultan Husayn, with whom they had close connections, by surrounding him textually with biographies of poets, learned scholars, and other important figures. In this way, we may view the narrative as a historiographical extension of Sultan Husayn's star-studded court. Khvandamir and his grandfather Mirkhvand, of course, had close connections to Sultan Husayn Bayqara's court. One of Mirkhvand's patrons was ʻAli Shir Nava'i, who was himself intimately associated with Sultan Husayn Bayqara, and an important patron in his own right.[73]

Moreover, Khvandamir betrays his pro-Timurid bias in choosing the rulers to whom he attached biographies. By adding a fairly small number of *tazkirah*s for the Mongol and post-Mongol dynasties, and a much larger number of *tazkirah*s for Timurid rulers, he lends prestige and legitimacy to the entire Timurid dynasty. At the same time, however, he singles out Shahrukh and Sultan Husayn Bayqara as significant Timurid rulers, with Ulugh Beg, Mirza Abu al-Qasim Babur, and Sultan Abu Saʻid receiving less attention.

As for Shah Ismaʻil, Khvandamir provides comparatively fewer biographies for his reign, especially when we take into consideration the fact that he combines the notices under Ismaʻil with those of the Aq Qoyunlu into a subsection entitled "The sayyids, ʻulama', and nobles, some of whom attained high positions with the Aqqoyunlu and others of whom flourished during the shah's glorious time." While this could simply be due to the fact that Shah Ismaʻil was still alive at the time of Khvandamir's writing and his court had not yet been fully established or developed, it is also the case that Khvandamir had closer ties with the Timurid rulers than with the Safavid founder.[74]

72 See David J. Roxburgh, "Art and Literature in Timurid Herat, 1469–1506: The Life and Times of Sultan ʻAli Mashhadi," in *Pearls on a String: Artists, Patrons, and Poets at the Great Islamic Courts*, ed. Amy S. Landau, 115–140 (Baltimore, MD: Walters Art Museum, 2015); and Maria Eva Subtelny, "Art and Politics in Early 16th Century Central Asia," *Central Asiatic Journal* 27 (1983): 121–148.

73 For more on this topic, see Maria Eva Subtelny, "ʻAlī Shīr Navāʾī: Bakhshī and Beg."

74 This pro-Timurid sentiment continued in the family; Maria Szuppe has demonstrated that Khvandamir's son, Amir Mahmud, showed equal admiration for Babur and Humayun as for Safavid kings in his Safavid history, the *Zayl-i habib al-siyar*, a continuation of his father's history. Maria Szuppe, *Entre Timourides, Uzbeks et Safavides: Questions d'Histoire politique et sociale de*

The Next Generation: Dughlat and Lari

The next example we see of a chronicler blending *tazkirah* information into a chronicle appears in Mirza Haydar Dughlat's *Tarikh-i Rashidi.* We have already shown in Chapter 2 how Dughlat highly praises and quotes from Sharaf al-Din 'Ali Yazdi's Timurid history, the *Zafarnamah*, in his preface. In addition to this, he also makes references to both Mirkhvand and Khvandamir in his history. Dughlat includes only one set of biographies in his *Tarikh-i Rashidi*, and this appears after a section where he explains how he and his father left Shahrisabz and fled to Khurasan in approximately 977/1506 because his father learned that the Uzbeks were plotting to kill him. This occurred toward the end of Sultan Husayn Bayqara's life. Dughlat tells us of the magnificence of Sultan Husayn's court, describing how he "promoted and patronized all classes of persons to such a degree that in every field there were one or two world-renowned masters the likes of whom had never existed before."[75]

After this, Dughlat stops his narrative and makes a first person intervention. In the same way that he stated in his introduction that he was unable to write a proper preface, here he confesses that "think and contemplate as I may to make a sufficient report of the mystics who lived during that blessed time, I find that I am incapable." He quickly changes his mind, however, stating that "amazingly, however, I cannot find it within me to leave this page blank."[76] He then proceeds with his *tazkirah* section, which he organized into categories of twelve mystics, one learned man and a list of the scholars who were his students, nine poets, two enigmatists, one calligrapher, nine painters going back to the time of the celebrated miniaturist Bihzad, two illuminators, two singers, and four musicians.[77] The section on calligraphy consists of a number of mostly names – without biographies – of calligraphers, organized according to the type of script they specialized in and a biography of calligrapher Sultan 'Ali Mashhadi. While the biographies only appear in connection with Sultan Husayn Bayqara, as was the case with Mirkhvand's *Rawzat al-safa*, in terms of content,

Hérat dans la première Moitié du XVIe Siècle (Paris: Association pour l'Avancement des Études iraniennes, 1992), 147–148.

75 Dughlat, *Tarikh-i Rashidi*, 146; trans., 117.

76 Dughlat, *Tarikh-i Rashidi*, 146; trans., 117.

77 Dughlat, *Tarikh-i Rashidi*, 147–167; trans., 117–132.

Dughlat does not appear to have imitated either the *Rawzat al-safa* or the *Habib al-siyar*. The following biographical entries for the painter Mirak Naqqash shows the close relationship between the *Rawzat al-safa* and the *Habib al-siyar*, and also indicates how the *Tarikh-i Rashidi* diverges from these texts:

Rawzat al-safa	*Habib al-siyar*	*Tarikh-i Rashidi*
Khvajah Mirak Naqqash had no equal in depiction and illumination. In epigraphy he raised the standard of uniqueness, and most of the epigraphic inscriptions in the buildings of the abode of the sultanate of Harat are by him. He died during Muhammad Khan Shaybani's taking of Khurasan.[78]	Khvaja Mirak Naqqash had no equal in depiction and illumination. In epigraphy he raised the banner of uniqueness, and most of the epigraphic inscriptions in the buildings of Harat are by him. He died during Muhammad Khan Shaybani's occupation of Khurasan.[79]	Mawlana Mirak Naqqash is one of the wonders of the age. He was Bihzad's master. His sketching is more masterly than Bihzad's. Although his execution is not up to Bihzad's, still all his works were done outside in the open air, whether he was traveling, in attendance on the prince or at home; and he was never tied to a studio or portfolio. This is strange enough, but further yet he practiced all kinds of sports, and this is absolutely at odds with being a painter. In order to [indecipherable phrase] he often practiced body-building exercises and gained a reputation for that. It is quite strange to couple painting with such things.[80]

78 Mirkhvand, *Rawzat al-safa*, 11: 5974.
79 Khvandamir, *Habib al-siyar*, 4: 348; trans., 2: 524.
80 Dughlat, *Tarikh-i Rashidi*, 165; trans., 131.

Dughlat, then, while taking inspiration from Mirkhvand and Khvandamir by including a *tazkirah* section in the first place, and perhaps in terms of some of the names and categories he includes, does not imitate either text in his *Tarikh-i Rashidi*, but appears to include information he obtained elsewhere for this *tazkirah* section.

The biographies associated with Shah Isma'il in the *Habib al-siyar* provide a fascinating contrast when compared with Muslih al-Din Lari's *Mir'at al-advar va mirqat al-akhbar*, which demonstrates even more clearly how historians used *tazkirah*s for political purposes. Like Khvandamir, Lari added biographies throughout his chronicle, including the very early periods of Islamic history. For example, under the 'Abbasid caliph al-Mutawakkil, he provides short accounts of several individuals, including the hadith scholars al-Bukhari (194–256/810–870) and Muslim b. Hajjaj (204–261/819–875).[81]

Lari places, as does Khvandamir, the largest number of biographies in his narrative covering the Timurid era. For example, in the middle of his chapter on the Timurids, he inserts a specific, discrete section on adepts (*'urafā'*), shaykhs (*mashāyikh*), and clerics (*'ulamā'*) from the time of Timur, listing some fifteen individuals. A few of these names also appear in Khvandamir's *Habib al-siyar*, but there are no instances of imitative writing. After his biographies of these individuals, Lari goes on to narrate the accounts of other Timurid rulers. He next places *tazkirah* material in a section entitled "the lords of mystic states and the perfect companions" (*arbāb-i ḥāl va aṣḥāb-i kamāl*) and clerics (*'ulamā'*), listing fourteen individuals from the time of "Sultan Husayn Mirza [Bayqara] and the children of Sultan Abu Sa'id in Khurasan and Mavar al-nahr." This section appears at the end of his Timurid chapter. Although a couple of names in this section appear in Dughlat's *Tarikh-i Rashidi*, again we see no instances of imitative writing.

Lari devotes chapter nine to Uzun Hasan Aq Qoyunlu (r. 857–882/1453–1478), after whose account he lists some three individuals who were among the erudite scholars (*fużalā*) of the time and then five individuals under "shaykhs and mystic knowers (*'urafā'*)." It is important to note that Lari does not provide a separate, dedicated chapter to the Safavids. Rather, like Khvandamir, he combines his narrative on the Safavids with his account of Uzun Hasan. Lari's text provides an

[81] Lari, *Mir'at al-advar*, 1: 394.

instructive example of how our chroniclers used *tazkirah* for political purposes. After listing some eight erudite scholars (*fāżil*), shaykhs, and mystic knowers (*'urafa'*) during the period of Uzun Hasan, Lari continues to provide brief overviews of Uzun Hasan's descendants, ending with Shah Isma'il, who was Uzun Hasan's grandson via his daughter 'Alam Shah Begum.[82] Lari does not add any biographies at all to Shah Isma'il's account, which consists of a fairly straightforward narrative of the geographical regions that he brought under his control, and the year that each campaign took place. He ends by noting Shah Isma'il's defeat at the battle of Chaldiran and providing his birth and death dates.

In contrast with his account of Shah Isma'il, Lari writes a very different sort of narrative for Shah Tahmasb. While he says nothing about Shah Isma'il's religiosity, he states that Shah Tahmasb attempted, from the very start of his reign, to promote Twelver Shi'ism, and at the same time disallowed the works of Sunnis in the regions that were under his control. Lari complains that many were intent on destroying the Sunni 'ulama and in Shah Tahmasb's opinion, ignorant people were made to look like learned people, and learned people were called ignorant.[83] Most of the shah's territories, he continued, were emptied of people of erudition (*fażl*) and learning, and filled with ignorant people, such that only a few people among the erudite ones (*fużalā'*) were left in all of the territories of Iran. He ends his account of Shah Tahmasb by stating that only a few of the Sunni forebears (*salaf*) remained, who opened their mouths in guiding people. He names seven individuals in this group:

(1) Mir Ghiyas al-Din Mansur (Lari's teacher)
(2) Shams al-Din Muhammad Khafri
(3) Kamal al-Din Husayn Lari (Lari's teacher), student of Davani
(4) Husayn Ardabili (Kamal al-Din Husayn Ilahi Aradbili)
(5) Sayyid Jamal al-Din 'Ata Allah bin Fazl Allah Muhaddis (Husayn Ardabili's teacher)
(6) 'Abd al-'Ali Birjandi (astronomer) (d. 934/1527–1528)
(7) Muhammad Hanafi (Muhammad Amin al-Hanafi al-Tabrizi)[84]

[82] Lari, *Mir'at al-advar*, 2: 895–899.
[83] Lari, *Mir'at al-advar*, 2: 900.
[84] Lari, *Mir'at al-advar*, 2: 900–901.

He also lists the names of some of their works. Of these individuals, the first five are associated with the so-called Shiraz school of philosophy, and the first and third names were Lari's own teachers.[85] Three others were students of Ghiyas al-Din Mansur, his father Sadr al-Din al-Dashtaki, and his rival Jalal al-Din al-Davani, or individuals who had intellectual connections to these Shirazi philosophers. Although some of them actually were respected by Shah Isma'il and Shah Tahmasb, it is clear that Lari is naming them as a group to express his personal and political opinion about the Safavids and about those Shi'is who, he said, held "ugly and obscene beliefs" about wanting to do away with the Sunni learned, or the *'ulama-yi ahl-i sunnat.*[86] Ali Anooshahr outlines the main contours of this group of philosophers who originated in sixteenth-century Shiraz, went through a similar education, and came to dominate the religious position of *ṣadr.* Anooshahr further shows how a number of students of these Shirazi philosophers ended up in India, in places like Bijapur under the reign of 'Ali 'Adilshah (r. 965–988/1580–1627), the Shi'i ruler of Bijapur, and eventually at the court of Akbar, where one such scholar, Fath Allah Shirazi, helped Akbar devise a new calendar and taught the children of Mughal elites. Muslih al-Din Lari himself, while at Humayun's court, also wrote about time and the Islamic calendar.[87]

85 Lari, *Mir'at al-advar*, 900–901.

86 On the influence of these scholars, even in the Ottoman empire, see Khaled El-Rouayheb, *Islamic Intellectual History in the Seventeenth Century: Scholarly Currents in the Ottoman Empire and the Maghreb* (Cambridge: Cambridge University Press, 2015), 88–89. There appears to have been no love lost between Lari and the Safavid rulers. Hamid Algar suggests that Lari left Safavid territory because of "his father's habit, before the establishment of Safavid supremacy, of patrolling the streets of Lar to clip the luxuriant moustaches that characterized the Shi'is of the city." Hamid Algar, "Persian Literature in Bosnia-Herzegovina," *Journal of Islamic Studies* 5 (1994): 256. But it is also likely that Lari initially went to Mughal territory, before settling in the Ottoman empire, for the same reasons that the poets went, in search of better funding and intellectual support, especially during the 1530s–1570s, when "Dashtaki (and his students) lost access to court patronage in Safavid Iran." Ali Anooshahr, "Shirazi Scholars and the Political Culture of the Sixteenth-Century Indo-Persian World," *Indian Economic Social History Review* 51 (2014): 339.

87 Anooshahr, "Shirazi Scholars," 344. Lari's writings differed somewhat from those of Fath Allah Shirazi. See also Francis Robinson, "Ottomans-Safavids-Mughals: Shared Knowledge and Connective Systems," *Journal of Islamic Studies* 8 (1997): 151–184.

The Mughal Chronicles

Indo-Persian historiographical writing encompasses the most robust tradition of *tazkirah* writing in historical chronicles. Indeed, an argument could be made that the tradition began with Babur himself, who included in his memoirs written in Chaghatay Turkish, the *Baburnamah*, numerous biographical sketches of individuals associated with various rulers of the time. For example, in his account of Sultan Ahmad Mirza, a great great grandson of Timur and Babur's uncle (r. Samarqand and Bukhara 1469–1494), Babur lists his wives and concubines and then ends the section with short biographies of his principal officers.[88] This practice can also be seen in three narratives from the period of Akbar: the *Akbarnamah*, the *Tabaqat-i Akbari*, and the *Muntakhab al-tavarikh*.

The Akbarnamah

The *Akbarnamah* is a highly complex history, consisting of many volumes and sections, and written from a specific ideological perspective. Abu al-Fazl was primarily interested in portraying Akbar as "both the Iranian ideal of the divinely sanctioned monarch and the Sufi ideal of the Perfect Man," a project that he undertook in other ways as well.[89] In terms of *tazkirah* information, unlike Khvandamir, whose writings he was familiar with, Abu al-Fazl does not add biographical entries to the end of his accounts of various kings. Rather, he places this information into the third and final volume of the *Akbarnamah*. This volume is called the *Ain-i Akbari*, and it has often been described by scholars as a separate and distinct text from the *Akbarnamah*.[90] This is largely due its contents, which consist of a gazetteer and a highly detailed description of the workings of the Mughal government. However much the contents of the first two volumes of the *Akbarnamah* and the *Ain-i Akbari* differ, Abu al-Fazl considered the entire text collectively as one work, the *Akbarnamah*, as evidenced by his conclusion to the final volume of the *Ain-i Akbari*, where he states:

88 See Babur, *Baburnama*, Thackston trans., 24–25.
89 *EIR*, s.v., "Abu'l Fażl 'Allāmī," by R. M. Eaton.
90 See EIR, s.v., "Akbar-nāma," by R. M. Eaton, and M. Athar Ali, "The Use of Sources," 370–371.

It is my intention to write in four volumes (*daftar*) a record of the transactions of the royal house during one hundred and twenty years, which are four generations, that it may stand as a memorial for those who seek knowledge in justice, and with the Institutions (*ā'īnhā*) of His Majesty as the concluding book, I purposed the completion of the Akbarnāmah in these five volumes.[91]

That Abu al-Fazl incorporated a gazetteer as the final section of his history is not entirely without precedent. Khvandamir, for example, included at the end of his *Habib al-siyar* an account of the wonders of the world, and while this formed the conclusion (*khātimah*) of his history, the *Ain-i Akbari* could be seen as an extensive structural magnification of Khvandamir's organizational framework. It is for these reasons that we may consider the *Ain-i Akbari* as the last section of Abu al-Fazl's historical work, the *Akbarnamah*.

The *Ain-i Akbari* provides historians with valuable information about Mughal society and the people who were part of it during Akbar's reign. It is itself divided into five books. At the end of Book Two, Abu al-Fazl includes a section on the "grandees of the empire." This extensive portion of the *Ain-i Akbari* contains lists of commanders' names according to how many troops they commanded, from five thousand down to two hundred. Altogether, Abu al-Fazl lists some 370 individuals, although he provides no biographical information about them. He follows the amirs with a list of 115 "learned men of the time," organizing them into five classes: (1) those who have both inner and outer understanding (21 individuals), (2) those who pay less attention to the external world but acquire vast knowledge (15 individuals), (3) those whose understanding does not go beyond observation (11 individuals), (4) those who look upon testimony with suspicion (28 individuals), and (5) those who are bigoted and cannot move beyond revealed testimony (40 individuals).[92]

Abu al-Fazl follows these groups of names with two more sections: first, an account of fifty-nine poets, including samples of poetry for each, and second, a list of thirty-six musicians. These musicians, Abu al-Fazl states, came from Hindu, Iranian, Turkish, and Kashmiri backgrounds were both men and women, and were arranged according to days of the week (into

[91] Abu al-Fazl, *Ain-i Akbari*, 2: 257; trans., 2: 476.
[92] Abu al-Fazl, *Ain-i Akbari*, 1: 232–235; trans., 2: 606–617.

seven divisions). Abu al-Fazl states that Akbar "pays much attention to music and is the patron of all who practice this enchanting art."[93]

While Abu al-Fazl certainly draws on an already established tradition of blending genres in his *Akbarnamah*, the sheer numbers of individuals that he lists, names, and in some cases describes, surpasses any earlier chronicle. In doing this, Abu al-Fazl textually surrounds Akbar with many times more than the number of individuals at any previous court, including that of Sultan Husayn Bayqara. By presenting numbers and statistics, and by naming names, Abu al-Fazl attaches the entire court and government, in all its wealth and magnitude, and with specific named individuals, to his historical narrative on Akbar's reign. Furthermore, he also replicates the social hierarchy that the various groups represent by placing the most important group first and the least important group last.[94] The four categories that Abu al-Fazl organizes his *tazkirah* entries around extend beyond the traditional subject matter of *tazkirahs*, which focus primarily on saints and poets. Although these groups are represented in the *Ain-i Akbari*, Abu al-Fazl's adding the category of military commanders to the *Ain-i Akbari*, and listing them first, places them in an important social position.

Abu al-Fazl's history also served as a model text that subsequent chroniclers imitated, responded to, and referenced when writing their own histories. This assured the survival of the *tazkirahs* into the later Mughal period. Furthermore, the imitation began quite early on in Mughal history. Although Abu al-Fazl continued to work on his *Akbarnamah* until his death in 1602, Nizam al-Din Ahmad Bakhshi, author of the *Tabaqat-i Akbari*, refers to the *Akbarnamah* in his history, which he composed in 1001/1592–1593.[95]

The Tabaqat-i Akbari

Nizam al-Din did not have the resources that were placed at Abu al-Fazl's disposal when he composed his *Tabaqat-i Akbari*. The *Tabaqat-i*

93 Abu al-Fazl, *Ain-i Akbari*, 1: 262–263; trans., 1: 681.

94 M. Athar Ali suggests that Akbar himself, with his establishment of the *ṣulḥ-i kull*, or universal peace, transcended the "parallel coexistence of cultures" or a "mere synthesis of cultures." M. Athar Ali, "The Evolution of the Perception of India: Akbar and Abu'l Fazl," *Social Scientist* 24 (1996): 80–88.

95 Storey notes that the text has been extended to 1002/1593–1594. See Storey, *Persian Literature*, 433.

Akbari consists of an introduction, a conclusion, and nine genealogies or categories of rulers (*ṭabaqāt*). Nizam al-Din apparently intended to conclude his history with a geographical treatise but was unable to complete this portion of his text. Nizam al-Din employs a geographical/chronological framework in his history, with each category of ruler (*ṭabaqah*) devoted to one region in India. His introduction covers the Ghaznavid kings, beginning with Sebüktigin and ending with Khusraw Malik. The first and longest of nine sections is devoted to Delhi, beginning with Sultan Mu'izz al-Din Ghuri and ending with Akbar.[96] Nizam al-Din planned for his conclusion to consist of a geographical treatise but apparently did not complete it.[97]

At the time of his writing, Nizam al-Din already had access to the *Akbarnamah*, even though Abu al-Fazl was alive then and continued to work on his *Akbarnamah* until his death in 1602.[98] Nizam al-Din, like Abu al-Fazl, includes *tazkirah* information in his *Tabaqat-i Akbari*, but he places this material in a section appearing after his narrative on Akbar's reign. In fact, Akbar is the only ruler for whom Nizam al-Din provides *tazkirah* information. In doing this within the context of writing a general history of India beginning with the Ghaznavids, he distinguishes Akbar from the other rulers whose lives and dynasties he narrates, and like Abu al-Fazl, provides Akbar with an extensive textual cadre of military commanders, scholars, scientists, and poets.

Nizam al-Din introduces the *tazkirah* section by telling his readers that, having "completed the fortunate and auspicious history of his Majesty, the khalifa-i-Ilahi," he would now "commence with naming the Amirs of high rank, who during [the time of] this exalted dynasty have rendered great service."[99] He then references Abu al-Fazl and the *Akbarnamah* in his final comments introducing the *tazkirah* section:

> As the names (histories) of the amirs of his majesty, the khalifa-i ilahi, are more numerous than can be contained in this short history, and as that asylum of excellencies, the most learned Shaykh Abu'l Fazl has written in his wonderful style an account of each of them in his book (called the)

96 Storey, *Persian Literature*, 433–434.
97 See Storey, *Persian Literature*, 433–434.
98 *EIR*, s.v., "Akbar-nāma," by R. M. Eaton.
99 For more on the divine caliph (*khalīfah-i ilāhi*), see Chapter 2. Nizam al-Din Ahmad Bakhshi, *Tabaqat-i Akbari*, 2: 425; trans., 2: 653.

Akbarnama, I have confined myself to mention of the names (histories) of great amirs (*umarā-yi kubār*) only.[100]

Nizam al-Din organizes these individuals roughly according to rank, placing the most prominent military commanders at the beginning, starting with the commander-in-chief, then the great amirs, the *khānkhānāns*, and finally, the commanders of four, three, two, and one thousand horses. While some of the individuals listed here are also mentioned in the *A'in-i Akbari*, there are no instances of imitative writing. After listing the prominent military commanders, Nizam al-Din continues with different categories of biographies. He classifies these into five main groups: (1) military commanders (*amīr*s),[101] (2) learned and wise men (*'ulamā' va fużalā'*),[102] (3) the shaykhs of Hindustan,[103] (4) physicians (*ḥukamā'*),[104] and (5) poets (*shu'arā'*).[105]

Akbar is the only ruler for whom Nizam al-Din provides *tazkirah* information. In doing this within the context of writing a general history of India beginning with the Ghaznavids, he distinguishes Akbar from the other rulers whose lives and dynasties he narrates, and like Abu al-Fazl, provides Akbar with an extensive textual cadre of military commanders, scholars, physicians, and poets. The political significance of the *tazkirah* sections becomes more apparent when we examine the order in which individuals are named. In other words, the hierarchy discussed above in terms of the actual groups of individuals mentioned, from most to least important, is replicated in the list of names within a single category.

Nizam al-Din's account of military commanders tells us something about the larger context of rival Persianate empires, much as Lari's list did. Bayram Khan is the first military commander that Nizam al-Din mentions, and the first thing he says about him is that he was a descendant of Mirza Jahan Shah Qara Qoyunlu (r. 841–872–3/1438–1467–8/1438–1467/1468).[106] He says nothing about how Akbar removed him from this position when he became "suspicious

[100] Nizam al-Din, *Tabaqat-i Akbari*, 2: 425; trans., 2: 653. Translation slightly modified.
[101] Nizam al-Din, *Tabaqat-i Akbari*, 2: 425–457; trans., 2: 653–684.
[102] Nizam al-Din, *Tabaqat-i Akbari*, 2: 457–471; trans., 2: 684–699.
[103] Nizam al-Din, *Tabaqat-i Akbari*, 2: 471–480; trans., 2: 700–710.
[104] Nizam al-Din, *Tabaqat-i Akbari*, 2: 481–484; trans., 2: 710–714.
[105] Nizam al-Din, *Tabaqat-i Akbari*, 2: 484–520; trans., 2: 714–753.
[106] Nizam al-Din, *Tabaqat-i Akbari*, 2: 425; trans., 2: 653. For more on Bayram Khan, see *EIR*, "Bayram Khan." s. v., N. H. Ansari.

of Bayram's growing influence."[107] The next individual listed is Mirza Shahrukh, son of Mirza Ibrahim, son of Sulayman Mirza. Mirza Shahrukh's grandfather, Sulayman Mirza, was a cousin of Babur's and an adopted son of Humayun. He ruled Badakhshan and came to Akbar's court when the Uzbeks took over the city.[108] The third individual is Tardi Beg Khan, who Nizam al-Din says was one of Akbar's great amirs, but in the first year of Akbar's reign, "he was, on account of certain political reasons, put to death by the endeavours of Bairam (Bayram) Khan."[109] The fourth military commander that Nizam al-Din mentions is Mirza Rustam, whom he describes as Shah Isma'il's great grandson via Bahram Mirza and Sultan Husayn Mirza.[110] By placing these individuals at the beginning of his list of amirs, Nizam al-Din stresses Akbar's power and authority over what they represented in terms of their ancestry: the Qara Qoyunlu, the Badakhshan Timurids, and the Safavids.

Nizam al-Din continues to emphasize individuals who came to India in his *tazkirah* entries on scholars, shaykhs, physicians, and poets, listing these people first. Under his account of learned and wise men, he states that the individuals he intends to discuss either "lived in the great continent of Hindustan during the time of Akbar," or "have come from other countries to the threshold, which is the asylum of all people."[111] As in his section on military commanders, he begins with those who came from abroad. The first person he mentions is Amir Fath Allah Shirazi, who he says was "distinguished above all learned men of Khurasan and Iraq and India: and in his own time he had no one in the world similar and equal to him."[112] Fath Allah Shirazi was a Sufi and scholar who studied with individuals such as Ghiyas al-Din Mansur, who was one of Muslih al-Din Lari's teachers discussed above who was associated with the Shiraz school.[113] In naming him first, Nizam al-Din places him at the top of the hierarchy of "learned and wise men" and connects him to Mughal state service, thereby claiming him for Akbar.[114]

107 *EIR*, s.v., "Bayram Khan," by N. H. Ansari.
108 Michael Herbert Fisher, *A Short History of the Mughal Empire* (London: I. B. Tauris, 2016), 57, 77–78.
109 Nizam al-Din, *Tabaqat-i Akbari*, 2: 426; trans., 2: 654.
110 Nizam al-Din, *Tabaqat-i Akbari*, 2: 426; trans., 2: 654.
111 Nizam al-Din, *Tabaqat-i Akbari*, 2: 457; trans., 2: 684.
112 Nizam al-Din, *Tabaqat-i Akbari*, 2: 457; trans., 2: 684–685.
113 See *EIR*, s.v., "Fatḥ-Allāh Šīrāzī, Sayyed Mīr," by Sharif Husain Qasemi.
114 Ali Anooshahr has noted that "Fath Allah's career demonstrates that while imperial ideologies both reflected and were directed at local populations, they

The second individual that Nizam al-Din lists is Amir Murtaza Sharifi, a grandson of the great Timurid scholar Sayyid Sharif-i Jurjani, who he says "came to India in the year 972 A.H. [1563–4] corresponding with the 8th year of the Ilahi era, and received imperial benefactions." The third individual is Mulla Sa'id Samarqandi, who he similarly says "came to India in 970 A.H. [1561–2], and was distinguished by imperial favours. He was one of the very wise men of his age." The first person he mentions who did not come to India from somewhere else is the fourth name on the list: Abu al-Fazl, author of the *Akbarnamah*.[115] The political point that Nizam al-Din seems to be making with this hierarchy of names is that Akbar's court was international and surrounded with talented individuals who came to India just to be at the Mughal court. *Tazkirahs*, then, are clearly not politically neutral texts. Such was especially the case for another well-known Mughal chronicler, 'Abd al-Qadir Badauni.

The Muntakhab al-tavarikh

'Abd al-Qadir Badauni's (947–ca. 1024/1540–ca. 1615) *Muntakhab al-tavarikh* (1004/1595–1596) covers the same chronological ground as Nizam al-Din's *Tabaqat-i Akbari*. Furthermore, Badauni, who was associated with Akbar's court, yet highly critical of Akbar's religious persuasions, indicates familiarity with the *Tabaqat-i Akbari* and imitates this work in his history. Badauni includes *tazkirah* information in the final volume of his history, and he organizes the biographies using almost the exact same format as Nizam al-Din. Indeed, in his preface, Badauni explicitly states his reliance on the *Tabaqat-i Akbari* and an earlier history, the *Tarikh-i Mubarak Shahi*: "I have selected and

were simultaneously intended for a trans-regional elite audience that was steeped in its own tradition—one that was adamantly group conscious and deeply connected to state service and textual scholarship." Anooshahr, "Shirazi Scholars," 350–351. For an analysis of the Shirazi scholars and their ties to the Ottoman empire, see Judith Pfeiffer, "Teaching the Learned: Jalāl al-Dīn al-Dawānī's *Ijāza* to Mu'ayyadzāda 'Abd al-Raḥmān Efendi and the Circulation of Knowledge between Fārs and the Ottoman Empire at the Turn of the Sixteenth Century," in *The Heritage of Arabo-Islamic Learning: Studies Presented to Wadad Kadi*, eds. Maurice A. Pomerantz and Aram Shahin, 284–332 (Leiden and Boston: Brill, 205 [2016]).

[115] Nizam al-Din, *Tabaqat-i Akbari*, 2: 487; trans., 2: 685.

transcribed accurately a portion of the circumstances of some of the autocrat emperors of Hindustan from the *Tarikh-i Mubarak Shahi* and the *Nizam al-tavarikh* of Nizami ... and have also added somewhat of my own."[116]

The relationship between these two histories is something like the relationship between the *Rawzat al-safa* and the *Habib al-siyar*, and being aware of this connection allows us to understand what changes Badauni made to his overall *tazkirah* scheme. Indeed, we may view the *tazkirah* portion of Badauni's history as a "response" to the *Tabaqat-i Akbari*. Overall, Badauni organizes his *tazkirah* categories in a similar fashion to Nizam al-Din, with one significant difference: in this case, he completely removes an entire class of people and moves the category of holy men (shaykhs) to the top of the hierarchy. Badauni explicitly states that he has not followed the standard organizational pattern:

> I would here request my respected and critical readers and acute appraisers not to be unduly carping and censorious as regards the lack of arrangement in this work, for the famous names of the members of the two classes which I have mentioned, who have been specially chosen out from among the people for honour, are mentioned in these few pages as haphazard like scattered pearls, and without regard to precedence or place.[117]

The following table shows the comparative organizational schemes of Nizam al-Din and Badauni:

Nizam al-Din *Tabaqat-i Akbari*	Badauni *Muntakhab al-tavarikh*
1. Amirs	1. Holy men (*mashāyikh*)[118]
2. Learned and wise men (*'ulamā' va fużalā'*)	2. Learned men (*fużalā'*)[119]
3. Physicians (*ḥukamā'*)	3. Physicians (*ḥakīmān*)[120]
4. Poets (*shu'arā'*)	4. Poets (*shu'arā'*)[121]

Badauni explicitly explains this change in sequence, noting that he would not be starting with describing the nobles of the realm like

116 Badauni, *Muntakhab al-tavarikh*, 3: 3; trans., 3: 10.
117 Badauni, *Muntakhab al-tavarikh*, 3: 108; trans., 3: 21–22.
118 Badauni, *Muntakhab al-tavarikh*, 3: 3; trans., 3: 1.
119 Badauni, *Muntakhab al-tavarikh*, 3: 48; trans., 3: 109.
120 Badauni, *Muntakhab al-tavarikh*, 3: 111; trans., 3: 224.
121 Badauni, *Muntakhab al-tavarikh*, 3: 119; trans., 3: 239.

Nizam al-Din did, but rather he would begin with the "holy men" "who were regularly employed in the Imperial Service until their fame reached such a pitch that it was as manifest as the sun at mid-day."[122] He states that he did not include the nobles because

> It will not remain concealed that as the author of the *Tarikh-i Nizami* has given an account of the nobles of the realm immediately after his history of the empire, and as most of them are now dead, and gone to perdition ... I will refrain from polluting the nib of my pen with a description of such worthless wretches (*ḥashviyāt*).[123]

He goes on to say that he will instead "commence with the enumeration of some of the holy men of the age, for an account of noble men who have chosen the way of God is in every way to be preferred to an account of scoundrels and debauchees (*fisqah-i fajrah*)."[124]

In addition to replacing Nizam al-Din's amirs with holy men, Badauni also omitted specific individuals from his *tazkirah* entries and changed the wording in other instances. A close examination of his section on physicians demonstrates how Badauni rewrote the *Tabaqat-i Akbari*. Badauni's section on physicians consists of fifteen names, as opposed to Nizam al-Din's twenty six.[125] Nearly all fifteen on Badauni's list can be found, in approximately the same order, in the *Tabaqat*. The actual entries, however, differ. For example, Badauni's entry on Hakim Hasan Gilani adds a phrase that is critical of the physician but still imitative of the *Tabaqat-i Akbari*:

Tabaqat-i Akbari	*Muntakhab al-tavarikh*
Hakim Hasan Gilani is possessed of praiseworthy morals.[126]	Hakim Hasan Gilani. He was noted for his natural quickness of wit, but he had not learning in proportion, though he

122 Badauni, *Muntakhab al-tavarikh*, 3: 3; trans., 3: 2.
123 Badauni, *Muntakhab al-tavarikh*, 3: 3; trans., 3: 1. M. Athar Ali suggests that Badauni was relying on 'Ala al-Dawlah's *Nafa'is al-Ma'asir*, but Badauni himself states that he is relying on Nizam al-Din. See Ali, "The Use of Sources," 369–370.
124 Badauni, *Muntakhab al-tavarikh*, 3: 3; trans., 3: 1
125 This has been commented on by various scholars. See, for example, Mukhia, *Historians and Historiography*, 118. See also Badauni, *Muntakhab al-tavarikh*, trans., 3: 238.
126 Nizam al-Din, *Tabaqat-i Akbari*, trans., 2: 712.

	possessed excellent qualities and praiseworthy attributes.[128]
Ṣāḥib-i akhlāq-i ḥamīdah ast.[127]	*bih ḥazāqāt-i shihrat dāsht va 'ilmash nah chinān būd ammā ṣāḥib-i makārim-i akhlāq va maḥāmid-i awṣāf būd.*[129]

Badauni's own personal attitudes become more easily discernable when we know what text he used as a model. As noted above, he removed some eleven names from his list of physicians, naming only fifteen individuals in comparison with Nizam al-Din's twenty six. If we look at the names that Badauni removed, it is clear that approximately half at least of them are names of Indian origin and were mostly physicians and surgeons as opposed to other sorts of medical experts. Badauni himself alludes to his removal of names at the end of his section on physicians: "There are also among the physicians others, obscure Muslims and accursed Hindus, from writing of whom my heart revolts."[130]

The Safavid Revival of the Convention

The fully developed *tazkirah* convention that we see in the *Rawzat al-safa* and the *Habib al-siyar* does not appear again in Safavid historical writing until 1038/1629, when Iskandar Beg Munshi completed his *Tarikh-i 'alam-ara-yi 'Abbasi.*[131] Iskandar Beg inserts biographical *tazkirah* material in three different places in his history. The first

[127] Nizam al-Din, *Tabaqat-i Akbari*, 2: 482.
[128] Badauni, *Muntakhab al-tavarikh*, trans., 3: 234.
[129] Badauni, *Muntakhab al-tavarikh*, 3: 115.
[130] Badauni, *Muntakhab al-tavarikh*, 3: 117; trans., 3: 238.
[131] Although it seems that only one pre-Shah 'Abbas chronicler – Hasan Beg Rumlu – followed this convention, and he did so only partially in his *Ahsan al-tavarikh*. This chronicle was originally intended as a twelve-volume world history, but only the last two volumes (11 and 12) have survived. Rumlu, who completed his chronicle during the reign of Shah Isma'il II (r. 984–875/ 1576–1577), organizes the information in his chronicle annalistically, according to hijri years, and adds the *tazkirah* material in the form of approximately one to three obituary notices at the end of each year's entry. These obituary notices usually follow a section of "miscellaneous events." See Hasan Beg Rumlu, *Ahsan al-tavarikh*, ed. 'Abd al-Husayn Nava'i (Tehran: Bungah-i Tarjumah va Nashr-i Kitab, 1349 [1970]).

appears at the end of his narrative on Shah Tahmasb, where he appends a large collection of biographies in some fifteen categories and subcategories, including Qizilbash amirs, sayyids, shaykhs, clerics and theologians, viziers, accountants and secretaries, and poets, artists, calligraphers, and musicians. In total, he provides somewhere between 150 and 200 biographical entries. This stands in stark contrast to the dearth of biographies that we see in Lari's *Mir'at al-advar*, and his comments about the lack of learning and scholarship during the reign of Shah Tahmasb. It may be that Iskandar Beg was writing in response to Lari, though we have no evidence that he was familiar with the *Mir'at al-advar*. The second place where we find biographical information is at the end of each year's narrative where he includes obituaries of several individuals who died during that year, usually numbering some three to five people. In this way, Iskandar Beg's chronicle echoes Hasan Beg Rumlu's *Ahsan al-tavarikh*, which he cites as one of his sources elsewhere in his history. The third and final cluster of biographies appears in the last section of the chronicle before the formal conclusion (*khātimah*), where Iskandar Beg lists amirs of the Qizilbash tribes who lived during Shah 'Abbas's time, followed by ghulams who were khans or sultans, and then finally *ṣadr*s, viziers, comptrollers, and provincial viziers. All together they number approximately 112 individuals.

It appears that Iskandar Beg Munshi had plans to include even more such material in his chronicle, in the form of a *tazkirah* section on poets, had he not run out of time. He makes this point in his conclusion (*khātimah*), where he states "I had also hoped to conclude my history with a few quotations from some of the poets who wrote during the reign of Shah 'Abbas, but by the time I finished writing the history, I had not collected this material either, and so this project too must be postponed until another time."[132]

Historiographical and Historical Contexts

Why would Iskandar Beg Munshi include so much *tazkirah* information when most of his predecessors did not? Both historiographical and historical context helps us understand his motivation. In terms of historiographical context, we know that Iskandar Beg drew on a large

[132] Iskandar Beg, *'Alam-ara-yi 'Abbasi*, 1095; trans., 1326.

number of historical sources in composing his chronicle. As a court secretary (*munshī*), he had access to documentary sources and in narrating contemporary events, he also relied on eyewitnesses and personal knowledge. But for structuring his *tazkirah* sections, he appears to have been using Khvandamir's *Habib al-siyar* as his model. There are several reasons why we may presume this is the case. First, we know he was familiar with the *Habib al-siyar* because he cites it at the beginning of his chronicle. Second, he places his biographies into categories just as Khvandamir did in the Timurid section of his history. And finally, in the *khātimah* (conclusion) to his *Tarikh-i 'alam-ara-yi 'Abbasi*, Iskandar Beg tells us that he actually ran out of time for *two* projects. In addition to the account of poets and poetry from the time of Shah 'Abbas that he wanted to write, he also wanted to include as an appendix, "a selection of rare and choice anecdotes and strange tales" (*muntakhabī az navādir-i ḥikāyāt va khulāṣah va sar khūshī az gharāyib-i ravāyāt*) drawn on "the works of both the ancients and the moderns."[133] He names nine such texts in this regard. The "strange tales" appendix that Iskandar Beg hoped to write falls into the category of books of marvels (*'ajā'ib*).[134] The biography of poets and the *'ajā'ib* treatise were, therefore, supposed to be the last two items in his history. It is interesting to note that the last two items in the *Habib al-siyar* consist of (1) an account of "sayyids, ulama' and nobles," – a number of whom are poets – who wrote under the Aq Qoyunlu and Shah Isma'il, and (2) a concluding appendix (*khātimah*) on "the oddities and marvels of the four quarters and wondrous events in the world" (*dar ẕikr-i badāyi' va gharāyib-i rab' maskūn va 'ajāyib-i vaqāyi'-i jahān-i būqalamūn*) – in other words, an *'ajā'ib* treatise.[135] So Iskandar Beg planned for his history to contain a number of the same structural features that we see in the *Habib al-siyar*, even though he never could carry out his intentions.

While historiographical context helps us understand how Iskandar Beg Munshi's structural models led to his inclusion of *tazkirah*s in his chronicle, historical context provides some insights as to why, politically, he may have done so. In associating the reigns of Shah Tahmasb and Shah 'Abbas – arguably the two most important Safavid rulers –

133 Iskandar Beg, *'Alam-ara-yi 'Abbasi*, 1094–1095; trans., 1325–1326.
134 *EI2*, s.v., "'ajā'ib," by C. E. Dubler.
135 Khvandamir, *Habib al-siyar*, 4: 619.

with an extensive number of biographies of notable individuals, Iskandar Beg places these rulers within the same sort of intellectual milieu and historiographical tradition that Khvandamir did for the Timurids, especially Shahrukh and Sultan Husayn Bayqara. In other words, these rulers were surrounded with individuals who were great administrators, accomplished religious scholars, prominent elites, skilled poets, and powerful military men. While such people lent prestige to the ruler, including information about them could also serve as a way of showing the king the limits of his power. A similarly glittering array of people figured in the Safavid ruler's orbit and made up a court that equaled that of the Timurids in Herat, which could also indicate to the Safavid rulers that their power was not endless. In both glorifying the Safavid court and indirectly cautioning the ruler, Iskandar Beg provides us with yet another example of Safavid chroniclers attempting, during the period of Shah 'Abbas, to forge connections between the Safavids and the Timurids.[136]

In addition to mirroring the Timurid courts historiographically through use of *tazkirah*, Iskandar Beg may have also been responding to and influenced by the Mughal historiographical tradition. Writing after Abu al-Fazl, Iskandar Beg mentions the *Akbarnamah* in his history and was, therefore, familiar with that text. In order to present Shah 'Abbas as a king who could rival Akbar in terms of his court, Iskandar Beg would have compared his own chronicle to the *Akbarnamah* and chosen to include many of its same elements.

Iskandar Beg Munshi's inclusion of biographies in his history ensured the survival of this semiconventional historiographical practice into the late Safavid period. Muhammad Valah Isfahani composed his *Khuld-i barin*, a world history, in 1078/1667–1668 during the reign of Shah Safi II (Shah Sulayman; r. 1077/1078–1105/1666/1668–1694).[137] In choosing to write a universal history, Isfahani looks back to the early Safavid period, when so many of the chronicles produced were universal histories. However, Isfahani does not include biographies for his account of the Timurids or any pre-Safavid dynasty. Instead, he imitates Iskandar Beg Munshi and includes

136 I have written about this phenomenon extensively elsewhere. See, for example, Quinn, *Historical Writing*, 86–89.

137 Muhammad Yusuf Valah Isfahani, *Khuld-i barin: Iran dar ruzgar-i Safaviyan*, ed. Mir Hashim Muhaddis (Tehran: Mawqufat-i Duktur Mahmud Afshar, 1372 [1993]).

biographical sections after his accounts of Shah Tahmasb and Shah 'Abbas. Isfahani thus places at the center of his narrative the Safavid court and associates the Safavids with great poets, learned theologians, and able administrators, just as Mirkhvand did with the Timurids.

Conclusion

In conclusion, we may view the biographical sections of post-Timurid chronicles as a semiconventional hybrid element that had its roots in the pre-Timurid period. Placing this hybrid element in historical and historiographical contexts demonstrates just how influential Mirkhvand and Khvandamir were for chroniclers writing under the Ottomans, Safavids, and Mughals. When read alongside their models, we have a much better understanding of the political agendas underlying the chroniclers, as historians used *tazkirah* to highlight the royal courts where many of them wrote.

6 *Conclusion*

Early modern Persian chronicles spanned vast empires, both geographically and temporally, in terms of their scope and their depth. Many of their authors similarly moved across empires. This notion of movement existed in the writing process itself. Far from composing isolated and static histories, early modern historians participated in a process of active engagement with earlier texts, reshaping, reformulating, and revising the works of their intellectual predecessors in creative and interesting ways. This process appears to have defied political borders and boundaries, as long before the invention of the printing press, we may point to a community of chroniclers who used the Persian language, regardless of their location, to narrate the past. Understanding how this all took place is a complicated task. This study has uncovered only some of the methods that the chroniclers used to compose their histories and offered strategies that could be used to greater advantage than simply reading a chronicle in a positivistic manner.

The most important point to emerge from the analyses put forward in Chapter 2 is that we need to understand our chroniclers' historiographical inheritance in order to understand how they interacted with it. For the most part, that inheritance consisted of a Timurid tradition that they proceeded to modify in various ways. Certain conventional and formal elements formed part of that tradition and made their way into early modern chronicles. Chapter 2 explored just a few of those conventions, although many more exist, particularly in chronicle prefaces. Many of these elements are located at the beginning portions of the chronicles. They include accounts of the benefits of history, bibliographies, dream narratives, and genealogies. They do not appear in every chronicle because a great deal depends on which model a chronicler used for his narrative. Mirkhvand chose to include in his *Rawzat al-safa* a discussion of the benefits of history and a bibliography of sources he allegedly consulted. Although he was not the first chronicler to include this information in his chronicle, the popularity that the

Rawzat al-safa enjoyed across empires ensured the survival, in varying degrees, of that convention into early modern histories written under the Ottomans, Mughals, and Safavids. Chroniclers felt a certain amount of freedom to modify that account, sometimes using imitative writing, in order to provide a commentary on their own situations. Thus, in his *Sharafnamah*, Sharaf al-Din Bidlisi explicitly rejected one of Mirkhvand's benefits of history and rewrote the text to reflect his own position about the need, or lack of need in Bidlisi's case, to consult with wise ones about the past.

Another staple of conventional historiography was the dream narrative. While dream narratives abound in Persian historiography, even in the pre-Timurid period, its political benefit proved irresistible to many early modern chroniclers, who chose to include a dream of their dynastic founder or early ruler in order to make it seem that his rule was predestined to be world-encompassing, as legitimized by way of interpretation or confirmation by a mystic or other prominent religious figure. Often these dream narratives share certain common elements such as light or stars or a tree.

Finally, many Ottoman, Safavid, and Mughal chroniclers showed great interest in including their ruler's genealogy in their narratives. The Timurid heritage is particularly significant here, as evidenced by the production of many Timurid family trees and other "stand alone" genealogical works in the fourteenth and fifteenth centuries. While the Safavids emphasized their connection to Musa al-Kazim, the seventh Imam of the Twelver Shi'a, the Mughals stressed their connection to Timur. Akbar's chroniclers, however, downplayed Timur's supremacy in favor of Akbar's, as witnessed by the extensive genealogical digression we see in Abu al-Fazl's *Akbarnamah*. Taken together, these conventional elements provide some of the most important building blocks upon which the early modern chronicles rested and formed a launching point for them to innovate in later sections of their chronicles.

Having demonstrated the survival of Timurid conventional elements into the Ottoman, Safavid, and Mughal empires, we are now in a position to analyze a particular chronicle beyond the confines of the dynasty under which it was written. For example, we cannot encase within the borders of a particular political entity a chronicler originally from Iran who moved to Mughal India, then settled in the Ottoman Empire where he proceeded to compose an extensive universal history in imitation of a history written in Timurid Herat, even though the history itself is full of political commentary. Rather, we need to read extensively across empires as our authors read in order to understand the full historiographical landscape.

Chapter 3 demonstrated how one highly prolific chronicler who moved across empires wrote one portion of his text. Khvandamir employed several strategies in composing his *Qanun-i Humayuni*. Having left Safavid Iran for Mughal India, he repurposed part of his earlier *Habib al-siyar*, where he wrote about the significance of the number twelve in order to explain why there were twelve Shi'i imams, in order to explain why Humayun divided Mughal society into twelve groups. Rather than compose something new, perhaps due to factors such as time restraints and library access, he simply rewrote something he had already written, but even then, his rewriting process was sophisticated and nuanced. Furthermore, in order to write his original account in the *Habib al-siyar*, Khvandamir translated an Arabic text from the thirteenth century. In reading Khvandamir in light of these earlier models – al-Irbili's *Kashf al-ghumma* and his own *Habib al-siyar* – we can better understand how he wrote a text perhaps designed to provide the Mughal emperor Humayun with a preview of what he could write in a later work, which, due to his death, he was never able to accomplish. Khvandamir should be seen as one representative of many intellectuals who moved across empires in search of patronage and a place to do their work. In other instances, entire families moved, and subsequent generations, such as the descendants of Sayfi Qazvini, ended up serving at a rival court from that of their patriarch, who remained in Iran and died in a Safavid prison.

The techniques that Khvandamir employed to rewrite one of his earlier compositions for another patron are similar to the methodologies used in universal chronicles, the most common genre in the first generation of early modern Persian historiography. The sheer scale of these often multivolume extensive histories makes it impossible to undergo a comprehensive analysis, especially when the relationship between the texts has not yet been established. Chapter 4, therefore, presents a case study of the mythical first Persian king, Kayumars. Accounts about Kayumars form a portion of the chronicle where we would expect the most extensive word–for-word imitation of earlier texts. However, one of the main points that the analyses in this chapter made was that the chroniclers were every bit as invested in their narratives of the distant or legendary past as they were in narrating their own present. In other words, while many of them imitated earlier texts for their accounts of Kayumars, they creatively engaged with that earlier text, rewriting it, responding to it, and modifying it in a number of ways. Only one chronicler, Sayfi Qazvini, imitated in a word-for-word manner, and even in that instance he made a significant omission from his model text, suggesting that there is as much to be learned from textual silences as from textual additions. The case study of Kayumars also showed how, at the same time that Safavid universal history writing became less popular, under the Mughals the genre continued to enjoy great popularity, as Mughal chroniclers continued to emphasize a past that they shared with other parts of the Islamicate world.

The approach used here of reading a chronicle alongside its model text or texts was not only useful for analyzing accounts of Kayumars but also when applied to other parts of the early modern chronicles, namely those sections that draw on sources beyond historical chronicles, such as mirrors for princes texts and *tazkirahs*. The chroniclers used a wide range of sources, many of which lie outside the genre of chronicle or history, when composing their narratives, and this reliance caused the historians to bring those elements into their chronicles. Thus, in addition to providing an annalistic account of historical events, the chroniclers also discussed the qualities of the king under whose reign they were writing, representing him very much in line with the ideals established in the mirrors for princes literature. Those ideals could also have been a factor in determining what topics the chroniclers covered in the annalistic sections of their chronicles. The regnal year entries analyzed in Chapter 5 for Shah ʻAbbas in the *Tarikh-i Akbari* and the *ʻAlam-ara-yi ʻAbbasi* showed that many of the themes reflect the actions of an ideal king in the mirrors for princes literature, helping us better understand why we see certain information in the contemporary portions of the chronicles.

Chroniclers also found inspiration in the *tazkirah* genre when they included biographical information in their chronicles. These sections included biographies of a variety of individuals, going beyond the usual poets and saints that one finds in stand-alone works of *tazkirah*. The simple methodological approaches used in this section, which included counting the actual names listed under each ruler, examining the order in which they appear, and reading the texts in light of their models, allowed us to understand better how the chronicler viewed the society he was describing, as he reproduced the social hierarchy around him, or at least its upper levels, in his chronicle. In textually surrounding the king with a large retinue of learned and prominent figures, he also made a political statement about the king's power and authority, especially in relation to past kings.

Through the analyses presented here, it becomes clear that very few authors wrote "alone." Much that we have discovered here resembles contemporary scholarship or, rather, scholarly practices today echo the methods of early modern Persian historiography. Early modern chroniclers writing in Persian actively engaged with their intellectual ancestors by responding to their works, updating their earlier scholarship and doing what they could to preserve and carry forward knowledge. They expressed anxiety when they were unable to conform to a historiographical norm, and when pressed for time or facing challenging circumstances, they repurposed material they had previously written. Their narrative techniques are impressively sophisticated, as they could make significant political alterations to an earlier narrative with the change of just one word. They used a variety of sources for their information and chose carefully from those texts. While they made sure to present the king and dynasty under which they were writing in the best possible light, they managed to make political statements and express their views through the techniques explained in this study.[1] The histories under examination in this book, therefore, are highly political and dynamic documents.

This study has also shown that, in order to make sense of the chroniclers' relationship to their historiographical legacy, we must look beyond the political boundaries of empire, if only because the chroniclers themselves were doing so. Timurid chronicles such as Mirkhvand's *Rawzat al-safa* became a popular text in Ottoman, Safavid, and Mughal territories, as chroniclers of the next generation used this history as a model. The early modern Persianate historiographical world was a reality that the chroniclers discussed here created, one far more seamless than the political world it sought to narrate.

[1] The chroniclers certainly criticized rulers as well. For an example of how one might read the chronicles in order to draw out such criticisms, see E. A. Polyakova, "The Development of a Literary Canon in Medieval Persian Chronicles: The Triumph of Etiquette," *Iranian Studies* 17 (1984): 237–256. See also E. A. Polyakova and E. A. Poliakova, "Timur As Described by the 15th Century Court Historiographers," *Iranian Studies* 21 (1988): 31–44.

Future Studies

While a close analysis of texts reveals a great deal about historiographical methods and biases, more comprehensive studies of the various genres that flourished during this period, such as dynastic and universal histories, would help us place the close readings in a wider context. Whereas the chapters here focused on histories written in Persian, comparative studies of Ottoman chronicles written in Persian with those composed in Ottoman would deepen our understanding of the Persianate world. The critical study of manuscripts and libraries, including related topics such as manuscript distribution, colophons, and book lists, will further help us understand how the histories analyzed here circulated around the Persianate world. While book-length studies of individual historians have been published, many early modern chronicles remain little known, and their histories remain unedited and unpublished. The availability of large digital manuscript collections makes rich stores of primary texts previously held in often inaccessible libraries widely available and will certainly help accelerate the process of making the scholarly world even more familiar with the complexities of Persian historiography.

Appendix
The Chroniclers and the Chronicles

The following list includes the main chronicles discussed in this volume, along with some background information about the author and the text itself, and the reference number to Storey/Bregel's *Persian Literature*. They are listed in order of composition the date. The record number refers to Storey's *Persian Literature*, followed by the record number in Bregel's update in brackets [], if it exists. Information about editions and manuscripts can be found in the bibliography.

Author: Shukr Allah Rumi (778–894/1375/1376–1488/1489)
Chronicle: ***Bahjat al-tavarikh*** (855/1451)
Storey/Bregel: 122 [259]

Shukr Allah came from a family of religious scholars and worked for the Ottomans. Part of his diplomatic duties involved traveling to neighboring courts. In one instance, as a diplomat serving the Ottoman Sultan Murad II (r. 824–855/1421–1451), Shukr Allah traveled to the Qara Qoyunlu ("Black Sheep" dynasty) court in 1447, where he had an audience with Jahanshah, the Qara Qoyunlu ("Black Sheep" dynasty) ruler. He was also apparently held in high regard by Murad II's successor, Mehmet II (r. 855–886/1451–1481).[1] Shukr Allah's *Bahjat al-tavarikh*, which has not yet been fully edited or published, is the first historical work written in Persian under the Ottomans, and Shukr Allah one of the only nonemigres to have written a history in Persian.[2] In her insightful essay on Persian historical writing under the Ottomans, Sarah Yildiz, noting that most scholarly attention has focused on the short Ottoman portion of this chronicle, proceeds to analyze the section devoted to creation. She suggests that Shukr Allah "Ottomanized" the cosmology of the "great Shaykh," the

1 For background and an analysis of Shukr Allah's history, see Yildiz, "Ottoman Historical Writing," 443; and Woods, *The Aqquyunlu*, 175–176; Shukr Allah, "Bahjat," folio 51a. See also Storey, *Persian Literature* 1: 91.
2 The other was Ghubari. See Yildiz, "Ottoman Historical Writing," 438.

Seville-born Sufi Ibn al-Arabi (560–638/1165–1240) by equating the sultanate with the caliphate.[3] Baki Teczan has pointed out that Shukr Allah presented an Oghuz genealogy for Ertuğrul, the father of the Ottoman dynastic founder Osman Ghazi, and noted that his account of Ertuğrul coming to Anatolia with the Seljuqs (a chronological impossibility) was part of an attempt to connect the Ottomans to the Seljuqs.[4]

Author: Fazl Allah ibn Ruzbihan Khunji (860–925/1456–1517)
Chronicle: *Tarikh-i ʻalam-ara-yi Amini*, completed during reign of Baysunghur (r. 896–897/1490–1491)
Storey/Bregel: 370 [704]

Khunji was a Sunni Muslim who wrote a number of different works for different patrons. He composed his *Tarikh-i ʻalam-ara-yi Amini* for the Aq Qoyunlu Uzun Hasan's son Yaʻqub. The chronicle covers the years 882–886/1478–1481 and 890–896/1485–1491.[5] The chronicle also includes an elaborate preface which contains a great deal of information about the author's perspectives on historiography and the philosophy of history.

Author: Muhammad b. Khavand Shah b. Mahmud, Mirkhvand (837–2 Rajab 903/1433 or 1434–24 February 1498)
Chronicle: *Rawzat al-safa fi sirat al-anbiya' wa al-muluk wa al-khulafa'* (902/1497)
Storey/Bregel: 123 [260]

Mirkhvand spent most of his life in Herat, though his family on his father's side lived in Bukhara and migrated to Balkh. His father was Burhan al-Din Khavand Shah. Mirkhvand's patron was the poet Mir ʻAli Shir Nava'i.

Mirkhvand composed his *Rawzat al-safa* in ca. 902/1497, with the final volume finished by his maternal grandson Khvandamir in ca. 907/1502, who probably wrote the *khatimah* (conclusion) as well. The *Rawzat al-safa* is a universal history consisting of an introduction,

[3] Yildiz, "Ottoman Historical Writing," 444–449.
[4] Baki Teczan, "The Memory of the Mongols," in *Writing History at the Ottoman Court: Editing the Past, Fashioning the Future*, eds. H. Erdem Çıpa and Emine Fetvacı, 23–38 (Bloomington: Indiana University Press, 2013), 30. See also Woods, *The Aqquyunlu*, 176–177.
[5] See Woods, *The Aqquyunlu*, 220.

seven volumes, and a conclusion. In an important unpublished dissertation on early Safavid historiography that examines the sectarian perspectives of several universal chroniclers, including Mirkhvand and Khvandamir, Adam Jacobs has demonstrated that the *Rawzat al-safa* contains pro-Zaydi sentiment and incorporates Shi'i versions of early Islamic history into the narrative.[6] These diverse religious views contained within one historical work are a good example of the "confessional ambiguity" of the Middle periods of Islamic history, described above. The *Rawzat al-safa* is probably the single most influential work on the early modern Persian historians, many of whom looked to this text as a model.

Author: Ghiyas al-Din b. Humam al-Din Muhammad, Khvandamir (880–942/1475/1476–1535/1536)
Storey/Bregel 125 [262]

Khvandamir was the maternal grandson of Mirkhvand. He was born, most likely in Herat, in approximately 880/1475–1476. He was a prominent writer who produced a number of texts in multiple genres and for different patrons and ruling dynasties. The most distinguished of his patrons was the poet and courtier Mir 'Ali Shir Nava'i (844–906/1441–1501), who gave him access to his private library.[7] Another important patron was the Timurid prince Badi al-Zaman Mirza, the oldest son of Sultan Husayn. Khvandamir witnessed the city of Herat coming under the control of Shaybani Khan the Uzbek in 1507 and then Shah Isma'il the Safavid founder in 1510. In 935/1527, Khvandamir left Herat for Qandahar. He eventually met Babur, who mentions Khvandamir in his memoirs, the *Baburnamah*.[8]

Because he was a historian "on the move," Khvandamir served not only as the historiographical bridge between the Timurid and Safavid dynasties, but he also linked the traditions of Safavids and Mughal historical writing by writing for both.

6 See Jacobs, "Sunni and Shi'i Perceptions," 49. The *Rawzat al-safa* itself was translated for the first time into Ottoman Turkish in 957/1550. See *EI2*, "Mirkhwand."

7 See "Khwāndamīr," *EI2*, s.v., H. Beveridge and J. T. P. de Bruijn; Khvandamir, *The Makārim al-akhlāq: A Treatise on 'Alīshīr Navā'ī*, ed. T. Gandjeï, ix–xi (Cambridge: E. J. W. Gibb Memorial Trust, 1979).

8 See Babur, *The Baburnama*, trans. Thackston, 403, 442.

***Habib al-siyar fi akhbar afrad al-bashar* 930/1524**
Storey/Bregel 125.3 [262.3]

The *Habib al-siyar* is an important source for early Safavid history. Khvandamir based this universal chronicle on his maternal grandfather Mirkhvand's *Rawzat al-safa*. He completed the text in 930/1524, although he rewrote it in 931/1525 and 935/1529. He dedicated it to the vizier whom Shah Isma'il (r. 907–930/1501–1524), founder of the Safavid dynasty, appointed to the city of Herat, Karim al-Din Khvajah Habib Allah Savaji. Khvandamir divides his history into a prologue and three volumes. The final volume covers the reign of Shah Isma'il and the Safavids.

***Qanun-i humayuni* 940/1534**
Storey/Bregel 125.4 [262.4]

After Babur died, he was succeeded by his son Humayun, to whom Khvandamir dedicated his *Humayunnamah* (940/1534), also known as the *Qanun-i Humayuni*. Khvandamir enjoyed great prestige under Humayun, who eventually made him his chief chronicler.[9] Although Khvandamir states in the *Qanun-i Humayuni* that he hoped to write more historical works for Humayun, he died before this could happen.

Author: Mas'udi b. 'Usman Kuhistani
Chronicle: *Tarikh-i Abu al-Khayr Khani* (some time between 947–959/1540–1551)
Storey/Bregel: 128 [267]

Kuhistani served as secretary to the Shaybanid Suyunjuk Khan (d. 1525). While not much is known about Kuhistani, Jo-Ann Gross suggests that he had Sufi sympathies.[10] The *Tarikh-i Abu al-Khayr Khani* has not been utilized a great deal, nor has it been published. It is a universal history that covers creation, the pre-Islamic prophets, Muhammad's ancestors, the life of the Prophet, the early caliphs and the twelve imams, and the early kings of Persia from Kayumars to

[9] Khvandamir, *Qanun-i Humayuni*, xv.
[10] See Jo-Ann Gross, "Khoja Ahrar: A Study of the Perceptions of Religious Power and Prestige in the Late Timurid Period" (Ph.D. diss., New York University, 1982), 94, 105.

Yazdigard. It then continues with the middle period dynasties: the Saffarids, Samanids, Ghaznavids, Saljuqs, and Mongols, ending with an account of the history of Abu al-Khayr Khan.[11]

Author: Mir Yahya ibn 'Abd al-Latif Sayfi Qazvini (885–962/1481–1555)
Chronicle: *Lubb al-tavarikh* (948/1542)
Storey/Bregel: 129 [268]

Sayfi Qazvini was a Sunni historian who, unlike many of his contemporaries discussed here, never left Safavid territory. Sayfi Qazvini, a Naqshbandi Sufi, came from a sayyid family of "landed notables" in Qazvin. He composed his universal history, the *Lubb al-tavarikh*, in 948/1542, and dedicated it to Bahram Mirza, a younger sibling of Shah Tahmasb.[12] Despite giving a prominent position to the Twelve Imams after his section on the Prophet Muhammad in the *Lubb al-tavarikh*, Sayfi Qazvini was banished from Qazvin to Isfahan and imprisoned there by Shah Tahmasb (r. 930–984/1524–1576), who was trying to convert Qazvin to Shi'ism before making it his capital city.[13] Having been "denounced as chief of the Sunnis of Qazvin," Sayfi Qazvini died in prison in 962/1555. This is not the end of his family's story, however: two of his sons and a grandson all became important literary figures in Mughal India, as they either left Iran or were born in Mughal territory.[14]

Author: Muhammad Haydar Dughlat (905–958/1499/1500/1551)
Chronicle: *Tarikh-i Rashidi* (952/1546)
Storey/Bregel 349 [1068]

Muhammad Haydar Dughlat was, on his mother's side, a first cousin of Babur, the founder of the Mughal dynasty who served as mentor of sorts to Dughlat.[15] Born in Tashkent, Dughlat spent

[11] See Rieu, *Catalog of the Persian Manuscripts*, I: 102–103.
[12] See also *EIR*, s.v., "Sayfi Qazvini," by Kioumars Ghereghlou.
[13] See *EIR*, s.v., "Sayfi Qazvini," by Kioumars Ghereghlou.
[14] Mir 'Abd al-Latif Qazvini was teacher to the Mughal emperor Akbar, and Mirza 'Ala' al-Dawlah "Kâmî" Qazvini wrote the *Nafa'is al-ma'asir*. Qazvini's grandson Naqib Khan was one of the translators of the Indian text, the Mahabharata. For more on this family, see Chapter 2.
[15] Dughlat, *Tarikh-i Rashidi*, vii.

time with Babur in Kabul before heading military expeditions to places like Badakhshan and Tibet under the command of Sultan Sa'id Khan. Another historian on the move, Dughlat ended up in Lahore during the reign of Humayun. Dughlat eventually conquered Kashmir.

Dughlat completed his *Tarikh-i Rashidi*, an account of the khans of Moghulistan, in 952/1546. Moghulistan at that time referred to the eastern portion of the Ulus Chaghatay, encompassing modern day Kazakhstan, Kirghizistan, Chinese Sinkiang, and western Mongolia. The history covers the years 1329–1533.[16]

Author: Ibrahim bin Hariri (or Jariri)
Chronicle: *Tarikh-i Ibrahimi* or *Tarikh-i Humayuni* (956 or 957/ 1549 or 1550)
Storey/Bregel: 130 [269]

Although a number of manuscripts of this work exist, it still has not been edited. Elliot and Dowson indicate familiarity with it and suggest that a comparison of this history with the *Habib al-siyar* "may show that the Humayuni is an abridgement of the larger work."[17] This suggestion is made due to the biographical entries on important individuals that can be found throughout the text. For more on this *tazkirah* element, see Chapter 5. The *Tarikh-i Ibrahimi* is a "concise general history" ending in 956/1549 or 957/1550.[18]

Author: Qasim Beg Hayati Tabrizi
Chronicle: *Tarikh* (961/1554)

This only very recently discovered history has been known to scholars for some time, because Qazi Ahmad Qumi mentions it in his chronicle of Shah 'Abbas, the *Khulasat al-tavarikh*. The history covers the early history of the Safaviyyah Sufi order and the reign of Shah Isma'il I. Kioumars Ghereghlou discovered the manuscript in the National Library of Iran in Tehran and has prepared an edition of the text.[19]

16 Dughlat, *Tarikh-i Rashidi*, vii–ix.
17 Elliot and Dowson, *The History of India*, 4: 214.
18 Storey, *Persian Literature*, 1: 113.
19 See Ghereghlou, "Chronicling a Dynasty on the Make."

Author: Khvurshah b. Qubad al-Husayni (d. 972/1564–1565)
Chronicle: *Tarikh-i ilchi-yi Nizam Shah* (970/1562–1563)
Storey/Bregel: 131 [272]

The author of this history was an ambassador of Burhan Nizam Shah I of Ahmadnagar (r. 914–961/1508–1553). He went to the court of Shah Tahmasb, arriving in Qazvin in 952/1545. He stayed there until 971/1563–1564 and died in Golconda in 972/1565.[20] Qubad al-Husayni divides his universal history into an introduction (*muqaddimah*) and seven sections, as follows: (1) pre-Islamic Iran, (2) Muhammad to the end of the ʻAbbasid dynasty, (3) dynasties contemporary with the Abbasids,(4) the Mongols, (5) the Timurids, (6) the Qara Qoyunlu, Aq Qoyunlu, Shah Ismaʻil and Shah Tahmasb, and the Ottomans, and (7) the Mughal rulers.[21] The work was completed in 970/1562–1563. While a recent edition has been published, it is only a partial edition covering the last two sections of the chronicle.

Author: Qazi Ahmad Ghaffari (d. 975/1567–1568)
Chronicle: *Nusakh-i jahan-ara* (972/1564–1565)
Storey/Bregel: 132 [273]

Ghaffari was a well-known figure who is mentioned by Sam Mirza in his *Tuhfah-i Sami* as having been a guest in the prince's home. He came from a learned family in Qazvin; according to Storey, his father was the Qadi of Ray and he was a descendant of the thirteenth century Shafiʻi scholar, Najm-al-Din ʻAbd al-Ghaffar Qazvini (d. 665/1266). After undertaking a pilgrimage to the Hijaz, Ghaffari died in Dibal, Sindh, on his way to Agra and the Mughals. Ghaffari composed his *Nusakh-i jahan-ara*, also known as the *Tarikh-i jahan-ara*, in 972/1564–1565 and dedicated it to Shah Tahmasb. He divided his chronicle into an introduction "on the age of the world and prophetship" and three sections: (1) the prophets and the twelve imams, (2) pre-Islamic and Islamic kings, and (3) the Safavids. Before writing the *Nusakh-i jahan-ara*, Ghaffari composed the *Nigaristan*, an anecdotal universal history also dedicated to Shah Tahmasb. Judging by the large number of extant manuscripts of the *Nusakh-i jahan-ara*, this was a popular work, also apparently translated into Turkish.[22]

[20] Storey, *Persian Literature*, 1: 113.
[21] Storey, *Persian Literature*, 1: 113–114.
[22] These details all come from Storey, *Persian Literature*, 1: 114–116, and *EIR*, s.v., "Ǧaffārī Qazvini, Aḥmad," by Kioumars Ghereghlou.

Author: Muslih al-Din Lari (d. 979/1572)
Chronicle: *Mir'at al-advar va mirqat al-akhbar* (974/1566)
Storey/Bregel: 133 [274]

Muslih al-Din Lari, as his name indicates, was originally from Lar. He studied in Shiraz with Mir Ghiyas al-Din Mansur Shirazi, one time *sadr* under Shah Tahmasb and the son of Mulla Sadra, and Mir Kamal al-Din Husayn, a student of the famous theologian and philosopher from Shiraz, Jalal al-Din Muhammad Davani.[23] He also studied with Shams al-Din al-Khafri.[24] His subsequent travels took him beyond Safavid territory, first to Mughal India, where Humayun received him and made him *sadr*, and then to Mecca and Istanbul, where he enjoyed the patronage of Rustam Pasha, the Ottoman Grand Vizier.[25] He finally settled at the Madrasa of Khusraw Pasha in Amid (Diyarbakir).[26] Among Lari's writings is the *Mir'at al-advar*, an extensive general history ending in 974/1566, which he dedicated to Mehmed Sokollu (d. 987/1579), the Grand Vizier of Sultan Selim II (r. 974–982/1566–1574).[27] The *Mir'at al-advar* has recently been published in its entirety.

Author: Muhammad 'Arif Qandahari
Chronicle: *Tarikh-i Akbari* (988/1580)
Storey/Bregel: 707

Qandahari was a scholar and high-ranking official attached to the courts of Bayram Khan. He also served as a tutor to both the young prince Akbar and Muzaffar Khan, an important official in Mughal India who held various government ministerial positions. Qandahari probably completed his history in 988/1580.[28] The *Tarikh-i Akbari* includes a brief overview of the reign of Humayun (r. 937–947/1530–1540; 962–963/1555–1556), followed by a detailed account of

23 Storey, *Persian Literature*, 1: 116. See also *EIR*, s.v., "Daštakī, Amīr Sayyed Gīāt-al-Dīn Manṣūr," by Andrew J. Newman, and *EIR*, s.v., "Davānī, Jalāl-al-Dīn Moḥammad," by Andrew J. Newman.

24 See Reza Pourjavady, "Muslih al-Din al-Lari and His Sample of the Sciences," *Oriens* 42 (2014): 294–295.

25 Pourjavady, "Muslih al-Din al-Lari," 296.

26 Storey, *Persian Literature*, 1: 116–117. See also Yildiz, "Ottoman Historical Writing," 497–498; Algar, "Persian Literature in Bosnia-Herzegovina," 256; and Pourjavady, "Muslih al-Din al-Lari," 295.

27 Pourjavady, "Muslih al-Din al-Lari," 296–297.

28 Streusand, *The Formation of the Mughal Empire*, 20. See also Storey, *Persian Literature*, 1: 541.

Akbar's reign until the year 988/1580. It is divided into forty-four chapters (*guftārs*). The first six include introductory material such as dream narratives and accounts of miraculous events.

Author: Mir Muhammad Sharif Vuqu'i Husayni Nishapuri (d. 1002/1593–1594)
Chronicle: *Majami' al-akhbar* (1000/1591–1592)
Storey/Bregel: 136 [278]

The *Majami' al-akhbar* is one of the earliest universal chronicles produced under the Mughals. It was composed in 1000/1591–1592, approximately two years after Vuqu'i entered the court of Akbar (in 998/1590). Vuqu'i came from a notable family of sayyids of Nishapur, and his mother was the sister of Shah Tahmasb's assay master.[29] Vuqu'i seems to have been fairly well known, and a number of important Mughal sources mention him. The celebrated Mughal chronicler Abu al-Fazl, for example, quotes one of his poems in his *Ain-i Akbari*, and 'Abd al-Qadir Badauni also mentions him in his history, the *Muntakhab al-tavarikh*, stating that Vuqu'i was related to Shihab al-Din Ahmad Khan, a notable at Akbar's court.[30]

Badauni does not seems to have regarded Vuqu'i very highly. After stating that his name was Muhammad Sharif, he adds, "Alas, that such a noble name should be borne by such a vile person!" (*ḥayf ast kih īn nām-i sharīf bar ān kas̱īf*) because, he continues, "his heresy (*ilḥādash*) was more than any person who, in this brief age, was known by the same name." Condemning Vuqu'i for his religious beliefs, he states that the poet "was not amongst the Pasikhvānīs (i.e., Nuqtavis) alone nor was he amongst the Sahiban [an unidentified heretical sect, apparently], but was between these two sects, damned by the lord and cursed of the people, and he believed in cycles (*advār*) and held the doctrine of the transmigration of souls (*tanāsukh*), nay, he contended and strove for these doctrines."[31] Badauni tells us that Vuqu'i went to his lodging while staying in the Kashmir border highlands (*sarḥad-i kūhistān-i Kashmīr*), wanting Badauni to accompany him to Kashmir. When Vuqu'i saw some "slabs of rock, weighing over thirty-five tons each, lying about (*takhtah-sanghā-yi hizār hizār manī-i uftādah dīd*), he said

[29] Badauni, *Muntakhab al-tavarikh*, trans., 3: 512, n. 1.
[30] Abu al-Fazl, *Ain-i Akbari*, 1:254; trans., 1: 591. Badauni, *Muntakhab al-tavarikh*, 3: 256; trans., 3: 512–513.
[31] Badauni, *Muntakhab al-tavarikh*, 3: 256; trans., 3: 513, slightly modified.

sorrowfully, 'These unfortunates are awaiting the time when they shall put on human form' (*āh īn bīchārah'hā muntaẓir'and kih tā kay bih qālib-i insānī bar āyand*)." Badauni then concedes that "In spite of all these ugly beliefs (*i'tiqād-i zisht*) he has written odes (*qaṣīdahs*) in praise of the holy Imams (may the acceptance of God be on them all), but these must have been written when he was young."[32] Badauni also comments on Vuqu'i's knowledge of history, stating that while "he was not studious he had devoted some attention to Arabic works on history and had acquired familiarity with their style."[33]

Vuqu'i's history consists of two discourses (*maqālah*), the first of which is devoted to the pre-Islamic period, and the second to the Islamic period.[34] Between his sections on the Lodis and the Mughals, the author inserts accounts of the Qara Qoyunlu, Aq Qoyunlu, Uzbegs, Safavids, and Ottomans. In terms of periodization, Vuqu'i's chronological scheme parallels both Mirkhvand's *Rawzat al-safa* and Khvandamir's *Habib al-siyar*. All of this suggests to me an unsurprising connection between Mirkhvand, Khvandamir, and Vuqu'i and provides further evidence for a link between late Timurid/early Safavid historiography and Mughal historiography.

Nizam al-Din Ahmad Bakhshi (d. 1003/1594)
Chronicle: *Tabaqat-i Akbari* (1001/1593)
Storey/Bregel: 613

According to Storey, Nizam al-Din served as the *bakhshī* of Gujarat and then *bakhshī* of the entire Mughal Empire. His *Tabaqat-i Akbari* is a general history of India. Nizam al-Din divided his history, which he completed in 1001/1592–1593, into an introduction and nine sections or layers (*ṭabaqāt*), with each layer devoted to rulers of a particular region of India. The final portion section contains a number of biographical entries devoted to prominent figures during Akbar's reign.[35]

32 Badauni, *Muntakhab al-tavarikh*, 3: 256; trans., 3: 513, slightly modified.

33 Badauni, *Muntakhab al-tavarikh*, 3: 256; trans., 3: 513. For further information on Vuqu'i, see also Aḥmad Gulchīn Ma'ānī, *Kārvān-i Hind* (Mashhad: Āstān-i Quds-i Rażavī, 1369 [1990]), 3: 1531–1535.

34 See Hermann Ethé, *Catalog of Persian Manuscripts in the Library of the India Office*, 2 vols. (Oxford: Horace Hart, 1902), 1: 42–43.

35 Storey, *Persian Literature*, 1: 433. See also *EI2*, s.v., "Niẓām al-Dīn Aḥmad b. Muḥammad Muḳīm al-Harawī," by E. Berthels.

Author: ʻAbd al-Qadir Badauni (17 Rabiʻ II 947–ca. 1024/ 21 August 1540–ca. 1615)
Chronicle: *Muntakhab al-tavarikh* (1004/1595–1596)
Storey/Bregel: 614

Badauni was a well known figure at Akbar's court. After living in various regions of India, he eventually met Akbar in Agra in 981/1574. He became an imam and engaged in projects of translating mostly Hindu works into Persian. He strongly disapproved of Akbar's religious policies, which he criticized in his three volume *Muntakhab al-tavarikh*, a history of India starting with the period of Sebuktigin and ending in 1004/1595–1596, Akbar's fortieth regnal year. Badauni appends to his chronicle a biographical compendium of prominent figures at Akbar's courts, as discussed above in Chapter 5.[36] Badauni did not release his chronicle during his lifetime because of his criticisms of Akbar.

Author: Sharaf Khan ibn Shams al-Din Bidlisi (949–1012/ 1543–1603/1604?)
Chronicle: *Sharafnamah* (1005/1596)
Storey/Bregel 490 [964]

Sharaf Khan Bidlisi was chief of the Ruzagi tribe of Kurds in Bidlis, eastern Anatolia. His family's allegiances shifted between the Ottomans, for whom his grandfather worked, and the Safavids, who employed his father. He was educated alongside Shah Tahmasb's sons after his father lost rule of Bidlis, and held several important government positions. He seems to have fallen out of favor with the Safavids, however, because after Shah Ismaʻil II apppointed him to the position of *amīr al-umarā'* of the Persian Kurds, he sent him to Nakhjavan. Eventually, Bidlisi sided with the Ottomans, receiving the title of Sharaf Khan from Murad I, who returned to him his father's kingdom of Bidlis.[37] Sharaf Khan's shifting allegiance between the Ottomans and the Safavids is significant because it reflects the rather fluid nature of intellectual and political sympathies of the Persianate elite of the period.[38]

[36] Storey, *Persian Literature*, 1: 435–437. *EIR*, s.v., "Badā'ūnī, ʻAbd-al-Qāder," by A. S. Bazmee Ansari.
[37] See Storey, *Persian Literature*, 1: 367.
[38] See *EIR*, s.v., "Bedlīsī, Šaraf-al-Dīn, by Erika Glassen.

The *Sharafnamah* contains a preface (*muqaddimah*), four sections, or *ṣaḥīfah*, and a conclusion (*khātimah*). Each of the four sections is devoted to a particular region, and collectively forms a history of the Kurds. The conclusions covers the history of the Ottoman and contemporary rulers.

Author: Abu al-Fazl (6 Muharram 958–4 Rabi I 1011/14 January 1551–22 August 1602)
Storey/Begel: 709

Abu al-Fazl was a prominent official in Akbar's court. His father was Shaykh Mubarak, a scholar who moved to Agra in 95/1543 from Nagaur, Rajastan. His brother, the well-known poet Fayzi, introduced Abu al-Fazl to Akbar, and the two became close friends.[39] Abu al-Fazl served as Akbar's "spokesman par excellence," and played a very important role in shaping Akbar's religious and social policies. Many of the most well known and significant aspects of Akbar's reign were a result of Abu al-Fazl's influence and participation. These include the weekly religious debates in the *'ibādat-khānah* (house of worship), the decree (*maẓhar*) of 987/1579 giving Akbar the power to settle religious disputes. Abu al-Fazl was executed upon the orders of Akbar's son, Prince Salim, who saw the scholar as a hindrance to his own political ambitions.[40]

Storey/Bregel: 709.1
Chronicle: *Akbarnamah* (1011/1602)

Akbar commissioned Abu al-Fazl to write an official history of the Mughal dynasty from its origins, which he continued working on until his death in 1011/1602.[41] The Mughal king made certain that Abu al-Fazl had at his disposal a considerable amount of chancellory and archival information in order for him to write his history.[42] The *Akbarnamah* is an elaborate text, divided into three books, the first two of which form what is known as the *Akbarnamah*. The *Akbarnamah* includes a description of Akbar's horoscopes, accounts

[39] *EIR*, s.v., "Abu'l-Fażl 'Allāmī," by R. M. Eaton.
[40] *EIR*, s.v., "Abu'l-Fażl 'Allāmī," by R. M. Eaton.
[41] *EIR*, s.v., "Akbar-nāma," by R. M. Eaton.
[42] Mukhia, *Historians and Historiography*, 66–72.

of his ancestors going back to Adam, and an annalistic narrative of his reign.[43]

Storey/Bregel: 709.2
Chronicle: *A'in-i Akbari* (1011/1602)

The *A'in-i Akbari* is the third volume of the *Akbarnamah*, although it is usually treated as a separate work. This extensive account consists of five sections, each addressing a different aspect of the Mughal Empire, including the emperor's governing system, his military, his administrative order, a geographical description of India, and Akbar's sayings. Altogether, the *Akbarnamah* became an extremely influential history in subsequent generations.[44]

Author: Tahir Muhammad Sabzavari
Chronicle: *Rawzat al-tahirin*, or *Tarikh-i tahiri* (1014/1605–1606)
Storey/Bregel: 137 [281]

Sabzavari was a figure associated with Akbar. His oldest brother, a certain Khvajagi Sultan Ahmad, was a poet at Akbar's court. Akbar sent Sabzavari on a diplomatic mission to Burhanpur, and he also accompanied the prince, Sultan Khurram (who later became Shah Jahan) to Jahangir's court in Lahore.[45] While the manuscript of this has not yet been edited or published, it has been used by contemporary scholars such as Sanjay Subrahmanyam and Audrey Truschke, both of whom focus on the latter portions of the text.[46] Sabzavari divides his history into five parts: (1) Prophets and sages; early kings of Persia; Arab kings; (2) the first four caliphs; Hasan and the other imams from Jami's Shavahid al-nubuvvat; Umayyads in the East; Umayyads of Spain; the Abbasids; Abbasid offshoots; (dynasties contemporary to the Abbasids, from the Saffarids to the Ismailis); (3) the Turks before Chingiz; the Mughals before Chingiz Khan; Chingiz Khan and his successors; Shahrukh's embassy to China; the Ottomans; Timur and his successors, descendants of Umar Shaykh to death of Akbar, the Qara Qoyunlu and Aq Qoyunlu; the Safavids; (4) Hindu traditions: translations from Mahabharat into Persian at Akbar's order: Vishnu's

43 *EIR*, s.v., "Akbar-nāma," by R. M. Eaton.
44 *EIR*, s.v., "Akbar-nāma," by R. M. Eaton.
45 Storey, *Persian Literature*, 1: 122.
46 Subrahmanyam, "On World Historians," 26–57; Truschke, "The Mughal Book of War," 506–520.

Avatars, Abstract of the Mahabharat; (5) (abridged from the Tarikh-i Nizami [*Tabaqat-i Akbari*]): kings of Delhi; history of Akbar; verses of amirs and poets at Akbar's court; kings of India; (*khātimah*) the wonders and curiosities of islands and harbors in Bengal (in fourteen chapters, the last devoted to Portugal).

Author: Iskandar Beg Munshi (968 or 969/1560 or 1561–ca. 1043/1633)
Chronicle: *Tarikh-i ʻalam-ara-yi ʻAbbasi* (1038/1629)
Storey/Bregel: 387 [734]

Iskandar Beg was a secretary or "chancery scribe" at the court of Shah ʻAbbas. His duties probably included composing letters, documents, and diplomatic missives, and indeed, his collection of model letters (*inshāʼ*) has survived.[47] He is best known, however, for having composed the *Tarikh-i ʻalam-ara-yi ʻAbbasi*, a detailed history of the Safavid dynasty, focusing on the reign of Shah ʻAbbas. Iskandar Beg divided his chronicle into three volumes or *ṣaḥīfah*. He completed the first two volumes in 1025/1616 and the third in 1038/1629. The history became very popular and influential in later Safavid historiography.[48]

[47] *EIR*, s.v., "Akbar-nāma," by R. M. Eaton.
[48] See *EIR*, s.v., "Ālamārā-ye ʻAbbāsī," by R. M. Savory, and *EIR*, s.v., "Eskandar Beg Torkamān Monšī," by R. M. Savory.

Bibliography

Primary Sources

Abū al-Fażl ibn Mubārak. *Āʾīn-i Akbarī*. Edited by H. Blochmann. 2 Vols. Calcutta: Asiatic Society of Bengal, 1877. Translated by H. Blochmann as *The Ain-i-Akbari*. 3 Vols. Calcutta: Royal Asiatic Society, 1873.

Akbarnāmah. Edited and translated by Wheeler Thackston as *The History of Akbar*. 4 Vols. London: Harvard University Press, 2018.

Amīr Maḥmud. *Īran dar rūzgār-i Shāh Ismāʿil va Shāh Ṭahmāsb Ṣafavī*. Edited by Ghulām Riżā Ṭabāṭabāʾī. Tehran: Bunyād-i Mawqūfāt-i Duktur Maḥmūd Afshār, 1370 [1991].

ʿĀsaf Khān Qazvīnī and Qāżī Aḥmad Tattavī. *Tārīkh-i Alfī*. Edited by Sayyid ʿAlī Āl Dāvūd. Tehran: Intishārāt-i Kulbah, 1378 [1999]. Partial Persian edition.

Aşikpaşazade. *Die altosmanische Chronik des ʿasikpasazade*. Edited by F. Giese. Leipzig, 1929, 6–35. Translated by Robert Dankoff as *From ʿAshiqpashazada's History of the House of ʿOsman*. Edited and annotated by John E. Woods, TMS [photocopy].

ʿAṭṭār, Farīd al-Dīn. *Kitāb-i taẕkirat al-awliyāʾ*. Edited by Muḥammad Qazvīnī. Tehran: Intishārāt-i Markazī 1957. Translated by Paul Losensky as *Farid ad-Din ʿAttār's Memorial of God's Friends: Lives and Sayings of Sufis*. New York: Paulist Press, 2009.

Bābur. *The Baburnama: Memoirs of Babur, Prince and Emperor*. Translated and edited by Wheeler M. Thackston. New York: Oxford University Press, 1996. Translated by Annette Beveridge. London: Luzac, 1922.

Badāʾūnī, ʿAbd al-Qādir ibn Mulūk Shāh. *Muntakhab al-tavārīkh*. Edited by Mawlavī Aḥmad ʿAlī Ṣāḥib. 3 Vols. Tehran: Anjuman-i Ās̱ār va Muvākhir-i Farhangī, 1379 [2000]. Translated by W. H. Lowe as *Muntakhabu't-tawārīkh*. 3 Vols. Delhi: Idarah-i-Adabiyat-i-Delli, 1898.

Balʿamī, Abū ʿAlī Muḥammad b. Muḥammad. *Tārīkh-i Balʿamī*. Edited by Muḥammad Taqī Bahār and Muḥammad Parvīn Gunābādī. Tehran: Zavvār, 1379 [1990].

Bidlīsī, Sharaf Khān ibn Shams al-Dīn. *Sharafnāmah*. 2 Vols. Edited by Vlādīmīr Valīyāmīnūf Zarnūf. Pitrubūrgh: Ākādamiyah-ʾi

Impirāṭūriyah, 1862. Translated by M. R. Izady as *The Sharafnama, or, the History of the Kurdish Nation, 1597*. Costa Mesa, CA: Mazda, 2005.

Dūghlāt, Mīrzā Ḥaydar. *Tarikh-i Rashidi: A History of the Khans of Moghulistan*. Translated and annoted by W. M. Thackston, Sources of Oriental Languages & Literatures 38. 2 Vols. Cambridge, MA: Harvard University Department of Near Eastern Languages and Civilizations, 1996.

Fażl Allāh b. Rūzbihān Khunjī-Iṣfahānī. *Tārīkh-i 'ālam-ārā-yi Amīnī*. Translated and abridged by V. Minorsky. Revised and augmented by John E. Woods. London: Royal Asiatic Society, 1992.

Firishtah, Muḥammad Qāsim Hindū Shāh Astarābādī. *Tārīkh-i Firishtah*. Edited by Muḥammad Riżā Naṣīrī. 2 Vols. Tehran: Anjuman-i Āsār va Mafākhir-i Farhangī, 1387 [2008]. Translated by John Briggs as *History of the Rise of the Mahomedan Power in India*. 4 Vols. Calcutta: R. Cambray & Co., 1909.

Ghaffārī Qazvīnī Kāshānī, Qāżī Aḥmad. *Tārīkh-i jahān'ārā*. Edited by Ḥasan Narāqī. Tehran: Kitāb'furūshī-i Ḥāfiẓ, 1342 [1963].

Al-Ghazālī. *Naṣiḥat al-mulūk*. Edited by Jalāl al-Dīn Humā'ī. Tehran: Chāpkhānah-i Majlis, 1315–1317 [1936–1938]. Translated by F. R. C. Begley as *Ghazālī's Book of Counsel for Kings (Naṣīhat al-mulūk)*. London: Oxford University Press, 1964.

Gul-Badan Begum. *Humayun-nama, The History of Humayun*. Translated by Annette S. Beveridge. New Delhi: Goodword Boks, 2002.

Ḥayātī Tabrīzī, Qāsim Beg. *A Chronicle of the Early Safavids and the Reign of Shah Ismā'īl (907–930/1501–1524)*. Edited by Kioumars Ghereghlou. New Haven, CT: American Oriental Society, 2019.

The History of India as Told by Its Own Historians. H. M. Elliot and John Dowson. 8 Vols. London: Trübner & Co., 1867–1877.

Ḥusaynī Qazvīnī, Sharaf al-Dīn Fażl Allāh. *al-Mu'jam fī āsār mulūk al-a'jam*. Edited by Aḥmad Futūḥī'nasab. Tehran: Anjuman-i Āsār va Mafākhir-i Farhangī, 2005.

Ibn Funduq. *Tārīkh-i Bayhaq*. Edited by Aḥmad Bahmanyār. Tihran: Mu'assas va Mudīr-i Bungāh-i Dānish, 1317 [1938].

Ibrāhīm ibn Jarīr. "Tārīkh-i Ibrāhīmī." MS. British Library India Office ISL 1874.

Idrīs Bidlīsī. "Hasht Bihisht." MS. Istanbul Süleymaniye Kütüphanesi Nurosmaniye 3209-919.

"Hasht Bihisht." MS. Istanbul Süleymaniye Kütüphanesi Ayasofia 3541–918.

al-Irbilī, 'Ali b. 'Īsá. *Kashf al-ghumma fi ma'rifat al-a'imma*. 3 Vols. Beirut: Dār al-aḍwā', 1985.

Iṣfahānī, Muḥammad Yūsuf Vālah. *Khuld-i barīn: Īrān dar rūzgār-i Ṣafaviyān*. Edited by Mīr Hāshim Muḥaddis̱. Tehran: Mawqūfāt-i Duktur Maḥmūd Afshār, 1372 [1993].

Khuld-i barīn: Rawżah-i panjum az rawżāt-i hashtgānah. Edited by Mīr Hāshim Muḥaddas. Tehran: Pazhūhashgāh-i ʻUlūm-i Insānī va Muṭālaʻāt-i Farhangī, 1390 [2011].

Iskandar Beg Munshī. *Tārīkh-i ʻālam-ārā-yi ʻAbbāsī*. Edited by Īraj Afshār. 2nd ed. 2 Vols. Tehran: Amīr Kabīr, 1350 [1971]. Translated by Roger Savory as *The History of Shah ʻAbbas the Great*. 2 Vols. Boulder, CO: Westview Press, 1978.

Jahāngīr. *Jahāngīrnāmah: tūzuk-i Jahāngīrī*. Edited by Muḥammad Hāshim. Tehran: Intishārāt-i Bunyād-i Farhang-i Īrān, 1359 [1980]. Translated by Wheeler M. Thackston as *The Jahangirnama: Memoirs of Jahangir, Emperor of India*. New York: Freer Gallery of Art, 1999. Translated by Alexander Rogers as *The Tūzuk-i Jahāngīrī; or, Memoirs of Jahāngīr*. Edited by Henry Beveridge. London: Royal Asiatic Society, 1909–1914.

Khvāndamīr, Ghiyāṣ al-Dīn ibn Humām al-Dīn. *Dastūr al-vuzarā'*. Edited by Saʻīd Nafīsī. Tehran: Iqbāl, 1317 [1938].

Ma'āsir al-mulūk bih żamīmah-i khātimah-'i Khulāṣat al-akhbār va Qānūn-i Humāyūnī. Edited by Mīr Hāshim Muḥaddis̱. Tehran: Mu'assasah-'i Khadamāt-i Farhangī-i Rasā, 1372 [1993].

Makārim al-akhlāq. Edited by T. Gandjeï. London: E. J. W. Gibb Memorial Trust, 1979.

Qānūn-i Humāyūnī. Edited by M. Hidayat Hosain. Calcutta: Royal Asiatic Society of Bengal, 1940. Translated by Baini Prashad. Kolkata: The Asiatic Society, 1940.

Tārīkh-i ḥabīb al-siyar. 4 Vols. Edited by Jalāl al-Dīn Humā'ī. Tehran: Kitābkhānah-'i Khayyām, 1333 [1954]. Translated by Wheeler Thackston as *Habibu's-siyar*. 2 Vols. Cambridge, MA: Harvard University Department of Near Eastern Languages and Civilizations, 1994.

Khvurshāh ibn Qubād al-Ḥusaynī. *Tārīkh-i īlchī-i Niẓām Shāh: tārīkh-i Ṣafaviyah az āghāz tā sāl-i 972 hijrī qamarī*. Edited by Muḥammad Riżā Naṣīrī and Koichi Haneda. Tehran: Anjuman-i Āsār va Mafākhir-i Farhangī, 2000.

"Tārīkh-i īlchī-i Niẓām Shāh." MS. British Library ADD 23513.

Kūhistānī, Masʻūdī b. ʻUsmān. "Tārīkh-i Abū al-Khayr Khānī." MS. British Library ADD 26188.

Lārī, Muḥammad Muṣliḥ al-Dīn. "Mir'āt al-advār." MS. Istanbul Süleymaniye Kütüphanesi Nurosmaniye 3156.

Mir'āt al-advār va mirqāt al-akhbār. Edited by Jalīl Sāghravāniyān. Tehran: Markaz-i Nashr-i Mīrās-i Maktūb, 1393 [2014].

Mīrkhvānd, Muḥammad ibn Khāvandshāh. *Rawzat al-safa. Lithography.* Bombay: n.p., 1261 [1845].

Tārīkh-i rawżat al-ṣafā fī sīrat al-anbiyā' va al-mulūk va al-khulafā'. 7 Vols. Edited by 'Abbās Parvīz. Tehran: Khayyām, 1338 [1959]. Translated by E. Rehatsek as *Rauzat-us-safa or, Garden of Purity.* 3 Vols. Edited by F. F. Arbuthnot, Oriental Translation Fund, New Series 1. London: Royal Asiatic Society, 1891.

Tārīkh-i rawżat al-ṣafā fī sīrat al-anbiyā' va al-mulūk va al-khulafā'. 11 Vols. Edited by Jamshīd Kiyān'far. Tehran: Intishārāt-i Aṣāṭīr, 2001.

Muṣtawfī Qazvīnī, Ḥamd Allāh. *Tārīkh-i guzīdah.* Edited by 'Abd al-Ḥusayn Navā'ī. Tehran: Mu'assasah-i Amīr Kabīr, 1339 [1960]. Partial translation by Edward G. Browne. Leiden: E. J. Brill, 1913.

al-Naṣībī, Muḥammad ibn Ṭalḥah Abū Sālim. *Maṭālib al-su'ūl fī manāqib āl al-rasūl.* Edited by 'Abd al-Azīz Ṭabātabā'ī. Beirut: Mu'assasat al-Balāghah, 1999.

Niẓām al-Dīn Aḥmad Bakhshī. *Tabaqāt-i Akbarī.* Edited by Brajendranath De. 3 Vols. Calcutta: Asiatic Society of Bengal, 1913–1927. Translated by Brajendranath De and Baini Prashad as *The Ṭabaqāt-i-Akbarī: A History of India from the Early Musalmān Invasions to the Thirty-Eighth Year of the Reign of Akbar.* 3 Vols. Calcutta: Asiatic Society of Bengal, 1927–1939.

Niẓām al-Mulk. *Siyāsatnāmah.* Edited by 'Aṭā' Allāh Tadayyun. Tehran: Intishārāt-i Tihrān, 1373 [1994]. Translated by Hubert Darke as *The Book of Government or Rules for Kings.* London, Routledge and Paul, 1960.

Qandahārī, Ḥājjī Muḥammad 'Ārif. *Tārīkh-i Akbarī: ma'rūf bih tārikh-i Qandahārī.* Edited by Mu'īn al-Dīn Nadvī, Aẓhar 'Alī Dihlavī, and Imtiyāz 'Alī Khān 'Arshī. Rampur: Hindustan Printing Vurks, 1382 [1962. Translated by Tasneem Ahmad as *Tarikh-i Akbari.* Delhi: Pragati Publications, 1993.

Qazvīnī, Yaḥyá ibn 'Abd al-Laṭīf Ḥusaynī. *Lubb al-tavārīkh.* Edited by Mīr Hāshim Muḥaddis. Tehran: Anjuman-i Āsār va Mafākhir-i Farhangī, 1386 [2007.

Qumī, Qāżī Aḥmad. *Gulistān-i hunar.* Edited by Aḥmad Suhaylī Khvānsārī. Tehran: Intishārāt-i Bunyād va Farhang-i Īrān, n.d. Translated by V. Minorsky as *Calligraphers and Painters.* With an Introduction by B. N. Zakhoder. *Freer Gallery of Art Occasional Papers,* Vol. 3, no. 2. Washington: Smithsonian Institution, 1959.

Khulāṣat al-tavārīikh. 2 Vols. Edited by Iḥsān Ishrāqī. Tehran: Dānishgāh-i Tihrān, 1363 [1984].

Qūnavī, Muḥammad b. Ḥājjī Khalīl. "Tavārīkh-i āl-i 'Usmān." MS. Kayseri Raşit Efendi Eski Eserler Kütüphanesi Raşid Efendi Eki 11243.

Rashīd al-Dīn Fażl Allāh Hamadānī. *Jāmiʿ al-tavārīkh*. Edited by Bahman Karīmī. 2 Vols. Tehran: Iqbāl, 1338 [1959]. Translated by Wheeler Thackston as *Rashiduddin Fazlullah's Jameʿuʾt-tawarikh: Compendium of Chronicles: A History of the Mongols*. 3 Vols. Cambridge, MA: Harvard University Dept of Near Eastern Languages and Civilizations, 1998.

Laṭāyif al-Ḥaqāyiq. Edited by Hāshim Rajabzādah. 2 Vols. Tehran: Markaz-i Pazhūhashī-i Mīrās-i Maktūb, 1394 [2015].

Rūmlū, Ḥasan Beg. *Aḥsan al-tavārīkh*. Edited by ʻAbd al-Ḥusayn Navāʼī. Tehran: Bungāh-i Tarjumah va Nashr-i Kitāb, 1349 [1970].

Sabzavārī, Ṭāhir Muḥammad. "Rawżat al-ṭāhirīn." MS. Oxford Bodleian Elliot 314.

Sām Mīrzā Ṣafavī. *Tuḥfah-i Sāmī*. Edited by Vahīd Dastgirdī. Tehran: Armaghān, 1936.

Shāh Navāz Khān Awrangābādī and ʻAbd al-Ḥayy ibn Shāhnavāz. *Maʼāsir al-ʻumarā'*. Edited by ʻAbd al-Raḥīm and Mīrzā Ashraf ʻAlī. 3 Vols. Calcutta: Asiatic Society, 1888–1891. Translated by H. Beveridge as *The Maāthir-ul-umarā Being Biographies of the Muḥammadan and Hindu Officers of the Timurid Sovereigns of India from 1500 to about 1780 A.D.* 2 Vols. Calcutta: Asiatic Society, 1952.

Shukr Allāh Rūmī. "Bahjat al-tavārīkh." MS. Istanbul Süleymaniye Kütüphanesi Ayasofia 2990.

al-Ṭabarī, Abū Jaʻfar Muḥammad b. Jarīr. *Tārīkh al-rusūl wa al-mulūk*. Edited by M. J. de Goeje. Leiden: Brill, 1879–1901. Translated by Franz Rosenthal as *The History of al-Ṭabarī*, Vol. 1. Albany: State University of New York Press, 1989.

Three Memoirs of Homayun. Translated by Wheeler M. Thackston. Costa Mesa, CA: Mazda Publishers, 2009.

Vuqūʻī, Mīr Muḥammad Sharīf Ḥusaynī Nīshāpūrī. "Majāmiʻ al-akhbār." MS. British Library India Office 1758.

Yazdī, Mullā Jalāl al-Dīn Munajjim. *Tārīkh-i ʻAbbāsī yā rūznāmah-ʼi Mullā Jalāl*. Edited by Sayf Allāh Vaḥīd Niyā. Tehran: Intishārāt-i Vaḥīd, 1366 [1987].

Yazdī, Sharaf al-Dīn ʻAlī. *Ẓafarnāmah*. Edited by Sayyid Saʻīd Mīr Muḥammad Ṣādiq and ʻAbd al-Ḥusayn Navāʼī. Tehran: Kitabkhānah, Mūzah, va Markiz-i Asnād-i Majlis-i Shūrā-yi Islāmī, 1387 [2008.

Secondary Literature

Abisaab, Rula Jurdi. *Converting Persia: Religion and Power in the Safavid Empire*. London: I. B. Tauris, 2004.

Aḥmadī, Nużhat. *Ru'yā va siyāsat dar 'aṣr-i Ṣafavī.* Tehran: Nashr-i Tārīkh-i Īrān, 1388 [2009].

Alam, Muzaffar. "The Pursuit of Persian: Language in Mughal Politics." *Modern Asian Studies* 32 (1998): 317–349.

Alam, Muzaffar, and Sanjay Subrahmanyam. *Writing the Mughal World: Studies on Culture and Politics.* New York: Columbia University Press, 2012.

Aldous, Gregory. "Qizilbash Tribalism and Royal Authority in Early Safavid Iran, 1524–1534." Ph.D. diss., University of Wisconsin, Madison, 2013.

Algar, Hamid. "Persian Literature in Bosnia-Herzegovina." *Journal of Islamic Studies* 5 (1994): 254–267.

Ali, M. Athar. "The Evolution of the Perception of India: Akbar and Abu'l Fazl." *Social Scientist* 24 (1996): 80–88.

"The Use of Sources in Mughal Historiography." *Journal of the Royal Asiatic Society* 5 (1995): 361–373.

Amanat, Abbas. "Remembering the Persianate." In *The Persianate World: Rethinking a Shared Sphere*, 15–62. Edited by Abbas Amanat and Assef Ashraf. Leiden: Brill, 2019.

Ando, Shiro. "Die Timuridische Historiographie II: Šaraf al-Dīn 'Alī Yazdī." *Studia Iranica* 24 (1995): 219–246.

Anhegger, Robert. "Mehmed b. Haci Halil ül-kunevi'nin Tarih-i Âl-i Osman'i." *Tarih Dergisi* 2 (1951): 51–66.

Anooshahr, Ali. "Dialogism and Territoriality in a Mughal History of the Islamic Millennium." *Journal of the Economic and Social History of the Orient* 55 (2012): 220–254.

The Ghazi Sultans and the Frontiers of Islam: A Comparative Study of the Late Medieval and Early Modern Periods. London and New York: Routledge, 2009.

"Science at the Court of the Cosmocrat: Mughal India, 1531–56." *The Indian Economic and Social Review* 54 (2017): 295–316.

"Shirazi Scholars and the Political Culture of the Sixteenth-Century Indo-Persian World." *Indian Economic Social History Review* 51 (2014): 331–352.

Turkestan and the Rise of Eurasian Empires: A Study of Politics and Invented Traditions. Oxford: Oxford University Press, 2018.

Ansari, Ali M. "Mīrkhwānd and Persian Historiography." *Journal of the Royal Asiatic Society* 26 (2016): 249–259.

Arjomand, Said. "Perso-Indian Statecraft, Greek Political Science and the Muslim Idea of Government." *International Sociology* 16 (2001): 455–473.

The Shadow of God and the Hidden Imam: Religion, Political Order, and Societal Change in Shi'ite Iran from the Beginning to 1890. Chicago: University of Chicago Press, 1984.

Ashraf, Assef. "Introduction: Pathways to the Persianate." In *The Persianate World: Rethinking a Shared Sphere*, 1–14. Edited by Abbas Amanat and Assef Ashraf. Leiden: Brill, 2019.

Askari, Nasrin. *The Medieval Reception of the Shāhnāma as a Mirror for Princes*. Leiden: Brill, 2016.

Auer, Blain H. *Symbols of Authority in Medieval Islam: History, Religion and Muslim Legitimacy in the Delhi Sultanate*. London: I. B. Tauris, 2012.

"A Translation of the Prolegomena to Żiyā᾽ al-Dīn Baranī's Tārīkh-i Fīrūzshāhī." In *Essays in Islamic Philology, History, and Philosophy*. Edited by Alireza Korangy, Wheeler M. Thackston, Roy P. Mottahedeh, and William Granara, 400–418. Berlin: Walter de Gruyter GmbH, 2016.

Babayan, Kathryn. *Mystics, Monarchs, and Messiahs: Cultural Landscapes of Early Modern Iran*. Cambridge, MA: Harvard University Press, 2002.

Balabanlilar, Lisa. *Imperial Identity in the Mughal Empire: Memory and Dynastic Politics in Early Modern South and Central Asia*. London: I. B. Tauris, 2012.

Bashir, Shahzad."On Islamic Time: Rethinking Chronology in the Historiography of Muslim Societies." *History and Theory* 53 (2014): 519–544.

"A Perso-Islamic Universal Chronicle in Its Historical Context: Ghiyās̱ al-Dīn Khwāndamīr's Ḥabīb al-siyar." In *Historiography and Religion*. Edited by Jörg Rüpke, Susanne Rau, and Bernd-Christian Otto, 207–223. Berlin: Walter de Gruyter, 2015.

Bernardini, Michele. "The Shahnama in Timurid Historiography." In *Shahnama Studies III: The Reception of the Shahnama*. Edited by Gabrielle van den Berg and Charles Melville, 155–172. Leiden: Brill, 2018.

Binbaş, İlker Evrim. *Intellectual Networks in Timurid Iran: Sharaf al-Dīn 'Alī Yazdī and the Islamicate Republic of Letters*. New York: Cambridge University Press, 2016.

"Structure and Function of the Genealogical Tree in Islamic Historiography (1200–1500)." In *Horizons of the World. Festschrift for İsenbike Togan*. Edited by İlker Evrim Binbaş and Nurten Kılıç-Schubel, 465–544. Istanbul: Ithaki, 2011.

Bosworth, C. Edmund. "Historical Information from Ibn Funduq's Tarikh-i Bayhaq 563/1167–68." *Iran: Journal of the British Institute of Persian Studies* 48 (2010): 81–106.

Brack, Jonathan. "Was Ede Bali a Wafā'ī Shaykh? Sufis, Sayyids and Genealogical Creativity in the Early Ottoman World." In *Islamic Literature and Intellectual Life in Fourteenth- and Fifteenth-Century*

Anatolia. Edited by A. C. S. Peacock and Sara Nur Yıldız, 333–360. Würzburg: Ergon Verlag in Kommission, 2016.

Canby, Sheila R. *The Shahnama of Shah Tahmasp: The Persian Book of Kings*. New York: The Metropolitan Museum of Art, 2015.

Chan, Naindeep Singh. "Lord of the Auspicious Conjunction: Origins of the Ṣāḥib-Qirān." *Iran and the Caucasus* 13 (2009): 93–110.

Christenson, Arthur. *Les types du Premier Homme et du Premier Roi. Ie partie: Gajomard, Masyayet Masyānay, Hosang et Taxmoraw*. Stockholm: 1917. IIe partie: Jim. Leiden, 1934. *Archives d'Etudes Orientales*, 14:1–2.

Comstock-Skipp, Jaimee K. "Heroes of Legend, Heroes of History: Militant Manuscripts of the Shaybani Uzbeks in Transoxiana." Forthcoming.

Conermann, Stephan. *Historiographie als Sinnstiftung: Ind-persische Geschichtsschreibung während der Mogulzeit (932–1118/1516–1707)*. Weisbaden: Reichert Verlag, 2002.

Csirkés, Ferenc. "'Chaghatay Oration, Ottoman Eloquence, Qizilbash Rhetoric': Turkic Literature in Ṣafavid Persia." Ph.D. diss., University of Chicago, 2016.

"Historiography and the Sho'ubiya Movement." *Journal of Persianate Studies* 6 (2013): 216–234.

Dabiri, Ghazzal. "The *Shahnama*: Between the Samanids and the Ghaznavids." *Iranian Studies* 43 (2010): 13–28.

Dale, Stephen F. *The Garden of Eight Paradises: Bābur and the Culture of Empire in Central Asia, Afghanistan and India (1483–1530)*. Leiden: Brill, 2004.

"The Legacy of the Timurids." *Journal of the Royal Asiatic Society* 8 (1998): 43–58.

Daniel, Elton. "Manuscripts and Editions of Bal'amī's 'Tarjamah-i Tārīkh-i Ṭabarī." *Journal of the Royal Asiatic Society of Great Britain and Ireland* 2 (1990): 282–321.

"The Rise and Development of Persian Historiography." In *Persian Historiography*. Edited by Charles Melville, 101–154. London: I. B. Tauris, 2012.

Darling, Linda T. "'Do Justice, Do Justice, for That Is Paradise': Middle Eastern Advice for Indian Muslim Rulers." *Comparative Studies of South Asia, Africa and the Middle East* 22 (2002): 3–19.

A History of Social Justice and Political Power in the Middle East: The Circle of Justice from Mesopotamia to Globalization. New York: Routledge, 2013.

Dickson, Martin B. "Sháh Ṭahmásb and the Úzbeks: The Duel for Khurásán with 'Ubayd Khán (930–946/1524–1540)." Ph.D. diss., Princeton University, 1958.

Dickson, Martin B., and Stuart Cary Welch. *The Houghton Shahnameh*. 2 Vols. Cambridge, MA: Harvard University Press, 1981.

Donner, Fred. *Narratives of Islamic Origin: The Beginnings of Islamic Historical Writing*. Princeton, NJ: Darwin Press, 1998.

Eaton, Richard M. *India in the Persianate Age 1000–1765*. London: Allen Lane, 2019.

El-Rouayheb, Khaled. *Islamic Intellectual History in the Seventeenth Century: Scholarly Currents in the Ottoman Empire and the Maghreb*. Cambridge: Cambridge University Press, 2015.

Elliot, Henry M. *Bibliographical Index to the Historians of Muhammedan India*. 4 Vols. Calcutta: Baptist Mission Press, 1850.

Encyclopedia Iranica (EIR). Edited by Ehsan Yarshater. London; Boston: Routledge & Kegan Paul, 1983–.

Encyclopedia of Islam, 2nd ed. Leiden: Brill, 1960–2007.

Eryılmaz, Fatma Sinem. "From Adam to Süleyman: Visual Representations of Authority in 'Ārif's Shāhnāma-yi Āl-i 'Osmān." In *Writing History at the Ottoman Court: Editing the Past, Fashioning the Future*. Edited by H. Erdem Çıpa and Emine Fetvacı, 100–128. Bloomington: Indiana University Press, 2013.

Ethé, Hermann. *Catalog of Persian Manuscripts in the Library of the India Office*. 2 Vols. Oxford: Horace Hart, 1902.

Faruqui, Munis D. *The Princes of the Mughal Empire, 1504–1719*. Cambridge: Cambridge University Press, 2012.

Fetvaci, Emina. "The Office of the Ottoman Court Historian." In *Studies on Istanbul and Beyond*. Edited by Robert G. Ousterhout, 7–21. Philadelphia: University of Pennsylvania, Museum of Archaeology and Anthropology, 2007.

Fisher, Michael Herbert. *A Short History of the Mughal Empire*. London: I. B. Tauris, 2016.

Fleischer, Cornell H. *Bureaucrat and Intellectual in the Ottoman Empire: The Historian Mustafa Ali (1541–1600)*. Princeton, NJ: Princeton University Press, 1986.

Gallop, Annabel Teh. "The Genealogical Seal of the Mughal Emperors of India." *Journal of the Royal Asiatic Society* 9 (1999): 77–140.

Ghereghlou, Kioumars. "Chronicling a Dynasty on the Make: New Light on the Early Safavids in Ḥayātī Tabrīzī's History (961/1554)." *Journal of the American Oriental Society* 137 (2017): 805–832.

"On the Margins of Minority Life: Zoroastrians and the State in Safavid Iran." *Bulletin of the School of Oriental and African Studies* 80 (2017): 45–71.

Green, Nile. The Religious and Cultural Roles of Dreams and Visions in Islam. *Journal of the Royal Asiatic Society* 3 (2003): 287–313.

Gross, Jo-Ann. "Khoja Ahrar: A Study of the Perceptions of Religious Power and Prestige in the Late Timurid Period." Ph.D. diss., New York University, 1982.

Gulchīn Ma'ānī, Aḥmad. *Kārvān-i Hind*. Mashhad: Āstān-i Quds-i Rażavī, 1369 [1990].

Hagen, Gottfried. "Dreaming 'Osmāns: Of History and Meaning." In *Dreams and Visions in Islamic Societies*. Edited by Özgen Felek and Alexander D. Knysh, 99–122. Albany: State University of New York Press, 2012.

Hanaoka, Mimi. *Authority and Identity in Medieval Islamic Historiography: Persian Histories from the Peripheries*. New York: Cambridge University Press, 2016.

"Visions of Muhammad in Bukhara and Tabaristan: Dreams and Their Uses in Persian Local Histories." *Iranian Studies* 47 (2014): 289–303.

Hartman, Sven S. *Gayōmart: Etude sure le Syncretisme dans l'ancien Iran*. Uppsala: Almqvist & Wiksells Boktryckeri AB, 1953.

Hillenbrand, Robert. "The Iconography of the *Shāh-nāma-yi Shāhī*." In *Safavid Persia: The History and Politics of an Islamic Society*. Edited by Charles Melville, 53–78. London: I. B. Tauris, 1996.

Hirschler, Konrad. *Medieval Arabic Historiography: Authors As Actors*. London and New York: Routledge, 2006.

The Written Word in the Medieval Arabic Lands: A Social and Cultural History of Reading Practices. Edinburgh: Edinburgh University Press, 2012.

Hodgson, Marshall G. S. *The Venture of Islam: Conscience and History in a World Civilization*. 3 Vols. Chicago: University of Chicago Press, 1974.

Inalcik, Halil. "How to Read 'Ashik Pasha-zade's History." In *Studies in Ottoman History in Honour of Professor V. L. Ménage*. Edited by Colin Heywood and Colin Imber, 139–156. Istanbul: Isis Press, 1994.

"The Rise of Ottoman Historiography." In *Historians of the Middle East*. Edited by Bernard Lewis and P. M. Holt, 152–167. London: Oxford University Press, 1986.

Jacobs, Adam. "Sunni and Shi'i Perceptions, Boundaries and Affiliations in Late Timurid and Early Safawid Persia: An Examination of Historical and Quasi-Historical Narratives." Ph.D. diss., University of London, School of Oriental and African Studies, 1999.

Kafadar, Cemal. *Between Two Worlds: The Construction of the Ottoman State*. Berkeley: University of California Press, 1995.

Khan, Reyaz Ahmad. "Naqib Khan: Secretary to Emperors Akbar and Jahangir." *Proceedings of the Indian History Congress* 74 (2013): 240–244.

Kondo, Nobuaki. "Making a Persianate Society: Literati Migration to Mughal India." In *Crossing the Boundaries: Asians and Africans on the Move: Proceedings of the Papers Presented at Consortium for Asian and African Studies (CAAS) 7th International Conference*, 67–73. Tokyo University of Foreign Studies, October 22–23, 2016.

Lal, Ruby. "Settled, Sacred and All-Powerful: Making of New Genealogies and Traditions of Empire under Akbar." *Economic and Political Weekly* 36(11) (March 17–23, 2001): 941–943, 945–958.

Lefèvre, Corinne. "In the Name of the Fathers: Mughal Genealogical Strategies from Bābur to Shāh Jahān." *Religions of South Asia* 5 (2011): 409–442.

Losensky, Paul E. "Biographical Writing: Tadhkere and Manâqeb." In *Persian Prose, A History of Persian Literature*. Vol. 5, forthcoming.

Welcoming Fighānī: Imitation and Poetic Individuality in the Safavid-Mughal Ghazal. Costa Mesa, CA: Mazda Publishers, 1998.

Markiewicz, Christopher. *The Crisis of Kingship in Late Medieval Islam: Persian Emigres and the Making of Ottoman Sovereignty*. Cambridge: Cambridge University Press, 2019.

"History As Science: The Fifteenth Century Debate in Arabic and Persian." *Journal of Early Modern History* 21 (2017): 216–240.

Marlow, Louise. *Hierarchy and Egalitarianism in Islamic Thought*. Cambridge: Cambridge University Press, 1997.

"*The Way of Viziers and the Lamp of the Commanders (Minhāj al-wuzarā' wa-sirāj al-umarā*) of Aḥmad al-Iṣfahbadhī and the Literary and Political Culture of Early Fourteenth-Century Iran." In *Writers and Rulers: Perspectives on Their Relationship from Abbasid to Safavid Times*. Edited by Beatrice Gurendler and Louise Marlow, 169–193. Wiesbaden: Reichert, 2004.

McCants, William F. *Founding Gods, Inventing Nations: Conquest and Culture Myths from Antiquity to Islam*. Princeton, NJ: Princeton University Press, 2012.

Medieval Central Asia and the Persianate World: Iranian Tradition and Islamic Civilisation. Edited by A. C. S. Peacock and D. G. Tor. London: I. B. Tauris, 2015.

Meisami, Julie Scott. "The Past in Service of the Present: Two Views of History in Medieval Persia." *Poetics Today* 14 (1993): 247–275.

Persian Historiography to the End of the Twelfth Century. Edinburgh: Edinburgh University Press, 1999.

Melville, Charles. 'Ali Yazdi and the *Shāhnāme*. In *International Shāhnāme Conference the Second Millennium*. Edited by Forogh Hashbeiky, 117–133. Uppsala: Acta Universitatis Upsaliensis, 2015.

"From Adam to Abaqa: Qāḍī Baiḍāwī's Rearrangement of History." *Studia Iranica* 30 (2001): 67–86.

"From Adam to Abaqa: Qāḍī Baiḍāwī's Rearrangement of History (Part II)." *Studia Iranica* 36 (2007): 7–64.

"The Historian at Work." In *Persian Historiography*. Edited by Charles Melville, 56–100. London: I. B. Tauris, 2012.

"The Illustration of History in Safavid Manuscript Painting." In *New Perspectives on Safavid Iran: Empire and Society*. Edited by Colin P. Mitchell, 163–197. London: Routledge, 2014.

"New Light on Shah 'Abbas and the Construction of Isfahan." *Muqarnas* 33 (2016): 155–175.

Melvin-Koushki, Matt. "Early Modern Islamicate Empire: New Forms of Religiopolitical Legitimacy." In *The Wiley-Blackwell History of Islam*. Edited by Armando Salvatore, Roberto Tottoli, and Babak Rahimi, 353–375. Malden, MA: Wiley-Blackwell, 2018.

Mengüç, Murat Cem. "Histories of Bayezid I, Historians of Bayezid II: Rethinking Late Fifteenth-Century Ottoman Historiography." *Bulletin of the School of Oriental and African Studies* 76 (2013): 373–389.

Mitchell, Colin. *The Practice of Politics in Safavid Iran: Power, Religion, and Rhetoric*. London: I. B. Tauris, 2009.

Moin, A. Azfar. *The Millennial Sovereign: Sacred Kingship and Sainthood in Islam*. New York: Columbia University Press, 2012.

Morimoto, Kazuo. "The Earliest 'Alid Genealogy for the Safavids: New Evidence for the Pre-dynastic Claim to *Sayyid* Status." *Iranian Studies* 43 (2010): 447–469.

Mossadegh, 'Ali Asghar. "La Famille Monajjem Yazdi," in "Notes sur des Historiographes de l'Epoque Safavide," by Jean Calmard, 'Ali Asghar Mossadegh and M. Bastani Parizi, 125–129. *Studia Iranica* 16 (1987): 123–135.

Mottahedeh, Roy. *Loyalty and Leadership in an Early Islamic Society*. Princeton, NJ: Princeton University Press, 1980.

Mukhia, Harbans. *Historians and Historiography during the Reign of Akbar*. New Delhi: Vikas Publishing House, 1976.

Newman, Andrew J. *The Formative Period of Twelver Shī'ism: Ḥadīth As Discourse between Qum and Baghdad*. Richmond, Surrey: Curzon, 2000.

"The Myth of the Clerical Migration to Safawid Iran: Arab Shiite Opposition to 'Ali al-Karakī and Safawid Shiism." *Die Welt des Islams* 33 (1993): 66–112.

Safavid Iran: Rebirth of a Persian Empire. London: I. B. Tauris, 2006.

Ogasawara, Hiroyuki. "The Biblical Origin of the Ottoman Dynasty in the 15th and 16th Century." *Bulletin of the Society for Near Eastern Studies in Japan* 51 (2008): 110–139.

Ohlander, Erik. "Enacting Justice, Ensuring Salvation: The Trope of the 'Just Ruler' in Some Medieval Islamic Mirrors for Princes." *The Muslim World* 99 (2009): 237–252.

Orthmann, Eva. "Court Culture and Cosmology in the Mughal Empire: Humāyūn and the Foundations of the dīn-i ilāhī." In *Court Cultures in the Muslim World: Seventh to Nineteenth Centuries*. Edited by Albrecht Fuess and Jan-Peter Hartung, 202–220. London: Routledge, 2011.

"Ideology and State-Building: Humāyūn's Search for Legitimacy in a Hindu-Muslim Environment." In *Religious Interactions in Mughal India*. Edited by Vasudha Dalmia and Munis D. Faruqui, 3–29. New Delhi: Oxford University Press, 2014.

Peacock, Andrew. *Mediaeval Islamic Historiography and Political Legitimacy: Bal'amī's Tārīkhnāma*. London: Routledge, 2007.

Persian Historiography. Edited by Charles Melville. London: I. B. Tauris, 2012.

The Persianate World: The Frontiers of a Eurasian Lingua Franca. Edited by Nile Green. Berkeley: University of California Press, 2019.

The Persianate World: Rethinking a Shared Sphere. Edited by Abbas Amanat and Assef Ashraf. Leiden: Brill, 2019.

Pfeiffer, Judith. "Confessional Ambiguity vs. Confessional Polarization: Politics and the Negotiation of Religious Boundaries in the Ilkhanate." In *Politics, Patronage and the Transmission of Knowledge in 13th–15th Century Tabriz*. Edited by Judith Pfeiffer, 129–168. Leiden and Boston: Brill, 2014.

"Teaching the Learned: Jalāl al-Dīn al-Dawānī's Ijāza to Mu'ayyadzāda 'Abd al-Raḥmān Efendi and the Circulation of Knowledge between Fārs and the Ottoman Empire at the Turn of the Sixteenth Century." In *The Heritage of Arabo-Islamic Learning: Studies Presented to Wadad Kadi*. Edited by Maurice A. Pomerantz and Aram Shahin, 284–332. Leiden and Boston: Brill, 205 [2016].

Polyakova, E. A. "The Development of a Literary Canon in Medieval Persian Chronicles: The Triumph of Etiquette." *Iranian Studies* 17 (1984): 237–256.

Polyakova, E. A. and E. A. Poliakova. "Timur As Described by the 15th Century Court Historiographers." *Iranian Studies* 21 (1988): 31–44.

Pourjavady, Reza. "Muslih al-Din al-Lari and His Samples of the Sciences." *Oriens* 42 (2014): 292–322.

Pourshariati, Parvaneh. *Decline and Fall of the Sasanian Empire: The Sasanian-Parthian Confederacy and the Arab Conquest of Iran*. London: I. B. Tauris, 2008.

Quinn, Sholeh A. "The Dreams of Shaykh Safi al-Din in Late Safavid Chronicles." In *Dreaming Across Boundaries: The Interpretation of Dreams in Islamic Lands*. Edited by Louise Marlow, 221–234. Cambridge, MA: Harvard University Press, 2008.

Historical Writing during the Reign of Shah 'Abbas: Ideology, Imitation and Legitimacy in Safavid Chronicles. Salt Lake City: University of Utah Press, 2000.

"The Mu'izz al-Ansab and Shu'ab-i Panjganah As Sources for the Chaghatayid Period of History: A Comparative Analysis." *Central Asiatic Journal* 33 (1990): 229–253.

"Through the Looking Glass: Kingly Virtues in Safavid and Mughal Historiography." *Journal of Persianate Studies* 3 (2010): 143–155.

"The Timurid Historiographical Legacy: A Comparative Study of Persianate Historical Writing." In *Society and Culture in the Early Modern Middle East: Studies on Iran in the Safavid Period*. Edited by Andrew J. Newman, 19–32. Leiden: Brill, 2003.

Rieu, Charles. *Catalog of the Persian Manuscripts in the British Museum*. 3 Vols. London: British Museum, 1879.

Robinson, Chase F. *Islamic Historiography*. Cambridge: Cambridge University Press, 2003.

Robinson, Francis. "Ottomans-Safavids-Mughals: Shared Knowledge and Connective Systems." *Journal of Islamic Studies* 8 (1997): 151–184.

Rosenthal, Franz. *A History of Muslim Historiography*. 2nd revised ed. Leiden: E. J. Brill, 1968.

Roxburgh, David J. "Art and Literature in Timurid Herat, 1469–1506: The Life and Times of Sultan 'Ali Mashhadi." In *Pearls on a String: Artists, Patrons, and Poets at the Great Islamic Courts*. Edited by Amy S. Landau, 115–140. Baltimore, MD: Walters Art Museum, 2015.

Rüstem, Üner. "The Afterlife of a Royal Gift: The Ottoman Inserts of the *Shāhnāma-i shāhī*." *Muqaranas* 29 (2012): 245–337.

Şahin, Kaya. *Empire and Power in the Reign of Süleyman: Narrating the Sixteenth-Century Ottoman World*. Cambridge: Cambridge University Press, 2013.

Savant, Sarah Bowen. *The New Muslims of Post-Conquest Iran: Tradition, Memory, and Conversion*. Cambridge: Cambridge University Press, 2013.

Schimmel, Annemarie. *The Mystery of Numbers*. New York: Oxford University Press, 1993.

Sela, Ron. "Rashīd al-Dīn's Historiographical Legacy in the Muslim World." In *Rashīd al-Din, Agent and Mediator of Cultural Exchanges in Ilkhanid Iran*. Edited by Anna Akasoy, Charles Burnett, and Ronit Yoeli-Tlalim, 213–222. London: The Warburg Institute, 2013.

Şen, Ahmet Tunç. "A Mirror for Princes, a Fiction for Readers: The *Habnâme* of Veysî and Dream Narratives in Ottoman Turkish Literature." *Journal of Turkish Literature* 8 (2011): 41–65.

Sharma, Sunil. *Mughal Arcadia: Persian Literature in an Indian Court.* Cambridge, MA: Harvard University Press, 2017.

Simidchieva, Marta. "Kingship and Legitimacy in Niẓam al-Mulk's *Siyāsatnāma*, Fifth/Eleventh Century." In *Writers and Rulers: Perspectives on Their Relationship from Abbasid to Safavid Times.* Edited by Beatrice Gruendler and Louise Marlow, 97–131. Wiesbaden: Reichert Verlag, 2004.

Simpson, Mariana Shreve. *Sultan Ibrahim Mirza's Haft Awrang: A Princely Manusript from Sixteenth-Century Iran.* New Haven, CT: Yale University Press, 1997.

Southgate, Minoo S. "Portrait of Alexander in Persian Alexander-Romances of the Islamic Era." *Journal of the American Oriental Society* 97 (1977): 278–284.

Spooner, Brian, and William L. Hanoway. "Introduction: Persian As Koine: Written Persian in World-historical Perspective." In *Literacy in the Persianate World: Writing and the Social Order.* Edited by Brian Spooner and William L. Hanoway, 1–69. Philadephia: University of Pennsylvania Press, 2012.

Storey, C. A. *Persian Literature: A Bio-bibliographical Survey.* 3 Vols. London: Luzac & Co., 1927. Revised and Translated by Yu. E. Bregel as *Persidskaya literatura: bio-bibliograficheskii obzor.* 3 Vols. Moscow: Central Department of Oriental Literature, 1972.

Streusand, Douglas E. *The Formation of the Mughal Empire.* Delhi: Oxford University Press, 1989.

Islamic Gunpowder Empires: Ottomans, Safavids, and Mughals. Boulder, CO: Westview Press, 2011.

Subrahmanyam, Sanjay. "Connected Histories: Notes towards a Reconfiguration of Early Modern Eurasia." *Modern Asian Studies* 31 (1997): 735–762.

"Intertwined Histories: *Crónica* and *Tārīkh* in the Sixteenth-Century Indian Ocean World." *History and Theory, Theme Issue* 49 (2010): 118–145.

"Iranians Abroad: Intra-Asian Elite Migration and Early Modern State Formation." *The Journal of Asian Studies* 51 (1992): 340–363.

"On World Historians in the Sixteenth Century." *Representations* 91 (2005): 26–57.

Subtelny, Maria Eva. "'Alī Shīr Navā'ī: Bakhshī and Beg." *Harvard Ukranian Studies* 3–4 (1979–1980): 797–807.

"Art and Politics in Early 16th Century Central Asia." *Central Asiatic Journal* 27 (1983): 121–148.

"Between Persian Legend and Samanid Orthodoxy: Accounts about Gayumarth in Bal'ami's *Tarikhnama*." In *Ferdowsi, the Mongols and the History of Iran: Art, Literature and Culture from Early Islam to Qajar Persia*. Edited byA. C. S. Peacock Robert Hillenbrand and Firuza Abdullaeva, 33–45. London: I. B. Tauris, 2013.

Szuppe, Maria. *Entre Timourides, Uzbeks et Safavides: Questions d'Histoire politique et sociale de Hérat dans la première Moitié du XVIe Siècle*. Paris: Association pour l'Avancement des Études iraniennes, 1992.

Teczan, Baki. "The Memory of the Mongols in Early Ottoman Historiography." In *Writing History at the Ottoman Court: Editing the Past, Fashioning the Future*. Edited by H. Erdem Çıpa and Emine Fetvacı, 23–38. Bloomington: Indiana University Press, 2013.

Tor, D. G. "The Islamisation of Iranian Kingly Ideals in the Persianate Fürstenspiegel." *Iran* 49 (2011): 115–122.

Trausch, Tilmann. *Formen höfischer Historiographie im 16. Jahrhundert: Geschichtsschreibung unter den frühen Safaviden: 1501–1578*. Wien: Verlag der Österreichischen Akademie der Wissenschaften (ÖAW), 2015.

Truschke, Audrey. *Culture of Encounters: Sanskrit at the Mughal Court*. New York: Columbia University Press, 2016.

"The Mughal *Book of War*: A Persian Translation of the Sanskrit *Mahabharata*." *Comparative Studies of South Asia, Africa and the Middle East* 31 (2011): 506–520.

Tucker, Ernest. *Nadir Shah's Quest for Legitimacy in Post-Safavid Iran*. Gainsville: University Press of Florida, 2006.

Van Putten, Jasper C. "Jahangir Heroically Killing Poverty: Pictorial Sources and Pictorial Tradition in Mughal Allegory and Portraiture." In *The Meeting Pace of British Middle East Studies: Emerging Scholars, Emergent Research and Approaches*. Edited by Amanda Phillips and Refqa Abu-Remaileh, 101–120. Newcastle upon Tyne: Cambridge Scholars Publishing, 2009.

Welch, Stuart Cary. *The Shah-nameh of Shah Tahmasp*. New York: The Metropolitan Museum of Art, 1972.

Woodhead, Christine. "An Experiment in Official Historiography: The Post of Şehnāmeci in the Ottoman Empire." *Wiener Zeitschrift für die Kunde des Morgenlandes* 75 (1983): 157–182.

"Reading Ottoman 'Şehnames": Official Historiography in the Late Sixteenth Century." *Studia Islamica* 104/105 (2007): 67–80.

Woods, John E. *The Aqquyunlu: Clan, Confederation, Empire*, 2nd ed. Salt Lake City: University of Utah Press, 1999.

"The Rise of Timurid Historiography." *Journal of Near Eastern Studies* 46 (1987): 81–108.

"Timur's Genealogy." In *Intellectual Studies on Islam: Essays Written in Honor of Martin B. Dickson*. Edited by Michel M. Mazzaoui and Vera B. Moreen, 85–125. Salt Lake City: University of Utah Press, 1990.

Yildiz, Sara Nur. "Ottoman Historical Writing in Persian, 1400–1600." In *Persian Historiography*. Edited by Charles Melville, 436–502. London: I. B. Tauris, 2012.

Yılmaz, Hüseyin. *Caliphate Redefined: The Mystical Turn in Ottoman Political Thought*. Princeton, NJ: Princeton University Press, 2018.

Yücesoy, Hayrettin. "Ancient Imperial Heritage and Islamic Universal Historiography: al-Dīnawarī's Secular Perspective." *Journal of Global History* 2 (2007): 135–155.

Zaman, Taymiya R. "Instructive Memory: An Analysis of Auto/Biographical Writing in Early Mughal India." *Journal of the Economic and Social History of the Orient* 54 (2011): 677–700.

Index

'Abbas I, Safavid ruler, 17, 101, 132
  seventeenth regnal year of, 170–173
  and universal histories, 109
    in general, 167–168
    in *Tarikh-i 'alam-ara-yi 'Abbasi* (Iskandar Beg Munshi), 170–172
  virtues of, 159–160, 162, 165–166, 170–172
'Abd al-Razzaq Samarqandi, 24, 177
Abu al-Fazl 'Allami, **219**
  works of. *see Akbarnamah* (Abu al-Fazl); *A'in-i Akbari* (Abu al-Fazl)
Abu al-Fazl 'Allami, **219**
  on Mir 'Abd al-Latif, 103
  on Qachulay's dream narrative, 70–71
Abu Hanifa Dinvari, 107
Abu al-Qasim Babur, 180
Abu Sa'id, Timurid ruler, 75, 180
Adam
  al-Ghazali on, 124
  Kayumars as, 112, 115, 147
  Timur's genealogy and, 57, 62
Afzal al-tavarikh, 13
Ahd-i ardashir, 122, 124
Ahkam al-sultaniyya (al-Mawardi), 124
ahl-i dawlat (people of government), 83
ahl-i murād (people of pleasure), 84
ahl-i sa'ādat (people of happiness), 83
Ahsan al-tavarikh (Hasan Beg Rumlu), 197–198
A'in-i Akbari (Abu al-Fazl), **220**
  Abu al-Fazl on, 188–189
  gazetteer in, 189
  in general, 188
  tazkirah section in
    on commanders, 188–189
    innovativeness of, 190
    on learned men, 189
    as model, 190
    organization of, 189
    on poets and musicians, 189
Akbar, Mughal ruler
  mention of, 17
  and Mir 'Abd al-Latif, 103
  as renewer, 60
  seventeenth regnal year of
    in general, 167–168
    in *Tarikh-i Akbari* (Qandahari), 168–170
  virtues of, 156–158, 162, 165–170
Akbarnamah (Abu al-Fazl), **219–220**, *see also A'in-i Akbari* (Abu al-Fazl); ain-i
  benefits of history discussions in, absence of, 41
  dream narratives in, 69–71
  genealogies in
    cosmological contexts of, 61–62
    in general, 60–62
  mention of, 12
  referencing of
    in *Tabaqat-i Akbari* (Nizam al-Din Ahmad Bakhshi), 191
  re-use in
    of *Qanun-i Humayuni* (Khvandamir), 100–101
  re-use of
    in *Tarikh-i 'alam-ara-yi 'Abbasi* (Iskandar Beg Munshi), 200
Alam, Muzaffar, 10
Alan Qo'a, 56, 62
Alexander the Great, 149
Algar, Hamid, 187
'Ali Shir Nava'i, 177, 182
Amini Haravi, Sadr al-Din Sultan Ibrahim, 54–55, 66–67, 71, 109
  works of. *see Futuhat-i shahi* (Amini)

Amir Mahmud (son of Khvandamir), 79, 83, 109
Anbiyanamah ('Arif), 108
Anooshahr, Ali, 9–10, 193
Anvari, 80–81
Aq Qoyunlu chroniclers
  benefits of history discussions by, 28
  bibliographies of, 44–46
  lists of kingly virtues by, 161–162
'Arif, 108
Arjomand, Said, 166
Ashikpashazadah, 64, 67–68
autobiographies/memoirs, 142–143

Baba Fighani, 8
Babur, Mughal ruler
  autobiography of. *see Baburnamah* (Babur)
  and Khvandamir, 75
Baburnamah (Babur)
  in general, 142
  mentioning of Khvandamir in, 77
  tazkirah section in, 188
Badauni, 'Abd al-Qadir, **217–218**
  works of. *see Muntakhab al-tavarikh* (Badauni)
Bahjat al-tavarikh (Shukr Allah Rumi), **208–209**
  in general, 118–119
  on Kayumars, 119–120, 122–124
  mention of, 118
  organizational scheme of, *109–118*
  re-use in
    of *Tarikh-i Bal'ami*, 119–120
  re-use of
    in *Tarikh-i Bal'ami*, 123–124
Bal'ami, Abu 'Ali Muhammad Amirak, 107
  works of. *see Tarikh-i Bal'ami* (Bal'ami)
Balkh, 143, 147
Bayazid Bayat, 78
Bayram Khan, 192
Bayzavi, Nasir al-Din, 138
benefits of history discussions
  absence of, 41–42
  in general, 26–29, 40–41
  by Kurdish chroniclers, 38–42
  in *Majami' al-akhbar* (Vuqu'i), 35–37, 40–41
  by Mughal chroniclers, 34–38
  in *Rawzat al-safa* (Mirkhvand), 26, 28–29, 202
  by Safavid chroniclers, 29–34
  as semi-conventional element, 21
  in *Sharafnamah* (Sharaf al-Din Bidlisi), 38–41, 203
  in *Tarikh* (Hayati Tabrizi), 29–34, 40–41
  in *Tarikh-i 'alam-ara-yi Amini* (Khunji Isfanani), 28
  in *Tarikh-i Bayhaq* (Ibn Funduq), 26–27
  by Timurid chroniclers, 26–29
Bible verses, Isaiah 11:6, 132–133
bibliographies
  of Aq Qoyunlu chroniclers, 44–46
  divisions in, 44
  in general, 38–44, 52–53
  in *Mir'at al-advar va mirqat al-akhbar* (Lari), 46–50
  in *Rawzat al-safa* (Mirkhvand), 44, 46, 48–50
  in *Tabaqat-i Akbari* (Nizam al-Din Ahmad Bakhshi), 51
  in *Tarikh-i 'alam-ara-yi Amini* (Khunji Isfanani), 44–46, *45–48*
  in *Tarikh-i Bayhaq* (Ibn Funduq), 42, 43
Bidlisi, Idris, 64–66
Binbaş, Evrim, 37, 55–56
biographical compendia. *see tazkirah*s (biographical compendia)
Birjandi, 'Abd al-'Ali, 186
book of kings (*kwadāy-nāmag*), 107
al-Bukhari, 185

Cami'ül-kemalat (Mustafa Ali), 101
Central Asian chroniclers
  dream narratives by, 68–69
  genealogies by, 55–57
  universal histories by, 133–136
Chingiz Khan, 53, 55, 69
chroniclers/historians. *see also* Aq Qoyunlu chroniclers; Central Asian chroniclers; Kurdish chroniclers; Mongol chroniclers; Mughal chroniclers; Ottoman

chroniclers; Safavid chroniclers
moving between empires, 73–74, 101–105, 204
sources used by, 206
techniques used by, 206
chronicles
analyzed in this study, 12–13
as connected histories, 4–5
conventional/semi conventional elements in. *see also* benefits of history discussions; bibliographies; dream narratives; genealogies; *tazkirahs* (biographical compendia)
in general, 21, 202
overview of types of, 181
and Persianate World, 5–6
circle of justice, 17, 38, 165, 169
commanders, 189, 192–193
Culture of Encounters: Sanskrit at the Mughal Court (Truschke), 10

Daniel, Elton, 113, 116
Dastur al-vuzara (Khvandamir), 179
al-Davani, Jalal al-Din, 187
divine caliphate (*khilāfat-i ilāhī*), 47, 66
dream narratives
in *Akbarnamah* (Abu al-Fazl), 69–71
by Central Asian chroniclers, 68–69
in *Futuhat-i shahi* (Amini), 66
in general, 62–64, 203
in *Habib al-siyar* (Khvandamir), 66, 69
in *Hasht Bihisht* (Bidlisi, Idris), 64–66
by Kurdish chroniclers, 64–66
by Mughal chroniclers, 69–71
in *Muqaddimah* (Yazdi), 69–70
by Ottoman chroniclers, 64–66
in *Rawzat al-safa* (Mirkhvand), 69
by Safavid chroniclers, 66–68
in *Tarikh-i Rashidi* (Dughlat), 68–69
Dughlat, Muhammad Haydar, **212–213**
and Chingiz Khan, 56
and Timurid historiographical legacy, 25–26
works of. *see Tarikh-i Rashidi* (Dughlat)
writing style of, 23
Dust Muhammad (painter), 142
dynastic histories, 157, 181

Edebali, 64–65
Empire and Power in the Reign of Süleyman: Narrating the Sixteenth-Century Ottoman World (Şahin), 9
Encyclopedia Iranica, 8
Eryılmaz, Fatma Sinem, 108–109
Esau, 112
external caliphate (*khilāfat-i ṣūrī*), 37, 66

Fath Allah Shirazi, 193
Fazli Isfahani, 13
Firdawsi, 48, 81, 133, 135–136, 139, 152
works of. *see Shahnamah* (Firdawsi)
Formen höfischer Historiographie im 16. Jahrhundert (Trausch), 9
Futuhat-i Humayun (Siyaqi Nizam), 101, 141
Futuhat-i shahi (Amini)
dream narratives in, 66
genealogies in, 54
mention of, 109

genealogies
of Akbar, 57–62, 143
in *Akbarnamah* (Abu al-Fazl), 60–62, 143
by Central Asian chroniclers, 55–57
of Chingiz Khan, 53, 61
in *Futuhat-i shahi* (Amini), 54
in general, 203
in *Habib al-siyar* (Khvandamir), 55
in *Jamiʿ al-tavarikh* (Rashid al-Din Fazl Allah), 53
of Kayumars, 113–117, 119–120, 143, 150–153
by Mughal chroniclers, 57–60
by Safavid chroniclers, 54–55
in *Tarikh-i Akbari* (Qandahari), 57–60
in *Tarikh-i Rashidi* (Dughlat), 55–57
by Timurid chroniclers, 53
of Tughluq Timur, 55–57

Ghaffari, Qazi Ahmad, **214**
works of
Nusakh-i jahan-ara, 141, **214**
al-Ghazali
on kingship and religion, 124–125
works of
Ihya 'ulum al-din, 124
Nasihat al-muluk. *see Nasihat al-muluk* (al-Ghazali)
Ghazan Khan, 80, 161–162
The Ghazi Sultans and the Frontiers of Islam: A Comparative Study of the Late Medieval and Early Modern Periods (Anooshahr), 9
Ghereghlou, Kioumars, 29, 33, 140
Ghiyas al-Din Afzal b. Sayyid Hasan, 177
Ghiyas al-Din b. Humām al-Din Muhammad. *see* Khvandamir (Ghiyas al-Din b. Humam al-Din Muhammad)
Ghiyas al-Din Mansur, 186–187, 193
Ghunyah, 128
Gulbadan Begum, 78

Habib al-siyar (Khvandamir), **210–211**
benefits of history discussions in, absence of, 41
divisions in, 86
dream narratives in, 66, 69
gazetteer in, 189
genealogies in, 55
on Kayumars
in general, 125, 128
and *Ma'asir al-muluk* (Khvandamir), 128–130
and ommissions, 126–128, 130–133
and *Rawzat al-safa* (Mirkhvand), 125–133
mention of, 15
number twelve in
fifth reason of importance of, 97–99
first reason for importance of, 91–92
fourth reason for importance of, 95–97
in general, 89–91, 99
second reason for importance of, 92–93
third reason for importance of, 93–95
organization of, 118–127
re-use in
of *Kashf al-ghumma fi ma'rifat al-a'imma* (al-Irbili), 89–99
of *Ma'asir al-muluk* (Khvandamir), 128–130
of *Rawzat al-safa* (Mirkhvand), 83, 85–86, 125–133, 175–177
of *Tarikh-i guzidah* (Mustawfi Qazvini), 177
of *Zafarnamah* (Yazdi), 177
re-use of
in *Tarikh-i 'alam-ara-yi 'Abbasi* (Iskandar Beg Munshi), 199
in *Tarikh-i Abu al-Khayr Khani* (Kuhistani), 132–135
sources for, 88–89
tazkirah sections in
in general, 175
on Isma'il, 185
on Mirak Naqqash, 184
overview of, *180–201*
and politics, 179–182
reasons for writing of, 179
sources for, 177, *178–181*
twelve Imams in, 86–87
Hafiz Abru, 28
Haft awrang (Jami), 146–149
Hartman, Sven, 112
Hasan Beg Rumlu, 197–198
Hasan Gilani, 196
Hasht Bihisht (Bidlisi, Idris), 64–66
Hayati Tabrizi, Qasim Beg, **213**
works of. *see Tarikh* (Hayati Tabrizi)
historians. *see* chroniclers/historians
historical writing
in Persian language, 3–4, 8–10, *see* Persian historiography
Historical Writing during the Reign of Shah 'Abbas: Ideology, Imitation and Legitimacy in Safavid Chronicles (Quinn), 7–8
history. *see* benefits of history discussions

History of Persian Literature series (Yarshater), 8
Hodgson, Marshall G. S., 5, 18
holy men, 195–196
horoscopes, 61–62
Hujwiri, 68
Humayun, Mughal ruler, 1, 3, 15
  and Khvandamir, 77–79
  patronage of
    for *Qanun-i Humayuni*, 77, 81–82
  reorganization of Mughal society by, 83–85
Humayunnamah (Gulbadan Begum), 78
Husayn Ardabili, 186
Husayn Bayqara, Timurid ruler, 176, 180, 182–183

Ibn Funduq, 26–27, 42–44, 46, 52
  works of. *see Tarikh-i Bayhaq* (Ibn Funduq)
Ibn al-Muqaffa', 107
Ibn Qutayba, 107
Ibrahim bin Hariri/Jariri, **213**
  works of. *see Tarikh-i Ibrahimi* (or *Tarikh-i Humayuni*) (Ibrahim ibn Hariri/Jariri)
Ihya 'ulum al-din (al-Ghazali), 124
imām-i 'ādil (just imam), concept of, 130
imām-i 'ādil (just imam), concept of, 96–97
imitation, in Persian poetry, 8
imitative writing
  in general, 7, 110
  of Khvandamir, 90
  of Qubad al-Husayni, 145
  of Timurid chroniclers, 21–22
al-Irbili, 'Ali b. 'Isa
  on number twelve, 89, 91–99
  works of. *see Kashf al-ghumma fi ma'rifat al-a'imma* (al-Irbili)
Iskandar Beg Munshi, **221**
  works of. *see Tarikh-i 'alam-ara-yi 'Abbasi* (Iskandar Beg Munshi)
Islamization
  of Kayumars, 122
  Samanid dynasty and, 115
Isma'il I, Safavid ruler, 67, 182, 185–186

Jacobs, Adam, 86
Jahangir, Mughal ruler
  autobiography of, 142
  on Naqib Khan, 104
  paintings of, 132
Jamal al-Din Muhaddith, 47
Jami, 'Abd al-Rahman, 177
Jami' al-tavarikh (Rashid al-Din Fazl Allah)
  genealogies in, 53
  lists of kingly virtues in, 161–163
  mention of, 18, 24, 80
  referencing of, in biographies, 44
Japheth, 57, 112, 128
Jawhar Aftabchi, 78
just imam (*imām-i 'ādil*), concept of, 96–97, 133
justice, as kingly virtue, 169

al-Karaki, 97
Kashf al-ghumma fi ma'rifat al-a'imma (al-Irbili)
  mention of, 88
  number twelve in
    fifth reason for importance of, 97–99
    first reason for importance of, 91–92
    fourth reason for importance of, 95–97
    in general, 89–91
    second reason for importance of, 92–93
    summary of, 89
    third reason for importance of, 93–95
  re-use of
    in *Habib al-siyar* (Khvandamir), 89–99
Kashf al-mahjub (Hujwiri), 68
Kayumars
  as Adam, 112, 115, 147
  and Alexander the Great, 149
  anecdotes about, 117

Kayumars (cont.)
- family of, 115, 139, 148, 151, 153
- genealogy of, 113–117, 119–120, 143, 150–153
- in general, 14–17, 111–113, 204–205
- Islamization of, 122
- *khuṭbah* of, 120, 122–123
- kingmaking of
  - Bal'ami on, 120–122
  - Lari on, 147
  - Mirkhvand on, 131–132
  - Shukr Allah Rumi on, 122–124
- sayings of, 143–144, 151
- in *Shahnamah*, 141–142
- in universal histories. *see* universal histories

Kenan, 120–121, 123–124
Khafri, Shams al-Din Muhammad, 186
Khans of Mughulistan, 22–26
khilāfat-i ilāhī (divine caliphate), 47, 66
khilāfat-i ṣūrī (external caliphate), 37, 66
Khulasat al-tavarikh (Qumi), 30
Khuld-i barin (Muhammad Valih Isfahani), 200–201
Khunji Isfahani, Fazl Allah ibn Ruzbihan, **209**
Khusraw, Amir, 82
khuṭbah, of Kayumars, 120–123
Khvajah Humam al-Din Muhammad, 75
Khvandamir (Ghiyas al-Din b. Humam al-Din Muhammad), **210**
- and Babur, 77
- death of, 82
- family of, 75, 78
- in general, 82
- and Humayun, 77
- and Husayn Bayqara, 182
- on Imams, 86
- in later Mughal historiography, 100–101
- mention of, 54
- movement/travels of, 1, 4, 74–75
- on number twelve, 81–85, 88–92, 204
- works of
  - *Dastur al-vuzara* (Khvandamir), 179
  - in general, 74
  - *Makarim al-akhlaq*, 80
  - patronage for, 76–77

Khvandamir (Ghiyas al-Din b. Humam al-Din Muhammad)
- works of, 1, 4, 15–16, 23, 34, 37, 41, 55, 59, 66–67, 69–71, 74–101, 105–106, 109, 111, 125, 127–136, 139, 143–144, 146–148, 153, 156, 175–185, 188–189, 199, 200–201, 204, 209–211, 217
  - *Habib al-siyar. see Habib al-siyar* (Khvandamir)
  - *Qanun-i Humayuni. see Qanun-i Humayuni* (Khvandamir)

kingly appointments, 171–172
kingly virtues. *see also* lists of kingly virtues
- of ʻAbbas I, 159–160, 162, 165–166, 170–172
- categories of, 160
- of Akbar, 156–158, 162, 165–170
- in general, 205
- of Ghazan Khan, 80, 161–162
- of Malik Shah, 165
- piety as, 165–167
- of Yaʻqub Khan, 161–162

kingmaking
- of Kayumars
  - Bal'ami on, 120–122
  - Lari on, 147
  - Mirkhvand on, 131–132
  - Shukr Allah Rumi on, 122–124

kingship
- Hayati Tabrizi on, 32–34
- Idris Bidlisi on, 65–66
- and religion, 121–122, 124–125
- Vuquʻi on, 37–38

Kitab al-irshad (Shaykh Mufid), 88
Kuhistani, Masʻudi b. ʻUsman, **211–212**
- works of. *see Tarikh-i Abu al-Khayr Khani* (Kuhistani)

Kurdish chroniclers
- benefits of history discussions by, 38–42
- dream narratives by, 64–66

kwadāy-nāmag (book of kings), 107

Lari Ansari, Muslih al-Din, **214–215**
- movement/travels of, 102
- works of. *see Mir'at al-advar va mirqat al-akhbar* (Lari)

Lari, Kamal al-Din Husayn, 186
Lari, Muslih al-Din, 46–47
learned men, 193–194
lingua franca, Persian language as, 3–4
lists of kingly appointments, 171–172
lists of kingly virtues. *see also* kingly virtues
  by Aq Qoyunlu chroniclers, 161–162
  in general, 156–157
  influence of *Siyasatnamah* (Nizam al-Mulk) on, 165–167
  in *Jami' al-tavarikh* (Rashid al-Din Fazl Allah), 161–163
  and mirrors for princes, 163
  by Mongol chroniclers, 161
  by Mughal chroniclers, 156–158
  by Safavid chroniclers, 156–160
  similarities between different lists, 162–163
  in *Tarikh-i Akbari* (Qandahari), 157–158, 162–163
  in *Tarikh-i 'alam-ara-yi 'Abbasi* (Iskandar Beg Munshi), 158, 162–163
  in *Tarikh-i 'alam-ara-yi Amini* (Khunji Isfanani), 161–162
Losensky, Paul, 8, 175
Lubb al-tavarikh (Sayfi Qazvini), **212**
  on Kayumars
    in general, 137–138
    and ommissions, 139–140
    sources for, 138–154
  mention of, 102
  organization of, *127–154*
  re-use in
    of *Shahnamah*, 112
    of *Tarikh-i guzidah* (Mustawfi Qazvini), 140–154
  as transitional text, 140–141

Ma'asir al-muluk (Khvandamir), 128–130
Ma'asir al-umara (Awrangabadi), 102–103, 105
Mahdi, 98
Mahmud of Ghazna, Ghaznavid ruler, 80
Mahmud, Chaghatay ruler, 75
Majalis al-nafa'is ('Ali Shir Nava'i), 177
Majami' al-akhbar (Vuqu'i), **215–217**
  benefits of history discussions in, 35, 40–41
  in general, 34–35
  on Kayumars, 149–151
  on kingship, 37–38
  mention of, 110
  re-use in
    of *Rawzat al-safa* (Mirkhvand), 35–37, 150–151
Majma' al-tavarikh (Hafiz Abru), 28, 44
Majmu'ah al-tavarikh (Rashid al-Din Fazl Allah). *see Jami' al-tavarikh* (Rashid al-Din Fazl Allah)
Makarim al-akhlaq (Khvandamir), 80
Malik Ghiyas al-Din Kart, Kart ruler, 180
Malik Shah, Seljuk ruler, 163–165
Mansur I (Mansur b. Nuh), Samanid ruler, 107, 115
Markiewicz, Christopher, 27
Matalib al-su'ul fi manaqib āl al-rasul (al-Nisibini), 88
Matla'-i Sa'dayn ('Abd al-Razzaq Samarkandi), 24, 177
Mavahib-i Ilahi (Yazdi), 47
al-Mawardi, 124
Meisami, Julie, 116
Melville, Charles, 8, 140, 142, 175
messianic arisers (*qā'imīn*), 91, 93
Mihin Begum, 33
The Millennial Sovereign: Sacred Kingship and Sainthood in Islam (Moin), 10
Mir 'Abd al-Latif, 102–103
Mir 'Ala al-Dawlah Kami, 103
Mir Yahya Husayni Sayfi, 105
Mir'at al-advar va mirqat al-akhbar (Lari), **215**
  bibliography in, 46–50
  Kayumars in, 146–148
  mention of, 150, 198
  quotations in
    from *Haft awrang* (Jami), 148
  re-use in
    of *Rawzat al-safa* (Mirkhvand), 46–47
  tazkirah sections in
    in general, 185
    and politics, 185–187
    on Timurids, 185
    uniqueness of, 185

Mirat al-janan (Yafi), 177
Mirkhvand (Muhammad b. Khavand Shah b. Mahmud), **209–210**
connections with Timurid court, 182
mention of, 21
works of. *see Rawzat al-safa* (Mirkhvand)
mirrors for princes
in general, 11, 17–18, 155–156, 205
and lists of kingly virtues, 163
popularity of, 164–165
Mirza Rustam, 193
Mirza Shahrukh, 193
Mirza Umar Shaykh, 75
Moghulistan, 55
Moin, A. Azfar, 10, 60, 84
Mongol chroniclers
lists of kingly virtues by, 161
tazkirah by, 183
moon, 97–99
Mu'izzi, 80–81
Mughal chroniclers
benifit of history discussions by, 34–38
dream narratives by, 69–71
genealogies by, 57–60
lists of kingly virtues by, 156–158
and Ottoman chroniclers, 109–110
tazkirah by, 187–197
universal histories by, 143–153
Mughal dynasty
establishment of, 1–2
historiographical tradition of, 4
Mughal rulers
autobiographies/memoir of, 142–143
Mughulistan, 22–26
Muhammad Amin al-Hanafi al-Tabrizi, 186
Muhammad b. Hajji Khalil Qunavi, 13
Muhammad b. Khavand Shah b. Mahmud. *see* Mirkhvand (Muhammad b. Khavand Shah b. Mahmud)
Muhammad Muzaffar, Muzaffarid ruler, 180
Muhammad Valih Isfahani, 200–201
Muntakhab al-tavarikh (Badauni), 218
in general, 194
re-use in
of *Tabaqat-i Akbari* (Nizam al-Din Ahmad Bakhshi), 195–197
tazkirah sections in
on holy men, 195–196
organization of, 195–198
on physicians, 196–197
sources for, 194–195
al-Muntazam (Ibn al-Jawzi), 44
Muqaddimah (Yazdi)
citations from
in *Akbarnamah* (Abu al-Fazl), 69–70
dream narratives in, 69–70
re-use of
in *Tarikh-i Rashidi* (Dughlat), 56
Murad II, Ottoman sultan, 118
Murtaza Sharifi, 194
Musa al-Kazim, 54
Muslim b. Hajjaj, 185
Mustafa Ali, 101
Mustawfi, Hamd Allah, 24, 44
al-Mutawakkil, 'Abbasid ruler, 185
Muzaffar, Mubariz al-Din Muhammad ibn, 57

Nafahat al-uns (Jami), 177
Naqib Khan, Mir Ghiyas al-Din 'Ali, 103–105
Nasihat al-muluk (al-Ghazali), 122, 124
al-Nasir, Mamluk ruler, 180
Nava'i, 'Ali Shir, 80
Newman, Andrew, 96
al-Nisibini, Kamal al-Din Muhammad b. Talha al-'Adawi
on number twelve, 89
works of
Matalib al-su'ul fi manaqib āl al-rasul, 88
Nizam al-Din Ahmad Bakhshi, **217**
works of. *see Tabaqat-i Akbari* (Nizam al-Din Ahmad Bakhshi)
Nizam al-Din al-Awliya, 82
Nizam al-Mulk 18, 163–166, 173
works of. *see Siyasatnamah* (Nizam al-Mulk)
Nizam al-tavarikh (Bayzavi), 138, 143

numerology, 59–60
Nusakh-i jahan-ara (Ghaffari), 141, **214**

Osman Ghazi, Ottoman ruler, 64–68
Ottoman chroniclers
benefits of history discussions by, 38–42
dream narratives by, 64–66
on Kayumars, 118–125
universal histories by, 108–109
Ottoman dynasty
establishment of, 1–2
historiographical tradition of, 4
Ottoman rulers
types of authority of, 66
Ottoman Turkish language, 3, 9

patronage
of Humayun, 77, 81–82
for *Tarikh* (Hayati Tabrizi), 33
for works of Kvandamir, 76–77, 81–82
people of government (*ahl-i dawlat*), 83
people of happiness (*ahl-i sa'ādat*), 83
people of pleasure (*ahl-i murād*), 84
periodization, used in this study, 18
Persian historiography
in general, 3–4
studies on, 8–10
Persian Historiography (ed. Melville), 8–9
Persian language
historical writing in, 3–4, 8–10
as lingua franca, 3–4
Persian poetry, imitation in, 8
Persianate, use of term, 5
physicians, 196–197
piety, as kingly virtues, 165–167
politics
in *Habib al-siyar* (Khvandamir), 179–182
in *Mir'at al-advar va mirqat al-akhbar* (Lari), 185–187
in *Tabaqat-i Akbari* (Nizam al-Din Ahmad Bakhshi), 192–194
prefaces (*dībāchah/muqaddimah*), 22–26

qā'imīn (messianic arisers), 91, 93
Qachulay
dream narrative of, 69–71
Qamar al-Din, 24
Qandahari, Muhammad Arif, **215–216**
works of. *see Tarikh-i Akbari* (Qandahari)
Qanun-i Humayuni (Khvandamir), **211**
in general, 79–80
historiographical background of, 85–89
on Humayuni's reorganization of Mughal society, 83–85
introduction to, 80–82
mention of, 15
number twelve in, 84–85
fifth reason for importance of, 97–99
first reason for importance of, 91–92
fourth reason for importance of, 95–97
in general, 90–91, 204
second reason for importance of, 92–93
third reason for importance of, 93–95
patronage for, 77
poets & historians in, 80–81
re-use of
in *Akbarnamah* (Abu al-Fazl), 100–101
strategies in composing, 204
Qasim Khan, 79
Qazvini family, 102–105
Qisas al-anbiya (stories of the Prophets) genre, 142
Qubad al-Husayni, Khvurshah b., **213–214**
works of. *see Tarikh-i ilchi-yi Nizam Shah* (Qubad al-Husayni)
Qumi, Qazi Ahmad, 30, 34

Rahat al-sudur (Ravandi), 140
Rashid al-Din Fazl Allah
on number twelve, 87–88
works of
Jami' al-tavarikh. *see Jami' al-tavarikh* (Rashid al-Din Fazl Allah)
Risalah-i 'adad, 87–88

Rashid al-Din Fazl Allah (cont.)
Shuʿab-i panjganah, 53
Rawzat al-ahbab (Jamal al-Din Muhaddith), 47
Rawzat al-safa (Mirkhvand), **209–210**
benefits of history discussions in, 26, 28–29
bibliography in, 44, 46, 48–50
division in, 85–86
dream narratives in, 69
importance of, 28
mention of, 3, 21
organizational scheme of, *118–127*
re-use of
in *Habib al-siyar* (Khvandamir), 83, 85–86, 125–133, 175–177
in *Majamiʿ al-akhbar* (Vuquʿi), 35–37, 150–151
in *Mir'at al-advar va mirqat al-akhbar* (Lari), 46–47
in *Rawzat al-tahirin* (Sabzavari), 152–153
in *Sharafnamah* (Bidlisi), 38–40
in *Tabaqat-i Akbari* (Nizam al-Din Ahmad Bakhshi), 47–52
in *Tarikh* (Hayati Tabrizi), 30–34
in *Tarikh-i ilchi-yi Nizam Shah* (Qubad al-Husayni), 144–146
tazkirah sections in, 175–177, 183–185
Rawzat al-tahirin (Sabzavari), **220–221**
mention of, 110
on Kayumars, 151–153
stating of sources in, 151–152
religion
and kinship, 121–122, 124–125
Risalah-i ʿadad (Rashid al-Din), 87–88
Robinson, Chase F., 108

Saʿid Samarqandi, 194
Sabzavari, Tahir Muhammad, **220–221**
works of. *see Rawzat al-tahirin* (Sabzavari)
Sadr al-Din al-Dashtaki, 187
Sadr al-Din Savaji, 178
Safavid chroniclers
benefits of history discussions by, 29–34
dream narratives by, 66–68
genealogies by, 54–55
lists of kingly virtues by, 156–160
tazkirah by, 197–201
universal histories by
in general, 109
Kayumars in, 125–133, 136–141
overview of, 109
Safavid dynasty
establishment of, 1–2
historiographical tradition of, 4
and Sunni Islam, 186–187
and Twelver Shiʿism, 2, 186–187
Safavid poets, 73
Safi al-Din Ishaq Ardabili
dream narratives of, 66–68
genealogy of, 54–55
Safvat al-safa, 66
Şahin, Kaya, 9
Samanid dynasty, 115
Sanjar, Seljuq ruler, 80
Sayfi Qazvini, Yahya ibn ʿAbd al-Latif, 149, **212**
family of, 102, *see also* Qazvini family
in general, 15
Ghereghlou on, 140
works of. *see Lubb al-tavarikh* (Sayfi Qazvini)
Sayyid ʿAbd Allah Khan, 78
Sayyid Jamal al-Din ʿAta Allah bin Fazl Allah Muhaddis, 186
Şehnames, 11
sermons. *see khuṭbah*, of Kayumars
Seth, 124
seventeenth regnal year
of ʿAbbas I, 170–172
of Akbar, 168–170
Shah Ismaʿil
as just Imam, 96–97
Khvandamir on, 95–97, 99
Shahnamah (Firdawsi)
illustrated version of, 112, 142
importance of, 140
making extracts of, 152
re-use of
in *Tarikh-i Abu al-Khayr Khani* (Kuhistani), 133–135
in *Tarikh-i guzidah* (Mustawfi Qazvini), 112
in *Zafarnamah* (Yazdi), 140
Uzbek interest in, 136–144

Shahnamah-yi Al-i Osman ('Arif), 108
Shahrukh, Timurid ruler, 180
Shami, Nizam al-Din 'Ali, 21
Sharaf al-Din Bidlisi, **218**
  movement/travels of, 101
  works of. *see Sharafnamah* (Sharaf al-Din Bidlisi)
Sharafnamah (Sharaf al-Din Bidlisi), **218–219**
  benefits of history discussions of, 38–41
  mention of, 12
  re-use in
    of *Rawzat al-safa* (Mirkhvand), 38–40
Shaybani Uzbeks, 3
Shaykh Mufid, 88
Shaykh Safi al-Din, 7
Shiraz school of philosophy, 186–187, 193
Shu'ab-i panjganah (Rashid al-Din Fazl Allah), 53
Shukr Allah Rumi, **208–209**
  on Kayumars, 122–124
  works of. *see Bahjat al-tavarikh* (Shukr Allah Rumi)
Siyamak, 139, 148, 151, 153
Siyaqi Niza, 101
Siyasatnamah, 163
Siyasatnamah (Nizam al-Mulk)
  in general, 163–164
  influence of, 165–167
  mention of, 18
  reasons for writing of, 163–164
Sokollu, Mehmed, 46
sources, used in this study, 11
Subrahmanyam, Sanjay, 4, 10
Subtelny, Maria, 115–117
Sulayman Mirza, 193
Sultan Ahmad Mirza, 188
Sultan Muhammad (painter), 112, 142
sun, 99–100
Sunni Islam, 2, 186–187
Szuppe, Maria, 182

Tabaqat-i Akbari (Nizam al-Din Ahmad Bakhshi), **217**
  bibliography in, 51
  in general, 190–191
  referencing in
    of *Akbarnamah* (Abu al-Fazl), 191
  re-use in
    of *Rawzat al-safa* (Mirkhvand), 47–52
  re-use of
    in *Muntakhab al-tavarikh* (Badauni), 195–197
  tazkirah sections in
    on commanders, 192–193
    in general, 191
    introduction to, 191–192
    on learned men, 193–194, 196
    organization of, 192, 195
    and politics, 192–194
Tahmasb I, Safavid ruler, 33, 102, 186–187, 198
Tardi Beg Khan, 193
Tarikh (Hayati Tabrizi), **213**
  benefits of history discussions in, 29–30, 40–41
  citations of, 30, 34
  patronage for, 33
  re-use in
    of *Rawzat al-safa* (Mirkhvand), 30–34
  role of kingship in, 30–34
Tarikh al-rusul wa al-muluk (al-Tabari)
  on Kayumars, 113–115
  mention of, 44, 107
  re-use of
    in *Tarikh-i Bal'ami* (Bal'ami), 115–116
Tarikh-i 'alam-ara-yi 'Abbasi (Iskandar Beg Munshi), **221**
  appendix to, 199
  conclusion of, 198–199
  in general, 155
  lists of kingly appointments in, 171–172
  lists of kingly virtues in
    and 'Abbas' seventeenth regnal year, 170–172
    in general, 158
    influence of *Siyasatnamah* (Nizam al-Mulk) on, 165–167
    innovativeness of, 172–173
    reasons for inclusion of, 158–159
    and similarities between different lists, 162–163

Tarikh-i ʻalam-ara-yi ʻAbbasi (Iskandar Beg Munshi) (cont.)
space devoted to, 159–160
mention of, 12
re-use in, 160–161
of *Akbarnamah* (Abu al-Fazl), 200
of *Habib al-siyar* (Khvandamir), 199
section on anecdotes in, 199
sources for, 198–200
tazkirah sections in
in general, 158–198
reasons for writing of, 199–200
Tarikh-i ʻalam-ara-yi Amini (Khunji Isfahani), **209**
benefits of history discussions in, 28
bibliography in, 44–46, *45–48*
in general, 161–162
lists of kingly virtues in, 161–162
on universal histories, 108
Tarikh-i Abu al-Khayr Khani (Kuhistani), **211–212**
on Kayumars, 133–136
mention of, 12
re-use in
of *Habib al-siyar* (Khvandamir), 132–135
of *Shahnamah* (Firdawsi), 133–135
Tarikh-i Akbari (Qandahari), **215–216**
in general, 57–58
genealogies in
in general, 58–60
numerology in, 59–60
lists of kingly virtues in
and Akbar's seventeenth regnal year, 168–170
influence of *Siyasatnamah* (Nizam al-Mulk) on, 165–167
innovativeness of, 172–173
reasons for inclusion of, 157–158
and similarities between different lists, 162–163
space devoted to, 158
re-use of, 160–161
Tarikh-i alfi, 13, 60
Tarikh-i al-i Muzaffar, 57
Tarikh-i al-i Osman (Ashikpashazadah), 64
Tarikh-i Balʻami (Balʻami)
on Kayumars, 116–118, 120–122
re-use in
of *Bahjat al-tavarikh* (Shukr Allah Rumi), 123–124
of *Tarikh al-rusul wa al-muluk* (al-Tabari), 115–116
re-use of
in *Bahjat al-tavarikh* (Shukr Allah Rumi), 119–120
sources for, 116
Tarikh-i Banakati (Banakati), 44
Tarikh-i Bayhaq (Ibn Funduq)
benefits of history discussion in, 26–27
bibliography in, 42, 43
Tarikh-i Firuzshahi (Ziya al-Din Barani), 12, 27
Tarikh-i guzidah (Mustawfi Qazvini), 24
citation of
in bibiographies, 44
on Kayumars, 138–140
re-use in
of *Habib al-siyar* (Khvandamir), 178
of *Shahnamah* (Firdawsi), 112
re-use of
in *Habib al-siyar* (Khvandamir), 177
in *Lubb al-tavarikh* (Sayfi Qazvini), 140–154
tazkirah in, 175
Tarikh-i Humayun (Bayazid Bayat), 78
Tarikh-i Humayuni (Ibrahim ibn Hariri/Jariri). *see Tarikh-i Ibrahimi* (or *Tarikh-i Humayuni*) (Ibrahim ibn Hariri/Jariri)
Tarikh-i Ibrahimi (or *Tarikh-i Humayuni*) (Ibrahim ibn Hariri/Jariri), **213**
on Kayumars, 143–144
mention of, 110
references in
to *Nizam al-tavarikh* (Bayzavi), 143
re-use in
of *Tarikh-i ilchi-yi Nizam Shah* (Qubad al-Husayni), 144–146

Tarikh-i ilchi-yi Nizam Shah (Qubad al-Husayni), **214**
on Kayumars, 144–146
re-use in
of *Rawzat al-safa* (Mirkhvand), 144–146
re-use of
in *Tarikh-i Ibrahimi* (Ibrahim ibn Jarir), 145–146
Tarikh-i jahan-ara (Ghaffari). *see Nusakh-i jahan-ara* (Ghaffari)
Tarikh-i jahangusha (Juvayni), 140
Tarikh-i Manzum ('Abd al-Razzaq), 24
Tarikh-i Rashidi (Dughlat), **212–213**
citations in
of *Muqaddimah* (Yazdi), *56–57*
dream narratives in, 68–69
explanation of methodology in, 25
genealogies in, *55–57*
in general, 183
literary review in, 24–25
mention of, 12, 22–26
prefaces in, 22
quotations in
from *Kashf al-mahjub* (Hujwiri), 68
reasons for writing of, 22–23
re-use in
of *Zafarnamah* (Yazdi), 23–24
re-use of
in *Muqaddimah* (Yazdi), *56*
tazkirah section in
in general, 183
uniqueness of, 183–185
Tarikh-i tahiri (Sabzavari). *see Rawzat al-tahirin* (Sabzavari)
Tarikh-i Vassaf, 47
Tarikh-i Yamini (al-'Utbi), 50
Tashih al-masabih, 177
Tavarikh-i Al-i Osman (Muḥammad b. Hajji Khalil Qunavi), 13
*tazkirah*s (biographical compendia)
in general, 11, 18, 155–156, 174, 205–206
in *Habib al-siyar* (Khvandamir), 175, 177–182, *178–181*, *180–201*, 184–185
in *Muntakhab al-tavarikh* (Badauni), 194–197
in *Mir'at al-advar va mirqat al-akhbar* (Lari), 185
by Mongol chroniclers, 185
by Mughal chroniclers, 187–197
origin and development of, 175
in *Rawzat al-safa* (Mirkhvand), 175–177, 183–185
by Safavid chroniclers, 197–201
in *Tabaqat-i Akbari* (Nizam al-Din Ahmad Bakhshi), 191–196
in *Tarikh-i 'alam-ara-yi 'Abbasi* (Iskandar Beg Munshi), 158–200
Tazkirat al-vaqi'at (Jawhar Aftabchi), 78
terminology, used in this study, 18–19
Thackston, Wheeler, 23–24
time, 95–97
time periods, used in this study, 11–12
Timur, Timurid ruler, 180
Timurid chroniclers
benefits of history discussions by, 26–29
and genealogies, 53
imitative writing of, 21–22
Timurid dynasty, 4
Topkapı Palace Museum, 108–109
Tor, D. G., 124
transliteration system, used in this study, 19
Trausch, Tilmann, 9
Truschke, Audrey, 10
Tughluq Timur, Chaghatay ruler
conversion to Islam of, 23–24, 68–69
dream narratives about, 68–69
genealogy of, *55–57*
Tuhfah-i Sami (Sam Mirza), 155
Turkestan and the Rise of Eurasian Empires (Anooshahr), 10
twelve (number)
al-Irbili on, 89, 91–99
Khvandamir on, 81–85, 88–99, 204
Mustafa Ali on, 101
al-Nisibini on, 89
Rashid al-Din on, 87–88
Siyaqi Niza on, 101
Twelver/Imami Shi'ism, 2, 186–187

Ulugh Beg, Timurid ruler, 180
Ulus-i arba'ah (attr. Ulugh Beg), 24

universal histories, 16–17
 and corresponding dynasties, 111
 in general, 107–108, 110, 204
 Kayumars in
  early universal histories, 113–118
  in general, 204–205
  Habib al-siyar (Khvandamir). *see* *Habib al-siyar* (Khvandamir)
  Lubb al-tavarikh (Sayfi Qazvini), 137–154
  Majami' al-akhbar (Vuqu'i), 150–151
  Nusakh-i jahan-ara (Ghaffari), 141
  Rawzat al-tahirin (Sabzavari), 151–153
  Tarikh al-rusul wa al-muluk (al-Tabari), 113–115
  Tarikh-i Abu al-Khayr Khani (Kuhistani), 133–136
  Tarikh-i Bal'ami (Bal'ami), 116–118, 120–122
  Tarikh-i guzidah (Mustawfi Qazvini), 140–154
  Tarikh-i Ibrahimi (or *Tarikh-i Humayuni*) (Ibrahim ibn Jarir), 143–144
  Tarikh-i ilchi-yi Nizam Shah (Qubad al-Husayni), 144–146
 Mughal chroniclers and, 109–110, 142–153
 Ottoman chroniclers and, 108–109, 118–125
 overview of types of, 181
 Safavid chroniclers and, 109, 109, 125–133, 141–148
 in Topkapı Palace Museum, 108–109
'Unsuri, 80
'Utbi, 80
al-'Utbi, Abu Nasr, 51
Uyghur khans, 22–26
Uzbeks, 133, 136
Uzun Hasan, Aq Qoyunlu ruler, 185

Venture of Islam (Hodgson), 18
virtues. *see* kingly virtues
Vuqu'i Husayni Nishapuri, Muhammad Sharif, **216–217**
 works of. *see Majami' al-akhbar* (Vuqu'i)

Woods, John, 21, 55
Writing the Mughal World: Studies on Culture and Politics (Alam & Subrahmanyam), 10

Ya'qu b. Uzun Hasan, 44
Ya'qub Khan, 161–162
Yafi, 'Abd Allah ibn Asad, 177
Yarshater, Ehsan, 8
Yazdi, Sharaf al-Din 'Ali, 12
 genealogies in, 53
 interpretation of Qachulay's dream narrative, 70–71
 on kingship, 37
 mention of, 21
 mentioning of
  by Khvandamir, 81
 works of
  Mavahib-i Ilahi, 47
  Zafarnamah. see Zafarnamah (Yazdi)
Yucesoy, Hayrettin, 108

Zafarnamah (Shami), 21
Zafarnamah (Yazdi), 12
 citations of
  in biographies, 47
 importance of, 21
 Khvandamir's mentioning of, 81
 mention of, 21, 24
 re-use in
  of *Shahnamah*, 140
  of *Zafarnamah* (Shami), 21
 re-use of
  in *Habib al-siyar* (Khvandamir), 177
  in *Tarikh-i Rashidi* (Dughlat), 23–24
Zayd b. Zayn al-'Abidin, 86
Zayl-i habib al-siyar (Amir Mahmud), 79, 109
Zayn al-akhbar, 51
Ziya al-Din Barani, 12, 27
zodiac, 97–99
Zoroastrianism, 112

Lightning Source UK Ltd.
Milton Keynes UK
UKHW021446091220
374873UK00003B/58

9 781108 842211